Dedicated to H
who is largely ?
for this book

READ THIS FIRST

It's frightening how some people, though adept at walking and scrambling, have none of the mountain sense usually learned through decades of mountain wandering, problem solving and familiarity with mountains in all weather. This is particularly true of people using AllTrails.

Learn to read topo maps, use a GPS, be wary of apps. Turn back if it looks too hard for you, if you can't handle loose rock, if the river is too high, if you can't hack a 10-hour day, or if the route-finding is out of your league. Turn back from a summit or ridge if a thunderstorm is approaching or if conditions are made dangerous by rain, snow and ice. **At all times use your own judgment.** The author and publisher are not responsible if you have a horrible day or you get yourself into a fix.

In this book there are no dos and don'ts. It is assumed that users of this book are caring, intelligent people who will respect the country they are travelling through.

Be aware that in Kananaskis Country trails can change in an instant owing to logging and the search for oil and gas. Please notify me of any changes you find so I can make revisions in future editions. Use **Contact Us** under the **About** tab at kananaskistrails.com.

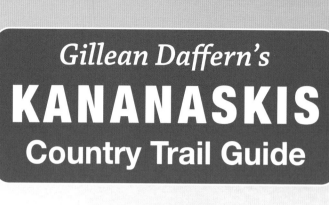

Gillean Daffern's
KANANASKIS
Country Trail Guide

VOLUME 1

For information on purchasing bulk quantities of this book, or to obtain media excerpts or invite the author to speak at an event, please visit rmbooks.com and select the "Contact" tab.

RMB | Rocky Mountain Books Ltd.
rmbooks.com
@rmbooks
facebook.com/rmbooks

Cataloguing data available from Library and Archives Canada
ISBN 9781771605984 (softcover)
ISBN 9781771605991 (electronic)

All photographs are by Gillean Daffern unless otherwise noted.

Book design and layout by Gillean Daffern
Cover design by Chyla Cardinal
Maps by Tony and Gillean Daffern
Topographical maps His Majesty the King in right of Canada

Printed and bound in China

We would like to also take this opportunity to acknowledge the traditional territories upon which we live and work. In Calgary, Alberta, we acknowledge the Niitsítapi (Blackfoot) and the people of the Treaty 7 region in Southern Alberta, which includes the Siksika, the Piikuni, the Kainai, the Tsuut'ina and the Stoney Nakoda First Nations, including Chiniki, Bearpaw, and Wesley First Nations. The City of Calgary is also home to Métis Nation of Alberta, Region III. In Victoria, British Columbia, we acknowledge the traditional territories of the Lkwungen (Esquimalt, and Songhees), Malahat, Pacheedaht, Scia'new, T'Sou-ke and W̱SÁNEĆ (Pauquachin, Tsartlip, Tsawout, Tseycum) peoples.

We acknowledge the financial support of the Government of Canada through the Canada Book Fund and the Canada Council for the Arts, and of the province of British Columbia through the British Columbia Arts Council and the Book Publishing Tax Credit.

Disclaimer

The actions described in this book may be considered inherently dangerous activities. Individuals undertake these activities at their own risk. The information put forth in this guide has been collected from a variety of sources and is not guaranteed to be completely accurate or reliable. Many conditions and some information may change owing to weather and numerous other factors beyond the control of the authors and publishers. Individuals or groups must determine the risks, use their own judgment, and take full responsibility for their actions. Do not depend on any information found in this book for your own personal safety. Your safety depends on your own good judgment based on your skills, education, and experience.

It is up to the users of this guidebook to acquire the necessary skills for safe experiences and to exercise caution in potentially hazardous areas. The authors and publishers of this guide accept no responsibility for your actions or the results that occur from another's actions, choices, or judgments. If you have any doubt as to your safety or your ability to attempt anything described in this guidebook, do not attempt it.

Contents

5th Edition Changes

New in this edition are designated winter walking trails that are also used for fat-tire biking. Summer trails are becoming increasingly multi-use, though less so in Volume 1 compared to other areas of K Country.

The devastating flood of 2013 damaged all the access roads into this area. Since then they have all been repaired and new bridges built. Trailheads and day-use areas were also affected and trails most of all. Some trails have been completely rerouted, others just partially and a few abandoned.

New trail building continues apace. Terrific new trails in this edition include the Guinns Pass trail and the High Rockies section of the Trans Canada Trail. And as before,, I continue to give up-to-the-minute information, which means that almost every trail has had to be rewritten.

As before, trails run the gamut from short interpretive trails to long day scrambles rated easy and backpacks.

For up-to-date info as changes occur, visit our website at kananaskistrails.com.

Acknowledgements

The following have been extremely helpful and supportive in giving out information in their areas of expertise: James Cieslak, Jeff Eamon, Jeff Gruttz, Matt Hadley, Gord Hurlburt, Gérard LaChapelle, Sara Lilley and Masaki Hayashi, and Alex Mueller.

All photos are by the author unless credited otherwise. The following have provided the rest of the photos in the effort to get the best possible. Thanks once again to long time K Country compatriot Alf Skrastins, who gives me free rein with his extensive photo collection. A close second in terms of numbers are Bob Spirko and Dinah Kruze, who contribute to all the volumes. Thanks are also due to the following: Sonny Bou (for the cover and title page images), Sharon Cairns, George Chan, Matt Clay, Clive Cordery, Eric Coulthard, Teresa Daffern, Wendy Devent, Vern Dewit, Rich Dodds and Jeremy Philips, Brenda Everitt, Gillian Ford, Maurice Gaucher, Matt Hobbs, Ron Hunter, Gord Hurlburt, Pete Irwin, Tanya Koob, Leon Kubbernus, Stephen Larsen and Nikita Paskiewich, Annette Le Faive, Sara Lilley, Dave Macdonald, Angélique and Allan Mandel, Roy Millar, Harold Muller, Bernie Nemeth, Andrew Nugara, Rachel Oggy, Carl Potter, Jody Robbins, Bill Rowe, and finally, Greg and Karen Smith who came to the rescue at the last minute. Thank you all.

PHOTO CAPTIONS

Front cover: Mt. Joffre from Northover Ridge. Photo Sonny Bou

Page 1: Taiga and Sierra at Frozen Lake.

Title page: The crux section of Northover Ridge. Note the figure on the northernmost high point. Photo Sonny Bou

Contents page: The tarn between upper and lower Birdwood Lakes reflects Mt. Birdwood and Snow Peak.

Page 17: The view from Piggy Plus Bluffs of Piggy Plus in front of Mt. Robertson, Robertson Glacier and Sir Douglas.

Page 391: Larch on North Kent.

Back Cover: Alpines on Birdwood Pass. Photo Alf Skrastins

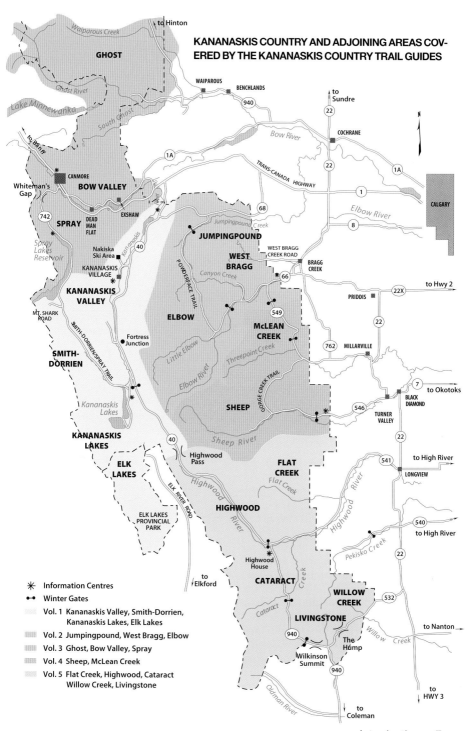

KANANASKIS COUNTRY AND ADJOINING AREAS COVERED BY THE KANANASKIS COUNTRY TRAIL GUIDES

GHOST

WAIPAROUS

BENCHLANDS

to Hinton

to Sundre

940

22

Bow River

COCHRANE

1A

TRANS-CANADA HIGHWAY

22

1

1A

CALGARY

CANMORE

BOW VALLEY

Whiteman's Gap

742

SPRAY

DEAD MAN FLAT

EXSHAW

68

Jumpingpound Creek

JUMPINGPOUND

Elbow River

8

Nakiska Ski Area

40

WEST BRAGG

WEST BRAGG CREEK ROAD

BRAGG CREEK

Spray Lakes Reservoir

KANANASKIS VILLAGE

Canyon Creek

66

549

PRIDDIS

22X

to Hwy 2

KANANASKIS VALLEY

ELBOW

McLEAN CREEK

22

MT. SHARK ROAD

Fortress Junction

762

MILLARVILLE

SMITH-DORRIEN

SMITH-DORRIEN/SPRAY TRAIL

Little Elbow

Elbow River

Threepoint Creek

GORGE CREEK TRAIL

546

7

to Okotoks

BLACK DIAMOND

Kananaskis Lakes

SHEEP

TURNER VALLEY

22

KANANASKIS LAKES

40

Sheep River

ELK LAKES

Highwood Pass

Highwood River

FLAT CREEK

Flat Creek

541

to High River

LONGVIEW

Highwood River

ELK LAKES PROVINCIAL PARK

ELK RIVER ROAD

HIGHWOOD

540

to High River

Pekisko Creek

22

to Elkford

Highwood House

CATARACT

WILLOW CREEK

532

to Nanton

LIVINGSTONE

The Hump

Willow Creek

940

Wilkinson Summit

940

Cataract Creek

Oldman River

to Coleman

to HWY 3

✳ Information Centres

•–• Winter Gates

Vol. 1 Kananaskis Valley, Smith-Dorrien, Kananaskis Lakes, Elk Lakes

Vol. 2 Jumpingpound, West Bragg, Elbow

Vol. 3 Ghost, Bow Valley, Spray

Vol. 4 Sheep, McLean Creek

Vol. 5 Flat Creek, Highwood, Cataract Willow Creek, Livingstone

Kananaskis Country

THE NAME

Since the previous edition the whole world has learned to pronounce the name 'Kananaskis': CTV's Lloyd Robertson, US president George W. Bush, British prime minister Tony Blair, Russian president Vladimir Putin. One wonders what explorer John Palliser would have thought of it all.

The strange name dates back to 1858 when Palliser named the pass he was about to cross 'Kananaskis' ...*after the name of an Indian, of whom there is a legend, giving an account of his most wonderful recovery from the blow of an axe which had stunned but had failed to kill him, and the river which flows through this gorge also bears his name.* Possibly the Indian in question was the great Cree Koominakoos who lost an eye and part of his scalp in a battle with the Blackfoot in the Willow Creek area but made a miraculous recovery and showed up at Fort Edmonton some weeks later ...*ready to take to the warpath again.*

Since then, the name has been cannibalized in various ways: can'-un-ask'-us, Koonanaskis, Cannanaskis (better as Cannabiscus surely?).

THE CONCEPT

Today, the Kananaskis Passes, Kananaskis Lakes and the Kananaskis River form the heart of Kananaskis Country (or K Country as it is more commonly called), a provincial recreation area owned by Albertans and established on October 7, 1977, to ...*alleviate congestion in National Parks, and to provide greater recreation opportunities for Albertans.*

Let's give credit to architect Bill Milne, who got the ball rolling. Alberta premier Peter Lougheed and Clarence Copithorne, then minister of highways, quickly came on board and a new Hwy. 40 was built. Their vision for the Kananaskis Valley was one of strenuous physical outdoor activity accessible from a good road but with minimal services. As we all know, that simple idea turned into a grand plan called Kananaskis Country, encompassing a lot more country (over 4000 square kilometres) and a lot more development, with facilities for every conceivable outdoor sport.

Many people forget that Kananaskis Country has always been multi-use, meaning it is also open to logging, cattle grazing and oil and gas exploration.

LOCATION

K Country is located on the eastern slopes of the Canadian Rockies, west and south of the Olympic city of Calgary, Alberta. From the city outskirts the eastern boundary is only a 20-minute drive away.

The western boundary adjoins Banff National Park, then runs down the Continental Divide. The northern boundary is delineated by Hwy. 1A and the fringe communities of Exshaw, Dead Man Flat and Canmore. The eastern boundary coincides neatly with the Bow-Crow Forest reserve boundary, while the southern boundary is marked by Hwy. 732.

GETTING THERE

Calgary is served by major airlines, several bus companies and by train from the east. That's it as far as public transportation goes. You need a car.

The core area described in Volume 1 is usually accessed from the Trans-Canada Highway via Hwy. 40. It can also be reached from the town of Longview on Hwy. 22 via Hwys. 541 and 40 over Highwood Pass. Another way in is along Hwy. 68 from the Trans-Canada or via Hwy. 742 from Canmore.

The northern portion of Elk Lakes Provincial Park is most often reached from Peter Lougheed Provincial Park on foot. The alternative is to drive to Sparwood on Hwy. 3, then take Hwy. 43 north to Elkford. From Elkford a gravel road follows the Elk River Valley to the park entrance.

What to Expect

Volume 1 centres on the Kananaskis River Valley and its tributary Smith-Dorrien Creek, most of which now lies within Peter Lougheed and Spray Valley provincial parks. The junction of the two rivers is the heart of K Country at Kananaskis Lakes.

Radiating out from the lakes are a number of passes: Highwood Pass, which carries the highest paved highway in Canada, Elk Pass, which leads over to Elk Lakes Provincial Park in B.C., and the infamous North and South Kananaskis passes to the west.

A large portion of the mid-Kananaskis Valley is taken up by the Evan-Thomas Provincial Recreation Area, which features Kananaskis Village, Nakiska Ski Area, Ribbon Creek ski trails, Kananaskis Country Golf Course and Boundary Ranch. Farther up the valley is Fortress Ski Resort (closed at time of writing).

The Fisher and Opal Ranges lining the east side of the valley provide exploratory trips up canyons and along rocky ridges.

Separating the Smith-Dorrien and Kananaskis valleys is the Kananaskis Range, which offers something for every level of hiker — numerous lakes within cirques, meadows and passes, easy ascents and classic ridgewalks, Mt. Allan being the prime example. Old Logging roads often give access. In fact, the Smith-Dorrien and Mt. Shark ski, snowshoe and bike trail systems are based on logging roads.

In the west along the Great Divide, the K Country scenery reaches its zenith — high peaks (up to 3449 metres on Mt. Joffre), glaciers, waterfalls, extensive alpine meadows, lakes, boisterous streams and old-growth forest. This is the scenario for the Canadian Rockies' most spectacular backpack the exciting Northover traverse.

This volume also covers the north end of Elk Lakes Provincial Park, which is known for its lakes and B.C. bush.

WEATHER TRENDS

The present trend is to hike all year round using microspikes in winter. Off-snow hiking generally starts in May in a few valleys at the north end of Hwy. 40. The Smith-Dorrien and Kananaskis Lakes area starts to open up much later, around the beginning of July. May is often a dry month, with rains starting in June. The flower months of July and August are the best for big trips, but be aware of late afternoon thunderstorms should that be the trend that particular year. Indian summers through September and October can be glorious. The mornings may be cold but the sunny, stable weather is a relief and the larches may have turned.

As in any mountain areas, snow can fall in any month of the year. In the rotten summer of 1992, for instance, snow fell on three consecutive weekends through late July into mid-August. Conversely, the summer of 2021 was consistently hot with the temperatures hovering around the mid-30s. At such times the area can be locked down to prevent forest fires. Generally, low cloud is not the problem it is in other, wetter ranges of the world and navigating blind is an unusual event.

NATURAL HISTORY IN A NUTSHELL

I urge you to buy the appropriate field guides or Ben Gadd's all-in-one *Handbook of the Canadian Rockies*.

Mammals Most commonly seen: bighorn sheep along Hwy. 40, moose along Hwy. 742, mule deer, elk, black bear and grizzlies, which often close down the Bill Milne bike path. Grizzlies most often frequent the valleys on either side of the Smith-Dorrien Valley, the high passes to the west and the area about Highwood Pass and Ptarmigan Cirque trail. Less commonly seen are wolves, goats, lynx (mainly in winter), and cougars at the north end of the valley. In the wet valley bottoms are muskrats, beavers and the odd river otter. Other critters include porcupines, ground and tree squirrels, and chipmunks, picas and marmots among the rocks.

Birds Most common—whiskey jacks (the ones that gather around when you stop to eat), Clark's nutcrackers, hummingbirds (wear red), ravens, thrushes, chickadees, kingfishers, owls, grouse in the forest, ptarmigans up in the alpine, loons on the lakes and various waterfowl in the valley wetlands. Dippers are common in fast running creeks. Golden eagle counting occurs during spring and fall migrations around the Ribbon Creek area.

Fish Trout in the lakes, which are stocked annually. Bull trout spawn at the mouth of Smith-Dorrien Creek.

Vegetation Trees range through fire succession lodgepole pine in the east to spruce and fir mixed with larch in the west. Balsam poplars grow in the more arid valley bottoms of the Fisher Range and are associated with dryas flats.

For too brief a time alpine meadows and grassy ridges are crammed with flowers in July and August. In particular, overseas visitors will be intoxicated by the gaudy colours of North America's Indian paintbrush. Glacier lilies cover glades near treeline.

Nibble on strawberries, raspberries, gooseberries and blackcurrants.

NATURAL HAZARDS & NUISANCES

River crossings The once wild Kananaskis River is part of the Bow River's hydro-electric scheme. Flow is no longer controlled by seasonal variations, but by the touch of a button, which has led to a few people getting benighted on the opposite bank. Upstream of Kananaskis Lakes this glacier-fed river and its tributaries can be impassable for much of the season.

Smith-Dorrien Creek and the Elk River in B.C. are impassable during spring runoff and after prolonged heavy rain, as are many creeks running east from the Divide and the Kananaskis Range. Conversely, creeks running west toward Hwys. 742 and 40 are much smaller and more manageable.

Caribbean water it is not, as Anthony Hopkins found out during the filming of *The Edge*. If cold water makes you feel sick to your stomach, wear neoprene booties.

Bears and other beasts At all times be aware of bears, but particularly in early spring after hibernation and in fall when the berries ripen. Most of the area described in this book is a high bear area. Many hikers carry a repellent and bear bangers where they can reach them in a hurry.

In the paranoia over bears we often forget that elk and moose should be given a wide berth too, especially in spring when with young and in fall during the mating season when males get very ornery. Lately cougars have become a year-round worry.

Hunters Hunting is allowed outside the provincial parks and provincial recreation areas, Marmot Basin being a prime example. Wildland Provincial Parks allow hunting, but generally the territory covered by Volume 1 is not a big hunting area.

Ticks Between about March and mid-June (and in certain areas right through to November) ticks are abroad and are found mainly in places where there are lots of sheep.

Loose rock In Calgary an insurance company's ad on a billboard once read "As firm as the Rockies," which made me laugh aloud. The "Rotten Rockies" aren't called that for nothing, the sedimentary limestone being subject to extremes of heat and cold. Of course there is firm limestone, but it's safer to expect the worse. On scrambling pitches, develop the technique for pushing handholds back into place. Be particularly aware of rockfall in gullies. You will run into scree—lots of it. Utilize game trails where the scree is more stabilized and watch for the occasional bounding rock from people scrambling above you.

Facilities

Hwy. 40 (Kananaskis Trail)
The **Stoney Nakoda Resort Casino** has a hotel and three eateries. Peaks Cafe is open for breakfast at 7 a.m. Sidelines Lounge (pub fare, pizza etc.) is open until 11 pm. The adjoining **Bearspaw Travel Centre** has a gas station and a Tim Hortons which sells groceries. In the same complex, **Goodstoney Meadows** has a gas bar, take-out restaurant, convenience store and shops.

Barrier Lake Information Centre is open 8 a.m.–6 p.m. April 1 to the end of October, then 9 a.m.–4.30 p.m. the rest of the year.

Sundance Lodges offers unique accommodation in tipis and trappers tents. Bring your own bedding and cooking supplies or rent. Attached is a coin laundry, small grocery store and gift shop. Open mid-May to near the end of September.

Boundary Ranch, run by Rick and Denise Guinn (son and daughter-in-law of Alvin Guinn of Guinn's Pass fame), is the place to go for trail rides. Rick's Steakhouse is open during July and August for lunch and early dinner until 6 p.m. on weekdays and 7 p.m. on weekends. One of the few eateries where corn on the cob is a staple. Gift shop attached.

Kananaskis Village has three hotels: Pomeroy Kananaskis Mountain Lodge, Mount Kidd Manor and Crosswaters Resort featuring a nordic spa, upscale restaurants and bars, and shops. Woody's Pub is popular for pub-type food. The Village Centre houses Moose Family Kitchen, which provides snacks and light meals with a Japanese touch, an information counter, a post office and Kananaskis Outfitters, who, besides selling outdoor gear and guidebooks, rent out bikes, bike racks, canoes, hiking equipment and ski gear during the winter. They also offer guided hikes.

Down the road at Ribbon Creek is **Kananaskis Wilderness Hostel** with fully equipped kitchen, coin laundry and volleyball court.

The **Summit Restaurant at Kananaskis Country Golf Course** is open for breakfast between 8 a.m. and 12 p.m. A wide selection of food is offered for lunch and dinner up to 9 p.m. The **Mount Kidd Snack Shack** is located on the Bill Milne bike path.

Fortress Junction sells gas, fresh coffee, snacks including breakfast sandwiches that can be heated up in the microwave, groceies, camping supplies, locally made gifts and mammoth ice cream cones. They also have a cash machine. Open year-round, until 10 p.m. in the summer.

Mount Kidd RV Park has a snack bar, groceries and hot tubs.

Kananaskis Lakes Trail/Road
The **Peter Lougheed Discovery Centre** dispenses information and has a comfortable lounge to relax in. The displays are a must see. Open 9 a.m.–6 p.m. mid May to mid October.

William Watson Lodge offers accommodation and a campground specifically for seniors and people with disabilities.

Boulton Creek Trading Post sells groceries, guidebooks and all manner of camping supplies, including sleeping bags. A small concession sells ice cream, pizza slices, hot dogs, sausage rolls and squares. Boulton Creek Rental rents out canoes and kayaks (parked at Lower Kananaskis Lake). Open mid May to mid September, 9 a.m.–10 p.m. at the height of summer.

Elk Lakes Provincial Park
Elk Lakes Cabin at the entrance is operated by the Alpine Club of Canada (ACC), and is open year-round for accommodation. Provided are stoves (bring white gas), mattresses, pots, dishes and cutlery. Reservations required. Pay here for campgrounds.

Hwy. 742 (Smith-Dorrien/Spray Trail)
Mount Engadine Lodge offers year-round accommodation in the lodge or in luxurious glamping tents. All meals provided. Walk-in afternoon tea is available from 2–5 p.m. between mid-June and Thanksgiving. Reservations recommended. Sunday brunch—available all year-round—must be reserved. Guided hikes can be arranged.

Camping

HIGHWAY ACCESSIBLE CAMPING

Park campgrounds fill up quickly in the summer. It's galling to find every campsite full of campers whose idea of exercise is the walk to the biffy, so book ahead if you can. Overflow areas with minimal facilities are often available. After Labour Day the situation eases. Prices vary depending on amenities offered and the number of vehicles in your party. Either phone 1-403-678-0760 or go online at reserve.albertaparks.ca and a permit will be emailed to you.

Hwy. 68 (Sibbald Creek Trail west end)
Stoney Creek group (beginning of May to the first week in October).

Hwy. 40 (Kananaskis Trail)
Porcupine group (May 1–mid October).
Eau Claire (mid May–Sep. 1).

Kananaskis Lakes Trail/road
Canyon (mid June–Sep. 1)
Elkwood (mid May–Sep. 1)
Lower Lake group (year-round)
Pocaterra group (mid May–mid October)
Boulton Creek (May 1–mid October)
Lower Lake (mid May–mid September)
Mount Sarrail (mid June–Sep 1)
Interlakes (mid May–mid October)

OTHER SITES

Hwy. 40 (Kananaskis Trail)
Sundance Lodges (Mid-May to near the end of September). Besides tipis and trapper's tents, Sundance also has regular campsites. Call 403-591-7122.
Mount Kidd RV Park (year-round). Campers Centre features a grocery store, coffee bar, laundromat, showers, saunas. Outside area children's wading pool, tennis courts, horseshoe pits, volleyball court. Call 403-591-7700.
Canoe Meadows group and individual. Check the Alberta Whtewater Assn. site under campgrounds. Camp kitchen with freezer.

Elk Lakes Provincial Park
Park entrance next to the parking lot.

BACKCOUNTRY CAMPING

For official sites you need a permit costing $12 per person, plus a camping pass, plus maintenance fee, plus GST. Children under 16 are free, but still require a permit. Either phone 1-403-678-0760 or go online reserve.albertaparks.ca and a permit will be emailed to you. It will have occurred to you that backcountry camping can cost considerably more than highway-accessible camping.

Off Hwy. 40
Jewell Bay, regular and equestrian, Ribbon Falls, Ribbon Lake, Lillian Lake, Elbow Lake.

Off Kananaskis Lakes Trail/road
Point, Forks, Three Isle Lake, Three Isle Creek, Turbine Canyon, Aster Lake.

In Elk Lakes Provincial Park
Lower Elk Lake, Pétain Creek, Pétain Basin bivouac. Cost is $5 per person per night. Children under 16 go free. Pay at the Elk Lakes Cabin. Random camping is not allowed.

Off Hwy. 742
(Smith-Dorrien/Spray Trail)
Rummel Lake winter only.
Along High Rockies Trail, non-bookable hiker/biker sites are available for through backpackers and bikepackers at Buller Mountain day-use area, Sawmill parking lot and Pocaterra overflow. All have food lockers.

RANDOM BACKCOUNTRY CAMPING

Random camping is not allowed in provincial parks and provincial recreation areas. Outside of these areas you can camp almost anywhere as long as you are 1 km away from a road. Memorial Lakes requires a special permit.

Other Information

ROAD CLOSURES

Hwy. 40 between Kananaskis Lakes Trail (road) and Highwood Junction is closed between Dec 1 and Jun 14. During this time, skiing, snowshoeing,walking and biking are allowed.

Valleyview Trail/road is permanently closed between Elpoca day-use area and Little Highwood Pass day-use area. Walking and biking are allowed except at specified times when the road is used as a dumping ground for roadkill. Check the K Country website.

ONLINE INFORMATION

CHECK THE K COUNTRY WEBSITE

Check the K Country trail report for trail conditions. Especially useful are the "Important Notes," which among other things give warnings about bear or cougar sightings and temporary trail closures. See kananaskis-country.ca.

BEWARE OF ALLTRAILS

According to Kananaskis Public Safety, many of the accidents they are called out to happen to hikers willy nilly following lines on their iPhones into potentially dangerous terrain for which they are ill prepared. Some trails follow the correct line, others do not and sometimes there is no trail at all. And what little information is given can be wildly wrong. For example, are you really going to take your bichon frise for walkies up Mt. Smuts, a difficult scramble with 5th class climbing?

BEWARE OF OPEN STREET MAPS

It has been my experience that trails marked on these maps can be not only wrong but often non-existent, posted by users who have bushwhacked.

CHECK OUR BLOG

The blog site maintained by Gillean and Tony Daffern covers all things Kananaskis, including notification of new trails, trail changes and trail issues.
See kananaskistrails.com

CHECK OUT OUR KANANASKIS TRAILFINDER APP

Kananaskis Trailfinder is a web app linked to a database that contains over 500 trails in K Country. When you select an area you are presented with a list of all the trails in the area. Tabs refine the list to Easy, Moderate, Strenuous and Winter trails. Very useful when deciding where to go. Clicking on a trail will give you some basic information and a reference to the trail guide. There are also lists of trails such as "Best Ridge Walks," "Favourite Hikes" and more.
See kananaskistrails.com/trailfinder/

CHECK REPUTABLE BLOGS

Blogs maintained by experienced hikers and scramblers are generally reliable..

CHECK THE WEBCAMS

The only webcam in this area is at Nakiska.

FRIENDS OF KANANASKIS COUNTRY

The Friends is a not-for-profit registered charity that works in partnership with Alberta Tourism, Parks & Recreation "for the benefit of Kananaskis Country and its visitors." One of its mandates is to repair trails, for which it is always looking for volunteers. See kananaskis.org.

CONSERVATION PASS

At present, vehicles parked in K Country and the Bow Valley need a conservation pass. Single-day and yearly passes can be bought online or at visitor information centres at Barrier and the Discovery Centre in Peter Lougheed Park. With a change in government, this requirement could change.

Using the Book

ARRANGEMENT OF TRAILS

Trails are arranged by highway and are colour coded. Refer to the map on page 16.

TYPES OF TRAILS

Official Trails officially maintained in Kananaskis Country by Alberta Environment and Parks are a mix of new and old trails, logging and exploration roads, fire roads and cutlines. Expect parking lots at trailheads with biffies and the occasional picnic table. Junctions are marked with signposts of the "You are here" variety. Some trails have directional arrows or coloured markers on trees or posts. Unless the trail is equestrian, expect bridges over creeks.

Unofficial Trails are similar to the above, but sometimes have no obvious trailhead and are neither signposted nor marked in any way except perhaps for the occasional flagging, cairn or trimmed branches. Creek crossings are the norm. For the first time, this category includes trails that have been demoted from official status.

Routes either have no trails or have long trail-less sections where you have to navigate from one intermittent game trail to another. Often there is some bushwhacking.

Scrambles can have official or unofficial status or be routes. They range from ridge walks to gruelling uphill flogs in excess of 1000 metres to the top of a mountain. You can be sure of scree, and possibly a pitch or two of easy scrambling. There may be mild exposure. Special equipment is unnecessary in optimum conditions when the mountain is devoid of snow and the weather is good. Under snow, leave the scrambles for the experts.

HEIGHTS, HEIGHT GAINS

Heights and height gains are given in both metric and imperial.

RATING TRAILS

No attempt has been made to classify trails. What's difficult for one person is easy for another. It's all relative. Also coming into play is the length of a trail, its gradient, its remoteness from a trailhead, conditions underfoot and so on. Read the introductory description carefully. If you're having a horrible time, it's up to you to turn back and try something easier.

RATING TIMES

Times are dependent on too many variables — everybody chugs along at a different rate. Some will be carrying heavy packs; some people, like me, like to make frequent flower stops. And then there are the underfoot conditions to consider, the weather and so on.

- Half day, up to 3 hours
- Day, up to 6 hours
- Long day, up to 10 hours plus. (Take headlamps.)
- Backpack, overnight camping.

Some of the trips are designated "bike 'n' hike" and even "paddle 'n' hike." Biking the first part of the trail can cut down the time considerably. In this way I've often squeezed a weekend trip into one day.

DISTANCES

Distances are given in kilometres. Distances shown between each segment of trail are not cumulative, but show the distance between segments.

TRAIL DESCRIPTIONS

Descriptions are arranged according to the character of the trail. Most trails lead to a single destination. But sometimes the destination is the springboard for further options under headings like "going farther," "making a loop," "optional descent route" etc. I sometimes describe the same mountain with different ways up and down, or an area with a number of trails or peaks radiating out from the same access. Occasionally loop trails can be extended into longer loops. Long-distance trails, rarely hiked in their entirety, are described by segment.

DIRECTIONS

Left and right refer to the direction of travel. Skier's left/right refers to descent, climber's left/right to ascent.

GRID REFERENCES & GPS RECEIVERS

Where I give grid references you can follow along on your topo map if you don't have a GPS receiver.

Maps have blue grid lines running east/west and north/south. Each line is numbered. The first two numbers indicate the grid line forming the west boundary of the kilometre square in which your point is located, and the third number gives the estimated number of tenths of a kilometre your point is east of that line. The fourth and fifth numbers indicate the south boundary of the square and the last number is the estimated number of tenths of a kilometre your point is north of that line.

GPS receivers are useful when bushwhacking or for finding your way back to a trail or a trailhead. However, be aware that neither grid references on maps nor waypoints on GPS receivers are dead accurate.

MAPS

Sketchmaps in the text are not always to scale and serve only to clarify complex areas where you might go wrong. Maps at the back of the book are based on today's topo maps, which come in a mix of imperial and metric. Therefore, the contour intervals vary. There are also errors like missing creeks, lakes, mountains and glaciers. Because of this, these maps are intended as a guide only. Still, trails and routes are marked as accurately as possible.

- Red line: a trail, official or unofficial
- Red dash: a route
- Black line: other trails
- Dashed black line: other routes

BUYING MAPS

Maps in the back of this book are for reference only. You need to carry a bona fide topo map. The latest editions of Gem Trek maps come close to being the perfect maps for the area, with contour intervals at 25 metres. They show grid lines, up-to-date road alignments, official trails, some unofficial trails, and major powerlines.

Government topo maps, depending on the edition, are in both imperial and metric, with contour lines at 100-foot and 40-metre intervals respectively (not so good). Occasionally, features like small lakes, streams, glaciers and even mountains are omitted, which leads to exciting discoveries.

Provincial Resource Base Maps from Alberta Energy & Natural Resources are updated fairly regularly and show what the other maps don't — all cutlines, all powerlines and exploration and logging roads. Unfortunately, the reality is sometimes nothing like what is shown on the map.

MAPS FOR VOLUME 1

Gem Trek

- Canmore and Kananaskis Village: scale 1:50,000, contour interval 25 m.
- Kananaskis Lakes scale 1:50,000, contour interval 25 m.

Government topo maps
Scale 1: 50,000
Contour interval 40 metres
- 82 O/3 Canmore
- 82 J/11 Kananaskis Lakes
- 82 J/14 Spray Lakes Reservoir

Contour interval 100 feet
- 82 J/10 Mount Rae
- 82 J/15 Bragg Creek
- 82 J/6 Mount Abruzzi

ABBREVIATIONS USED IN TEXT

TCT Trans Canada Trail
GDT Great Divide Trail
HRT High Rockies Trail

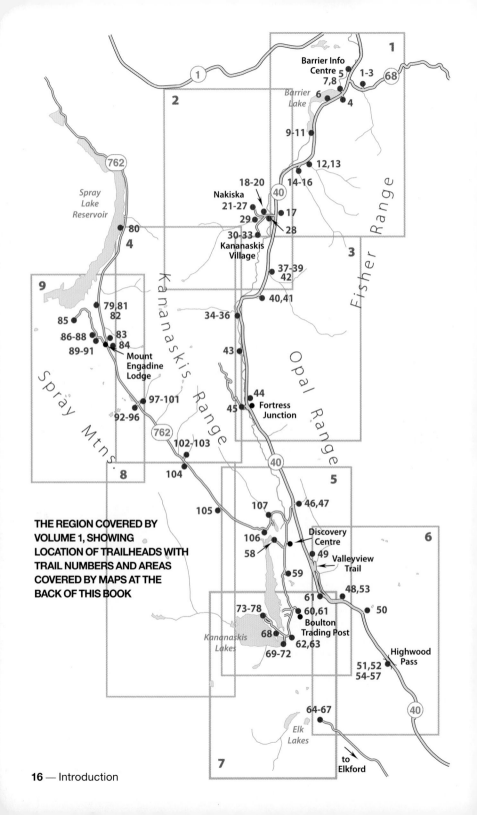

THE REGION COVERED BY
VOLUME 1, SHOWING
LOCATION OF TRAILHEADS WITH
TRAIL NUMBERS AND AREAS
COVERED BY MAPS AT THE
BACK OF THIS BOOK

Trail Descriptions

1 Horton Hill

map 1

Short day hikes
Route, unofficial trails
Height gain 320 m (1050 ft.)
High point 1722 m (5650 ft.)
Map 82 O/3 Canmore

Access Hwy. 68 (Sibbald Creek Trail) at Lusk Creek day-use area.

"It took a lot of mussels to do it."

Comments You'll have fun reading some of the comments in the summit register atop Horton Hill, the forested hill rising behind Tim Horton's Children's Ranch off Hwy. 40.

Nowadays the hill is fairly popular all year round with two moderately steep trails of the game trail variety leading to the saddle where you pick up the better ranch trail. Go for the exercise and the views.

Trail history The original trail started from the ranch. But because the ranch didn't want the hiking public traipsing through their lease, they suggested we come in via a logging road which joined the trail a third of the way up the hill. When the logging road was reclaimed in 2009, the ranch further suggested we use their disused horse trail, but unfortunately a derecho (straight-line wind)

felled a whole swath of trees over the top of it. So now we must start from the opposite side of the hill off Hwy. 68.

Naming Miles Gilbert "Tim" Horton, a hockey hall of famer, proved there was life after hockey by founding Canada's largest coffee and doughnut franchise. After his untimely death, the Tim Horton's Children's Foundation was established to offer summer camps for underprivileged kids. This particular ranch opened in 1991.

Geology The trees hide a series of descending ribs and draws, some steep-sided, that all end abruptly at the same contour line around the southwest slope, likely signifying the top of the lake that formed when the great Bow Valley Glacier receded some 10,000 years ago. Interestingly, drainage from the glacier at its maximum height flowed northeast along the line of today's Hwy. 68.

1A Southwest Slope
Distance 1.8 km one way

Comments The usual winter route heads straight up the southwest flank to join with 1B near the saddle. Watch for flagging, beaten down juniper bushes, footprints in shale and yellow wooden arrows.

Horton Hill trails.
Dashed lines are routes.

trail
ranch 1
viewpoint
aspens
1A
LUSK
CREEK 1B
Lusk Creek
68

Getting to the start of the climb

A lot of people have trouble finding the bottom of this climb. So here's how to do it without beating through the bush.

From the parking area walk down to the loop road where you pick up the trail heading down Lusk Creek valley. At the first obvious junction go left and cross a sandy area in the open. At the next obvious junction go right and pass a yellow Alberta Provincial Boundary sign. Just before the trail ends above the banktop (washout after the 2013 flood), turn right up the hillside on a trail that starts between two flagged trees.

The climb to 1B

Go right initially, then following flagging, wind up out of the trees to the left of rocks and climb step no. 1. After a grassy flat area the trail climbs up a rib to the left of a draw, first on the left side, then trampling across juniper bushes up the right side to another easing. At step no. 2 the trail splits and does a figure 8. Keeping right is easier, but there's still some juniper to plow through.

Continue more easily uphill, ultimately diagonalling left, right and up to a large tree fallen across the trail. Cross at the one place where the side branches have been cut.

Continue uphill on another rib to the bottom of a steep shale slope. The trail follows the right edge of it to a viewpoint on the top. Walk flat aspen meadow, beyond which is step no. 3. Arrive at a small circle of shale.

From here the trail follows open, shaley avenues between trees to a T-junction with 1B. Turn left. But before you do, step right a few metres to enjoy the best viewpoint the hill has to offer: the vista ranging from Hunchback Hills to left, through Lusk Pass and the Fisher range to the Baldy Peaks, Barrier Lake and Yates Mountain.

To Ranch trail

The flat bit of trail soon enters pine forest and divides. Go left per the flagging. Step over some deadfall to a trail leading to the very much clearer ranch trail at a yellow arrow. Turn right.

Opposite: Heading down the man-made clearing below the summit you get a view of Barrier Lake enclosed by Mt. Baldy to left and Yates Mountain.

Above: #1A The flat section through the aspens.

To summit
On the ranch trail descend slightly to a saddle, then start what is really step no. 4 to the summit ridge, en route crossing a man-made clearing. At the top the trail heads right to a small clearing with cairn and ammunition box enclosing geocache goodies like Halloween masks, the summit register and the ranch book used for "thoughts or views of inspiration and courage."

DESCENT OPTION

1B Southwest Ridge

Distance 1.7 km one way

Comments A fast descent trail (also used as an ascent trail) with interesting variations at the end. No flagging or markers.

Return to the outstanding viewpoint near the junction with #1A.

From the viewpoint descend a trail in shale, lower down veering right through an avenue and a few trees to another open area. Again, wend slightly left and into the open forest of the southwest ridge. The steepness eases off the lower you get, until ultimately you're traversing rightward between the forest edge and the mouth of a wide, open draw to the left. Climb a little onto a grassy prominence overlooking Hwy. 68.

The trail continues down a gentle slope to the left of a forested draw. At the steepening cross the draw on a trail to a rib and descend it. Near the bottom, look for a trail heading right onto an aspen bench with one bright blue prayer flag. From here, getting off onto the day-use area access road is easiest from the far end of the bench.

Return options to Hwy. 68
Descend the wide open draw to its abrupt end. Traverse left to a small open gully, descend by the side of it and cross it on game trail to a small ridge that offers an easy way down to the blue road sign. Alternatively, from the prominence, descend the easy grass ridge to the right of the wide draw, at the end picking your way down to the access road at the edge of slope stabilization matting.

Top: Summit cairn and view to Midnight Peak across the cutblocks.

Bottom: #1B Climbing up the shale trail toward the outstanding viewpoint at the top.

2 Kananaskis Integrated Forest Interpretive Trail

map 1

Half day hike
Official trail
Distance 2.7 km one way from official access, 2.4 km from popular access
Height gain 180 m (590 ft.)
Maps 82 O/3 Canmore

Official access Hwy. 68 (Sibbald Creek Trail) at Lusk Creek day-use area,
Popular access Park 300 m west of Lusk Creek crossing at the widening of Hwy. 68 below a sign "No Motorized Vehicles." Deduct 360 m from trip.
Campground access from Stoney Creek group campground via a connecting trail starting from the kiosk. Park at the closed gate without blocking it. Distance to the interpretive trail is 440 m. Deduct 360 m
Also accessible from #3 Baldy Pass from the north.

Comments An easy uphill trail built in 2009 offering good views, interpretive signs and benches to sit on. The walk can be extended by returning via Old Mill Road (6.1 km), this little loop better as a winter walk or snowshoe. A much more interesting 8.2 km loop, summer or winter, takes in Lusk Pass trail and the original finish. See ##2A and 2B and the sketchmap on the next page.

Also check out Lusk Pass in Volume 2.

To Interpretive trail turnoff 800 m

From Lusk Creek day-use area, follow the access road out to Hwy. 68. Turn right, cross Lusk Creek on culvert, then follow the trail up the grassy bank to the flat above, which is the site of a gravel pit. At a 4-way go straight and pass between boulders onto an old road leading to the U of C's BGS Institute field research station. (Trail to left is the return route for #2B, the Lusk Pass trail original finish. Trail to right has come in up the bank from the popular access.)

In another 440 m is a 4-way. Turn left on the signed interpretive trail. (Trail to right has come in from Stoney Creek group campground.)

The final interpretive sign and Mt. Baldy, the south peak to its left.

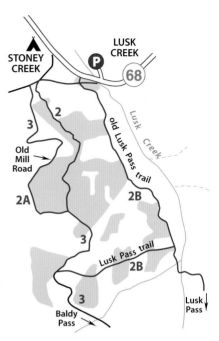

Kananaskis Integrated Forest interpretive trail, Lusk Creek loop, Lusk Pass trail and Baldy Pass from the north trail

Interpretive trail 1.9 km

The trail starts a twisting climb through mixed forest and cutblocks displaying the bright green foliage of young aspens. As you climb, Horton Hill and the Hunchback Hills come into view to your left. To your right rises the long wall of Mt. Baldy with South Baldy to its left.

Come to the first set of benches at Barrier Lake Viewpoint, as it's optimistically called. After more winding and climbing come to the final two signs and benches, the view now including distant peaks of the Bow Valley and the Ghost.

The trail continues climbing into a big flat cutblock where it heads across to the forest edge to join Baldy Pass trail at a signpost. This is also the Old Mill Road and the Trans Canada Trail. From here you can make two loops

Top: Trail en route to the Old Mill Road. Midnight Peak ahead, showing the ascent route facing.

Bottom : #2B View from Lusk Pass trail of cutblocks and the peaks of the Fisher Range.

Opposite: #2B Descending the old Lusk Pass trail (née highway).

2A Old Mill Road Loop

Official trail
Distance 6.1 km loop to official start

Comments The easiest and least attractive option is all through trees.

Turn right and simply follow the dirt road winding down the forested hillside. At the T-junction, turn right to return to the trailhead.

2B Lusk Creek Loop

Official, unofficial trails
Distance 8.2 km loop to official start
Total height gain 214 m (702 ft.)
High point 1830 m (6004 ft.)

Comments A very popular add-on , summer or winter, that climbs higher into more open country with fine views of the Fisher Range, then returns down Lusk Creek valley.

To Lusk Pass trail 1.1 km
Turn left. Follow the Old Mill Road uphill through forest and cutblocks to signed T-junction 388531 with boulder close under the logged slope of Mt. Baldy. Turn left. (Straight on is Baldy Pass North following the Old Mill Road.)

Lusk Pass trail 1.5 km
The old road now growing grass makes a very pleasant downhill walk through alternating forest and growing plantations allowing views to the right of the Fisher Range and ahead to the Hunchback Hills. On coming to T-junction 401534 with signpost on the banktop above Lusk Creek, turn left onto what was once a driveable road running between Hwy. 68 and Powderface Road. (To right the old road continues as Lusk Pass trail over Lusk Pass. See Volume 2.)

Lusk Creek trail 2.3 km
The going is straightforward, the old road varying between track and sandy trail as it heads downhill at the edge of cutblocks and

through woodlands with pines and poplars, After the final stony descent curving right, the trail runs flat through an older forest to the old gravel pit, now a grassy basin. Here it turns left and runs along the top of the basin to a 4-way with Baldy Pass/Integrated Forest interpretive access trail. Go right for Lusk Creek day-use, straight for the popular access below the bank.

3 Baldy Pass from the north

map 1

Half-day or long day hike
Official trail
Distance 10.9 km from official access
Height gain 564 m (1850 ft.) to pass
High point of trail 1890 m (6200 ft.)
Maps 82 O/3 Canmore, 82 J/14 Spray
Lakes Reservoir

Official access Hwy. 68 (Sibbald Creek
Trail) at Lusk Creek day-use area.
Popular access Most people park 300 m
west of Lusk Creek at the widening of Hwy.
68. Deduct 400 m.
Campground access from Stoney Creek
group campground via the connecting trail
starting from the kiosk. Distance 'tween
gate and trail is 440 m. Deduct 560 m.
Also accessible from #9 Baldy Pass from
the south at the high point, from the west
terminus of Lusk Pass trail (see Volume 2)
via the TCT from #4 Barrier Lake Forestry
Trails parking lots.

Comments Relatively few people walk the
Baldy Pass trail from one end to the other,
which requires two vehicles. This is the longer, northern half which traverses miles of
forest and cutblocks on logging roads of

The old mill road and Yates Mountain.

various ages best tackled by bike. The pass
between Midnight Peak and Mt. Baldy is
usually reached by hikers from the south via
the very much shorter #9 trail.

The northerly section of the Old Mill Road
to Lusk Pass trail junction is part of the Trans
Canada Trail and duly signed.

Trail note It will have occurred to hikers
that if you take the very much more interesting Kananaskis Integrated Forest Interpretive
Trail to T-junction 389538 on Old Mill Road,
the route will be shorter by 650 m. Old Mill
Road? This name is used interchangeably
for Baldy Pass North trail for the first 7.4 km.

Logging history Baldy Pass North trail
uses the Old Mill Road, initially bulldozed in
1951 by the Olorenshaw Logging company
lusting after 300 acres of spruce at the head
of Lusk Creek's south fork. Around the same
time, the Forest Experiment Station (later the
Forestry School for field employees, now
the University of Calgary's Biogeoscience
Institute field research station) began a
research project on the northern slope of
Mt. Baldy above Lusk Creek, and for a while
in the road's history it became part of a
driving loop to look at cutblocks called the
"Lusk Creek Tour of Logging and Reforestation Areas" — similar to today's loop in the
Jumpingpound. As the trees grew up the old
signs faded and fell down and the roads were
closed to vehicles.

After becoming part of Kananaskis Country in 1979, Old Mill Road was conscripted
into Baldy Pass trail and for a long period in its
history hikers, bikers, skiers and researchers
quietly went about their business on the old
roads that were gradually reverting to trails.

This all changed in the winter of 2007/08
when Spray Lakes Sawmills moved in and in
anticipation of pine beetle attack, logged a
large area of 80-year-old pines, in so doing
dramatically changing the landscape into a
temporary parkland (if it wasn't for all the
slash). Old Mill Road was widened, spur
roads were built, the upper cut-off to Lusk
Pass trail disappeared in a cutblock, but the
lower one was spared and became the new
Lusk Pass trail.

By the summer of 2009 the logging roads had been reclaimed and mini lodgepoles planted in the cutblocks. The building of the interpretive trail in 2009 opened up new possibilities for loops with Baldy Pass trail, which was conscripted into the Trans Canada Trail. Then in 2020 another extensive round of logging in the upper reaches of Lusk Creek reopened 4.5 km of Old Mill Road to logging trucks. And once again the look of the trail changed with the addition of even bigger cutblocks.

In the latest biggest cutblock, Boundary Peak rises above Boundary Ridge in the background. The trail follows the fringe of trees from right to left across the cutblock.

To Old Mill Road turnoff 800 m
From Lusk Creek day-use area, follow the access road out to Hwy. 68. Turn right, cross Lusk Creek on culvert, then follow the trail up the grassy bank to the flat above, which is the site of an old gravel pit. Cross a grassy track (popular access to right, #2B Lusk Creek Loop to left) and pass between boulders onto an old road leading to the U of C's Biogeoscience Institute field research station. In another 460 metres is a 4-way. Go straight. (Left is the signed interpretive trail. Right is the access trail from Stoney Creek group campground.)

Continue ahead for another few metres, then turn left on Old Mill Road. (The old road ahead is the Trans Canada Trail making for Barrier Dam. See the sketchmap on page 28.)

To the interpretive trail 2.5 km
In aspen and spruce forest the Old Mill Road climbs uphill in great windings. At the end of a long left-hander, the interpretive trail comes in from the left at 389538 in a cutblock.

To Lusk Pass trail junction 1.1 km
The road continues climbing through cutblocks and plantations dating back to 1972 and 2007. Close in under Mt. Baldy is an important T-junction 388531 with trail sign and boulder. Keep straight. (To left is Lusk Pass trail.)

To end of Old Mill Road 3.8 m
A flat section of road winds below a low grassy ridge on the left and the connecting ridge between the two Baldys up to the right. An uphill brings you into 2020 cutblocks where the road climbs up right beside a belt of trees into the biggest cutblock of them all. This the road crosses in a fringe of trees before descending to the bridged crossing of Lusk Creek's southwest fork. En route look left to Hunchback and Lusk Pass and ahead to Boundary Peak,

the view gradually extending to "Quarter to One" and Midnight Peak.

A few metres farther on cross the stony south fork (usually dry at this point) and climb a stony hill. In the following dip recross the south fork via a culvert, then climb to junction 395505. This is where you abandon Old Mill Road, which turns left and is overgrown. (See SIDE TRIP to Mill Site.) Keep straight on another road.

To Baldy Pass 2.5 km

The new road gains height quickly through mature spruce forest. From its end, a trail traverses out left, then back right to the route's high point on the north ridge of Midnight Peak. To left is a foreshortened view of the route to the summit. To right is a new view of Baldy's west peak and the south ridge route up South Baldy.

At a partially dismantled cairn the trail turns right and descends 62 vertical metres (203 ft.) of shale to the actual pass in the trees. At a cairn you meet Baldy Pass South trail come up from the other side.

Top: The high point of the Baldy Pass trail looking north to West Baldy (left) and South Baldy described in #11.

Right: The loggers' cabin in the woods. Photo Pete Irwin

SIDE TRIP TO MILL SITE

Distance 480 m

Turn left at km 8.4 and follow the last leg of Old Mill Road through old spruce to the sawmill site, where you might still find relics left over from Olorenshaw logging days.

The loggers' cabin is still standing, though the roof is looking a bit iffy. In 1984 it starred in CBC's made-for-TV movie called *Ernest Thompson Seton: Keeper of the Wild*. Starting a year earlier it was used for a number of years by researchers from the BGS Institute studying bumble bee foraging and other esoteric subjects. To seek out the cabin see the 4th edition of Volume 1, #3.

4 Barrier Lake Forestry Trails map 1

Half day hike
Official trail
Distance 2.5 km of biggest loop
Height gain 40 m (130 ft.)
High point 1417 m (4650 ft.)
Map 82 O/3 Canmore

Access Hwy. 40 (Kananaskis Trail). Just south of Barrier Dam Road turn onto James Cragg Road. Turn first left into the Veteran's Loop parking lot. If that is full, turn second left into the Colonel's Cabin parking lot.

Comments Two interpretive trails — the Forestry Ecology loop and the Forestry loop — can be joined to make one enjoyable forest walk. There's plenty of interpretive signage to read. There are also 18 numbered signs that are explained in booklets produced by the U of C's BGS Institute field research station and available May to November from the two kiosks and from the front of the Colonel's Cabin. The trails are open year-round, but the 76-year-old cabin is currently closed.

The south leg of the Ecology loop acts as a substitute for the nearby Trans Canada Trail (TCT), in that it connects the Baldy Pass North trail to Veteran's Loop parking lot. See 4A for details.

History The Dominion's Forest Experiment Station opened in 1934 and was accessed by the fledgling Hwy. 40. (See #18 Stoney trail.) Shortly after, during the Second World War, it became POW Camp #130 for alien internees, Canadian conscientious objectors and prisoners of war. (See #44 Opal traverse.) After the war the bunkhouses were moved to serve as youth hostels up and down the Icefields Parkway and the eighth guard tower was taken onto McConnell Ridge, painted white and renamed Pigeon Lookout. (See #7 Prairie View trail.) After 1952 the station returned to its original purpose for the most part and today is used for research and education.

The eighth guard tower during its time as a fire lookout on what is now Prairie View trail.

ANTI-CLOCKWISE

From just beyond the Veteran's Loop parking lot a trail heads right, past a kiosk, to a T-junction of sorts. Turn left. (To the right a trail leads to the History Loop, which includes the Colonel's Cabin and the eighth guard tower, now painted grey.)

Pass another kiosk, then go straight at a 4-way junction marked with a TCT sign. Cross Barrier Creek by bridge to a T-junction, then turn immediately right.

The trail climbs through a mixed forest of lodgepole pine, white spruce, Douglas fir, aspen and Scots pine from Sweden. Interestingly, the pines were planted in the 1940s, and though thriving, their seeds don't ever germinate. Just after sign 09 turn right on a narrower trail that crosses a track (old road) onto the smaller loop.

Wander through a grove of Norway spruce to the shelter at the far end of the loop, where you can stop for a rest. Then continue on past the hole (soil exhibit), recross the track and climb up to the big loop. Turn right.

After an initial climb, pass the site of a viewing platform (the trees grew up) and meander along and downhill to a junction. Detour right to a viewpoint for McConnell Ridge and Yates Mountain, where you learn about which trees grow where. Return to the main trail and turn right down a hill which deposits you back at the Barrier Creek T-junction. Cross the bridge and return the same way you came to the parking lot.

Typical scene along the interpretive trail.

4A Trans Canada Trail Connector

Distance 1 km to parking lot

FROM OLD MILL ROAD

To Veteran's Loop parking area Drop off Baldy Pass trail (Old Mill Road) to the station road and turn left. Follow it down through a gate into the complex of buildings. Turn first right. At a 4-way trail junction with TCT sign, turn left. Pass a kiosk and climb to a T-junction near the Colonel's Cabin. Turn right and in a few minutes arrive on the Veteran's Loop road. Turn left for the parking area.

Alternatively, on reaching station road, turn right, then in 5 m turn left down a trail that intersects the south leg of the Ecology Loop at a fence. Go left. At the far end go left and cross a bridge over wee Barrier Creek to the 4-way with TCT sign. Go straight etc.

If heading to Barrier Dam, go straight (or right) at the 4-way with TCT sign and cross Barrier Creek on stepping stones. The trail rises gradually across grass to Hwy. 40 beyond the guard rail. Walk left down the highway a short way, then turn right onto Barrier Lake Road.

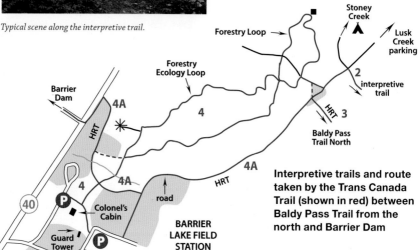

Interpretive trails and route taken by the Trans Canada Trail (shown in red) between Baldy Pass Trail from the north and Barrier Dam

5 Widowmaker Trail map 1

Half, short day
Official, unofficial trails
Distance from Access 1 to 4, 4.4 km via banktop trail
Height gain N-S 46 m (150 ft.)
Map 82 O/3 Canmore

Access Hwy. 40 (Kananaskis Trail)
1. Canoe Meadows day-use area.
2. Barrier Lake Information Centre. From opposite the front entrance, the 160-m-long access trail heads through trees, crosses the loop road (more parking spots), then descends to Widowmaker trail.
3. Widowmaker day-use area opposite Hwy. 68.
4. Barrier Dam parking areas via Barrier Lake Rd.

Comments An easy riverside walk along the east bank of the Kananaskis River between Access 1 at Canoe Meadows and Access 3 at Widowmaker day-use area. An unofficial trail carries on to Access 4 at Barrier Dam.

There's plenty to watch on a weekend: novice canoeists dumping in the water, kayakers practising rolls, paddle boarders and river surfers playing in the waves, rafters floating by — but ONLY when TransAlta turns on the tap. High water is guaranteed on long weekends and during slalom competitions held the last weekend in May and in the middle of September. For competition dates see the website of the Alberta Whitewater Association.

Facilities All accesses have biffies and picnic tables. Access 2 has indoor toilets. Access 1 features a group campground in the meadow with shelter and individual walk-in sites close to a parking area, all of which have to be booked beforehand.

River history The bed of the Kananaskis River below Barrier Dam has been almost completely reconstructed, first by TransAlta Utilities and then by the Alberta Whitewater Association and members (i.e., the LKRUA and the ARSA, the Alberta government and Lafarge Canada, who donated rocks) to create a playground for whitewater enthusiasts. Refashioning the bed is an ongoing activity, with enhancements to rapids and the creation of eddies, ledges and holes — all of which has to be done at low water. Coming up in the next few years is the innovative 12 metre-wide "Perfect Surf and Kayak Wave" that is fully adjustable!

NORTH TO SOUTH FROM ACCESS 1

The shorter route follows the new trail through the trees, the more interesting route the trail alongside the river built for competition watching. See the sketchmap on the next page .

1. Widowmaker official start 300 m From the left side of the parking lot at the sign "Widowmaker" follow a wide gravelled trail through the trees to the left of the big meadow. At a junction turn left and keep left down a hill above the Kananaskis River. En route, steps on the right lead down to the top of the slalom course, which is also the way up from the riverside trail.

Looking down on the slalom course in O'Shaugnessy Canyon from the banktop trail.

Mountain Wave from the viewing platform.

On the map: plaque, problem area at high water, course, slalom, rocks, Group Camp, 5, Widowmaker trail, steps, Kananaskis River, Canoe Meadows, P, rocks, 40, Widowmaker

2. Riverside trail 450 m Start from the trail sign between a biffy and the picnic area on the right side of the parking lot. Turn right and descend steps to the Kananaskis River at the take-out.

Turn left upstream, walking a strip of gravel between the river and steep banks. As you can see from the slalom gates, this is the race course through O'Shaugnessy Canyon. Note the memorial plaque at the first rocky bluff. A little farther along, a trail heading up the bank is an escape route should you be unable to get around the next bluff because of high water. Continue to Miami Beach where a trail climbs the bank to campsites. Round Cartwheel Corner where the river turns left and a gravel track comes in down the bank. Continue on track between crags and rapids past the well-named Green Tongue rapid and its wavy outflow Green Gullet to the beginning of the slalom course. Just downstream of the Point Break surfing feature, climb steps up the bank to Widowmaker trail. Turn right.

NOTE: If the river is high, turn left at the start and walk past viewpoints of O'Shaugnessy Canyon to the beginning of the campsites. Here turn right down a hill onto Miami Beach. Then turn left.

To Access 2, Barrier Information Centre junction 700 m
The track narrows to forest trail and soon descends to river level. A little way along is a staging area and viewing platform at Mountain Wave, a feature built by the Alberta River Surfing Association for river surfers.

Continue on stepping stones between river and water pooling from springs to the next rapid. Here the trail climbs up steps away from the river. At the top go right and along to a junction. Go straight. (Left leads to Barrier Lake Information Centre.)

To Access 3, Widowmaker 1.1 km
The trail once again descends to river level, this time travelling an open flat between-aromatic wolf willows and hedysarums. On coming to a Y-junction keep right and cross Lusk Creek on a bridge. After crossing a dry, stony channel, the trail climbs and meanders along clifftops with views of rapids down below. At a junction, going left brings you to the north end of Widowmaker

parking lot, which was the site of Lusk Creek Cabin. Going straight, then left gains you middle of the lot at picnic tables. (If you descend steps down right you'd join the trail to Shingle Cove.)

The route (a track) continues from the far end of the parking lot beyond a gate. Pass the trail to Shingle Cove, the staging area steps below Widowmaker rapid and a flow measurement station. This is where you can walk out along a promontory to view rafts bobbing through Widowmaker in close-up. Continue along the track to the 2020 parking lot for commercial outfitters. On your right 55 steps lead down to the put-in above Widowmaker.

GOING FARTHER

To Access 4 at Barrier Dam 2.1 km

Initially, the unofficial section is a flat track. After passing a flow monitor cable strung across the river, the track climbs around a river bend and descends to water level where it narrows to trail. To your left rises a line of high crags; to your right the river is squeezed into a narrow, rocky channel with signs warning of fluctuating water levels. Cross the outflow from springs on a couple of planks, then pass below the nine springs that tumble down steep banks even in the middle of winter. The water is thought to

Looking down on the Kananaskis River from the high point of the trail south of Lusk Creek crossing.

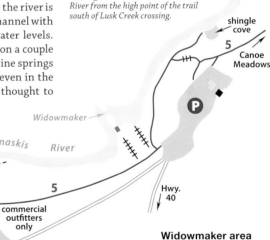

Widowmaker area

have percolated through glacial debris below the Hunchback Hills, en route passing under Lusk Creek.

Come to Barrier substation 325. Pass behind the building and join the access road from Barrier Dam. Cross the spillway, then curve up left to join the road across the dam.

Either continue along the road to lower parking lots, or climb steps to the left of the gate to the middle and upper parking areas. Most people parked in the upper lot use a shortcut trail that climbs directly to the biffy from the junction of substation and dam roads. See the map on the next page.

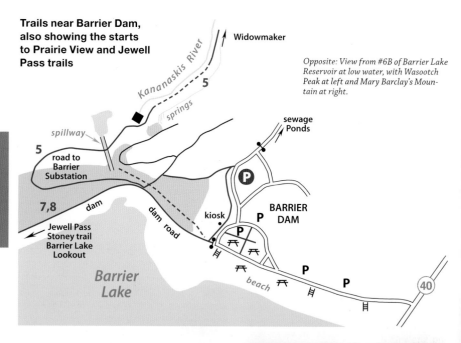

Trails near Barrier Dam, also showing the starts to Prairie View and Jewell Pass trails

Widowmaker

Kananaskis River

5

springs

spillway

5

road to Barrier Substation

7,8   dam

dam road

kiosk

sewage Ponds

P

BARRIER DAM

P

P

P

Jewell Pass
Stoney trail
Barrier Lake
Lookout

Barrier Lake

beach

P

P

40

Opposite: View from #6B of Barrier Lake Reservoir at low water, with Wasootch Peak at left and Mary Barclay's Mountain at right.

Above left : Between Widowmaker and Barrier Dam you cross the creek from the springs. Kananaskis River is corralled in a narrow channel to right. Mount Baldy in the background.

Above right: One of many springs pouring down the left bank below the dam. To reach the top of the springs leave the substation access road just before the dam road and head down left on grass. A trail starts to the right of posts and descends onto a terrace at the end of which is a mossy bank from which issues the spring shown in this photo.

6 Barrier Lake Trails

map 1

Half day hikes
Official and unofficial trails
Map 82 O/3 Canmore

Access Hwy. 40 (Kananaskis Trail).
1. Barrier Lake day-use area. Keep straight at a junction and ascend to the upper parking lot located in a gap between two hills.
2. Barrier Lake day-use area. Keep right at a junction and descend past A parking lot to B and C parking lots.
3. Shortly before the turnoff to Barrier Lake day-use area, turn right into a small lot.

Comments Choose from short pleasant trails ending at viewpoints on east and west hilltops or take Barrier Lake trail to the beach or combine forest and beach walking with East Beach Loop.

Facilities Picnic sites at the upper parking lot and between the middle and lowest parking lots with steps leading down to the west beach. The two lowest parking lots access the Brian Targett boat ramp which doesn't extend into the lake at low water. The 2021 boat ramp at near parking lot A *does* reach the lake at all water levels, but unfortunately, the ramp's gated parking lot is for the exclusive use of rescue personnel, which means the shortest access to the water is via steps down to the beach. Nearby. Kananaskis Outfitters operates a canoe and kayak rental from July 1 to Labour Day.

6A Connection trail

Official trail
Distance 280 m one way

Comments Wheelchair accessible.

FROM ACCESS 1

Start from the loop. After passing a glut of picnic tables, the route follows the line of the old Hwy. 40 down a gentle, gravelled incline where visitors are "invited to experience nature in silence." (Hopefully, a posse of motor bikers will not be zooming down the nearby highway at the same time.) The trail splits at the end, the uphill fork to left leading to viewpoints.

The original plan called for a scattering of individual hand-made chairs at trails' end from which "to reflect," a nice idea but obviously impractical, so we now have the usual hard rock seats. Bring a cushion.

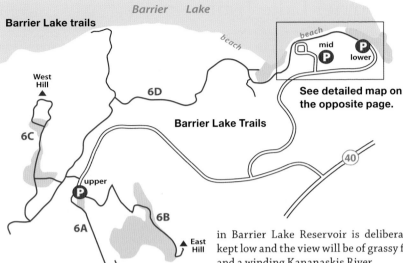

Barrier Lake

West Hill ▲

6D

6C

6B

6A

East Hill ▲

upper

See detailed map on the opposite page.

Barrier Lake Trails

beach

mid P

lower P

40

6B East Hill Lookout Interpretive trail

Official trail
Distance 580 m
Height gain 60 m (197 ft.)
High point 1508 m (4947 ft.)

Comments. A short uphill walk to the hilltop southeast of the upper parking lot — a great viewpoint.

FROM ACCESS 1

Start from the loop road by climbing a few steps. From the top the trail zigs up the west side of the hill under a canopy of aspens, which the Barrier Lake info centre calls "the Bride's Arch." On reaching a T-junction on the open ridge crest turn right and walk past a couple of interpretive signs to the rocky top overlooking Hwy. 40.

Look across the highway to Mt. Baldy, née Barrier Mountain, née Sleeping Buffalo Mountain. Maybe there'll be climbers on Barrier Bluffs. The calendar views, though, are from the open ridge lower down the trail where you look south along Barrier Lake and the Kananaskis valley to Wasootch Peak. Just know that in summer the water

in Barrier Lake Reservoir is deliberately kept low and the view will be of grassy flats and a winding Kananaskis River.

NOTE: Return the same way. At the T-junction where you start down the zigs, the trail continuing along the ridge crest appears to offer a different way off. Don't bother trying it.

6C West Hill

Unofficial trail
Distance 1.2 km loop
Height gain 70 m (230 ft.)
High point 1528 m (5013 ft.)

Comments This is the prominent hill seen across Barrier Lake from Jewell Pass and Stoney trails in the vicinity of Jewell Bay.

This slightly higher and craggy hill northwest of the parking lot gives excellent views of Mt. Baldy and Barrier Lake looking north to Horton Hill. Two ways onto the ridge can be combined to make a loop. Expect a few steep hills and stony ground.

FROM ACCESS 1

Start from the trail sign at the parking lot. Walk out to an arrow pointing to the right and turn left. Almost immediately turn right and climb a steep, narrow trail onto the ridge. Turn right up the ridge on a shaley trail with alternating steep bits. The terrain eases off at a Y-junction in a bit of meadow.

Loop

Go right around the east edge of the summit plateau which gives the best viewpoints of Barrier Lake, Mt. Baldy and Barrier Bluffs. On a skimpier trail continue around the north end and back on the more open west edge with views down across the lake to Jewell Bay and Jewell Pass. On arriving back at the Y-junction turn right.

Return

Descend the steep shaley bit. Instead of following your ascent trail off the left side of the ridge, stay ahead, descending a scree trail that very quickly transforms into an easy trail winding through aspen woods. On coming to a junction, turn left to return to the parking lot.

But before doing the return run, I urge you to follow the trail to the right for 60 m to a great viewpoint of the winding Kananaskis River. The point on a bluff is identified from above by a decades-old picnic table lying in pieces.

6D Barrier Lake trail

Official trail
Distance 1.1+ km
Height loss 85 m (279 ft.)

Comments An easy descending trail connecting access 1 to parking lots A, B and C. Supposedly, in reverse this is the lower section of 6B.

View from the west hill of Mt. Baldy. West Baldy to right. In the middle ground is the east hill.

FROM ACCESS 1

To A parking lot 1 km
Start from the trail sign at the parking lot. Walk out to a sign with arrow and turn right. At the next unmarked junction be sure to turn right and begin the descent through a pleasant forest of pine and aspen. Low down, climb to a signed junction and go left. (Trail to right has been discontinued beyond a picnic table.) The trail then dips around a grassy bay and after rising, heads left to the boat ramp, where you transfer to the banktop trail.

Getting to parking lots
See the map at left for trails through the picnic area to the parking lots.

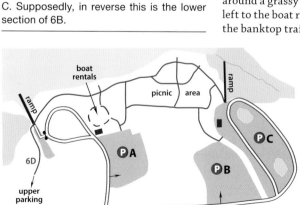

Trails accessed from parking lots

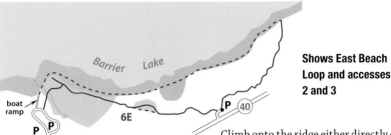

Shows East Beach Loop and accesses 2 and 3

6E East Beach Loop

Unofficial trails
Distance ~2.1 km loop
Height gain/loss ~46 m (150 ft.)

Comments A varied walk through woodlands and along Barrier Lake's sandy east shoreline. Great for the kids in all of us.

FROM ACCESS 2 OR 3

To Access 3, 700 m
From either parking lot B or C walk down the Brian Targett boat ramp. At its end cross a wee creek and head for the low, grassy ridge ahead. I'm assuming the water level is low. At high water you'll have to skirt around to the right

Climb onto the ridge either directly or from its tip, enjoying a view of your return route from atop a steep slope of sand plunging to the water's edge. Follow the ridge trail into the trees where it climbs up a draw. Higher up, where the trail has grown in, detour to the left where necessary and finally deke right into the west end of the parking lot at access 3.

Return 1.4 km
From the far east end of the lot a good trail heads out to the right. Keep right and in a short distance start a twisting descent through trees to Barrier Lake's empty shoreline at flagging. Turn left.

Safe from high water levels, follow the highest bench of softest sand below steep banks of sand. Round the tip of the ridge and head back to the boat ramp.

7 Prairie View Trail

map 1

Day hike
Official trail
Distance 7.8 km one way
Height gain E-W 500 m (1640 ft.)
Height loss E-W 240 m (790 ft.)
High point 1875 m (6150 ft.)
Map 82 O/3 Canmore

Access Hwy. 40 (Kananaskis Trail) at Barrier Dam day-use area reached via Barrier Lake Rd.
Also accessible from #8 Jewell Pass trail and #18 Stoney Trail, and from Quaite Creek trail in Volume 3.

Comments A very popular trail with one steep section that connects Barrier Dam day-use area to Jewell Pass via McConnell Ridge. Most obviously the trail can be part of a 14.5 km circuit from Barrier Dam incorporating #8, Jewell Pass trail. If you want to be surprised by the surprise view, hike the loop clockwise. See also the map on page 40.

Opposite: #6E The sand trail above Barrier Lake.

Below: Looking up the last lap to McConnell Ridge. To right is Yates Mountain topped by a fire lookout.

More popular than the loop is the foray from the trail's high point to Barrier Lake Lookout atop Yates Mountain — an irresistible objective at 12.3 km return.

Trail history The first part of the route is a fire road that once accessed Pigeon Lookout (see #4). Perhaps many of you remember the white fire tower, even sat on its steps to eat lunch. In 1984, made redundant a year earlier by Barrier Lake Lookout, it was taken down to the Colonel's Cabin, painted grey and stocked with artifacts. The lookout that first saw service as guard tower 8 at POW Camp 130 in the early 1940s had returned to its birthplace. The name caused an immense amount of confusion with hikers during its 24 years — Pigeon Lookout is not on Pigeon Mountain. Ruthie believes the name alluded to stool pigeons.

Barrier Dam to Jewell Pass trail 1.3 km
From the parking areas walk around a gate onto Barrier Dam. Either keep left on the stony road that crosses the dam crest, or go right on the substation road and after a few metres turn left onto a narrow trail that traverses the sloping downstream face. On

coming to a gravel road, turn left, then right to join the dam road.

The road, originally the fire road to Pigeon Lookout, crosses under a powerline into a reclaimed meadow. Follow either the road or a trail to its right up a hill to the Nadiya bench. A few metres on is a 4-way intersection with a powerline access road. Go straight. (To left is #8 Jewell Pass trail.)

Continue uphill for another 300 metres to a T-junction with Stoney trail. Turn right, then straightaway left.

To McConnell Ridge 4.3 km

Closeted in trees, the fire road winds uphill in easy zigs with shortcuts not worth taking. At the end of the 11th and final zig turn left onto the northeast ridge. It's here, at the bend, where the unsigned trail from Camp Chief Hector joins in from the right.

The road continues up the ridge and ends at a levelling above meadows sloping south, a popular rest spot with a view of Barrier Lake. The flat to your right between road and forest is the Pigeon Lookout site. Nearby are Stoney prayer flags. For some people this is the end of the road—literally.

McConnell Ridge viewpoint, looking southeast to Barrier Lake Reservoir and Mt. Baldy.

A trail carries on along the ridge, then makes a short, steep climb, zigging left, right and up a rocky step below a TransAlta repeater station. Keep left of the repeater station (right is #7A) to an arrow sign on McConnell Ridge, the trail's high point. Just beyond is the surprise viewpoint at the top of a cliff. Pose a friend on the edge and you have yourself a great pic with Barrier Lake and Mt. Baldy in the background.

McConnell Ridge to Jewell Pass 2.2 km

Another arrow points the way down a badly eroded ridge above the line of crags. Watch for marmots doing sentry duty on the rocks. At a low point, the trail turns right into the trees and it's here where the very much better shortcut from the lookout trail joins in from the right.

Now heading northwest, you make a gradual descent into the pine forest of Jewell Pass. Come to a 5-way junction with signpost. Left is Jewell Pass trail, second right is Quaite Creek trail.

7A Barrier Lake Lookout

Unofficial trail
Distance 1.1 km return to Prairie View
Height gain 145 m (476 ft.)
High point 2016 m (6614 ft.)

Comments Who can resist a detour to the high point of McConnell Ridge (Yates Mountain) for the view of the prairies, finally, and for a chance to say hello to the lookout. A short, steep trail.

Naming The Stoney name of Tokyapebi îpa, meaning "lookout point for Blackfeet," is very apt. Its English name of Yates Mountain comes from Emily Yates, who ran the Diamond Cross ranch located on the site of today's Camp Chief Hector, seen down below to the right of Chilver Lake.

Some G8 history In 2002 the summit offered a grandstand view of another kind: the arrival by helicopter of US president George W. Bush into the Kananaskis Valley for the G8 Summit. Were you allowed up there? Lookout Chip McCullough was designated head of security on the summit, and all known trails to the top had security forces stationed at the bottom to stop people from hiking up. It seems security never read the guidebook, though, because on this momentous day

Chip at the lookout.

"the summit was crowded with gawking kids" come up the connector trail from Camp Chief Hector!

After passing the repeater station turn right (northwest) on an unmaintained trail which becomes clear as you climb up the broad, forested ridge. The first section is very steep, then the gradient eases right off. Go either way at a split: left on a scree trail or right along the ridgetop above a deepening cliff. After they join, one uphill burst gains you the summit, a big open area of grass and rocks.

Since the previous edition the summit has had several important additions and now sports a helipad, shed, private biffy, two wireless masts, a brightly coloured wind sock, a Stevenson screen, blobs of cement inscribed "pilot mistake #1," "pilot mistake #2" et al., and a pink flamingo.

To save asking, the fencing above the big north-facing cliff — the Diamond X Face — is not to stop people falling off but to protect nesting prairie falcons from rocks being kicked off by the hordes straining for a bird's-eye view of the prairies.

DESCENT NOTE: Anyone bound for Jewell Pass can take the shortcut trail that leaves the right side of the lookout trail just above the repeater station.

8 Jewell Pass

map 1

Day hike, paddle 'n' hike
Official trail
Distance 6.9 km one way
Height gain 259 m (850 ft.)
High point 1631 m (5350 ft.)
Map 82 O/3 Canmore

Access Hwy. 40 (Kananaskis Trail) at Barrier Dam day-use area on Barrier Lake Rd.
Also accessible from #7 Prairie View trail, #18 Stoney trail and from Quaite Creek trail in Volume 3.

Comments As a destination, forested Jewell Pass isn't up to much, although the walking is pleasant enough. Most people use this trail in combination with Prairie View (#7) to make a 14.7 km loop. This trail also connects the Kananaskis Valley to the Bow Valley via the trail in Quaite Valley.

It's a two-parter. The least interesting first section of under-the-powerlines walking can be avoided by a quick paddle across Barrier Lake from the boat launch at Barrier Lake day-use area. Aim for Jewell Bay, where a short stint right on Stoney trail sees you at section two in a few minutes. For this section see the map to right and on page 68.

Trail reroute The second section is a forest walk alongside Jewell Creek with a few steepish hills, a large portion of it rerouted after the flood of 2013 and made more exciting for bikers doing the trail in reverse.

Naming The pass is named after Bud Jewell who had a lease to log Douglas firs still standing there after a fire.

Barrier Dam to Jewell Creek 3.8 km
From the parking areas walk around a gate onto Barrier Dam. Either keep left on a stony road that crosses the dam crest, or go right on the substation road and after a few metres turn left onto a narrow trail that traverses the sloping downstream face to a gravel road. Turn left and on joining the dam road turn right.

The first section of Jewell Pass trail after leaving Barrier Dam

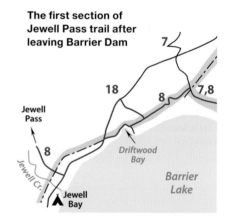

The road, also Prairie View trail, crosses under a powerline into a reclaimed meadow. Follow either the road or a trail to its right up a hill to the Nadiya memorial bench. A few metres on is a 4-way intersection with the powerline access road. Turn left under another set of powerlines.

The track heads southeast, winding and undulating to a T-junction with signpost. There are two routes on:

1. Keep straight on another track. Very shortly the route, temporarily reverting to trail, turns right into the trees and dipsy-doodles in short, steep hills around the edge of Driftwood Bay. A final climb gains you a big meadow. Walk a track under the powerlines to a Y-junction with Stoney Trail (gravel road). Turn left.

2. The longer, easier route turns right up the powerline access road. On reaching Stoney Trail (gravel road) turn left. Route 1 comes in from the left at a Y-junction just before the road bends to the right.

As you round the end of McConnell Ridge, you're treated to fine views of Barrier Lake backdropped by Mt. Baldy and Mary Barclay's Mountain. The road then rises into trees, flattens and passes the "God is Love" boulders scattered along the powerline right-of-way to your right. At the signed T-junction at 347542, turn right onto Jewell Pass trail. (The road continuing ahead is Stoney Trail. Only 200 metres distant across Jewell Creek bridge lies Jewell Bay backcountry campground.)

To Jewell Pass 3.1 km
The trail crosses the right-of-way and follows a terrace above Jewell Creek a short way before dropping into the valley bottom. A new section of trail undulates along to the first bridge. Cross and on coming to Jewell Falls Creek wind up a hill to its left and cross the creek directly above the falls. Climb some more, making use of a few stone steps, the trail then seesawing across a steep slope to a bridge over a north fork. The trail veers right and on reaching the original trail turns left.

After crossing the east fork the trail climbs a hill, then is flat all the way to Jewell Pass at a 5-way junction with signpost. Prairie View trail is to the immediate right, Quaite Valley trail is second right.

Opposite: Sharing the route with Stoney Trail alongside Barrier Lake.

Top: Crazy paving in Jewell Creek.

Bottom: Jewell Falls in spate.

9 Baldy Pass from the South   map 1

Day hike
Official trail
Distance 4.2 km to pass,
4.4 km to high point of trail
Height gain 411 m (1347 ft.) to pass
High point 1828 m (5997 ft.) at pass
Map 82 J/14 Spray Lakes Reservoir

Usual access Hwy. 40 (Kananaskis Trail). At 10.3 km south of the K Country boundary, turn right (west) into the Baldy Pass parking lot.
Also accessible from #3 Baldy Pass from the north and from #16 the Wasootch-Baldy connector.

Comments Well marked with signs and cairns, this trail up an unnamed valley is the usual hiking route to Baldy Pass. It is considerably shorter than route #3 from the north, and leaves time for a little ridge wandering onto Midnight Peak or the south summit of Baldy. (See the next two entries, #10 and #11.) No water. Also note that in early spring the forest section where you gain most of the height can still be snowed in and icy, so at such times carry microspikes.

Straightaway cross the highway at the trail crossing. For the first 730 metres head south though trees to a junction with sign. Turn left. (The flagged trail ahead is route #16 to Wasootch Creek parking lot.)

Your trail heads east into a valley confined between the west peak of Baldy and the west ridge of Midnight Peak. The going is flat at first, the valley floor wide and stony, the creek nowhere to be found except during its resurgence in times of flood when it adds to the stone count. The trail stays on the left (north) side of the creekbed all the way to the narrows, where after passing the remains of a bridge, it crosses to the right bank and, guided by cairns, crosses a side creek that is the source of all the stones.

In mossy spruce forest with rotting log piles the valley narrows to a V. After passing the scree slopes of West Baldy, the trail steepens as you climb across the steep southern slope of the valley, en route crossing two narrow avalanche gullies not far below the watershed. A last uphill ends directly at the cairn on the pass. On the far side are cliffs. Barely rising above the trees, the pass is not the greatest viewpoint. The best view is to the south of the ongoing trail and the grossly foreshortened north ridge of Midnight Peak described in the next entry.

Going farther for the view
It pays to continue up the trail for another 200 metres, climbing 62 vertical metres (203 ft.) up the open ridge to the south to another cairn marking the trail's high point where it slips over onto the north slope. This is a far superior viewpoint for the Mt. Baldy massif — you can even trace the trail up the south end of Baldy described in #11. (See the pic on page 25.)

Opposite: The valley trail at the narrows where it crosses to the right (south) bank. Shows the bridge after the 2013 flood! Above rises the west ridge of Midnight Peak.

Top: #9. Looking up to the high point of Baldy Pass trail from the pass. At upper right rises the north ridge of Midnight Peak, showing the scree hump at centre.

Bottom: #10. Nearing the summit of Midnight Peak via the normal north ridge and face route.

10 Midnight Peak normal route   map 1

Day scramble
Unofficial trail
Distance 1.6 km from Baldy Pass
Height gain 511 m (1676 ft.) from #9,
927 m (3041 ft.) from trailhead
High point 2339 m (7674 ft.)
Map 82 J/14 Spray Lakes Reservoir

Access Via #9 Baldy Pass from the south at the trail's high point.
Also accessible from #16 the Wasootch-Baldy connector.

Comments This is the mountain to the south of Baldy Pass, a fine-looking peak when viewed from the northeast. Only the standard ascent route up the north ridge has a trail to the top. A more solid variation exists up the northwest ridge. Combine them to make a small loop, but NOT when snow covered as it entails crossing avalanche slopes. Alternatively, descend the long west ridge, which prolongs the enjoyment of being up high and makes a loop of about 9.1 km.

Technically, all routes are about the same easy standard of scrambling on moderately steep slopes of scree, rubble and broken rock with no exposure. WARNING: The two north slope routes retain the snow until late spring and are prone to wet avalanches.

Naming Its unofficial name comes courtesy of Art Davis, who led a group of Rocky Mountain Ramblers up to its top on October 21, 1973. Attempting to find another way down, they got hung up above cliffs and didn't get back to their cars until midnight.

To treeline 1.2 km
Start from the high point on Baldy Pass trail at the cairn, continuing up the broad north ridge of your mountain on a good trail. On coming to a flat meadow with a surfeit of cairns indicating variations of all sorts, it's best to head right. At the farthermost and biggest cairn a trail climbs easily to where one of the steeper variations joins in.

Up next is the steep, twisting climb in trees to the left of the big scree hump. Twice the trail touches the scree, after the second one heading away left to the top of the hump. After a dip, endure another steep, twisting climb to treeline. High up, keep left at a split.

To the summit 370 m
At the start of the rock continue uphill. After one or two zigs, the trail and its equally messy variations climb diagonally right onto the north face across very loose, tippy rubble. At a concave steepening one would

wish for a few of Ha Ling's rock steps, but after this the angle falls back a little and a twisty trail straight up the fall line on much better rock leads to the long summit ridge just left of the summit cairn.

The view is incredible in every direction. Where to begin? Of more immediate interest to scramblers is the slightly higher summit to the southeast that is yoked to Midnight by a seductively curving ridge that takes half an hour to negotiate, hence its most common name of "Half Past Midnight." (For me it's more likely to be "Quarter to One.") Others call it "Twilight Peak," "Midday Peak," "Half Past Noon Peak."

OPTIONAL DESCENT

10A Northwest Ridge

Walk to the west end of the summit ridge and turn right down the northwest ridge. The ridge is narrower than one might suppose. Scree and crags fall away from the left side, but the upper ridge itself is a solid staircase of grass and rock that offers easy going. Next, choosing whatever line appeals, descend into the basin to your right via grassy ribs with outcrops to manoeuvre around.

Cross the basin toward the north ridge. The only problem is the central gully that splits the seamed north face. Because it's steep-sided at this point, you need to cross it above a slabby step, then head down the far side of it a way before traversing right through meadow and trees below the scree hump of the north ridge to your ascent trail.

SHORTCUT TO BALDY PASS TRAIL

Do not cross the central gully. Instead, head left (north) toward a treed ridge. Wend left between the trees and the northwest ridge into a low-angled scree gully cum creekbed that is easy to follow down to its intersection with the Baldy Pass trail. Alternatively, stay in the trees on the right side of the creekbed. NOTE: This is NOT the outrun from the central gully, but a smaller one to the west, but just as avalanche prone under snow.

Opposite: Midnight Peak from the south peak of Baldy. shows two routes. The usual north ridge route goes up the left-hand skyline above the big scree hump. Higher up above treeline the northwest ridge route takes to the ridge to its right.

Above: The north ridge. Transferring to firmer rock and an easier gradient.

10B West Ridge

Mainly route
Distance 3 km to intersection with #9
Height loss 930 m (3050 ft.)

Comments A GPS receiver is useful for finding the correct way off the end of the west ridge.

From the summit, walk west along the summit ridge past the northwest ridge turnoff and descend the rubbly west ridge. On the second, steeper drop, a few slabs near the top can be circumnavigated by a trail on the right side that winds all the way down to an area of orange shale.

Ahead is the up step. When seen in profile from Baldy Pass trail in the valley below, this rockband appears to present a problem. But it's really an imposter, and while you can scramble safely over the top, you can also sneak around the left side.

A little farther along, the ridge bends left, then back right. Here a really good game trail leaves the crest and traverses the right flank down into trees at dip no. 1.

Hike over a bump to dip no. 2 with fire circle, then ascend to 369490. This is where you drop off the end and lose almost 610 m (2000 ft.) in one fell swoop. Whatever you do, don't follow the logical extension of

the ridge to the left. Besides being booby-trapped with cliffs, the southwest ridge doesn't take you in the right direction. Your route is the northwest rib at the demarcation of the north and west slopes, which lower down curves more to the west. Looked at from Hwy. 40, it's the partially grassy rib to the left of the gully.

After an easy start the going becomes progressively steeper and rockier, until a third of the way down you reach the white pinnacles at a narrowing. Thread together pieces of trail on the left side. Below this the gradient gradually eases and the rocks dwindle to small areas of talus on a predominantly grassy slope.

Where trees brush across the rib there are two ways to reach official trails at the bottom of the slope:

1. Simply bash on down through open pine forest to intersect #16 the Wasootch-Baldy Connector. Turn right and some time later come to the 4-way junction with Baldy Pass trail. Go straight.

2. Follow a cutline at 2 o'clock down through open pine forest to Baldy Pass trail, which you meet a little way up from the 4-way junction at some deadfall. Turn left.

Top left: #10A Going up the northwest ridge.

Top right: #10B The step on the West Ridge can be avoided by slipping through the gap to its left.

11 South Peak of Baldy

map 1

Day scramble
Unofficial trail
Distance 2.1 km from pass,
6.2 km from trailhead
Height gain 379 m (1244 ft.) from pass,
806 m (2644 ft.) from trailhead
High point 2193 m (7195 ft.)
Maps 82 J/14 Spray Lakes Reservoir,
82 O/3 Canmore

Access Via #9 Baldy Pass from the south at the actual pass.

Comments The south summit of the Mt. Baldy massif at 372519 is gained from Baldy Pass via its long south ridge — an enjoyable ridgewalk with one scramble step. Of course, there is the odd steep section and some scree, but a trail makes things easy. Nearly halfway along, the south end of Baldy is the perfect stopping place for those who want to call it a day. Unlike Midnight Peak, the mountain dries out early in spring.

To the south end of Baldy 900 m

Starting from the cairn at the pass, a good trail winds up the pine-sprinkled ridge to the north. At the top of the first and longest rise the ridge narrows. The trail stays right of the first rocky step. Next up is "The Tower" with orange screes leading up to its base. Arriving at the rock, DO NOT follow the trail that traverses right above a steep gully. DO scramble up diagonally left.

Descend the far side of the tower to a gap, then climb in zigs to the south end of Baldy at 2082 m (6830 ft.) which features a cairn.

Behind you is Midnight Peak displaying its various ascent and descent routes, and ahead the South Peak of Baldy. Who can resist?

To the South Peak of Baldy 1.2 km

The ridge descends into trees (small hiatus at a low point), then rises slightly over a series of rocky humps which can be taken direct. After a flat section the ridge steepens, stacking up in great rocky steps that

Top: Descending The Tower.

Bottom: Looking up at The Tower, which is climbed direct. To its left is the south end of Baldy.

Top: Crossing rocky humps en route to the final steepening. A trail in scree climbs below the crest on the left side to the prominent shoulder.

Above: The ever-growing summit cairn. Photo Matt Hobbs, shown here with Crux

look a little imposing. Bypassing the rock is very easy. Just don't be lured onto the right side of the ridge by a trail. Follow the scree trail that runs below the crest on the left side. Higher up, it wriggles up a short scree slope to a shoulder on the skyline. Above it the ground lies back, and it's an easy walk up grass and stones to the summit cairn above eastern cliffs. Since we first visited, the cairn has grown to an enormous size, but still has quite a way to go before equalling the height of Mt. Baldy.

Into sight comes the rocky head of Mt. Baldy — 34 metres higher — and the whole of its scramble route in profile. For hikers, going for the main summit is easily resisted when you know it's a difficult scramble from this side. The same applies to the West Peak of Baldy off to the west.

Without doubt the most depressing view of the whole day is of cutblocks to the east, their vast extent finally revealed from this high vantage point.

Return the same way.

12 Porcupine Creeks

map 1

Long day hikes, backpack
Unofficial trails, routes
Maps 82 J/14 Spray Lakes Reservoir,
82 J/15 Bragg Creek

Access Hwy. 40 (Kananaskis Trail). At Porcupine Creek crossing a track leads down from the southbound lane to a parking area at the start of the trail.
Also accessible from #16 the Wasootch/Baldy connector. The north fork is accessible from Boundary Ridge. (See Volume 2.)

Comments Both forks of Porcupine Creek are enticing to adventurers wanting to get off the beaten track. As a bonus, several ridges and tops are available for scramblers, including Porcupine Ridge (#13). Unless you're a super runner/scrambler into enchainments, for farther back mountains take a tent; nothing is as maddening as finding yourself within 150 metres of an attainable summit when time runs out. Creek crossings often require wading.

Standing below the crag Blind Man's Bluff that can be circumvented at low water. If necessary cross the creek on branches. Into view ahead are the lower slopes of Porcupine Ridge.

To the Forks 1.3 km
Step out along the left bank trail of Porcupine Creek. At a T-junction go right on the Wasootch-Baldy Connector. Where the connector crosses a bridge over Porcupine Creek, stay left.

On coming to the creekside crag Hyperion, use a scrambly bypass trail about 3 metres up from the water. A second crag, Blind Man's Bluff, can usually be passed at creek level. Walk cobbles to the forks.

12A Southeast Fork

Distance 5.2 km from forks
Height gain 317+ m (1040+ ft.)
High point 1722+ m (5650+ ft.)

Comments An easy walk between Porcupine and Wasootch ridges. For the most part the valley floor is flat and wide, dead-ending in cul-de-sacs below the main axis of the Fisher Range. Several scramble peaks are available, as well as a high col over to Wasootch Creek at 384431.

Just above the forks, crossing the northeast fork gets you started along the left bank of the southeast fork. After the 2013 flood it may be easier to cross the southeast fork on logs and head up the right bank.

The valley is typical of the eastern slopes: wide floors of arid dryas mats alternating with woody narrows with running water. Farther in, densely forested side slopes on the left give way to lighter sprinklings of trees and grass which lure you onto the unnamed summit east of Porcupine Ridge. But only if you have time.

It's here at the most scenic part of the valley at 384442 that 90% of people turn around and go back. If you've brought along a tent, it's good to know there's always water around this point.

The upper valley 1.7 km

Upstream of 384442 the main valley curves round to the left and narrows. Cross and recross the creek. After passing the stony side creek on the left at 396445, you hit an obstacle: a long and impenetrable canyon with waterfalls. To circumvent, get onto the left-hand bank just after the side creek and climb diagonally through trees to a forested notch about 130 vertical metres higher up at 400444, where you can pick up ticks in September and the change fallen out of Tony's pocket. Don't all rush at once; it was only a dollar's worth.

From the notch it's a short, easy descent to the valley beyond the impasse. The valley definitely ends around the next bend, below peak 412443.

Incidentally, at the notch scramblers are in position to tackle Tiara Peak via its southwest ridge, which appears a relentless bash up orange-coloured screes for 564 vertical metres (1850 feet).

Above: The southwest ridge of Tiara Peak. Trees at bottom right indicate the forested notch. The normal route from the Jumpingpound joins in at the bottom of the summit block just below the right-hand skyline.

Top: #12A The dry midsection of the southeast fork.

12B Northeast Fork

Unofficial trail, route
Distance 5.7 km from forks
Height gain 783 m (2570 ft.)
High point 2180 m (7150 ft.)

Comments The northeast fork takes you through Red Fox Canyon with its spectacular rock scenery to an unnamed pass on Boundary Ridge at 402482. Improbable as it seems, this is one of only a handful of routes crossing the Fisher Range to the Jumpingpound and Elbow. Combine it with routes #3 and #9 (Baldy Pass North and South), or walk out to Powderface Trail (the road) via South Lusk Meadows, which is described in Volume 2. Or follow the ridges on either side over the tops.

Although the terrain is continuously stony, the gradient is never steep and there's no scrambling. Unlike most canyons, there are no hidden horrors waiting around the next bend. There are, however, a great many creek crossings.

To Boundary Ridge

From the forks, a trail heads left up the east fork, following the left bank into the first narrows. Like the southeast fork, the valley floor alternately narrows and widens, necessitating lots of back and forth creek crossings. As you can see from the fixed protection on a slab named "The Hedgehog," sport climbers are gradually working their way in from the road.

At 381471 the valley splits. Keep left up the magnificent northeast fork. (The waterless fork ahead ends in a box canyon 2.5 km distant.)

Straight off, enter lower Red Fox Canyon, where perpendicular walls topped by wafer-thin ridges winging upwards to unseen summits will have your mouth hanging open. There are actually two parts to the canyon, separated by side slopes of scree. Both are quite easy to walk through aside from the creek crossings, the water supplemented by springs bubbling out of mossy banks. Above the canyon, the slopes on either side fall back a little. At a questionable fork at 394478, take the right-hand fork.

Lower Red Fox Canyon.

The creekbed narrows as it approaches Boundary Ridge. Head up the last forested rib on the left, a very moderate slope despite converging contours shown on the topo map. On shale near the top, traverse right to a low point on the ridge which is marked by a cairn.

This is where you join the route coming up the other side from the east. Bookending the long ridge to the south is Boundary Peak at 403471, which is an easy plod. Conversely, Half Past Midnight at the north end is definitely a scramble.

13 Porcupine Ridge

map 1

Day scramble
Unofficial trail
Distance 4.6 km to from Hwy. 40
Height gain 760 m (2231 ft.) from hwy.
High point 2108 m (6916 ft.)
Map 82 J/14 Spray Lakes Reservoir

Access Hwy. 40 (Kananaskis Trail) at Porcupine Creek bridge. Via #12 Porcupine Creeks to the forks.

Comments The seemingly forested ridge between the two forks of Porcupine Creek is a fun trip for experienced hikers who can hack some easy scrambling. Look for flagging.

As seen from Wasootch, Porcupine is actually a prickly ridge characterized by staggered cliffs on one side or the other and two massive pinnacled ribs stepping down the west slope from the ridge crest. Most people stop at a fabulous viewpoint just short of the high point. Since the previous edition there is a route change at the beginning.

To the rock ridge 2.8 km

Start off by following Porcupine Creek trail to the forks. Cross the northeast fork to the base of the treed ridge between the forks. You're going to be following this ridge all the way.

The initial step is steep, the ridge narrowish with a drop on the left side. After a brief easing tackle the longer second step, the trail a slippery mix of slabs, scree and dirt. As the ridge widens, the going gradually gets easier with the odd steep hill. Descend past a cairn and climb back up to the ridge crest at grass. Up next is the long haul up grass to the start of the rock ridge.

To the viewpoint 1.2 km

The trail rounds a free-standing crag to the right and ends below a welter of slabs that are steeper and higher to your right. Scramble up an easy groove on the left edge. Walk right along a ledge between the

Climbing the easy slab above the groove.

This groove is the key to the rock ridge.

Clambering up to the viewpoint from which there is a fabulous view of the middle pinnacle. For many this is the logical stopping point, as the way on to high point is a bit of an anticlimax.

lower and upper slabs. Climb the easy slab above to a ledge, walk left, then right and up onto the ridge crest. The ridge is a mere walk with a view of your objective ahead. Get off the far end bump via a crack or the slabby terrain to its left. The resurrected trail descends to a col.

The trail then climbs through a belt of trees to an open area below turnip-shaped nubbins marking the start of the first pinnacle rib. At the trail junction go straight and on a faint trail weave around rocks and up to the highest nubbin for an incredible

Top: Your objective from the rock ridge. The arrow marks the viewpoint.

Bottom: Looking back to the rock ridge.

view of the middle pinnacle, which one would swear is higher than the summit. (It's not, says Gérard.) In the other direction is a panorama stretching from Tiara Peak through to Midnight Peak with its west ridge in profile.

To the summit 600 m

Going farther seems pointless when you've enjoyed the best view on offer. But if you must, at the last junction go left on a trail that bypasses the pinnacle rib and climbs the forested ridge to a top where the second pinnacled ridge takes off down the west slope. From here the summit's a little way on, at the point where the ridge narrows above a cliff band on the left side.

14 Wasootch Creek map 1

Half-day, day hike
Unofficial trail, route
Distance ~7.7 km to valley head
Height gain 472 m (1550 ft.) valley head
High point 1890 m (6200 ft.) valley head
Map 82 J/14 Spray Lakes Reservoir

Access Hwy. 40 (Kananaskis Trail) at Wasootch Creek parking lot.

Comments While the walking to the forks is easy, it's debatable whether the upper valley is worth the tedium of the endless stony plod to get there. Most people just go to Wasootch Slabs to watch the climbers.

Naming The valley's most interesting aspect is its name, which derives from the Stoney word "wazi," denoting uniqueness and solitariness. Possibly it's connected with Wasootch Tower, a valley landmark that would have been seen from a prehistoric campsite now demolished by the highway.

The flats of Wasootch Creek. Wasootch Slabs to left, Wasootch Tower to right.

To the forks 6.3 km

From the far end of the loop road, a trail leads past the kiosk onto a wide, stony flat. Continue along the trail, delineated by bigger rocks on either side, to Wasootch Slabs on the left, a popular trad and sport climbing area for just about everyone from small kids to seasoned experts. The large white letters A to G at the bottom of various slabs were painted on by the Canadian army, who used the crags for mountain warfare training during the 1950s when the guidebook by Ben Gadd was still 30 years in the future. The spectacular rock outlier on the opposite side of the valley is Wasootch Tower.

From the slabs, pass through a comparative narrows onto another stony flat completely rewritten during various floods that tore up dryas mats (unfortunately for the walker) but spared the balsam poplars. Usually, water is intermittent here, disappearing underground for long stretches at a time. On either side the slopes rise steeply:

Wasootch Ridge on the left and a long stream of summits heading southeast from Wasootch Peak on the right to Mt. McDougall.

Upper valley ~1.4 km

At the forks overlooked by Mt. McDougall the scenario changes. The main left-hand valley narrows and the trees close in. A trail along the left bank leads to a small canyon with waterfall steps. To circumvent, scrabble up a gully to the left, then cut back right over a rib to the creekbed. A little farther on, cross a stony side creek at 378423.

NOTE: This side creek leads to the col separating Wasootch Ridge from the main axis of the Fisher Range. While it can be crossed to the southeast fork of Porcupine Creek at 384442, or even used as a way on or off Wasootch Ridge, know that both sides of the col are very steep.

From here on, stream hopping, awkward side hill traverses around small waterfalls and fights with willow bush are the norm. There seems no easy ways over the ridges to Upper Canyon Creek.

Top: Climbing school at Wasootch Slabs.

Bottom: Upper Wasootch Creek looking toward unnamed mountains between Wasootch and upper Canyon creeks.

Opposite: #15 Wasootch Ridge. The undulating forest section. The summit at top left still looks a long way distant. To its right you can see the two open tops, which is where most people stop.

15 Wasootch Ridge

map 1

Day hike, Long day scramble
Unofficial trail
Distance 6.9 km to summit
Height gain ~975 m (3200 ft.) to top
High point 2332 m (7650 ft.)
Map 82 J/14 Spray Lakes Reservoir

Access Hwy. 40 (Kananaskis Trail) at Wasootch Creek parking lot.

Comments The long ridge dividing Wasootch Creek from the south fork of Porcupine Creek has evolved into one of K Country's classic ridgewalks with a delectable little summit at the end of it. It may be almost as straight as a ruler, but in profile it's as wavy as a rough sea with many tops. Unfortunately, maps, especially metric maps with contour lines at 40-m intervals, show none of this. Regardless, all this up and down hiking puts Wasootch Ridge in the strenuous category, especially when you factor in all the uphills of the return trip.

In terms of technical difficulty, it depends how far you go. Most people wander along to wherever it suits them, then sunbathe for the rest of the day. Others end the trip on the open top with cairn at 365447. Thus far you have been on a really good trail.

To go for the summit at 375438 is more difficult. Expect one pitch of easy scrambling and lots of rock rubble and some route-finding difficulties eased here and there by an intermittent trail and occasional cairn. But no exposure. That's reserved for serious scramblers who on the final approach climb the rock ridge. (Because of its odd dicey move, a rope is advised for novice scramblers tagging along in a group.)

To top 365447, 5.3 km

The trail starts from the trail sign for the Baldy Connector. From picnic tables, turn right off the trail and without preamble twist very steeply up the gable end of the ridge, forest alternating with a few slabby sections out in the open. A long flat follows. The second rise is higher and just as steep: scree and slab, then forest. It's good to know that when you reach the top you've put the worst of the climbing behind you.

The ridge makes a brief jog to the left, then turns right and resumes its straight-line progress. A shorter climb gains you

Opposite: The usual finish at top 365447, looking over sundry rocky tops to the summit.

what might be called top no. 1, which is broad and fairly open, offering views across Porcupine Creek to prickly Porcupine Ridge on the left and down to Wasootch Creek on the right, its stony bed presided over by the conjoined Wasootch Tower and Wasootch Peak. Ahead, the highest summit of your ridge looks far, far away.

The view changes little as you progress along the ridge, climbing up and down the numerous tops. Expect three longish descents and a brief moment of excitement where the trail traverses a narrow ledge above a small cliff. Care is needed here.

Ultimately, the ridge rises gracefully out of the trees to an open top with cliffs plummeting down the Wasootch Creek side. Continue easily to the next top with cairn — a very fine viewpoint for the final section of ridge to the summit. After about 762 m (2500 ft.) of height gain this is the end of the road for most people. The ridge beyond is for scramblers.

GOING HIGHER
To the summit 1.6 km

Continue on trail to the foot of the rock fin. This obstacle is bypassed to the left by a scramble down a rockband. Use either a slab or a crack a little farther on. Either way, you end up on a black shale trail near the base of the rockband. Turn right and follow it up onto the ridge crest again, then down to the col between the fin and the rocky top at 369444, which is where another percentage of hikers call it a day.

Climb a little, then traverse below the rocky top to another col on the far side. From here a good trail climbs up over another small top and down to a man-made wind shelter — a fabulous viewpoint for the summit, which looks terrifying or interesting depending on your point of view. Be assured that the route up the southwest face gets you to the summit without turning you into a gibbering jellyfish begging for a rope.

Walk a little farther along the ridge, then descend right, following the base of slabs. (Scramblers who continue along the ridge crest at this point nearly always come unglued at the notch.)

The view of the summit from near the rock shelter. The normal route descends to the foot of the rock ridge and follows it along to easier terrain.

Hwy. 40 — **59**

Left: *Summit block, showing the approximate route. The dashed line indicates route hidden by the buttress. To left is the scrambler's narrow ridge crest.*

Above: *On the last stretch to the summit.*

Opposite: *#16 The trail above Porcupine Flats, Mary Barclay's Mountain in the background.*

At a gap in the slabs continue on the same line and pick up a good trail descending scree. Then go on as before below slabs to a cairn. This marks the notch up left. There are actually two notches divided by a pinnacle. Ridge scramblers should head for the right-hand one.

Everyone else, continue along the trail below the slabs. Shortly the trail traverses right, then heads uphill to round the base of a rock buttress. When the buttress is outflanked, scrabble the broken slope up left to cairns — an exceptional photo viewpoint for the airy, scary-looking ridge crest, especially if you can catch someone climbing up it. Continue up on easier ground, then, just below the crest, traverse right below slabs to gain the ridge above all difficulties.

All that remains — and this section takes longer than you might think — is to pick your way among large rocks on the right side of the crest to the summit. At a protruding wall en route, it's easier to stay on the crest.

Apart from revealing the long length of the ridge you've just come up, the summit view is not substantially different from before. You are, however, much closer to the myriad of unnamed peaks at the head of Wasootch and Porcupine creeks, which are more easily reached from Upper Canyon Creek. (See Volume 2.)

16 Wasootch-Baldy Connector   map 1

1 to 2 hours one way
Official trail
Distance 3.3 km
Height gain 90 m (295 ft.)
High point 1500 m (4920.)
Map 82 J/14 Spray Lakes Reservoir

Access Hwy. 40 (Kananaskis Trail) at Wasootch Creek parking lot.
Also accessible from #9 Baldy Pass from the south and #12 Porcupine Creeks.

Comments This easy forest trail with more height gain than you might expect, connects Wasootch Creek parking lot to Baldy Pass South trail. Officially it's called Baldy Pass trail and officially is another start to #9. But who wants to walk all those extra kilometres when you don't have to?

Better uses: **1.** Short forest walks for hot days. **2.** If you're doing a circuit with both Baldy Pass trails and Porcupine Creek over the Fisher Range, this is the connector. **3.** part of the Midnight Peak west ridge loop (#10B).

Wasootch to Porcupine 1.7 km
The trail starts from the trail sign at the left side of the parking lot. At picnic tables note Wasootch Ridge trail turning off to the right up steep hillside. Stay ahead.

Your trail parallels the parking lot access road, then turns away from it, climbing gradually around the end of Wasootch Ridge in bushy lodgepole pine forest. From a high point descend into Porcupine Creek Valley and cross the 2017 bridge over Porcupine Creek.

Porcupine to Baldy 1.6 km
On the far side turn left. (Right is the trail up Porcupine Creek). At the next T-Junction, in 100 m, keep right as per the arrow. (The trail to left leads to Porcupine Creek parking area 700 m distant.)

Straight off the trail climbs onto a bank giving nice views across Porcupine flats to Mary Barclay's Mountain. Keep right twice at arrows and climb into a traverse across the skirts of Midnight Peak. Cross three springs. On the way down, cross a dry side valley on stones rolled down in the 2013 flood. A better section of trail, recognizable as old logging road, leads to the 4-way with Baldy Pass trail. Straight leads to Baldy Pass parking lot.

17 Wasootch Peak (G8 Summits)   map 2

Day scramble
Unofficial trail
Distance 5.8 km return
Height gain 898 m (2947 ft.)
High point 2349 m (7707 ft.)
Map 82 J/14 Spray Lakes Reservoir

Access Hwy. 40 (Kananaskis Trail). About 200 m north of the Kananaskis Village/ Nakiska Ski Area junction, park on the east side of the highway or in the shallow ditch. A cairn and flagging atop a branch marks the start of the trail.

Comments This twin-headed mountain presents a bold front to the west, so it's all the more remarkable that there is a trail to the higher south summit via the southwest and south ridges. Nevertheless, there is still scree to contend with and the odd bit of easy scrambling. All in all, a very enjoyable route you'll want to do more than once. Often in condition by May.

Below: Looking up the south ridge from the top of the rock ridge.

Opposite top: Looking down the screes of the south ridge to the rocky southwest ascent ridge.

Opposite bottom: The trail has crossed the gap in the rock crest to the east side of the ridge.

Naming "Let it be named in honour of the G8 Summit held at Kananaskis Village in June of 2002," suggested scrambler Sonny Bou. Over the last few years, the names "Wasootch" and "Winnipeg Peak" have also appeared in the summit register, the latter after it was climbed by two busloads of high school students from Winnipeg. Eagle counters in the valley below call it "Patrick." Who knows what name it will officially end up with: Eagle Mountain? Mt. Sherrington after the chief eagle counter? But for now we can have some fun with the name.

To Six Flags junction 660 m

The trail leads to the flat, stony bed of an unnamed creek. Walk up-creek for 280 m, then at a very large cairn, transfer to a trail on the left bank. After running close to the creek for a way, the trail rises past trails descending to the creekbed. Just beyond the yellow wildland park boundary sign is the junction with the access trail to Six Flags Bouldering Park, also the route to #17A, the plunge waterfall. That trail, blazed at the junction, descends down right. Your trail keeps left uphill.

To summit 2.2 km

A few uphill zigs leads into a traverse above Collossus Wall. At the end of the traverse turn left up the fall line, the trail making a longer, twistier climb to the edge of a perpendicular cliff where the trail has nowhere to go but up. This steepest section ends at a fabulous viewpoint for the Kananaskis Valley and Kananaskis Village, an obvious halting place before tackling the rocky southwest ridge.

The trail dips into a few trees before starting a meandering climb up the ridge to avoid small crags (or not, your choice). On reaching the base of a cliff, traverse right on scree, scrabble over a few rocks, then climb up behind the cliff to a bit of a saddle. After this the trail continues much as before, keeping left of the crest, the many wonderful situations calling out for photos. At last trees the ridge butts against the west-facing slope of the south ridge.

Zig up pale-orange scree, gradually bearing left up the south ridge. High up, the trail stays close to a mane of rock on the ridge crest. A cairn signals both an easing of the gradient and the place where you cross the rock to the east side of the ridge via an obvious gap with easy scrambling both sides.

The far slope drops away very much more steeply but the trail is good and after a couple of minutes you're walking a short, rubbly ridge to the summit cairn with register.

Suddenly revealed is the lower north summit, which is not as easy to reach as it looks. Heading southeast and yoked to your summit is a string of nameless mountains culminating in Mt. McDougall.

17A Plunge Waterfall

Unofficial trail
Distance 2.3 km return from Hwy. 40
Height gain 190 m (623 ft.)

Comments A rough flagged trail through Six Flags Bouldering Park leads past a waterfall where the casual wanderer will stop. The fall is most spectacular in winter when you can walk behind thick sheets of blue ice, hopefully having got there in someone else's footsteps.

Follow #17 for 660 m. Just past the yellow Wildland Park boundary sign turn off right on a blazed trail. After only a few steps turn first left and round the bottom of a broken crag, taking care where the trail is breaking away down the eroded bank. All is then safe going between the creek and the 400-m long Collossus Wall high up to your left. Go right at a Y-junction, cross a wee side creek and pass boulders Sangay and The Banjo Amp. Climb a little alongside the creek, now running and alternately picking its way between boulders and gliding down long slabs. A steeper climb brings you to the falls viewpoint, where a side trail descends to the creek below the fall. As you will see, the water, having glided down more slabs, plunges over the lip of a horizontal rockband with a cave behind it. In summer the flow can be minimal; in winter the ice extends from one end of the band to the other.

18 Stoney Trail

Day hike, bike
Official trail
Distance 22.2 km
Height gain ~80 m (260 ft.)
High point 1470 m (4820 ft.)
Map 82 O/3 Canmore,
82 J/14 Spray Lakes Reservoir

South access Hwy. 40 (Kananaskis Trail). Turn west onto Mt. Allan Drive (signed "Kananaskis Village, Nakiska Ski Area"). Keep straight at the first junction with Centennial Drive, then turn next right into Troll Falls parking lot.

North access Hwy. 1 (Trans-Canada Highway) at Bow Valley Provincial Park South. At the Seebe interchange (exit 114A) follow signs to Rafter Six Ranch Resort and the Rocky Mountain YMCA. At the T-junction go straight ahead into a parking lot.

Also accessible from Hwy. 40 (Kananaskis Trail) at Barrier Dam. Via #8 Jewell Pass and #7 Prairie View Trail.

Comments Walking a powerline access road and the old Hwy. 40 is tedious, though views are really good and you travel past a large number of unnamed valleys and ridges up and down the west side of the lower Kananaskis Valley. So use it as access to better things and don't grumble when overtaken by horses or bikes. Some side creeks are unbridged. Most people use the trail in conjunction with Prairie View and Jewell Pass trails. The south end is heavily used by birders accessing Powerline Beaver Ponds and by climbers and scramblers biking to Mt. Lorette. In this southern area keep an eye out for cougars.

Facilities Jewell Bay backcountry campground, which can also be reached by a paddle from Barrier Lake day-use area. Closed from April 15-June 15. During this time, no random camping is allowed. After July 15, camping is only permitted at Jewell Bay.

Trail note The northerly section in Bow Valley Provincial Park South passes through

Below: A boring section better biked than hiked. Mary Barclay's Mountain up ahead.

Right: Treetop heron at the beaver ponds.

Opposite top: #17 Final ridge to the summit.
Opposite bottom: #17A The waterfall. Photo Bob Spirko

a network of trails which are described with a sketchmap in Volume 3 under "Bow Valley Provincial Park South."

Regulations The section between Evan-Thomas Recreation Area boundary just north of Lorette Creek and Jewell Pass trail junction is closed April 15–June 15 to protect the spring movement of elk.

SOUTH TO NORTH

To Powerline Beaver Ponds 2.3 km

Walk to the far end of the parking lot and around the gate onto the powerline access road. A long, slightly downhill straight leads into meadows used as parking lots during the 15th Olympic Winter Games in 1988. (Up the hill is Nakiska ski area.) Here the road semicircles to the left to a junction. Stay ahead. (The better road to right leads to two pumphouses.) On the way up an incline, cross Hay Meadow trail.

On top of the alluvial fan cross Marmot Creek by culvert. On the descent, note #22A Balam trail to left just before you pass the Mt. Allan substation. Up next is the boring section shown on the previous page pic.

Eventually the road descends below the craggy east face of Hummingbird Plume Hill to Powerline Beaver Ponds and undulates along the west shore of the biggest pond. There are many more ponds worth getting off the beaten track for. According to local birders, you might find such rarities here as Cassin's finch and black swifts. In early spring look for a heronry of about seven birds.

To Lorette Creek/mountain 1.9 km

Shortly after the road leaves the ponds, a faint trail heading left through the aspens is the climber's access to the south ridge of Mt. Lorette and the hiker's access into Lorette Creek Canyon.

Climb another vegetated alluvial fan and on top cross Lorette Creek, which is sometimes dry by this point. Continuing on, the road avoids a steep descent by looping down right into the forest, then back left onto the powerline right-of-way directly under K Country's killer mountain, Mount Lorette, which throws down two spectacular rock ridges toward the road. The left-hand ridge, a classic 5.6 climb famous for its hand traverse, has been the scene of several fatalities.

Stoney trail approaching Jewell Bay backcountry campground. McConnell Ridge ahead.

A God is Love boulder.

The scenic stretch alongside Barrier Lake Reservoir where you can access the water. Mt. Baldy to left; to right the west hill climbed by #6C, Barrier Lake trails.

To Jewell Bay backcountry campground and Jewell Pass trail 7.5 km

As you cross the creek north of Lorette you finally get a close-up view of a mountain much admired for its beautiful orange and grey colouring by Mary Barclay, co-founder with sister Catherine of the Canadian Youth Hostel movement. The moderately difficult scramble up Mary Barclay's Mountain starts up the south ridge from the track.

Then follows a long uneventful stretch below the mountain's steep eastern slopes, boring if it wasn't for the good view across the Kananaskis Valley to the twin valleys of Porcupine and Wasootch divided by Wasootch Ridge, and of Mt. Baldy showing some of the ascent route.

The road makes a big detour to the left to avoid a boggy valley bottom, then on regaining the right-of-way climbs to a first viewpoint for Barrier Lake Reservoir, a depressing scene at low water in the spring and summer when a vast expanse of mud flats is revealed.

Undulate high above the reservoir to a side creek crossing at 344524. If you're into geological structures, this valley is worth a day trip to view excellent examples of horses and duplexes (a mass of rock completely boxed in by thrust faults). Apparently, this structure is something every prospector dreams of finding should it occur in oil-bearing rock. Which is not the case here.

After another ho-hum stretch, come to Jewell Bay backcountry campground on your right. Then cross Jewell Creek bridge at the head of Jewell Bay. In only another 200 m near the top of a hill, Jewell Pass trail turns off to the left at a signed T-junction.

There are two ways to end this route: 1. At Barrier Dam and 2. At Bow Valley Provincial Park South. See the map on the next page.

ENDINGS

1. To Barrier Dam 3.9 km

Continue to follow the road, passing "God is Love" boulders on your left. To your right is Barrier Lake and easy ways down to its shore. After the road bends to the left, the capricious powerline trail with hiking sign turns off to the right under the powerlines. Better to stay on the road and turn next right down the powerline access road to the powerlines, THEN turn left and undulate under the wires to the 4-way with Prairie View. Turn right and cross Barrier Dam to parking lots.

2. To north access 10.8 km

Continue to follow the road, passing "God is Love" boulders on your left. To your right is Barrier Lake and easy ways down to its shore. After the road bends to the left, ignore the powerline trail with hiking sign turning off to the right. Stay on the road that climbs into the trees. After passing the powerline access road heading right, Stoney trail narrows to trail width and continues climbing, a very pleasant section with Douglas firs and views through the trees of McConnell Ridge and its crags. On coming to the staggered 4-way with the wider Prairie View trail, stay straight.

After a bend to the left, watch for a meadow on the right side that leads to the Powerline right-of-way—another way forward. At last visit it had picnic tables.

Descend to a junction where Stoney trail makes an acute turn to the right, heading wrong way southeast. (The track ahead is the western boundary of Bow Valley Provincial Park South.) The trail coming in from the right through some trees just before you cross the N-S powerline right-of-way is the powerline route from the meadow joining back in. Enter the provincial park, for which there is a map in Volume 3.

The road swings left up a hill, then makes a long, gradual descent past a spate of trails peeling off to right and left as you approach the Kananaskis River. Nearly there, note a grassed-over road joining in from the right. This is the original Hwy. 40 built in 1934 between Seebe and Kananaskis Field Station, which was a camp for the unemployed.

On reaching the river bank, go left, following a strip of dark forest below a steep bank. For a period in its history this stretch was also known as the "River Road."

The road eventually climbs the bank into Sundance Meadow at a 4-way. Go straight. Reverting to grass in many places, the old highway heads southwest between a drumlin on the right and an array of Sundance Lodges in various states of disintegration. The one nearest the trail has an interpretive sign "Ti-jurabi-chubi."

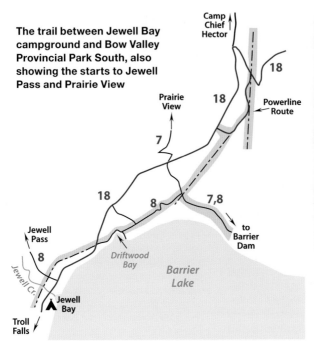

The trail between Jewell Bay campground and Bow Valley Provincial Park South, also showing the starts to Jewell Pass and Prairie View

#18A Pictograph in Lorette Creek canyon.

Pass under the powerlines and curve right around the end of the drumlin into a vast grassy flat called Scouts Field, the site of Canadian and World Scout Jamborees in 1981, '83 and '93. As you walk the final 1.1-km straight to north access, imagine the whole area filled with tents and flagpoles with flags flying in the usual stiff west wind. Commemorative plaques are affixed on boulders near the parking lot.

OPTION
18A Lorette Creek Pictographs
**Distance to falls 3 km,
5.6 km from trailhead**

Comments Lorette Creek is hard going. However, people actually exist like Alf who love pushing through willows and deadfall, risking rockfall from overhanging cliffs, thrutching up a horribly steep slope to get around the waterfall step and side-hilling for hours above a clogged V-shaped valley bottom. Hardly the quickest way to get to Skogan Pass! However, there is one good reason for venturing into the canyon.

The start is easy enough. From the end of the beaver ponds follow the climber's access trail toward Mt. Lorette. Then before hitting Lorette Creek, head along the left bank.

Progress slows, and for most people little Lorette Falls and back is more than enough. The rock scenery is amazing, though, especially the weeping wall on the right that transforms into a frozen waterfall come winter.

But the main reason for persevering is to find pictograph wall, an exceedingly overhanging cliff on the left beyond the narrows. You are looking at tally marks and human stick figures that appear to be falling headfirst down the cliff. Most intriguing is a rock protuberance shaped like a flying eagle and below it curved red lines and two dots that could by the feet on either side of the head. But who knows? No expert has ever given their opinion about the site.

Top: Stoney Trail passes through Douglas firs below McConnell Ridge.

Bottom: #18A Frozen waterfall at the weeping wall in Lorette Creek canyon.

Half day hike
Official trails
Distance 3.7 km loop
Height gain 30 m (100 ft.)
Map 82 J/14 Spray Lakes Reservoir

Access Hwy. 40 (Kananaskis Trail). Turn west onto Mt. Allan Drive (signed "Kananaskis Village, Nakiska Ski Area"). Keep straight at the first junction, then turn right into Troll Falls parking lot with biffy.
Also accessible from #18 Stoney Trail, #21 Skogan Pass from the south, and from Nakiska Ski Area via Hidden trail and Ruthie's.

"If you haven't been to Troll Falls, you haven't been to Ribbon Creek" goes the saying.

Comments The trail to Troll Falls is wide and undulating — a far cry from the narrow forest trail pre-1982—and likely packed with families and kids and couples with dogs and tourists from Kananaskis Village. Runoff is the best time to visit, but it's equally popular as a winter walk when the falls freeze over.

Troll Regulations In the last few years, little tykes have had a wonderful time searching for mini doll trolls hidden at the base of trees and tucked into bridges. Now the grinches of Troll Falls Present have declared it littering.

Birding The optional return loop takes in the Mount Lorette Site, the valley's premier eagle-counting venue. It was here in 1992 that Des Allen and Peter Sherrington demonstrated to the world that the Kananaskis corridor is a major eagle migratory route between the sunny south and breeding grounds in Canada's far north during spring and fall migrations. Incredibly, in the spring it takes birds zooming up the Highwood and Opal Ranges only half an hour to get from Highwood Junction to Wasootch Peak, or "Patrick" as the eagle counters call it. Because this is the narrowest part of the Kananaskis Valley, most birds cross here to Mt. Lorette before continuing northward.

To Troll Falls 1.7 km
The trail starts from behind the biffy and climbs a hill. At the first junction go straight. (Trail to left is the south connector to Skogan Pass trail.) At the next junction atop another hill, again keep right. (Trail to left is the north connector to Skogan Pass trail.) A longer stretch through pines and across a swath of meadow with buried water pipe ends at the always flowing spring creek. Look for fossil oyster shells on the boulders to your left. From here a gradual rise through aspens brings you to the staggered 4-way junction with Hay Meadow trail (right) and Ruthie's trail (left), named after Ruth Oltmann, author, historian of the Kananaskis Valley and hostel house

Opposite top: Troll at the parking lot. Summer or winter, looking for trolls hiding among the trees lured little kids along the more boring sections of the trail.

Opposite bottom: The original troll of Troll Falls.

Above: Toll Falls in April is still half frozen. The trail to the ledge and the troll is now cut off by a wooden fence.

parent at Ribbon Creek in the days when hostellers were avidly exploring the trails left behind after mining and logging.

Turn left, then immediately right at the 4-way with bike rack, following the trail along the left bank of Marmot Creek. In 140 m a side trail to right signed "Upper Falls" is #20. Stay ahead and enter a gloomy recess where Troll Falls plunges over a cliff. Keeping an eye on the falls through huge empty eye sockets is the rock troll himself, which prompted Don Gardner to name the falls Troll back in 1973. Sadly, most people won't get to see it. After recent rockfall from the cliffs above, the public has been corralled by fences into a viewing area with rock seats.

Return the same way or cross the 2020 bridge below the falls to more stone seats. At the next junction with #20 a right turn over a bridge returns you to Troll Falls trail. (NOTE: It's here that anyone wishing to view the upper falls would turn left.)

Hay Meadow trail 2 km

Return to the staggered 4-way intersection and turn left on Hay Meadow trail. Cross Stoney Trail (access road) into aspen forest, then cross the pumphouse road between the primary and secondary pumphouses where water from the Kananaskis River is pumped uphill to Nakiska for snow-making purposes.

Between Hay Meadow on the right and the bank of the Kananaskis River is the Mount Lorette Site with kiosk, bench and plaques erected by the Rocky Mountain Eagle Research Foundation in September of 2017. Though unlikely to see Peter these days, you are bound to encounter locals like Cliff who have their telescopes trained on "The Big Smile" and "The Bumps." There's always binoculars to spare for passing hikers, so be careful! It could be hours before you get back to your car.

Top: Eagle counters in Hay Meadow, where horses once grazed during the early days of the coal mine. Mt. Lorette to left.

Bottom: Ruthie Oltmann and her bench at the Mount Lorette Site on September 16, 2017, during the dedication ceremony.

Recross the spring and head into the trees for a long straight stretch, finally curving right to emerge into the centre of the parking lot opposite Troll Falls trail.

20 Upper (Marmot Creek) Falls   map 2

Short day hike
Official trail
Distance 3.7 km return from parking
Height gain 70 m (230 ft.)
Map 82 J/14 Spray Lakes Reservoir

Access Hwy. 40 (Kananaskis Trail). Turn west onto Mt. Allan Drive (signed "Kananaskis Village, Nakiska Ski Area"). Keep straight at the first junction, then turn right into Troll Falls parking lot.

Comments Between Marmot Basin Road and Troll Falls trail, Marmot Creek skips and plunges its way down the hillside to its ultimate drop-off at Troll Falls. It's a gorgeous piece of water to be savoured by all waterfall lovers, at its spectacular best during snowmelt in June. Also popular in winter when the falls are frozen. At such times wear microspikes.

Most people just go as far as Triple Falls at the end of the Upper Waterfalls sanctioned trail. Seasoned hikers can carry on all the way past the canyon to Marmot Basin Road and make a 5.3 km loop with Skogan Pass and Ruthie's back to the parking lot.

Trail history A whole mess of trails gradually came into being as adventurous hikers, experienced or not, were running around visiting the various waterfalls. After a serious accident in 2018 when a girl fell over Troll Falls, the "upper waterfalls trail" was built in 2019/2020 in an effort to steer rookie hikers away from the dangers of the lower trails and to make it harder for people to look over the edge of bigger falls like Troll and Marmot. Winter users will appreciate the new handrails and the rock and wooden steps.

Below left: Triple Falls in spate in early June.

Below right: Triple Falls at low water in August. Now is the time for a short swim in the pool below.

To start of Upper Falls trail
Follow #19, Troll Falls trail.
1. 140 m along the last leg, turn right and cross Marmot Creek on a bridge to a junction. Go straight
2. **Alternatively,** after visiting Troll Falls cross the bridge below the falls and follow the trail downstream to the aforementioned junction, then turn left.

Upper Falls trail 360 m
At the split either go straight up the hillside (steeper with handrail) or zig left (easier). The trail then wends left, making a rising traverse to a junction which is really a split. Go left on the lower trail.

The trail traverses to an uphill zig, after which it descends to the bottom of Marmot Falls, purposely joining the ledge taking you behind the falls.

From Marmot, climbs rock steps to the upper trail and turn left. A new trail shortcuts to Boulder Falls. Wooden steps made from old telephone poles make the passage of the boulders easy through you may get a soaking when the falls are in spate. The series of small falls above culminates at beautiful Triple Falls where people are sure to congregate, even taking a dip in the pool below the upper fall. Here ends the official trail.

On the return keep left on the upper trail. See #20A if going on.

SIDE TRIP
Below Marmot Falls a very rough trail descends to the bottom of Lower Canyon Falls.

Opposite top: An unfound troll.

Opposite bottom left: Marmot Falls.

Opposite bottom right: Marmot Falls in early April when you can still walk behind the frozen falls.

Above: The steps alongside Boulder Falls, named for the huge boulder the creek dashes against as it makes a sharp right-hand turn.

20A Making a Loop

Unofficial trail, creek crossing
Distance 5.3 km loop from parking lot
Height gain 170 m (560 ft.)

Comments The trail carrying on from the end of the sanctioned trail is no more difficult than what has gone before and allows a loop with Skogan Pass trail and Ruthie's. The creek crossing is difficult at spate.

To the canyon 350 m
Climb a steep step to another flat area. (A side trail to left is the safest way to the slabs atop Triple Falls.) The creek and a split trail then bend right. At the next junctions keep left on the flagged trail nearest the creek. At the far end impasse is a view of the high fall exiting the canyon.

At the impasse the trail climbs easily above the rising walls of the canyon to a Y-junction. Go left and carefully walk the canyon edge. The canyon is featured in the long-running German TV series *Forsthaus Falkenau* (*Ranger Station Falconfield*), this segment made in 2006. A wooden bridge with key slats made of balsa wood for easy breaking was slung across the narrowest part and for a very short while provided hikers with a dizzying view of "Upper Canyon Falls." See *Staffel* (season) 18, *Filge* (episode) 1 to view the exciting denouement.

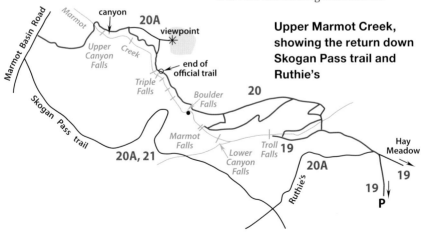

Upper Marmot Creek, showing the return down Skogan Pass trail and Ruthie's

Descend slightly to a calm stretch of creek just before its plunge into subterranean blackness. At the right-hand bend is a Water Survey of Canada groundwater site measuring water flow. A little upstream the remains of a footbridge is tangled up in debris brought down by the 2013 flood. In between, a line of rocks offers a dry passage at low water to a grassy track on the other bank. Follow it out past a groundwater well to Skogan Pass trail on Marmot Basin Road. Turn left, then left again down Skogan Pass trail. At a 4-way, turn left and descend

Ruthie's trail to the 4-way with Troll Falls and Hay Meadow trails. Turn right to return to the parking lot.

DESCENT VARIATION

Via the Viewpoint

If the creek at the crossing place is impassable, try this variation on the way back down. Walk back along the canyon edge, then at the Y-junction go left. The trail heads more gradually downhill, then levels off. Ignore the first steep descending trail to right and the second more reasonable one. Ahead is a meadow out on a ridge with a really fine view of the Kananaskis valley, Wasootch Peak to left, The Wedge ahead and Mt. Kidd to right. Return and at the first side trail you come to turn left and follow it slightly downhill to a junction. Go left to another junction, then return the way you came up.

Top: #20A Hiking the canyon edge. This is the site of the bridge scene in the German TV series.

Left: Screenshot from Forsthaus Falkenau of the bridge built by a K Country crew.

Day hike, bike 'n' hike
Official trails
Distance 10.5 km via Access 1 and 2,
9.4 km via Access 3
Height gain 625 m (2050 ft.) from
Access 1 and 2, 585 m (1919 ft.)
from Access 3
Height loss 49 m (160 ft.)
High point 2063 m (6765 ft.)
Map 82 J/14 Spray Lakes Reservoir

Access Hwy. 40 (Kananaskis Trail). Turn west onto Mt. Allan Drive signed "Kananaskis Village, Nakiska Ski Area."
1. Ribbon Creek Turn first left onto Centennial Drive, then at the 4-way turn right onto Ribbon Creek Road. Drive past Kananaskis Wilderness Hostel to the upper Ribbon Creek parking lot at the end of the road. Park near the picnic shelter.
2. Troll Falls Keep straight at the first junction, then turn next right into Troll Falls parking lot.
3. Nakiska, summer only When the ski area closes, you can still use their parking lots as long as you're out of there before 5 p.m. when the gate closes. If you don't think you can make it, park just before the gate on the right side of the road.

Comments A long uphill plod following 4-m-wide ski trails, then a powerline access road to the watershed between Lorette and Pigeon creeks. Most of the route is closeted in forest of various ages offering few views. You can of course follow it right through to Hwy. 1 (see Volume 3), but most people use it to access Hummingbird Plume Lookout and Marmot Basin. Higher up, Skogan Loop offers a third option. Maps at all junctions.
Starting points The access from Ribbon Creek parking lot works well all year round. Do NOT follow the X-C ski access which starts up Hidden trail; it's three times as long. Access from Troll Falls parking lot is very slightly longer. Access from Nakiska gate is very much shorter with less height gain, but can only be used after the ski area closes.

About the pass and its trail Just over a hundred years ago Pigeon Pass, as it was called then, was a quiet place crossed by an Indian trail shown on George Dawson's map from 1886. Likely it was the same trail, by then called the Kananaskis Pack Trail, which was widened in 1936 by the Forest Service to carry the telephone line linking Dead Man Flat ranger cabin to Boundary ranger cabin near the mouth of Ribbon Creek. Henceforth it was known as the Canmore Boundary Telephone Line trail over Dead Man Pass.

Since then, the trail, and the whole hillside on the south side of the pass has been carved up by the powerline right-of-way and its access road and by a proliferation of logging roads and cutblocks, coal mine access roads, Marmot Basin project roads, all of which were used as cross-country ski trails by the early hostellers. By 1986 Nakiska Ski Area was up and running with the 1988 Winter Olympics in mind. The lower Marmot Basin Road was incorporated into the ski area and access road, thus forcing a new start to Skogan Pass trail that today undulates all around the ski area's perimeter.

Naming It was skier Don Gardner who named the pass "Skogan" in 1973, the older names having never caught on. Skogan is a Norse word meaning "magic forest with elves and trolls."

There are three starting points. All converge on Marmot Basin Road.

FROM ACCESS 1
Longest from Ribbon Creek 2.6 km
The official trail starts from the back of the picnic shelter. After crossing a wee creek (no bridge), the track traverses right, then climbs to a junction with the X-C ski trail. Stay ahead and in a minute cross Mt. Allan Drive. Continue along Skogan Pass trail, which dips to the junction with the south connector (access 2). Keep left.

In 340 metres the north connector comes in from the right. Keep straight and climb to a Y-junction where you climb up

right. (Left climbs up to north parking lot at Nakiska.) The trail then eases and crosses a swath of meadow with buried water pipe. The next point of interest is the 4-way with Ruthie's. Go straight and climb. After a dip to cross the southwest fork of Marmot Creek, embark on a longer climb alongside the creek to gain Marmot Basin Road. Turn right.

FROM ACCESS 2

Just as long from Troll Falls 2.6 km.
Halfway along the parking lot at the biffy turn left onto Troll Falls trail and climb to a junction. Turn left on the south connector, which brings you to Skogan Pass trail in 550 m. Turn right and read the second paragraph of access 1.

FROM ACCESS 3

Shortest via Marmot Basin Road, 1.5 km
From the gate walk up the access road to Nakiska and walk in front of the day lodge. Just before Olympic Chair's bottom terminal pick up an old road (the original Marmot Basin Road) that heads left, then diagonals up right, passing under Olympic Chair, the Bronze Chair and across assorted downhill ski runs.

After leaving the ski runs, the road bends left, then right (ignore tracks to left) and crosses the southwest fork of Marmot Creek just before the junction with Skogan Pass ski trail come in from the right. Go straight.

To Upper Marmot Creek Road 100 m
Where the road levels are junctions. First on the right is a grassy track leading to Marmot Creek canyon (see #20A). A few metres on, the Marmot Basin Road turns left uphill, making for Mid Mountain Lodge and Marmot Basin (see #23). Go straight on the powerline access road past an old gate.

To Sunburst trail 1.8 km
Around a bend is a third junction with churned-up Marmot Creek Road to left that washed out in 2013. Go right here and cross Marmot Creek on Two Ton Culvert.

The three starts to Skogan Pass trail

Resuming the uphill grind again, the access road winds above a steep bank to a groundwater well on the second bend, then diagonals right below steep hillside to the powerline right-of-way. This is where Sunburst trail turns off to the right to Hummingbird Plume Hill. And also where Balam plummets down the powerline's right-of-way access road to Stoney Trail. (See #22A.)

To High Level trail 900 m
Swing back left and then right to a signed junction with High Level trail which also leads to Hummingbird Plume Hill.

To Skogan Loop junctions 2.8 km
Again you swing left, then gradually turn right and climb a long straight. You're about 50 years too late to see the view and a string of historic wooden tripods holding up the telephone line between ranger stations. At the top of the hill is the lower junction of Skogan Loop trail at 1.2 km.

Keep straight and thread "Spruce Avenue" to the powerline right-of-way. Here the road turns sharp left and climbs, twining about the right-of-way. At the top of the hill is the upper junction with Skogan Loop which is NOT the pass.

To Skogan Pass 1.9 km
The access road leaves the powerline right-of-way and DESCENDS to a gate signifying the northern boundary of the Marmot Basin Project. Keeping left, you swing around all the heads of Lorette Creek and cross the powerline right-of-way. The road then turns left and paralleling the right-of-way climbs to its high point, an indeterminate place in the pines just beyond where the old pack trail turns off to the right. Look for telephone wire trailing on the ground.

From the road's high point it's worth detouring left onto the right-of-way for a view through the powerlines to Old Baldy and the peaks around Mt. McDougall.

Opposite: #21 "Spruce Avenue" between the two junctions of Skogan Loop

OPTIONAL END LOOP
21A Skogan Loop

Distance 2.8 km, total return distance from Nakiska gate 15.3 km
High point 2066 m (6778 ft.)

Comments Skogan Loop makes a fine alternative to Skogan Pass because it has the odd view and is higher than the pass by 3 m.

Turn left at the lower junction. The track (ski trail) makes long, easy windings with viewpoints en route of Mt. Collembola and a few other peaks glimpsed from the picnic table at Vista View. At a meadow offering a foreshortened view of Collembola, the track climbs more steeply up right between snow fences to a T-junction in dark, old forest. Turn right. (Left leads to more meteorological instruments.)

From the high point the old road descends a long hill to the upper junction with Skogan Pass trail at the powerline right-of-way. Turn right.

Above: #21A foreshortened Mt. Collembola from the point where you climb up to the right past snow fences to the high point of Skogan Loop.

22 Hummingbird Plume Lookout map 2

Day hike
Official trails
Distance 5.2 km from Nakiska gate
Height gain 700 m (2300 ft.)
High point 1865 m (6120 ft.)
Map 82 J/14 Spray Lakes Reservoir

Access Via #21 Skogan Pass from the south.

Comments Mostly a forest walk following 4-m-wide ski trails to an historic lookout atop Hummingbird Plume Hill.

Naming It was named in 1973 by Don Gardner but dates back well before that, possibly to the mid-1930s.

Skogan Pass trail 3.3 km

Start by following #21 Skogan Pass trail from access 3 to the Sunburst trail junction. Add on 1.1 km from Accesses 1 and 2.

Via Sunburst to High Level trail 1.2 km

Turn right onto Sunburst trail, which crosses the powerline right-of-way, then climb ever more steeply to the junction with High Level trail.

To Hummingbird Plume Hill 500 m

Turn right onto High Level and on flat ground walk to the small meadow atop Hummingbird Plume Hill.

You missed the lookout in the rush to get seats at the picnic table? The "lookout" is the tarpapered shack on the right that doesn't appear to be worth a second glance unless there's an imminent thunderstorm, and then it pays to know the shack is grounded. But take a closer look inside. On the walls are inscribed the names and initials of German POWs from Camp 130: Erich Petrinski POW 17.11.1939, JQ 1941, PW July 6/41.

At the time, the POWs were salvaging burnt timber from the 1936 fire that started in the upper reaches of Galatea Creek. Since that time the pines have grown high, so what you do now is follow a two-minute trail to the other end of the meadow and through a few trees to an overlook above the craggy east slope of the hill. Before you is the same view of the Kananaskis Valley, Mt. Lorette to the left, the Fisher Range opposite and to the right a clutch of ridges rising to Wasootch Peak. Return the same way or try High Level, which adds on another 1.1 km.

OPTIONAL RETURN TO ACCESS 2

22A Balam

Distance 3.3 km to access 2

Comments A powerline shortcut to access 2 that cuts off 1.2 km. Back in early hostel days, it was a crazy fast downhill ski run named Balam after the three-headed king of the demons who rode a ferocious bear.

Balam 1.7 km

Backtrack toward Skogan Pass trail, but this time keep going down the powerline right-of-way, following the old road that starts to the left of a draw. The road twines about the right-of-way and has some very steep hills during its thousand-foot-drop, but as of 2023 no obstacles to worry about. Finally it spits you out on Stoney trail just south of the Mt. Allan substation.

Stoney trail 1.6 km

The easy half turns right and crosses Marmot Creek on a bridge. Descend past the 4-way with Hay Meadow trail, then rise very gradually to Troll Falls parking lot.

TO OTHER TRAILHEADS?

See the sketchmap on page 78. My view is that the extra height gain up Ruthie's or Troll Falls trail and the north connector is not worth the bother.

Opposite: Wasootch Peak from the viewpoint. The snow-covered mountain to right is peak 356417.

Top: The lookout, now surrounded by pine forest.

Centre: One of the POW's names carved into wood inside the lookout.

Bottom: Old road sign at the bottom of Balam.

23 Marmot Basin

map 2

Long day hikes
Official & unofficial trails, route
Distance 7.6 km to Marmot Creek
Height gain 797 m (2614 ft.) to Marmot Creek
High point 2275 m (7464 ft.) at Marmot Creek
Map 82 J/14 Spray Lakes Reservoir

Access Via #21 Skogan Pass from the south.
Also accessible from Collembola traverse in Volume 3.

Comments A steep climb on access roads followed by another steep climb on a forest trail through the Marmot Basin Project area gives access to the cirque between Mt. Allan and the lower Collembola. The trip from bottom to top is definitely strenuous with lots of height gain if going on to Fisera Ridge. On the plus side the past navigational problems with the forest trail have been solved by flagging put up in 2019. All trails stop at treeline but the open terrain above the larch belt is straightforward. You can, if you want, climb both these peaks from the basin, or make a loop with the Centennial trail or a point to point with the Collembolas.

Trail update Since the last edition the south leg of upper Marmot Basin road has been absconded by Nakiska Ski Area and renamed Mid Mountain Road. In winter it acts as a snowmobile cat track to deliver supplies to Mid Mountain Lodge and as a private snowshoe trail for guided trips organized by Nakiska, not that this elite status is recognized by any self-respecting backcountry skier, snowshoer and walker.

History So what WAS the Marmot Basin Project? Basically, it was a hydraulic study of the whole watershed by the Forest Experiment Station that began in the mid-1950s and lasted almost 30 years. The forest was logged in various ways to see what the effect would be on snowpack depth, snowmelt and water flow. Since 2004, the studies, now part of the *Improved Processes and Parameterization for Prediction in Cold Regions* research network, have been revived by the University of Saskatchewan and Environment Canada working out of the University of Calgary's Kananaskis Field Station. Nearly all the instruments you see now as you wander around are recent.

Naming And how DID the cirque come by its name? Even his friends might be surprised to learn the basin and creek were named by Gordon Scruggs, who as a young university student, assisted M.B.B. Crockford during the geological survey of 1947 prior to the opening of the Ribbon Creek coal mine. According to Gordon, their camp was overrun by marmots looking for easy pickings. In mountaineering circles, Gordon was best known as a member of the Grizzly Group who specialized in first ascents in remote areas of the Rockies.

Right: Instruments in Marmot Creek.

Opposite: Typical view of the forest trail above Upper Marmot Basin Road. First appearance of the larches. Photo Bob Spirko

Skogan Pass trail 2.8 km

Start by following the Skogan Pass trail from whichever access to the Marmot Basin Road. Turn right.

After the road levels, a grassy track heading right to a groundwater well is the route taken by #20A after viewing the Marmot Creek waterfalls. Just before a gate, turn left onto the upper Marmot Basin Road/ Nakiska's Mid Mountain Road.

Upper Marmot Basin Road 2.7 km

Most of this uphill section is a snowmobile access road to Nakiska's mid-mountain lodge and is totally enclosed in trees. Right near the start stay straight (cat track to left leads to ski runs), then keep left four times in a row as you climb around two sweeping bends, ignoring signs saying "cat track." At the next T-junction keep straight. (Cat track to left leads to Gold Chair.) Continue climbing—the uphill grind is relentless, calling for a collapse next to a fuel tank where another cat track turns left toward Mid Mountain Lodge (unfortunately closed in summer).

Keep straight on the old road that descends and turns right to cross South Twin and North Twin creeks. The bridge over South Twin got washed aside during the 2013 flood, but the moss-covered bridge

over North Twin still stands. The trail up #23B South Twin Creek takes off to the left between the two. After the second crossing leave the road and at flagging turn left onto a narrow trail. (NOTE: In 2013 the continuing road, called Marmot Creek ski trail down Marmot Creek was washed out and is unlikely to be rebuilt.)

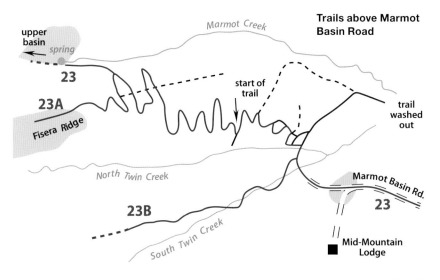

Trails above Marmot Basin Road

upper basin
← spring

23

23A

Fisera Ridge

Marmot Creek

start of trail

trail washed out

North Twin Creek

Marmot Basin Rd.

23

23B

South Twin Creek

Mid-Mountain Lodge

What joy to finally follow an easy-angled trail winding through spruce forest and patchworks of mini-cutblocks. Look for the first larch. High up you cross a straight-up shortcut trail three times. After the last intersection a long traverse right leads into willowy Marmot Creek at the site of instruments measuring stream flow. Where you go next depends on your destination.

1. For Fisera Ridge Zig back left on the flagged trail. See #23A.

2. For upper Marmot Basin Follow a less distinct trail up the left bank of Marmot Creek to the spring where Marmot Creek emerges in boisterous flight. Ahead are meadows dotted with boulders, rocky outcrops and spruce thickets.

People with energy to spare can continue climbing another 270 metres (886 ft.) of height gain to the Allan/Collembola col to look down on Jubilee Tarns, and even tack on Mt. Allan via its east ridge or, more easily, the lower summit of Mt. Collembola, which is just a grassy walk.

To Marmot Basin trail junction 2.1 km
The trail initially follows the north bank of North Twin Creek. This first (and worst) section has gotten rather bushy — thank god for the flagging — as it twines about and uses sections of old logging roads. You're on logging road as you approach North Twin Creek for the second time. Just before the road peters out above the bank, turn right onto original trail in a flurry of flagging.

Top: #23A Weather instruments on Fisera Ridge. Photo Bob Spirko

Bottom: #23 Upper Marmot Basin. In the background game trails climb onto Fisera Ridge. Photo Alf Skrastins

Opposite: #23A Relaxing on Fisera Ridge. Mt. Allan in the background.

TWO OPTIONS

23A Fisera Ridge

Distance ~1.2 km from Marmot Creek
Extra height gain ~145 m (476 ft.)
High point ~2420 m (7940 ft.)

At Marmot Creek, the better-used flagged trail swings back left past a metal sign reassuringly stamped "Fisera Ridge."

Recross the straight-up shortcut trail and wind up the backbone of the ridge through larches (always a thrill) where in ages past Zdenek "Denny" Fisera tended to his instruments. Nowadays, researchers still hike up the trail to three hydrometeorological stations measuring everything from soil temperature to snow depth and wind speed, i.e., blowing snowstorms. Not for nothing did FES employees call Mt. Allan "Storm Mountain."

Continue to where the ridge levels in a meadow with views all around of Olympic Summit through to Mt. Allan and the lower summit of Collembola.

23B South Twin Creek

Distance ~1.3 km from Upper Marmot
Basin Road
Height gain ~228 m (750 ft.) from Upper
Marmot Basin Road
High point ~2133 m (7000 ft.)

Comments A direct route to open slopes on the south side of the cirque.

Start from Upper Marmot Basin Road between South Twin and North Twin creeks. Turn left up what was once a grassy logging road that crosses South Twin Creek twice before ending in a tangle of deadfall. A trail continues and crosses the creek another two times.

Then follows a long stretch along the north bank to a V-shaped valley bottom where the trail is forced into a steeply rising traverse to gain the rib between the twin creeks. The trail ends at an instrument site in the larches about 60 metres below treeline. This puts you in a good position to cut across to Fisera Ridge, which is one ridge over to the north, and return that way.

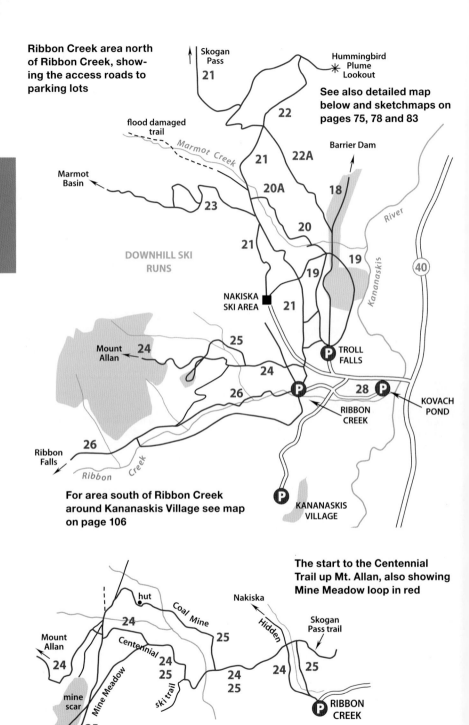

Ribbon Creek area north of Ribbon Creek, showing the access roads to parking lots

Skogan Pass
21

Hummingbird Plume Lookout

See also detailed map below and sketchmaps on pages 75, 78 and 83

flood damaged trail

Marmot Creek

22

Barrier Dam

21   22A

Marmot Basin

20A

18

23

20

River

21

DOWNHILL SKI RUNS

19

Kananaskis

19

40

NAKISKA SKI AREA

21

Mount Allan

24

25

24

TROLL FALLS

26

28

KOVACH POND

RIBBON CREEK

Ribbon Falls

26

26

Ribbon Creek

For area south of Ribbon Creek around Kananaskis Village see map on page 106

KANANASKIS VILLAGE

The start to the Centennial Trail up Mt. Allan, also showing Mine Meadow loop in red

hut

Coal Mine

Nakiska

Skogan Pass trail

Mount Allan

24

Centennial

25

Hidden

24

mine scar

Mine Meadow

24
25

Ski trail

24
25

24

25

RIBBON CREEK

25

#24 Mount Allan Centennial Ridge. Photo by Roy Millar of the Claw

24 Mount Allan Centennial Ridge map 2

Long day scramble
Official trail
Distance 7.8 km to summit,
18.6 km to north trailhead
Height gain 1369 m (4491 ft.)
High point 2832 m (9,291 ft.)
Map 82 J/14 Spray Lakes Reservoir

Access Hwy. 40 (Kananaskis Trail). Turn west onto Mt. Allan Drive signed "Kananaskis Village, Nakiska Ski Area." Turn first left onto Centennial Drive, then next right onto Ribbon Creek Road. Drive to the upper Ribbon Creek parking lot at the end of the road.
Also accessible from Mount Allan from the North in Volume 3.

Comments The Centennial trail over Mt. Allan extends all the way from Ribbon Creek to Wind Valley. Not many people do the whole traverse, because it requires two vehicles and a spare pair of feet, knees, hips etc. The vast majority of summiters prefer a there and back trip via the southern half of the route from Ribbon Creek, an entertaining ridgewalk with two pitches of very easy scrambling. Signposts, cairns and red paint splodges on rocks make navigation easy. Bearing in mind the strenuous nature of the trip and the humongous height gain, start early from the parking lot.

Regulations Upwards of Mine Scar the trail is closed for lambing April 1–June 21.

Trail history It was 1966. The next year was Canada's centennial and to mark this momentous occasion the Rocky Mountain Ramblers, spearheaded by Wally Drew, decided to build a trail up the long southeast ridge of Mt. Allan to the summit and down the even longer north ridge to Dead Man Flat. It would be the highest trail ever built in the Canadian Rockies, higher even than Jasper's celebrated Skyline trail. The work took three summers to complete and culminated in a champagne ceremony on the summit during a snow squall. A large wooden sign was erected but didn't stand for long. Within three months the picas had chewed away the supporting poles and in another two years the sign itself was fully digested. In 1983 an inedible bronze plaque was placed in the Mushroom Garden along the southeast ridge — or the Centennial Ridge as it is called

nowadays. In 2018 Alberta Parks made a welcome improvement to the steep section below Mine Scar. Thanks, Jeff.

Naming After geologist John Allan, who is credited with the founding of Alberta's energy industries.

Opposite: Looking up the second step to Olympic summit. The rockband is surmounted on the right side.

Top: The ridge between Olympic Summit and the top. The Mushroom Garden at the halfway point.

Bottom: The conglomerate pinnacles lining the trail on the left side. Photo Bill Rowe

To top of Mine Scar 2.5 km

Luckily, the complicated start through a maze of old coal mine roads is now very well signed.

From the kiosk halfway along the parking lot, follow Hidden trail curving up and left. In 390 metres at a 4-way with map turn left onto Centennial trail/Ribbon Creek ski trail. In 500 metres keep left at a Y-junction. (Coal Mine to right is used by #25 Mine Meadow Loop .) At the next T-junction turn right off the ski trail onto the narrower Centennial Trail. See the map on page 86.

After a winding ascending traverse, the trail turns left up the fall line. Keep right where #25 comes in from the left and shortly cross a vegetating road. Climb even more steeply to the first of three parallel "truck driven roads" heading left to various levels of the strip mine, now reclaimed and known as Mine Meadow. The trail crosses this road and climbs to the second one, crosses that and climbs to the third road. Here turn left. Keep right (unless headed for the upper level of Mine Scar) and come to signs overlooking the meadow.

Centennial Ridge 5.4 km

The trail winds up right to another "road" and follows it to the left. Watch for where a narrow trail turns right into the trees.

On emerging from the trees, the sight of the trail crawling upwards, climbing 610 metres in less than 2 km, is a real downer, but the grassy rib it follows has its compensations in the marvellous views that unfold, and summer's succession of flowers ending in late August with a purple colour scheme of asters and harebells. Take a breather on a shoulder, then zig some more up a shaley slope to the apex of three grass ribs.

Step no. 2 features a rock step that looks alarming but is easily turned on the right side by a series of broad ledges and a gully that calls for hands in a few places. Under snow, however, this section can be tricky. Maybe you'll find a rope rigged up to the left of the gully.

Continue more easily to grassy Olympic Summit which is topped by a meteorology station. Having spent much energy getting there it's discouraging to find the main summit looks as far away as ever. But the worst of the climbing is behind you and the most scenic part of the whole route is yet to come. This is where the trail winds through the Mushroom Garden (note the plaque), a mere prelude to the passage between the rocky ridge crest and a row of 25-m-high conglomerate pinnacles, the most striking of which is called The Claw. Through gaps look down on Memorial Lakes.

Some interesting down-scrambling follows and brings you to a section of scree ridge where you can either follow the crest or keep to the trail on the left slope. Tackle the final rise to the summit direct. (The trail traversing below the summit block to the north ridge is a sheep trail.)

The view from the summit cairn is little different from that seen on the way up. The greater height of Mt. Lougheed's four peaks effectively blocks all views to the west.

25 Mine Meadow Loop

map 2

Half day hike
Official trail
Distance 5.3 km loop
Height gain 270 m (890 ft.)
High point 1695 m (5560 ft.)
Map 82 J/14 Spray Lakes Reservoir

Access Hwy. 40 (Kananaskis Trail). Turn west onto Mt. Allan Drive signed "Kananaskis Village, Nakiska Ski Area." Turn first left onto Centennial Drive, then next right onto Ribbon Creek Road. Drive to upper Ribbon Creek parking lot at the end of the road.

Comments A fairly easy uphill hike to Mine Scar meadow, a worthy viewpoint at the site of the Ribbon Creek strip mine/underground mine. And while primarily a winter walking/snowshoe loop, It also works well in summer for hikers who don't want to climb Mt. Allan.

You get there by walking mine access roads in a figure 8 configuration, the junctions well signed with maps and snowshoe/biking markers. As you can see from the lower map on page 86, there is a choice of up and down routes. My preference in winter is to plod up the easier gradient of Coal Mine.

History In brief the mine operated between 1948 and 1952.

From the north side of the parking lot head out on Hidden trail beyond the gate. To avoid conflict with downcoming skiers in the winter, transfer to the trail on the right side of the small creek (actually the original Marmot Basin Road) and on reaching Skogan Pass ski trail turn left across a bridge to the 4-way junction. Go straight. In summer, you can walk up Hidden trail and turn left at the 4-way.

Plod up Centennial Ridge/Ribbon Creek ski trail, the start of a long climb through forest. In 600 m turn right onto Coal Mine and follow its windings past a hut clad in metal to a flat traversing road once used by trucks rumbling up and down from "Ribbon Crick" village. Turn left, still on Coal

Mine. After the gully the road splits into three. Take the lowest road to the left. After intersecting the staggered Centennial trail it descends slightly to an X junction. Go straight, still descending slightly to the far end of the mine scar, then at posts climb up and across the meadow to the right for the view of the Kananaskis Valley.

Back in trees descend to the X junction on Coal Mine. Maps suggest you turn left, then right down the very steep hill on Centennial trail. I prefer to cross Coal Mine and walk a very gently inclined mine road, at its low point cutting right through a bit of bush onto Centennial trail below the steep bit. Turn right. Descend the winding Centennial trail to the Ribbon Creek ski trail where you turn left. At the junction with Coal Mine keep straight and return the way you came up.

Opposite: #24 The easy upper section of the ridge leading to Mt. Allan's summit. Photo Roy Millar

Top: Crossing Mine Meadow.

Bottom: The metal-clad hut can be used as a shelter.

26 Ribbon Falls

Long day hike, backpack, bike 'n' hike
Official trail
Distance 9. 2 km to Ribbon Falls
backcountry campground,
9.4 km to Ribbon Falls
Height gain 311 m (1020 ft.) to
Ribbon Falls
High point 1814 m (5950 ft.)
Map 82 J/14 Spray Lakes Reservoir

Access Kananaskis Trail (Hwy. 40). Turn west onto Mt. Allan Drive signed "Kananaskis Village, Nakiska Ski Area." Turn first left onto Centennial Drive, then next right onto Ribbon Creek Road. Drive past Kananaskis Wilderness Hostel to the upper Ribbon Creek parking lot at the end of the road.
Also accessible from #81 Buller Pass.

Comments This long and popular trail follows a spectacular valley hemmed in by cliffs to Ribbon Falls backcountry campground and Ribbon Falls. Your companion for the whole journey is the disgracefully behaved Ribbon Creek, its rapids and waterfalls at their very best after June rains and snowmelt. Don't go for a first visit in late fall or you'll be disappointed.

Biking is allowed to 1 km beyond the North Fork/Memorial Lakes junction. It all helps to get you to Ribbon Falls and back in one day, and scramblers to the summit of Mt. Bogart.

Trail update The 2013 flood wiped out the first two sections of trail to the north fork confluence. Both were rebuilt and almost completely rerouted in 2014 and 2015, the old wooden bridges replaced by expensive fibreglass models.

History Eau Claire logging was busy in this valley and in the north fork at various times from 1886 to the beginning of the Second World War. By the 1940s a winter logging road zigzagged up the creek, snaking up the north fork a way, then continuing on to where the bike racks used to be. In the meadow of the north fork was a logging camp with bunkhouse, cookhouse, office and garage. A

Logjam bridge no. 4.

barn could still be seen here in the late 1950s. Then came the flood of 2013.

The opening of the Ribbon Creek Youth Hostel in 1960 started the recreational ball rolling. Getting up the first section of Ribbon Creek was not the easy walk it is now. No bridges, of course, the uncrossable creek forcing hostellers to devise a tortuous route along the north bank. Who can forget the perilous shale traverse!

To Link junction 2.5 km

The trail leaves the end of the parking lot at interpretive signs and climbs onto a berm protecting the parking lot from floods. Straightaway cross a meadow, once a Rundle rock quarry opened by Elmer Smith in the 1960s, maybe pausing en route at the Vera M. and Michael B.B. Crockford memorial bench. In 1948, M.B.B named Mt. Allan and one year later wrote report no. 52 for the Research Council of Alberta giving a detailed description of the geology of the Ribbon Creek area.

Ribbon Falls in spate.

After dropping to creek level at a narrows, cross bridge no. 1. The trail runs alongside the creek, crosses a year-round spring by boardwalk, then cuts off a bend to bridge no. 2. Go left. Shortly veer right alongside the old channel to a massive logjam. To its left, steps wide enough to take snowshoes lead onto bridge no. 3.

Now on the south bank, cross two log bridges spanning an old channel. In between them, look across Ribbon Creek to Eleanor's lonely memorial bench left stranded by the flood. Back on wide old trail, the view ahead is dominated by Ribbon Peak, which through many editions of the government topo map was incorrectly marked as Mt. Bogart.

Just before the old trail vanishes in the creek, turn right and cross bridge no. 4. On coming to a 4-way junction with the 4-m-wide ski trail at 1.6 km, go straight on a bypass trail. NOTE: At the junction detour into the creek debris to look at the twisted remains of the old no. 4 bridge.

Turn next right onto the ski trail, then right again onto the old trail arisen from the creek. The trail continues close to the creek, passing two picnic tables en route to the signed T-junction with Link trail. Stay ahead. (Link turns left down a hill and bridges Ribbon Creek.)

To Memorial Lakes trail 1.1 km

At the Lorax stump (representing the Dr. Seuss character who speaks for the trees), diagonal up the bank, cross a bridge over a draw, then settle into an enjoyable walk along a bench from where you can look down on Toad Forest as the hostellers called it and the flood-wrecked trail. Seats are plentiful. At T-junction 272430 with cairn keep left. (Trail ahead is #27 to Memorial Lakes.)

To bike racks 1 km

More banktop wandering leads to a bridge over the north fork. Descend onto a cobble flat. Sadly, most of the meadow was washed away in the 2013 flood, taking with it the picnic table, interpretive plaque and tastefully strewn pieces of metal at the site of the logging camp.

Top left: The Lorax stump.

Top right: Dipper Canyon.

On flat old logging road, head between Ribbon Peak and the cliffy west side of Mt. Kidd to road's end at a bike rack—the end of the trail for bikers.

To Ribbon Falls 4.9 km

A narrower trail carries on, soon climbing to get above stony banks. Descend into a grassy, willowy section where you cross side creeks on assorted bridges. Again the trail rises and follows a bench above chutes and waterfalls, merely a prelude for what is to come. Allow extra time for forays to viewpoints. At 1.8 km from the bike rack, look for the ruins of log cabins to your right, their walls a popular place for a sit-down and snack. There's a flat area for tents and a trail down to the creek.

The trail then undulates and traverses steep hillsides above Dipper Canyon, named by early hostellers after "a chubby grey songbird with an amazing adaptability to rough water," their progeny still bobbing about on mist-sprayed ledges. It features the highest waterfall below Ribbon Falls.

After this, the creek calms down somewhat and the going is uneventful below the avalanche slopes of Mt. Bogart. Pass below the big cirque between Mt. Kidd and its south summit. At snowmelt, waterfalls step-plunging down the cliffs of South Kidd are an arresting sight. A stony side creek crossing with no bridge signals your imminent arrival at Ribbon Falls backcountry campground. Site #13 is the desired view lot if you can stand the increased decibel count of Ribbon Falls.

From the campground it's a short climb to Ribbon Falls viewpoint, identified by a memorial seat to 18-year-old Simon White. En route, pass side trails leading to the bottom of the falls, a place to avoid when the falls are in spate unless equipped with full storm gear.

This is what you can expect if continuing along the trail to Ribbon Lake. Looking up the first pitch of the headwall safeguarded with metal rungs and a cable. For further pictures turn the page. Photo Karen and Greg Smith

GOING FARTHER

26A To Ribbon Lake

Scramble
Distance 1.9 km from campground
Height gain 277 m (910 ft.)
High point 2076 m (6810 ft.)

Important Comments The cliff bands responsible for a spectacular series of waterfalls, cause much difficulty to the backpacker bound for Ribbon Lake. The trail beyond Ribbon Falls viewpoint is steep, difficult and even dangerous. So I wrote in the 4th edition. Then In 2022, iron rungs were drilled into the rock and the four chains replaced by cables to which safety gear can be attached should you so choose. It's now K Country's first Via Ferrata!

If hauling yourself plus pack up the cliff doesn't appeal, leave your camping gear at Ribbon Creek and make Ribbon Lake a side trip. If you must camp at Ribbon Lake take easier routes: Buller Pass (#81) or Guinn's Pass (#35). Lately, it's become the fad to run a one-day circuit using Ribbon Creek, Guinn's Pass and Galatea trails.

From the falls, the trail heads up right into dark forest, climbing quite steeply, then arcs back left below a scree slope and across the creek bounding down from the cirque southwest of Mt. Bogart (scrambler's ascent route). Continue traversing, at the last crossing a scree slope to the bottom of the headwall with yellow warning sign.

With the help of rungs and cable no. 1, climb a corner until level with a large ledge on the left, then traverse 3 metres of intervening slick slab (cable no. 2). Walk along a wide ledge to cable no. 3 and instead of heaving yourself up 5 metres of difficult rock, bulging in the middle, simply climb up rungs. On easier ground above wend

Opposite: #26A the Via Ferrata page.

Top left: The trail leading to the rock face, showing the numbered cables. Photo Tanya Koob

Top right: Looking back down the corner from the first ledge (second cable). Photo Jeremy Philips

Bottom left: Climbing difficult rock with the aid of rungs and cable no. 3. Photo Greg and Karen Smith

Bottom right: The exposed horizontal ledge. Photo Greg and Karen Smith

right, then left onto a long horizontal ledge protected with cable no. 4. As you edge above the big drop, it's disquieting to know a fall from here would definitely kill you. Don't relax your vigilance on the easy steps that follow; the rock is greasy smooth and a slip could send you perhaps not over the edge into the creek, but to the very brink, hanging on to a few bushes like the hero of a 1920 Harold Lloyd movie. Luckily, the rungs and cable have been extended to include this seemingly innocuous section. After all the excitement, the series of cataracts, falls and pools in the now nearby creek are well-worth a detour.

At the top, look back for a thrilling view of Ribbon Creek Valley hemmed in by the cliffs of mounts Bogart and Kidd. In the other direction is Ribbon Lake with its calendar backdrop of peak 217373.

The trail continues around the north shore to Ribbon Lake backcountry campground at the far end in the shelter of trees. As you go, look for springs bubbling out of circular depressions at the lake edge.

Ribbon Lake from the east shore and Peak 217373. Photo Roy Millar

27 Memorial Lakes map 2

Day hike
Unofficial trails
**Distance from trailhead: waterfalls
7 km, First Lake 7.5 km, Second Lake
8.2 km, Third Lake 8.8 km
Height gain 624 m (2047 ft.) to Second
Lake, 770 m (252 ft.) to Third Lake
High point 2240 m (7350 ft.)
above Third Lake
Map 82 J/14 Spray Lakes Reservoir**

Access Via #26 Ribbon Falls trail.

Comments Waterfalls, tarns, cliffs. The head of Ribbon Creek's north fork is a magical place and reasonably easy to get to now the trail is well trodden. Beyond First Lake, though, the way remains rough and steep in spots, particularly the slope below Third Lake, which is almost a scramble. Know also that by September Third Lake has drained underground, so go early in the hiking season — mid-July is about right when the waterfalls are also at their finest. Many people just go as far as the canyon waterfalls. For scramblers this trail doubles as the access route to Bogart Tower, Ribbon Peak and the fourth peak of Mt. Lougheed.

Trail update In 2017, 800 m of trail near the beginning was realigned to miss out the dreaded shale traverse that had gotten so bad someone had slung a rope across it for people to hang on to! So the first two creek crossings are now bridged. The rest are easy.

Naming The three tarns were named Memorial Lakes on September 27, 1986, as a reminder of the tragic events of the previous June when 13 people died in three separate plane crashes, 11 of them searchers out looking for biologist Orval Pall and pilot Ken Wolff. Contrary to what some people believe, none of the crashes occurred in this beautiful valley. To learn more, read #35 Guinn's Pass, Cox Hill in Volume 2 and Connolly Lake in Volume 3.

Regulations The valley is closed Dec. 1– Jun. 21 and camping is by permit only.

To Canyon Waterfalls 3.4 km
Follow #26 Ribbon Falls for 3.6 km. At T-junction 272430 with cairn stay ahead.

Easy going leads to the north fork. Continue on stony trail alongside the creek; then, just before the start of eroded banks, cross the creek on a bridge. Follow the mossy left bank to a second bridge that returns you to the right bank. Two short zigs puts you back on the original trail. Turn left.

Undulate across hillside back down to creek level. Not much farther on go either way at a split across a side creek. Then note a camping area on the left. A badly eroded side creek kicks off a small mess of stones and trees brought down by the flood. Aim for flagging, and at a T-junction go left. (The trail ahead offers a worse alternative to the side creek crossing.)

Lower canyon waterfalls in spate. Photo Alf Skrastins

Travel alongside the north fork, then along the banktop, gradually settling into a long, easy uphill climb away from the creek through menziesia bushes. Not long after the trail flattens, returning you back to the creek at the start of the canyon, come to a Y-junction. As you can see, the lakes trail climbs steeply up right to get above the canyon.

But first, go left on the flagged trail to the lower canyon waterfalls. In an open area climb up right, then descend a little into the canyon between falls. This is a fabulous place for a stopover and at low water you can walk slabs right up to the second fall.

To First Lake 500 m

From the falls a side trail returns you to the lakes trail above the first steep step. Turn left and grovel up steep dirt with the odd high step to a T-junction. IMPORTANT: Your trail turns LEFT into a traverse. This junction is where some people go wrong. Continuing uphill is the climber's access trail to the valley between Sparrowhawk and Lougheed under "Nopasseron Col" as Pete F calls it.

I love the next section of trail that follows the canyon rim around. The ribbon fall is impressive, but don't kill yourself trying to see to where the water lands Continue around a bend and up short steep steps to flat ground where the water is calmly gliding along like nothing's going to happen. Past a confluence is a T-junction. Turn left and cross the tributary on logs. (The trail ahead is another variation of the climber's access trail.)

The trail crosses easy ground to First Lake, reached about halfway along its north shore at a camping area. It may be the least attractive of the three lakes, but its setting under Bogart Tower is undeniably grand.

Top left: The green waters of First Lake. Most people get a pic with Bogart Tower in the background, but here we are looking across to Ribbon Peak.

Top right: The falls below Second Lake, which most people omit in their haste to get to Third Lake. This is what they look like when in spate in mid July. Screen shot from George Chan's video "Explore Memorial Lakes and the History behind the Scenes."

To the tower's left, Memorial Falls tumbles down the headwall from Third Lake. (Or to be scrupulously correct, the lake's water drains underground and bursts forth about a third of the way down the headwall and drops over a cliff.) To its right is the scrambler's descent from Third Lake — the top to toe scree gully immediately left of the tower.

To Second Lake — the Emerald 700 m

Coming up is an occasionally steep slog of about 137 vertical metres up a headwall with a confusing network of cairned and flagged trails.

But first continue along the north shore, then head left and cross the ingress on logs. (NOTE: The rough trail up the near bank leads to a more difficult crossing higher up.) Follow cairns through flat creekside willows, stones and a few trees to an open hillside sprinkled with rocks below Bogart Tower.

At the T-junction turn right, heading upstream between the hillside and the creek. I'm happy to report that the dirt slope traverse at the bend by the cataracts now has its tread back after washing out in 2013. A little beyond, keep left at a junction and plod up scree to a lightly treed bench.

For the ascent, most people follow the bench below the scree slope to a cairn on a boulder at the tree edge where you can choose from two onward routes. But first, go and see what the creek is doing by heading right on a trail. When in spate, the waterfall splaying out from between steep canyon walls is the most beautiful of all the falls — another reason to do this trail before the end of July.

1. Scree trail The most direct route climbs up left on vegetation to the right of the steep upper scree slope, then traverses left below a rockband onto the scree. Forgoing steep shortcuts, stay on the main trail, which shortly zigs right and diagonals across the scree to the top of the headwall. In trees route 2 joins in from the right. Go straight.

2. Forest trail Climb up vegetation to the right of the steep upper scree slope; then, below the rockband, double back right into the trees. At a gap in the band the trail climbs straight up the treed slope and joins the scree trail at the top of the headwall. This junction is flagged, but the trail heading into the trees is obvious should you want to return this way.

Either way, descend to second Memorial Lake. If, like me, you've looked down on this gorgeous piece of water with great longing from the summits of Sparrowhawk or Allan, this is a special moment. The unusual clarity of the water and its brilliant emerald colour coupled with its setting are great inducements for calling it a day.

To Third Lake 600 m

Out of sight in a cirque behind Bogart Tower, Third Lake is more difficult to access, despite the deceptively easy contour lines shown on the topo map.

The trail continues on, rising to the base of cliffs, then running below them to the bottom of a gully system. People who follow apps are still scrambling up the first rotten gully, or the side gully to its right that is marginally safer, either way risking a rock on the head. Then, unwilling to descend the same scary route, they descend fans of scree far, far to the right. Why risk injury when the ramp route is available?

The safe trail crosses the gully and follows a wide ramp that rises slowly between cliff bands. (See the top photo on page 103.) The ramp narrows sensationally, but luckily the top band ends at this point, enabling the trail to zig left. A couple more zigs and a long, easy traverse above the gullies leads to a verdant hanging valley rimmed by steep slopes. The trail climbs the grassy slope up ahead onto scree. At the top, head left, aiming for the lightly treed neck of land connecting Bogart Tower to Mt. Bogart — the day's high point.

From the neck, the trail diagonals down scree into the cirque enclosed by the cliffs of Ribbon Peak and Mt. Bogart. At its outer

*The emerald waters of Second Memorial Lake.
Rising behind is Bogart Tower.*

edge lies Third Lake with its signature promontory of spruce trees. Hopefully by the time you get there the afternoon shadow cast by high rock walls will not yet have spread its pall over the scene, and equally hopefully the lake will be filled to the brim. On a hummock at the edge of the drop-off is a memorial cairn and plaque. Read the first and last lines of the sonnet "High Flight," written by 19-year-old fighter pilot John Magee. Strange how something scribbled on the back of a letter sent to his mother two months before he died during the Battle of Britain in 1941 has endured all this time. US president Ronald Reagan quoted this very sonnet after the loss of the Challenger astronauts. It was also Brad Washburn's favourite recitation.

OPTIONAL DESCENT

A steep scrambler's route down to First Lake.

Starting immediately right of Bogart Tower as you look out is a scree gully. If uncomfortable at the top, wade through dense spruce thickets on the right side where it's hard to get any downward momentum going at all. Where the gully splits, follow the neck between the two, then continue easily down the right side of the left-hand gully, thus bypassing a small rockband in the gully bed. Level with the bottom of Bogart Tower, cross to the left side to avoid a small cliff. Below the cliff wend back right (Memorial Falls comes into view) and follow a dribble of scree into forest where game trails continue to the valley bottom. On the flat, a game trail heading left intersects Memorial Lakes trail at a cairn.

Top left: First view of Third Memorial Lake backdropped by Ribbon Peak. By fall the lake is completely dry.

Bottom left: The memorial.

Opposite top: The best route to Third Memorial Lake follows the white line marked on by photographer Harold Muller. Note the size of three hikers following the correct line. Do not climb up the loose gully to left.

Opposite bottom: Third Lake at high water. In the background, the left-hand ridge of Bogart Tower which is the scrambler's ascent route. Photo Alf Skrastins

28 Kovach Pond interpretive trail map 2

Hour walk
Distance 470 m
Map 82 J/14 Spray Lakes Reservoir

Access Kanaskis Trail (Hwy. 40). Turn west onto Mt. Allan Drive signed "Kanaskis Village, Nakiska Ski Area." Turn first left onto Centennial Drive, then at the 4-way turn left onto the Kovach Pond access road that leads to the parking lot.

Comments A very short stroll with benches, picnic tables and interpretive signs around a gravel pit with a tiny pool of water at the bottom.

History In the early days of K Country, a ditch was gouged out to bring water from Ribbon Creek into a nearby gravel pit. For years the attractive pond was very popular spot for picnics. Then came the 2013 flood. The creek banks were shored up to protect infrastructure and, sadly, the ditch dried up, resulting in the sorry state of the pond today.

Naming Joe Kovach was the Canmore and district forest ranger between 1940 and 1953. One of his jobs was to capture escapee POWs. Hike #22 to learn more.

From the biffy walk out to the trail circling the old pit. Go left. Pass picnic tables en route to the bridge over the inlet "creek." On either side are memorial benches and an interpretive sign about the strip mine on Mt. Allan. To visit the site read #25.

The trail continues past the Troll Falls connector trail to an interpretive sign about "Ribbon Crick," which is what locals called the village of Kovach. It was situated where the Ribbon Creek parking lots are now. Interestingly, the schoolhouse was left standing and became the youth hostel. Inland from the sign look for the concrete foundations of Norman Holt's trucking camp.

Cross a bridge over the "outlet" and walk around to the south bank where two trails head left to the parking lot.

Top: Kovach Pond before the water source was cut off.

Bottom: Kovach Pond today, an unattractive puddle at the bottom of a pit. Ah well, the interpretive signs are interesting.

Opposite: A typical view of Shinrin. To the right the slope falls steeply to Ribbon Creek.

29 Studless and Shinrin   map 2

Half day
Distance 2 km
Height gain/loss 200 m (656 ft.)
Map 82 J/14 Spray Lakes Reservoir

Access Kananaskis Trail (Hwy. 40). Turn west onto Mt. Allan Drive signed "Kananaskis Village, Nakiska Ski Area." Turn first left onto Centennial Drive, then at the 4-way right onto Ribbon Creek Road. Drive past Kananaskis Wilderness Hostel to the upper Ribbon Creek parking lot at the end of the road.
Also accessible from #30B Village Winter Trails, #31 Village Summer Trails.

Comments Touted as a winter forest walk with a few easy hills along the rim of Ribbon Creek's high south bank. Also a fat-tire bike trail. Walkable all year round. See the map on page 106.
   Naming Shinrin-yoku is a Japanese term used in ecotherapy "taking in the forest atmosphere."

Terrace trail 220 m
From the upper parking lot cross the bridge over Ribbon Creek onto the multi-use section of Terrace trail, Follow it up to the junction with Studless on the right.

Studless to Shinrin 900 m
The trail climbs in long easy stretches and short steep steps, with a flat bit in the middle, to a T-junction with #30A. Turn right.
   Follow an undulating section of Village North Loop to a picnic table on the top of Ribbon Creek's bank with a view of Mt. Lorette. Where 30A circles left back out to Kovach, stay ahead on Shinrin that continues along the banktop.

Shinrin trail 1.2 km
Initially the trail descends, then rises gently through trees festooned with old man's beard. A post signals a side trail to a so-so viewpoint out on a point. After an unavoid-

able few metres of walking on Kovach trail, it's back to banktop walking with occasional views across the valley to Mt. Allan's Olympic summit. A steeper climb wending left ends at the Kovach/Link junction.

RETURN LOOP
Now what? Most obviously, make a 5.4 km loop with Link and Ribbon Creek multi-use trails. Link could be a problem with skiers coming down fast behind you to the bridge over Ribbon Creek. So it's good to hear that one day we might have a very interesting single track squeezed in between the ski trail and the drop-off to the creek.
   On gaining Ribbon Creek trail turn right. The boring section ends after the ski trail goes off up the hill to the left and you criss-cross the creek on an assortment of bridges the rest of the way down to Ribbon Creek parking lot. See #26.

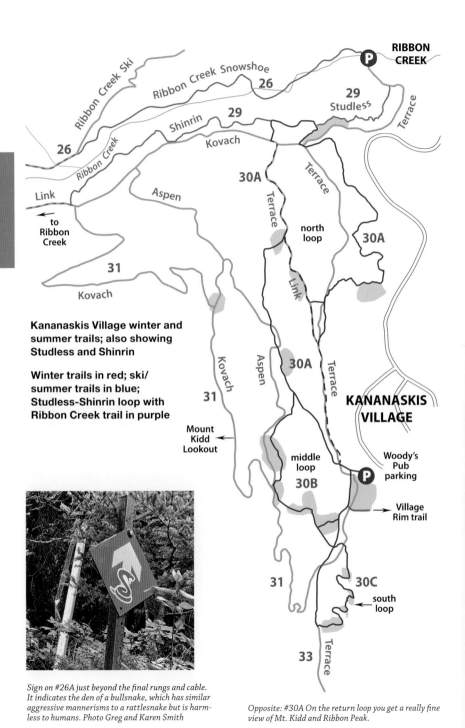

RIBBON CREEK

26 Ribbon Creek Ski

Ribbon Creek Snowshoe 26

29 Shinrin

29 Studless

26

Ribbon Creek

Kovach

Terrace

30A

Link

to Ribbon Creek

Aspen

Terrace

Terrace

north loop

30A

Link

31

Kovach

Kananaskis Village winter and summer trails; also showing Studless and Shinrin

Winter trails in red; ski/ summer trails in blue; Studless-Shinrin loop with Ribbon Creek trail in purple

Kovach

31

Aspen

30A

Terrace

KANANASKIS VILLAGE

Mount Kidd Lookout

middle loop

30B

Woody's Pub parking

Village Rim trail

31

30C

south loop

33

Terrace

Sign on #26A just beyond the final rungs and cable. It indicates the den of a bullsnake, which has similar aggressive mannerisms to a rattlesnake but is harmless to humans. Photo Greg and Karen Smith

Opposite: #30A On the return loop you get a really fine view of Mt. Kidd and Ribbon Peak.

30 Village Winter Trails   map 2

Half day loops
Map 82 J/14 Spray Lakes Reservoir

Access Hwy. 40 (Kananaskis Trail) at Kananaskis Village. Turn west on Mt. Allan Drive signed "Kananaskis Village, Nakiska Ski Area." Turn first left onto Centennial Drive and follow it up the hill to Kananaskis Village. At the top turn second right onto Terrace Drive and drive to a parking lot for Mount Kidd Manor and Woody's Pub.
Also accessible from #29 Studless and #31 Village Summer Trails.

Comments Initially touted as snowshoe trails, these single-track trails are now equally popular with winter walkers and fat-tire bikers. Possibly, the tread is visible all year round. They undulate and wind about the ski trails and though travelling mainly through trees, have a few really fine viewpoints. All are well signed.

There is one loop of 4.4 km, and two smaller loops of 1.4 and 1.7 km, all of which can be joined up to make an outside loop of 6.1 km with a stop for lunch at Woody's Pub.

30A North Loop

Distance 4.4 km
Height gain/loss 30 m (98 ft.)

Comments The longest, hilliest loop, with views and a picnic table in the middle.

CLOCKWISE

To Terrace Link

From the top of the parking lot head through the gate onto Terrace North trail. Cross a paved trail. Take a signed trail to right that cuts off the bend on Terrace.

Cross Terrace and start the longest climb of the loop, a long diagonal across a steep hillside. In 400 m the middle loop turns off to the left.

Keep straight and climb some more to a 4-way with Aspen ski trail at the top. Cross, then after paralleling Aspen, recross the ski trail.

After a dip to the left, start the descent to Terrace Link. The steepness soon moderates and before you know it you've reached the junction with Terrace Link.

At Terrace Link, a multi-use trail, you have the option of turning right and joining Terrace trail for the last leg back to the parking lot. But its a pretty flat, boring shortcut and you miss out what I consider is the best part of the loop. So turn left.

To the northernmost point
A slight descent brings you to a T-junction with Kovach trail. Walk left a few steps, then turn right onto a single-track that leads (going left at the split) to the east end of Shinrin. Turn right past a picnic table on the edge of Ribbon Creek's south bank with a view of Mt. Lorette.

Return
Continue on the same line, keeping left on undulating Studless to a junction. Stay ahead and circle back right to Kovach at its junction with Terrace North at a bend with map. Cross Terrace at the bend.

Almost straightaway the trail heads into the trees to the left, shortly descending in increments to a straight alongside the access road to Kananaskis Village. A sharp right-hand bend signals my favourite section where the trail follows low, rolling ridges to an open banktop above a draw with great views of Mt. Kidd. Turn right along the undulating top of the draw, too soon climbing back into forest and winding along to Terrace trail. Turn left on Terrace. (Trail ahead is a shortcut to Terrace Link.)

Walk the left side of Terrace for a few metres, then head back into the trees, following a rib. The next time you reach Terrace turn left. This is shortly before Terrace Link comes in from the right at a Y-junction. Follow Terrace to left for 600 metres back to the parking lot.

30B Middle Loop

Distance 1.4 km return
Height gain/loss 60 m (197 ft.)

Comments Go anti-clockwise for the fun descent.

ANTI-CLOCKWISE

From the parking lot start out on north loop. Cross Terrace trail and in 400 m on the diagonal climb turn left.

The middle loop traverses a steep side slope and climbs to the top of it. Easy going through trees brings you to a big meadow. Head down the left side of it. Climb a little through trees to briefly touch Aspen ski trail at a picnic table in a small meadow. Go left and downhill through trees to an open slope where you swing left to EPCOR's water treatment plant, the hill on the left that also holds two potable water reservoirs.

Cross the access road and turn right, paralleling the road. On coming to a wide, open slope on the left, head down it to the snowshoe sign, then enjoy a fun finale down a much steeper slope to the EPCOR road.

Turn left on the road. On joining the paved rim trail go straight, passing between picnic tables and a biffy to the 4-way with Terrace trail. Turn right through the gate into the parking lot.

Above: #30B in the big meadow also crossed by Aspen.

Opposite: #30C The best viewpoint looks across the Kananaskis Valley to the Mackay Hills, The Wedge at right, and up Evan-Thomas Creek to Fisher Peak at left.

NOTE: If connecting to the south loop, walk down the EPCOR access road to the 4-way on the bend. Go ahead down the hill. (Trail to right is the return leg.) See the map below.

30C South Loop

Distance 1.7 km return
Height gain/loss 65 m (213 ft.)

Comments Go either way on an interesting trail with views of the Kananaskis valley.

CLOCKWISE

From the parking lot, go through the gate to a 4-way .Turn left on a paved trail (Rim trail) passing between a biffy and picnic tables. Where it curves left go straight on the EPCOR road toward the water treatment plant. Keep following snowshoe signs to the bend in the road at a 4-way. Turn left down a hill.

East leg
South Loop crosses Kovach ski trail en route to the banktop above the Kananaskis River. Here it turns right and for the next kilometre weaves a very wavy course between headlands (look for blue posts), all the while descending to the trail's low point. The second headland is the one with the best view. Finally, start the climb back up alongside a draw to Terrace South trail.

Terrace South
Turn right and climb up Terrace to a 4-way with Kovach. Cross, and in a minute or two reach the 4-way on the EPCOR road at the bend. Go straight along the road to return the way you came.

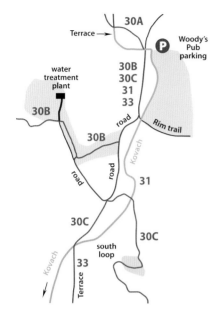

The start to 30A/30B, the finish to 30B and the start and finish to 30C; also showing the start to 33 Terrace trail heading south

Blue indicates ski trails Kovach and Terrace, which are crossed at various points

Half-day walks
Official trails
Longest distance 7.5 km loop
Height gain ~150 m (492 ft.)
High point 1675 m (5495 ft.)
Map 82 J/14 Spray Lakes Reservoir

Access Hwy. 40 (Kananaskis Trail) at Kananaskis Village. Turn west on Mt. Allan Drive signed "Kananaskis Village, Nakiska Ski Area." Turn first left onto Centennial Drive and follow it up the hill to Kananaskis Village. At the top turn second right onto Terrace Drive and drive to a parking lot for Mount Kidd Manor and Woody's Pub.
Also accessible from #29 Studless and Shinrin, #26 Ribbon Falls

Comments Easy but hilly forest circuits with occasional views. Because you're following well-signed 4-m-wide ski trails, these loops are a good introduction to the area for novice tourists who have absolutely no chance of going astray with maps at every intersection. See the map on page 106.

Kovach 4.5–5 km

Start from the top end of the parking lot on a dirt road that is Terrace trail. Beyond the gate is a 4-way junction with Rim trail. Turn left on a paved trail that leads past a biffy and picnic tables into a big flat meadow. At junctions on the left-hand bend, do not follow the EPCOR road ahead which has snowshoe signs. Around the bend turn right onto a descending track (former logging road), which is Kovach ski trail. Cross the South Loop of the winter trails, then go straight at a 4-way. (To left is Terrace South trail.)

Kovach winds uphill, then heads north to a junction with Aspen and the Middle Village Loop in a damp, mosquito-ridden meadow with picnic table. Keep left on Kovach and continue climbing. The next sweeping left-hand bend has a cairned shortcut trail. After the following right-hand bend, a large cairn on the left side indicates the unofficial trail to Mt. Kidd lookout site (see #32).

Below: The very pleasant Aspen trail, looking toward Mt. Allan's Olympic Summit.

Continue on Kovach to a look-alike junction with Aspen Link at picnic tables and again stay left. As you climb the hill look back for a fine view of The Wedge before rounding a bend and disappearing into spruce forest indicating the upper limit of the 1936 fire. At the loop's high point join a logging road built to salvage timber after the fire.

On your way down, trees obscure the mountain vista of past years, though you can see Ribbon Peak ahead and at the bend with picnic table is a view of Mt. Allan. This marks the start of two long downhill zigs to the T-junction with Link trail. Should you go left here you'd link up with Ribbon Creek trail.

But for today turn right on Kovach and descend Buffalo-berry Alley.

Coming up are three different ways back to the parking lot. For nos. 2 and 3 you can substitute Shinrin trail, then at the picnic table walk out on North Village Loop to Kovach, reached opposite Terrace Link.

ENDINGS

1. Aspen trail 3 km (7.5 km loop)

Turn first right on Aspen trail and climb to a junction with Aspen Link. Keep left onto the nicest stretch of trail in the area: aspens, of course, flowery meadows and two viewpoints, one with a picnic table at the junction with Middle Village Loop. On rejoining Kovach, keep left and return the same way you came up.

2. Terrace Link 1.8 km (6.7 km loop)

Turn second right onto Terrace Link. After climbing to a junction with North Village Loop, the trail rolls across strips of damp willowy meadows before joining Terrace trail. Keep right and in 600 m reach Kananaskis Village.

3. Terrace trail 1.8 km (6.8 km loop)

Follow Kovach all the way down the hill to a T-junction with map at the intersection with Terrace trail. Turn right and return on Terrace to Kananaskis Village. Watch for Terrace Link joining in from the right 600 m before the end.

Below left: On the descent of Kovach from the high point there used to be a fine view extending from Ribbon Peak and Mt. Sparrowhawk all the way across the Kananaskis Valley to Wasootch Peak.

Below right: By 2022, on the same stretch of trail around the high point of Kovach, the trees had obscured the view, limiting it to Ribbon Peak.

32 Mount Kidd Lookout Site map 2

Half-day, short day
Unofficial trail
Distance 3.1 km one way from village
Height gain 579 m (1900 ft.) from village
High point 2103 m (6900 ft.)
Map 82 J/14 Spray Lakes Reservoir

Access Hwy. 40 (Kananaskis Trail) at Kananaskis Village. Turn west on Mt. Allan Drive signed "Kananaskis Village, Nakiska Ski Area." Turn first left onto Centennial Drive and follow it up the hill to Kananaskis Village. At the top turn second right onto Terrace Drive and head to a parking lot for Mount Kidd Manor and Woody's Pub.

Comments A lookout, even the site of one, is a magnet for view aficionados. At one time K Country had plans to access the lookout by a nice winding trail at the forest edge. That never happened and now a trail made by K Village staff goes straight up the steep east front on grass. Cruelly tiring it is, and not one to do when the temperature is hitting 30°C. NOTE: The meadows are a grizzly hotspot.

Lookout The Mount Kidd Lookout, sited on the northeast shoulder of Mt. Kidd at 286418, was an unusually short-lived lookout that saw service between 1982 and 1992, then was removed in 1997.

Kovach access 1.9 km

Start from the top end of the parking lot on a dirt road that is Terrace trail. Beyond the gate is a 4-way junction with Rim trail. Turn left on a paved trail that leads past a biffy and picnic tables into a big flat meadow. At junctions on the left-hand bend, do not follow the EPCOR road ahead, which has snowshoe signs. Around the bend turn right onto a descending track (former logging road), which is Kovach ski trail. Cross the South Loop of the winter trails, then go straight at a 4-way. (To left is Terrace South trail.)

Kovach winds uphill, then heads north to a junction with Aspen and the Middle Loop of the winter trails in a damp meadow with picnic table.

Keep left on Kovach and continue climbing. The next sweeping left-hand bend has a cairned shortcut trail. After the following right-hand bend, a large cairn on the left indicates the route to the lookout site. Here you turn left onto a much narrower trail.

To the Lookout Site 1.2 km

Shortly the trail steepens dramatically. At a division go either way and climb through a small rockband to gain the meadows. Then grovel (and I use that word deliberately) up steep grass to the right of a shallow, bushy gully. Arrive on the northeast ridge and follow it up left at the edge of trees to the shoulder. A concrete pad marks the lookout site.

As expected, the lookout site is a superior viewpoint for the Kananaskis Valley and surrounding mountains: Bogart, Sparrowhawk, Lougheed, Allan displaying its Centennial Ridge in profile, Wasootch Ridge, Old Baldy, The Wedge and Fisher Peak up Evan-Thomas Creek.

GOING FARTHER

Having done the vertical, who can resist wandering farther along the grassy northeast ridge to the foot of Mt. Kidd's northeast buttress?

Opposite: The lookout in 1983.

Top right: The lookout site and the grassy ridge extending to the foot of Mt. Kidd's northeast buttress.

Top left: Climbing steep grass.

Bottom: #33. Terrace trail south of Kananaskis Village runs below the east face of Mt. Kidd.

33 Terrace Trail

maps 2, 3, 4

Day hike
Official trail
Distance 9.9 km whole trail
Height gain N-S 40 m (130 ft.)
High point 1590 m (5217 ft.)
Map 82 J/14 Spray Lakes Reservoir

North accesses Hwy. 40 (Kananaskis Trail). Turn west onto Mt. Allan Drive signed "Kananaskis Village, Nakiska Ski Area."
1. Ribbon Creek parking lots Turn first left onto Centennial Drive, then next right onto Ribbon Creek Road. Just past Kananaskis Wilderness Hostel, drive past the lower parking lot and the picnic shelter into the upper parking lot
2. Usual start/finish at Kananaskis Village Turn first left onto Centennial Drive and follow it up the hill to Kananaskis Village. At the top, turn second right onto Terrace Drive and drive to the parking lot for Mount Kidd Manor.
3. South access Hwy. 40 (Kananaskis Trail) at Galatea Creek parking lot. Via #34 Galatea Creek trail just after the first crossing of Galatea Creek.
Also accessible from #30 Village Winter Trails, #31 Village Summer Trails

Comments Terrace is an easy but undulating trail that follows terraces of the Kananaskis River between Ribbon Creek and Galatea Creek. Most people start from either access 2 or the south access and put a vehicle at each end, the plan being to end the walk in one of the village's numerous watering holes. The trail's intricacies around the village are shown on the sketchmap on page 106.

The southern part of the trail is also the scrambler's access to Mt. Kidd and the ice climber's access to Mt. Kidd Falls.

Trail notes 1. Disregard all signs and trails pertaining to snowshoeing. **2.** Mountain bikers are plentiful. **3.** Expect one easy creek crossing. **4.** The annual spring closure of Galatea Creek trail does not apply to the section at the south end shared by both trails.

The gully between the two summits of Mt. Kidd is a popular tourist stop.

TERRACE TRAIL NORTH
Access 1 to Access 2, 2.4 km
This northern section is a 4-m-wide ski trail (logging road) that travels through forest within sound of vehicles revving up Centennial Drive to Kananaskis Village. In 2008 the section between Kovach and the village was widened further to accommodate horses and wagons.

At the top end of the parking cross the bridge over Ribbon Creek. On old road wind up the far bank for 800 metres to a T-junction with Kovach trail on a terrace. Turn left on the very much wider Terrace trail, which undulates along to a Y-junction with Terrace Link trail coming in from the right. Again stay left. Reach a signed 4-way junction with a paved trail close to the parking lot for Mount Kidd Manor. Head straight for Woody's Pub patio for a burger and beer.

If you've brought your own lunch turn right on the paved trail and find a picnic table.

TERRACE TRAIL SOUTH
Access 2 to Galatea Creek 7.5 km
The southern section is a scenic forest trail with one unavoidable creek crossing.

Start from the top end of Access 2 parking lot at a gated road with hiking icon. At the 4-way junction a little way in, turn left on a paved trail. (The dirt road ahead is Terrace North trail.)

Follow the paved trail (which is also Rim trail) past a biffy and picnic tables to where it bends left at the end of the big meadow. Do not follow the gravelled EPCOR road to the water treatment plant. Around the bend turn right onto Kovach trail, a 4-m-wide ski trail née logging road. Cross a snowshoe trail that is #30C South Loop, then turn left at the following 4-way onto Terrace South trail. See the sketchmap on page 109.

Head gradually downhill on an older, narrower track. Where the track turns left, go straight on a signed trail. Finally free of junctions, though not yet of tourists, follow the trail to the start of the scenic section where the trail winds and undulates along the terrace rim, now and then offering great views up Evan-Thomas Creek to Fisher Peak. Down below you are chains of beaver ponds and the K Country golf course. I've spent an enjoyable 10 minutes at one of these viewpoints watching golfers putt into the largest pond, a small and some might say petty revenge for being turfed off the golf course for wearing a Mo Zeegers T-shirt.

Thus far the mighty east face of Mt. Kidd, which acts like a giant reflector throwing the sun's heat back down onto a dry forest of pine, aspen and scrub, has always been in view. But then you enter a darker, cooler forest with deadfall where the trail flattens and you can see nothing at all. In spring listen for avalanches. At such time waterfalls leaping down gullies in the cliffs fill small streams crossing the trail.

Come to the one crossing possibly requiring a wade. This is the wide, stony gully separating North and South Kidd — the scrambler's jumping-off point for Mt. Kidd's highest point, which now sports Firenet's VHF repeater station no. 107 and two golf clubs in the cairn.

Continue through forest. Approaching the south end, you touch the Kananaskis River at a narrows where a rocky ridge slopes down to the water. Close by is a large, algae-green beaver pond. Then you cross another stony creekbed, which is Kidd Falls Creek (see #33A).

Five minutes later you reach the T-junction with Galatea Creek trail on the north bank of Galatea Creek. Only another half kilometre to go.

Turn left and cross Galatea Creek on a bridge. Shortly cross the Kananaskis River via suspension bridge and stagger up the hill to Galatea Creek parking lot.

OPTION

33A Kidd Falls Creek

Unofficial trails
Distance ~600 m to first falls
Height gain 137+ m (450+ ft.)
High point 1676+ m (5500+ ft.)

Comments Rough trails with confusing variations have developed over the years as a climber's access to Kidd Falls, a IV WI 4 ice climb. No need to go that far; many lower falls in the creek make this a pleasant diversion. Usually arrived at from access 3.

Geology From up close you're treated to a view of the dramatic north end of the Lewis thrust fault — a perfect example of an anticline and syncline pair. Located on the syncline is the falls. More amazing are the wafer-thin folds of the anticline, which are not quite as ethereal as they look from Hwy. 40.

Above: View from the first falls of the Spoon Needle. Some scramblers descend the facing ridge to the cliff, then head off into the valley to the west.

Opposite: Lillian Lake from the south shore. Galatea Lakes are located through the gap.

Leave Terrace South trail one creekbed north of the Galatea Creek trail junction.

Follow the right (north) side of the stony creekbed. After a trail develops, zig up a steep hill, then traverse left across a scree bank. At a fork, go left on stones. Climb a little to below the open bank. Again keep left (the much steeper right-hand trail is more often used as a descent route). At the right-hand bend in the creek the trail climbs the grassy ridge alongside to the base of the first fall. Contour right below a small rockband and meet the descent trail. Turn left along a ledge to the top of the rockband and waterfall. Already there is a fabulous view to the south of Spoon Needle (Aiguille de la Cuiller), a scrambler's peak usually approached from the Fortress ski area access road.

Above here the trail degenerates. If inclined, climb past three more falls. The higher you go the steeper and stonier the terrain but the better the view. Limber pines make an appearance and likely snow into June. Kidd Falls is not worth the final effort of grovelling up a whole lot of rubble and risking a rock on your head. Admire it from afar.

34 Galatea Creek to Lillian Lake map 4

Day hike, backpack
Official trail
Distance 6.3 km to Lillian Lake
Height gain 560 m (1837 ft.)
High point 2027 m (6650 ft.) at lake
Map 82 J/14 Spray Lakes Reservoir

Access Hwy. 40 (Kananaskis Trail) at Galatea Creek parking lot.
Also accessible from #33 Terrace Southtrail and #35 Guinns Pass.

Comments Galatea Creek was once a place for adventurers, being fraught with difficulty and uncertainty. In the early morning, low water in the Kananaskis River would entice people to wade across to the "trail." On returning in the late afternoon, they would sometimes find the river a raging torrent and be forced to spend the night trapped on the west bank within sight of their cars.

Since then, the trail has been rebuilt several times over with umpteen bridges, including a suspension bridge across the Kananaskis River. Now everybody and their dog goes to Lillian Lake, including the part-time conservation officer who ticks off anyone not having their dog on a leash and the woman playing "Hey Jude" and other Beatles favourites on the harmonica. So the clientele has changed. Nevertheless, it's worth dodging the crowds up this moderately strenuous trail to view Lillian Lake and maybe stay at its backcountry campground. Lovers of the alpine can climb higher to Galatea Lakes. Scramblers use this trail to access Mt. Kidd South.

Facilities Lillian Lake backcountry campground has been refurbished after the 2013 flood and over half the sites now sport wooden tent platforms with cables and hooks to which you can attach your tent and fly. The roomy Phoenix composting toilet is another plus.

Flood history The 2013 flood took out nearly all the bridges and forced reroutes. Most people gave a sigh of relief when "walking the tree" was replaced by a 60-foot -long fibreglass bridge in the fall of 2015. But not everyone. Some adventurers still use the tree.

Top left: The traverse below Mt. Kidd south.

Top right: No. 8 bridge over the northwest fork.

Left: The P Tree, more easily noticed on the descent.

To Terrace trail 500 m

Descend the steep hill everybody loves to hate to the memorial bench and suspension bridge over the Kananaskis River. Cross and wander the left bank of Galatea Creek to bridge no. 1. On the north bank is a junction with Terrace South. Turn left.

To the forks 3.8 km

After an up-down with zigs, you cross bridges 2 and 3 in the narrows below cliffs. More climbing and zigs across steep hillside leads to bridge no. 4. Then follows a long stint along the south bank. Trees give way to sand and cobbles alongside the creek to bridge no. 5.

Follow cairns along a cobble flat. Back in trees climb and cross a stony gully. In the following undulating stretch close to the creek look for the "P"-shaped tree on the

Naming The name of this disgracefully behaved piece of water is for once appropriate. It appears that Galatea, meaning "milk white," was a sea nymph who turned her beloved Acis (killed by Polyphemus with a rock), into a river that forever after bore his name. Okay, so it was named after a battleship named after the nymph.

Regulations The trail is closed April 1 to June 21.

right side where a low branch has grafted back onto the trunk higher up. This easy section ends in a stiffer, winding climb to a scree slope offering a backward view of The Wedge.

Descend, then again climb high across a rocky gully preceding the grass slope traverse. Just before re-entering trees, a steep side trail to left leads to a dicey viewpoint for the waterfall where the creek emerges from a canyon. Nearby, a scrambler's access trail marked by cairns takes off up the hillside bound for South Kidd.

Undulate within earshot of rushing water in the canyon below, finally descending into a belt of tall firs in the flood-ravaged valley bottom. Cross bridge no. 6. A hilly reroute brings you to the forks. Keep right and cross bridge no. 7. (The lesser used trail ahead with cairn leads to Alvin Guinn's Lost Lake. See #36.)

To Lillian Lake 2 km

Now following the northwest fork, begin a rambling, winding climb up and along its right bank. Cross a wide swath of avalanche debris that decimated the trail in the summer of 2017. Soon after comes crossing no. 8, the deep gulf of the creek spanned by the aforementioned 60-foot-long fibreglass bridge. Then follows a very much steeper climb up along the left bank where, inevitably it seems, at least one kind, concerned person on their way down will tell you you're "almost there." Well not quite.

After downhills, pass the old Guinns Pass trail junction, then psych yourself up for the very last climb. What relief when the terrain levels off and you walk the north shore of Lillian Lake with its numerous benches. Come to a T-junction. Right is the signed trail to Galatea Lakes. Straight on leads to the backcountry campground.

Every summer weekend, the environs of the lake take on a festive atmosphere from the mingling of campers and day trippers who are socializing, fishing and swimming in chartreuse-coloured waters shallow enough to retain a little of the sun's warmth.

Lillian Lake campground and route to Galatea Lakes

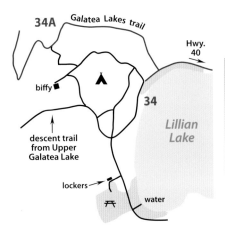

GOING FARTHER

34A Galatea Lakes

Official, unofficial trails
Distance 2.4 km to upper lake
Height gain 183 m (600 ft.)
High point 2210 m (7250 ft.)

Comments While Lillian Lake is beautiful, the surroundings don't turn me on and I have to climb higher to that fascinating alpine country about Galatea Lakes that, incidentally, were known as Engadine Lakes when we first knocked around the area. Getting there requires a steep initial climb, but after that the going is easy.

To Guinns Pass trail 1.1 km

As mentioned, the trail leaves the north shore before the camping area. En route to the Y-junction with the connecting trail from the campground, the trail crosses tongues of stones that decimated campsites in 2013. Keep right.

On butting against steep hillside, the trail zigs left, then right onto a more moderate slope where it winds through scrubby forest onto a scree slope and heads up its

Above: Lower Galatea Lake and The Tower. The upper lake lies beyond the low rock ridge. You can see the access trail rising from right to left to the grassy gap at left.

Opposite: Upper Galatea Lake showing the beach at the far end.

left side. After a brief levelling on grass, the route veers left to another scree patch, zigs right at a junction, then left across the *upper* scree trail that leads directly to a T-junction with cairn and signpost. Go straight. (Trail to right is #35 to Guinns Pass.)

To the lakes 1.3 km
Below lies Lower Galatea Lake, a blue body of water filling a rock-girt bowl. A steep side trail plummets to the east shore. A trail going left into trees leads to old camping areas at the terminus of the original trail, which can still be followed down the draw to the grassy levelling.

The main trail traverses steep scree above the lake, then gradually drops to the lake's far end. To your right rise the rugged south slopes of peak 217373, which is more readily climbed from Buller Pass if 396 metres (1300 ft.) of scree appeals. Ahead is a low rock ridge blocking the way to the upper lake. The trail sidesteps this by climbing leftward on the diagonal to a grassy gap. At the 4-way junction of trails go straight. (The trail heading left across a scree slope is the optional descent.)

Descend meadow above the brighter waters of Upper Galatea Lake, cradled in a hollow below The Tower. The trail ends with a steep drop to the stony beach at the far end. I hope you refilled your water bottles at the lower lake, because this lake is full of red freshwater shrimp. Just out from the beach is a moored raft used by anglers casting for cutthroat. Among the rocks of the west shore look for a white version of creeping beardtongue.

OPTIONAL DESCENT
Because of its steepness, this trail only works as a descent route. Its only asset, apart from being a shortcut, is the view of Lillian Lake.

Return to the 4-way junction and keep right. The trail traverses scree above the south shore of Lower Galatea Lake, then passes through the southernmost gap in the small ridge. Descend a very steep strip of grass between scree and the forest edge to a brief levelling. Here you turn left and, still on trail, slither down a nasty, stony slope to the campground trail between site 16 and the Phoenix composting toilet.

35 Guinns Pass

map 4

Long day, backpack
Official trail
Distance 2.6 km
Height gain 457 m (1500 ft.)
from Galatea Creek
Height loss 259 m (850 ft.)
to Ribbon Creek
High point 2423 m (7950 ft.)
Map 82 J/14 Spray Lakes Reservoir

South access Via #34 Galatea Creek to Lillian Lake, then #34A Galatea Lakes trail.
North access Via #81 Buller Pass trail 1.3 km west of Ribbon Lake.

Comments Connecting first Galatea Lake to upper Ribbon Creek valley via Guinns Pass is a "world class trail" as Alf calls it, that on the south side takes a spectacular line across the steep slopes of peak 217373. In combination with the lakes, the pass makes a magnificent day trip from Lillian Lake backcountry campground.

Regulations The southern half of the route usually opens up in late June.

Trail history Many years ago Alvin Guinn took a string of 20 pack horses over the ridge from Galatea Creek to Ribbon Lake. Not by the route of the first trail exactly. He went up the avalanche gully farther to the right. By the time he reached the ridge night was falling and in the need to hurry he led his horses straight down the scree slope to Ribbon Lake! Next morning he looked for a better route back and that's when he discovered Guinn's Pass.

Even after the first official trail replaced the game trail up the avalanche gully to the left of Guinn's ascent gully, gaining the pass was no pushover. From both sides the trail was a steep, demanding climb exposed to bad weather above treeline. Then, in the very hot August of 2017, the trail on the south slope was rerouted away from the dreadful avalanche gully to its present location, truly a tour de force by Jeff Eamon and his crew of volunteers from "Friends," who are said to have sweated away half their body weight.

SOUTH TO NORTH

To the Pass 1.4 km

Follow Galatea Lakes trail for 1.1 km. At the cairn with signpost turn right.

Straightaway, Jeff's trail backtracks across a boulder field below Submarine Rock as he calls it. Then, after after crossing a scree gully, it climbs steeply up scree and slab to friendlier slopes of grass at treeline. Keep looking back for views of Lower Galatea Lake and The Tower. At a levelling, the trail rounds the bottom of a crag and again climbs steeply up scree

Above: Alvin Guinn (1915-2006), father of Rick Guinn, who with his wife Denise runs Boundary Ranch in the Kananaskis Valley.

Opposite top: Rounding the crag on the south slope, with Lillian Lake below.

Opposite bottom: The final traverse to the pass on the south slope.

Above: The north slope of Guinns Pass from South Buller Pass, showing the zigzags on scree. At left is peak 237374, which is easily climbed from the pass. See #35A.

Left: Snow on the stony north slope in early summer can make the going easier. Photo Sharon Cairns, courtesy Carl Potter

Opposite: Looking down on Guinns Pass from peak 237374 before the new trail was built. The mountain is peak 217373, which is a scramble from the Buller Creek side. Buller Pass is visible to the right of the peak. Photo Ron Hunter

and "moondust"with widely spaced rocks, meant to act as foot stops when slithering down the stuff.

Round a corner in trees onto the second half of the trail, the traverse of a steep grass slope. Throughout is a panoramic view stretching from Mt. Galatea through The Fortress to the serrated Opals. It is only on reaching the cairn on the pass, however, that peak 217373, whose south slopes you have been trogging across, fully reveals its massive northeastern precipice. To its right look across to South Buller Pass and the red peak.

To Buller Pass trail 900 m

The north slope is mostly grassless and treeless, just plenty of stones and lots of snow early in the season. Under the eye of the precipice make long, sweeping zigzags on easy-angled shale and scree into a barren basin, all bumps and hollows, one of which holds a shallow tarn. On the bench an unofficial shortcut to Buller Pass heads left. The official trail descends the bench to the signposted junction with Buller Pass trail near Ribbon Creek Spring.

Go left for South Buller Pass, right for Ribbon Lake backcountry campground.

OPTION

35A Peak 237374

Route
Distance 900 m from pass
Height gain 180 m (590 ft.)
High point 2606 m (8550 ft.)

Comments The little top immediately east of the pass is a simple walk up scree to an even better viewpoint.

From the pass walk east up a wide, stony ridge to the top, which is marked by a cairn and a pole.

To the south is a welter of peaks, Mt. Galatea and The Fortress among them, shadowy shapes among which Lillian Lake and Lower Galatea Lake glow like bright jewels. In the opposite direction you can inspect both Buller passes, Red Peak, Mt. Bogart showing the scrambler's route, Ribbon Lake and the long connecting ridge to Mt. Kidd South, which makes you yearn to carry on.

This insignificant summit is the scene of momentous happenings, from Guinn's adventurous crossing, to the tragic loss of Orval Pall and Ken Wolff, which started off K Country's largest search. If you have time to spare, descend to the col to the east to see where Guinn first crossed over the ridge with his pack horses. You can trace his ascent route down the heathery hillside to the south and into the grassy avalanche gully that flows into Galatea Creek not far below the old Guinns Pass junction.

Some girlfriends and I once made the mistake of following the forested ridge to the left of the gully. Not only is it steep and rocky lower down but we suddenly realized we were looking down the cliff where Wolff's Cessna crashed exactly a year before to the day. To learn more about the tragic chain of events that followed, see #27 Memorial Lakes, Cox Hill in Volume 2 and Connolly Lake in Volume 3.

36 Lost Lake

map 4

Day hike
Unofficial trail
Distance 6.8 km from trailhead
Height gain 500 m (1640 ft.)
High point 2018 m (6620 ft.)
Map 82 J/14 Spray Lakes Reservoir

Access Hwy. 40 (Kananaskis Trail). Via #34 Galatea Creek to Lillian Lake at the forks. **Also accessible** from #84A Rummel Pass.

Comments Escape the crowds bound for Lillian Lake by taking a quiet forest walk to a lake in Galatea Creek's southwest fork. It's a much less strenuous alternative with some flagging and minor creek crossings. However, this trapline trail cut by Alvin Guinn is not a trail to be enjoyed by novices, there having been no deadfall removal for the last 60 years and more.

To peak 238342 turnoff 300 m

Just *before* you cross Galatea Creek on no. 7 bridge, leave the official trail and on a cairned trail head up the left bank to the ruins of Guinn's cabin. From here you're set for an easy walk along the left (southeast)

Alvin Guinn's cabin at the start of the trail.

bank all the way to the lake. Easy if it wasn't for all the deadfall.

Not too far along you come to a major side valley and trail junction. Keep straight and cross the side creek. (Trail to left is route #36A to peak 238342.)

To Lost Lake 2.3 km

After this, the trail accumulates height gradually in a forest strangely bereft of shrubs, only occasionally making forays down to the creek. Two side creeks on, keep left up a hill (logs have been laid across the false, yellow-flagged trail to the right). The only other recognizable landmark is a muddy side creek.

Not far beyond the muddy creek is another junction. Most people will go left up a hill into a glade and through a few willows to the northeast end of the lake. The colour? Olive green. I recommend you climb grassy bluffs above the south shoreline for the greatest view of the lake backdropped by Rummel Pass and The Tower.

But back to the last junction. If bound for Rummel Pass (and 99% of people do this route in reverse), head right and read #84A backwards.

OPTION
36A Peak 238342

Lost Lake from the northwest shore, looking towards Peak 238342 at left.

Unofficial trail, route
Distance 2.4 km to summit,
4.4 km to lake
Height gain 635 m (2080 ft.)
Height loss 466 m (1530 ft.)
High point 2493 m (8180 ft.)

Comments This is the big grassy hill that overlooks Lost Lake from the south. Most obviously it can be combined with trails #34 and #36 to make a 15.7 km loop. While not really a scramble despite a few rocks, this route does require you to be comfortable tramping about terrain with no trails and one minor creek crossing.

To the summit 2.4 km

Leave Lost Lake trail at the first big side valley. Turn left (south) onto a trail that yo-yoes along the left bank, then ends cold turkey in the creekbed. Cross. Continue up the V-shaped valley bottom between your hill on the right and a long, unnamed ridge to the left with grassy slopes. At the bend to the southwest stay on the right bank, us-ing game trails through willowy meadows. Directly opposite is the low point in the ridge, which is treed; you can bet your last dollar there's a game trail crossing over it into Fortress Lake Valley.

Farther round the bend is the forks, both of them deeply incised. Climb the slope to the right of the right fork through a sub-alpine forest of spruce and larch with small meadows you can connect up. Either aim for the pink shale col at 238336, then turn right and follow the south ridge to the summit, or make directly for the summit through fields of purple fleabane. Higher up, the gradient eases to short-grass meadows with just a few rocks to scramble up below the summit.

While you've been ogling the Opals, and The Fortress all the way up, the summit view now adds in Guinn's Pass, the big grey peak at 217373 and Rummel Pass between The Tower and Mt. Galatea.

Returning more or less the same way you went up is the shorter option. But why not take in the lake?

Descent to Lost Lake 2 km

Descend the west ridge on grass and rocks. Because of a big drop on the right side overlooking Lost Lake, you have to keep going a long way west, even into trees and all the way down to the lip of a hanging valley. Only then can you descend to the flat forest floor at the west end of the lake. Even so, the way down is steep, but at least you have trees to hang on to.

Regain Lost Lake trail by going either way around the lake. Clockwise is easier and you can pick up a trail. Just past the lake the trail crosses the southwest fork via a beaver dam and joins the main valley trail. Turn left.

Below top: Descending the west ridge, with Rummel Pass at far left below The Tower.

Below bottom: Flower meadows at treeline.

37 Evan-Thomas Creek to Pass   map 3

Long day hike, bike 'n' hike, backpack
Official, unofficial trails
Distance 14.3 km to pass
Height gain 760 m (2493 ft.)
High point 2180 m (7150 ft.)
Map 82 J/14 Spray Lakes Reservoir

Access Hwy. 40 (Kananaskis Trail) at Evan-Thomas Creek parking lot.
Also accessible from North Fork of the Little Elbow in Volume 2.

Comments Evan-Thomas Creek to Evan-Thomas Pass is one half of a route through to the Little Elbow. The other half is described in Volume 2 under "North Fork of the Little Elbow."

The route (exploration road, trail, cutline) is such a long trudge it's debatable whether the pass is worth the effort unless you're backpacking over to the Little Elbow or heading up to the tarn under Mt. Potts or crossing the delectable Paradise Pass into the west fork of the Little Elbow. Use this trail as a jumping off point for more interesting options such as Camp Creek (#38), the Mackay Hills (#41), Old Baldy (#42), Dead Horse Canyon (#39) and Fisher Peak as described in Alan Kane's *Scrambles in the Canadian Rockies*.

Biking is possible to first creek and would be possible to second creek if wearing an alder protection suit and a full face motorcycle helmet. Trimming is spasmodic.

Important flood note This was the creek that demolished the highway bridge and the celebrated Kananaskis golf course in 2013. So what to expect higher up the valley? Repairs have been made twice over to the section between the parking lot and the Wedge Connector. The section between second creek and Rocky Creek Pass junction has only snippets of road remaining, The creek moving east has either totally demolished it, gouged pieces out of it or is using it as a convenient channel. Additionally, side creeks at the crossings have been scoured from side to side and denuded of all vegetation. Early in the season you'll be doing a lot of wading

and may not get through. August on is a much better time to go, when creek levels are lower.

Naming The valley was called Porcupine Creek when George Pocaterra and his co-prospectors built the road section to coal prospects in Camp Creek. The Stoney called it Îthorhan Odabi Waptan, meaning "Abundance of porcupines valley." In 1922 it suffered a name change and the old name was moved to another, far less appropriate valley.

To Wedge connector trail 1.6 km
From the parking lot walk through to Shatto's exploration road, turn left and disregarding all side trails, follow it up-valley through pine forest. Before getting to where the creek gouged out the banks to a height of 30 feet, transfer to a brand new trail covered in wood chips. Walk the last bit on original road to a junction and turn left. (Wedge Connector, signed "No Horses" takes off to the right down a hill.)

To Old Baldy trail 300 m
Climb a slightly winding hill. At the top the horse trail from Boundary Ranch joins in from the left. A second trail turning left just before McDougall Creek crossing is the route to Old Baldy (#42).

To Dead Horse Canyon turnoff 2.1 km
Cross McDougall Creek on stepping stones and then the old creekbed. Shortly the road starts a long uphill climb through a narrow band of pines. Since the last edition the forest on both sides has been logged and burnt.

Near the summit of the hill, trail #39 to Dead Horse Canyon turns off to the right at blazed tree 336371.

To third side creek 4.2 km
Descend an eroded hill to first side creek at 4.3 km from the trailhead and cross its usually dry cobbled bed. (NOTE: The creek to right descends between steep walls to a drop-off above Dead Horse Canyon. So it's a no-go as a route. Of more interest to scram-

Top: Alder alley on the second uphill between first and second side creeks.

Bottom: Falls in the main creek at the third side creek crossing.

blers, the side valley to left is the jumping-off point for "Missing Mountain" omitted from every topo map. It was finally climbed by John Martin back in 1979. Rob Eastick, who brought the anomaly to everyone's attention in 2009, probably made the second ascent 30 years later.)

Climb a second hill into a long, flat traverse through "alder alley" as I call it. The problem here is one of over-the-head bushes. A longer downhill, even more gouged out by landslides than the first one, descends to the second side creek, where the road disappears among the boulders.

The bypass trail crosses the second creek upstream, then descends and after a short level stint delivers you to the cobbles alongside an attractive series of small cascades in the main creek. At the impasse climb a slab to a snippet of trail on the banktop. This morphs into a ditch, then a stony section of road, then trail which enters a field of cobbles at a right-hand bend. Walk a sandy road under the left hillside. This too ends in a great mess of cobbles at the third side creek, which appears to carry half the water in Evan-Thomas. (NOTE: Valley to left is the route over to Upper Canyon Creek. See Volume 2.) Wade across. On the far bank be sure to walk downstream a short way to look at falls in the main creek.

To Rocky Creek Pass turnoff 1.9 km

A recognizable section of road resumes on the far bank under the northwest ridge of Fisher Peak, but not for long. On coming to a washout, use the bypass trail up the hillside or at low water stumble between rocks at the water's edge. At deadfall take the bypass trail to right. The road then becomes increasingly stony and wet. Cross a wee channel of Evan-Thomas. BEFORE coming to the usual crossing place, turn right on a dirt trail and wade Evan-Thomas Creek to the west bank at 355338 below a small rapid.

The west bank trail skirts around flood debris, then turns left. Cross a large area of cobbles. The road resumes, then disappears in two more cobbled areas. In between cobbles 2 and 3 is a good camping area on

In the vicinity of the pass looking toward Fisher Peak (left) and Shoulder Peak. Photo Alf Skrastins

grass to the left. Climb slightly to an important junction at 355331 where Shatto's Road heads right up a tributary to Rocky Creek Pass. For Evan-Thomas Pass continue ahead on what is now a cutline.

To Evan-Thomas Pass 5.2 km

In a few metres the cutline dips to cross Evan-Thomas Creek at the confluence with Camp Creek. This cutline has all the foibles of its kind because after the crossing it climbs high, undulates awhile (bypass trails available), then plummets back to creek level. Coming up is the flat wet section, a muddy jaunt through willow brush below the runout zone of large avalanche slopes with seven creek crossings. This comes to an end on the east bank at the point where another major tributary joins in from the southwest from under Mt. Denny. In the angle of the forks is a grassy meadow with a fabulous view of the unnamed mountain in the angle of the west and north forks of the Little Elbow, its east ridge built like a ripsaw.

In front you'll see two low gaps in the forested watershed ridge. The trail heads toward the left-hand gap. Higher up, watch for a junction offering a choice of routes.

1. Gap trail The trail to right dekes neatly through the gap — the true pass — into the head of Little Elbow's north fork. In a meadow is a junction. Turn right for Potts Tarn; keep straight for the north fork of the Little Elbow, Boundary Ranch's "Happy Valley Camp" and Paradise Pass.

2. Cutline The cutline straight ahead climbs steeply, passing 50 vertical metres above the gap in open forest, the reward for extra climbing being a clear view of the northern Opals. From the high point, the cutline descends to another junction with the gap trail, then carries on as cutline down the north fork of the Little Elbow. See Volume 2 for ongoing routes.

38 Rocky Creek Pass and Camp Creek

map 3

Long day hike, bike 'n' hike, backpack
Unofficial trail
Distance 2.5 km to Camp Creek,
11.6 km to Camp Creek from trailhead
Height gain 207 m (680 ft.),
579 m (1900 ft.) from trailhead
High point 2103 m (6900 ft.) at Camp
Creek crossing
Map 82 J/14 Spray Lakes Reservoir

Access Via #37 Evan-Thomas Creek to Pass at 9.6 km. At 355331.

Comments The easy Shatto's exploration road (continuation of the road up Evan-Thomas Creek), leads to Rocky Creek Pass and on into Camp Creek.

Camp Creek has meadows and larches and the option of doing a short ridgewalk over Prospect Ridge into the bargain. Be aware it's a hunter hot spot, so at such times wear fluorescent pink and swear blind you haven't seen any elk.

History This is the place for George Pocaterra aficionados to come and look at his coal claims. Pocaterra spent much of his life trying to develop this site. Despite the coal testing superior to coal from Drumheller and Crowsnest, and interest expressed by the Brits, the Germans and the Japanese, access was a huge problem. That and trying to find backers, plus the interruption caused by two world wars. Finally the waning market sounded the death knell for Pocaterra's grand dream. I still wonder how he intended to get a railway to the site.

To Rocky Creek Pass 1 km

At the junction turn right, continuing up the Shatto coal exploration road, which is pretty well grassed over. (Note coal spoil down in the forks.) Alvin Guinn remembered as a youth persuading Pocaterra to build the track up the dry north bank of Camp Creek and not up the muddy south bank where it was likely to be washed out. Nevertheless, the deluge of 2013 has taken one big bite out of it.

Halfway up, at 350328, a modern offshoot of historic Prospect trail takes off up the hillside to right. (This trail climbs ~152 metres (500 ft.) to its high point on the NE ridge of the Mackay Hills south peak, but is of little use as a route to that summit when a better route exists from the pass itself.)

In another half kilometre the road levels off in a soggy longitudinal meadow on the watershed between Evan-Thomas and Rocky creeks. In the last edition I called the pass "Cloudburst" after the Cloudburst Coal Company, which did some prospecting under contract to Pocaterra in the early 1950s. Ruthie Oltmann says it was also known as Moose Wallow, likely referring to the black pool in the middle of the meadow. Nowadays, people refer to it as Rocky Creek Pass.

To Camp Creek 1.5 km

After leaving the meadow, the road doubles back left, rounding the edge of a ridge and turning south into the main fork of Camp Creek. This is where you run into the first of the hunter's camps and garbage dumps. Wait a hundred years and the dumps will become historic. I can imagine future hikers sifting excitedly through nose tags, bottles of Palm Breeze light rum and assorted plastic containers.

A little farther on, the road crosses the creek and splits into two grassy tracks. Possibly this was the site of Pocaterra's cabin. The track to right heads up-valley into meadows where a trail carries on to the valley head below the northernmost peaks of the Opals. Alternatively, turn left and keeping left, climb a meadow on the diagonal to Pocaterra's coal claims on north end of Prospect Ridge.

Opposite top: Prospect Ridge from Fisher Peak. Shows the old roads through Pocaterra's coal prospects on the left-hand ascent ridge.

Opposite bottom: Summit of Prospect Ridge. To left is "Ripsaw" also called "Mt. Sarcee," separated by Paradise Pass from the northerly peaks of the Opal Range: Potts and Denny. Photo Sonny Bou

38A Prospect Ridge Loop

Unofficial trails, route
Distance 4.2 km loop from Camp Creek
Height gain 488 m (1600 ft.) from Camp Creek
High point 2454 m (8050 ft.)

Comments A thoroughly enjoyable trip that incorporates the grassy ridge to the southeast at 348304 and the valley trail.

Set off toward Pocaterra's coal prospects, but at the far junction turn right up another track. Near track's end a trail heads left, gaining the north ridge much higher up.

The trail continues up the ridge to further prospects, then fades away at last trees. Clamber up rocks, prelude to a smooth grass slope interrupted at mid-height by a short horizontal ridge of tilted sandstone blocks. The actual summit (at km 1.6) is as broad as a soccer field and striped with rockbands you can step over.

You can now see over Evan-Thomas Pass to mounts Glasgow, Cornwall and Outlaw in the Elbow. To their right is the familiar profile of the ripsaw peak, and farther to the right Mt. Evan-Thomas, with Paradise Pass slung between them. In the opposite direction The Wedge and the Mackay Hills are naturally of most interest should you be headed that way.

Descend easily to the col at 347296. An elk trail runs across it and down to Camp Creek, then up an equally enticing ridge to the west. Before descending to Camp Creek, look southwards into the true head of Evan-Thomas Creek below Mt. Denny. This really is an elk's heaven, a mix of meadow, last trees, talus, and gullies criss-crossed with countless game trails, some of which emanate from this ridge. Nevertheless, heading cross-country to Evan-Thomas Pass or Paradise Pass is no simple matter, despite the elk trails luring you on.

So from the col turn right and descend the elk trail into Camp Creek at the flat. Leave it here and turn right down-valley, shortly picking up a grassy track which conveniently joins your outgoing track near the creek crossing.

OPTIONAL DESCENT

38B Rocky Creek

Distance 6.6+ km
Height loss ~442 m (1450 ft.)

Comments Descending Rocky Creek from Rocky Creek Pass to Hwy. 40 is not popular. In 1995 it took a mountain biker two days to get down to the highway; the bike was abandoned on a hillside and later picked up by helicopter.

The lush meadows of Camp Creek from the lower slopes of Prospect Ridge. In the background are the three summits of the Mackay Hills.

The problem is the section downstream of the forks where the valley narrows and is steep sided. There are two ways through: the creek and the hillside below The Wedge. Both routes are rough and demand that hikers be experienced in route-finding. Descending this way requires another vehicle to be parked at Hwy. 40. Just south of the highway bridge over Rocky Creek is a pull-off on the west side.

Because I have not done either of these routes for decades, the following write-ups lean heavily on Alf Skrastins's more up-to-date descriptions.

1. Via the hillside
Back in the 1970s, we found a traversing game trail high on the southwest-facing slopes of The Wedge. As of 2009 Alf found the trail in good condition still, but getting off remains unsatisfactory.

A trail starting from the north side of the pass heads west through the longitudinal meadow, then, keeping right of the west fork, follows the uppermost bench below the grassy slopes of the Mackay Hills. Cross a northeast fork, then climb across a small rib to the north fork, which is crossed lower down at the 1800-m contour at 320332.

To avoid a rockband, the trail climbs through trees, then up scree to a high point at about 313333 on the south ridge of The Wedge. From here it makes a long, gradually descending traverse of steep hillside, crossing the odd rocky gully and avalanche slope. On the way are great views of The Fortress ahead, looking its sharpest. Across the valley the eye is drawn to a textbook syncline valley off the north end of Opal Ridge with waterfalls.

At 1700 m in elevation, the trail divides, both forks gradually fading. Which way? The obvious thing to do is to drop 100 vertical metres down the right side of the avalanche slope to the creek and put up with a few creek crossings.

Alternatively, continue traversing, heading a little uphill to get above a diagonal cliff. On the other side pick up an intermittently flagged on/off trail on its way up Limestone Mountain (as we found out) and turn left. After the initial rocky step, the gradient eases off in the trees and it's a good trail that deposits you in the meadow at the mouth of the valley. Turn right and walk out to Hwy. 40. Cross the bridge to the parking area.

2. Via the creek

Basically a bush walk with many creek crossings. If you must try it, wait until the creek calms down and take Tevas.

Because there's a trail initially, it's best to follow the same route as no. 1 to the north fork. Read the second paragraph.

Descend the creek to the main fork and turn right. Straightaway you're into the narrows between The Wedge and North Opal Ridge. The creek swings from side to side between canyon walls, so there is much unavoidable wading.

The lower half of the route only seems endless — a narrow forested valley with many more creek crossings. At the mouth of the valley, under a diagonal rockband, you cross the creek one last time to the right bank and follow meadow out to Hwy. 40. Cross the bridge to the parking area.

Top: #38B 1. The traversing trail. Photo Alf Skrastins

Bottom: #38B 2. Rocky Creek narrows. Photo Alf S krastins

39 Dead Horse Canyon map 3

Day hike
Unofficial trail
Distance 2.1 km return from #36, 10.1 return from Evan-Thomas trailhead
Height gain 214 m (700 ft.) from trailhead
Height loss 116 m (381 ft.) from #36

Access Via #37 Evan-Thomas Creek to Pass at 4 km.

Comments The canyon of Evan-Thomas Creek, perhaps the easiest objective for a day trip up the valley, is reached by a well-used horse trail dropping in from above.

About the trail When the 2013 flood damage in Evan-Thomas Creek temporarily thwarted Boundary Ranch's pack trips to their camp at the pass, the Guinns found another objective for their clients: Dead Horse Canyon as they call it.

Near the top of the first long hill after the Old Baldy trail turnoff, turn right onto a narrow trail at blaze 336371. Shortly it turns left and travels slightly uphill between blackened trees to a grassy ridge.

Here it turns right and starts a winding descent of bushy hillside with some deadfall. At one right-hander it comes close to a vertiginous view into the canyon of first creek. Lower down, the trail travels on the canyon edge. Listen for the faint music of water falling over an undercut rock step, the reason why walking down first canyon from above is impossible. In winter it transforms into an ice climb called Exit Combo.

Reach the cobble flat of the valley bottom below a big cliff some distance upstream of the great ice climb Midnight Falls. The trail crosses first creek and heads left past a picnic area with rock seats to reach Evan-Thomas Creek below a small two-tier waterfall in the tight narrows at 333364. Across the creek starts the old Prospect trail, most useful as a shortcut to Rocky Creek Pass or as a way off the Mackay Hills.

Returning the same way is easier despite the height gain. However tempting it may look, heading downstream to the Wedge Connector bridge involves numerous creek crossings, impossible at high water. But see the next entry.

39A The Canyon in Winter
Day hike
Official/ Unofficial trails
Distance 9. 5 km return from
Evan-Thomas trailhead.
Height gain 250 m (820 ft.) from trailhead

Access Via #37 Evan-Thomas Creek to Pass at 1.6 km.

Comments In winter, when Evan-Thomas Creek is pretty well frozen you can walk there the flat way by following the creekbed from the Wedge Connector bridge site. The trail, the route of which varies a little from year to year, is well trodden by ice climbers and ends for us hikers in the spectacular cliff scenery of Dead Horse Canyon. But the main reason for going in winter is to ogle the frozen waterfalls, mere seepages in summer.

To Moonlight Falls 4 km from trailhead
At the 4-way at 1.6 km turn right onto Wedge Connector. Descend to the flats of Evan-Thomas Creek, en route crossing McDougall Creek with its smooth blue ice. Cross Evan-Thomas Creek and turn left.

The trodden trail, often a trench, heads along flats and through an extended narrows into a longer flat. Cross and recross the creek. Cliffs begin on the right side. Chantilly Falls is the first route you pass, then smaller pieces of ice culminating in the magnificent 360-foot-high Moonlight Falls. A side trail leads to its base.

To Dead Horse Canyon 800 m
A trail carries on along the right bank below an even higher cliff into Dead Horse Canyon. Opposite route #39, cross to the left bank and walk into the tight narrows where a small two-tier waterfall stops further progress. Above the overhanging anticline of the right wall you can spot the safety fence protecting Prospect trail at an exposed bend. The trail heading left is the controversial route to Green Monster. See the next page...

Return the same way. Don't bother with the summer route.

Top: Moonlight Falls.

Bottom: Hiker entering Dead Horse Canyon.

Opposite: The summer route into Dead Horse Canyon.

GOING FARTHER

We could have a heated discussion on whether hikers egged on by social media, should follow the ice climber's access route to the icefalls beyond the narrows. Green Monster (it really IS green) is the main attraction. Interestingly, the climber's longer and safer access route once followed the first section of Prospect trail on the south bank, then cut across and down through the trees. But because the direct route is now safeguarded by ropes and a cable, it's the one followed by today's climbers. The crux is a narrow, exposed ledge, followed by a slippery slide with rappel rope back into the creekbed. Some hikers have no problem, others get panicky and have to turn back.

The problem then is lack of passing lanes and weekends can be very congested. But if you must go, wearing Microspikes is a must. Overall, a fairly moderate route that is potentially hazardous depending on conditions, the state of the hardware and the grouchy mood of some ice climbers who are threatening to remove the safety gear.

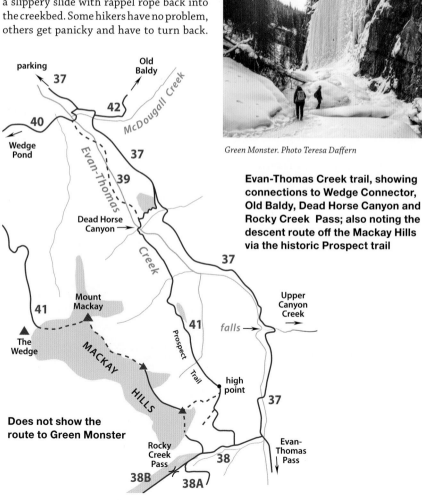

Green Monster. Photo Teresa Daffern

Evan-Thomas Creek trail, showing connections to Wedge Connector, Old Baldy, Dead Horse Canyon and Rocky Creek Pass; also noting the descent route off the Mackay Hills via the historic Prospect trail

40 The Wedge Connector map 3

Half-day hike, bike 'n' hike
Official trail
Distance 2.9 km
Height gain W-E 24 m (80 ft.)
High point 1580 m (5184 ft.)
Map 82 J/14 Spray Lakes Reservoir

Access Hwy. 40 (Kananaskis Trail) at Wedge Pond parking lot (far end).
Also accessible from #37 Evan-Thomas Creek to Pass.

Comments A short forest trail (once a 1940s logging road, now an official ski trail) connects Wedge Pond to Evan-Thomas Creek trail. Ridge walkers on the Mackay Hills use it as a connector. Bathers will head to McDougall Creek, the trail's newest attraction.

Is Evan-Thomas Creek bridged? After the old iron bridge was pushed aside in the 2013 flood, it was replaced by a footbridge (the sacrificial) that washed away a few years later. In 2022 it was decided that no more bridges should be sacrificed to the wayward creek. So this means wading from mid-July on. In the future a new leg of the trail will connect with the Bill Milne bike path south of the highway bridge, so opening up another winter approach route for #39.

WEST TO EAST

From the far end of Wedge Pond parking lot follow a paved bicycle trail (the Bill Milne trail) beyond the gate to a T-junction. Turn left on the bike path.

Where the bike path turns left, continue ahead on a grassy track. In 1 km, begin a gradual climb to the trail's high point at a Y-junction. Keep left. (Logging road ahead heads toward the Mackay Hills.) The track then descends to the cobble flats of Evan-Thomas Creek. Starting a half kilometre upstream are the great red cliffs of Evan-Thomas, best visited in winter when a trail is stamped out along the creekbed.

After bypassing the heavy duty iron bridge left high, dry and intact, wrapped up in branches, come to Evan-Thomas Creek itself. Wade across and wind up the bank, en route crossing the wonderfully scenic McDougall Creek above falls and pools. On arriving at the 3-way with Evan-Thomas Creek trail (exploration road), turn left for Evan-Thomas parking lot, which lies 1.6 km distant.

The last bridge over Evan-Thomas Creek. The Wedge and the three Mackay Hills in the background.

41 Mackay Hills Loop

map 3

Long day hike/scramble
Unofficial trails, route
Distance 18.4 km loop via descent 1,
20.2 km loop via descent 2.
Height gain 1400 m (4590 ft.)
High point 2460 m (8070 ft.)
Map 82 J/14 Spray Lakes Reservoir

Access Hwy. 40 (Kananaskis Trail).
1. Wedge Pond parking lot (far end).
2. Evan-Thomas Creek parking lot.
Also accessible from #38 Camp Creek at Rocky Creek Pass.

Comments A beautiful ridgewalk over three grassy summits with a touch of easy scrambling. But it's not for everyone — this is a strenuous undertaking because of the huge height gain. Best, then, to tackle it anti-clockwise to get the bulk of the climbing over with early, leaving you to plod mindlessly along easy trails later in the day. Expect two creek crossings via descent 1, four via descent 2.

The return leg off the hills takes in Prospect trail, Dead Horse Canyon trail, Evan-Thomas Creek trail and the Wedge Connector. A second vehicle left at Evan-Thomas trailhead will only shorten the loop by 1.3 km, BUT will reduce the creek crossings by one. See ##39, 37, 40.

About the route "The penalty for enjoying yourself is an ending so horrible only experienced bushwhackers with a talent for route-finding need think about doing the whole loop." So this was what I wrote in the last edition. Since then two things happened which made me do a complete route rethink. First, the 2013 flood badly damaged a large section of the approach trail up Evan-Thomas Creek and it was taking forever to get onto the hills from this direction. Second, Boundary Ranch, unable to get horses to "Happy Valley Camp" at Evan-Thomas Pass, made a trail into Dead Horse Canyon, then opened up the historic prospect trail used by Pocaterra and Mackay, from where they could reach Evan-Thomas Pass in a very roundabout way. Inadvertently, this offered an excellent way on and off the hills. See Getting off on page 142.

Naming According to James Ashworth's 1917 report on the coalfield, the northernmost top is called Mt. Mackay or Mackay's Mountain after claimant Walter Grant Mackay. It is not the highest of the three. That honour goes to the centre peak. Nevertheless, we know from a photo that Mackay, George Pocaterra and probably Paul Amos climbed all three peaks sometime between 1910 and 1917 during their search for coal prospects in Evan-Thomas Creek.

ANTI-CLOCKWISE FROM ACCESS 1

The Wedge access trail 3.2 km

From the end of the parking lot, pass through a gate onto the paved Bill Milne bike path. A few metres in, turn right on a gravel track. In 70 m turn left onto a trail heading into the forest. In 150 m the trail splits. Go either way, both having some step-over deadfall. Where they join up, go left from the left-hand split, straight from the right-hand split.

Coming up is the longest, steepest ascent of the day: 884 vertical m (2900 ft.). But first the going is easy to the left of a dry creekbed. Do NOT cross the creekbed on a wrong-way trail. Suddenly, the creek is noisy with water, this signalling an ever steepening climb up its left bank. Come to a flat section. Here the trail turns left, climbing diagonally up grass, then making two steep zigs onto the north ridge.

Turn right and follow the ridge, open sections of grass and stones alternating with steeper steps in spruce and larch. You'll be stopping often to admire the fabulous aerial views of Mt. Kidd and the Kananaskis Valley behind you. As you get higher the Mackay Hills and Fisher Peak come into sight. The top of the ridge at last vegetation is the place for a sit down. (The ongoing "trail" leads onto the rubbly northeast face of The Wedge, the start of a moderate scramble described by AllTrails as a popular hike and dog friendly!)

The Wedge traverse to Mt. Mackay 1.3 km
You, however, head left at rockline on an adequate trail traversing *below* the northeast face on scree. Don't linger; climbers on the summit ridge could be kicking off rocks. On reaching the top of a grassy ridge yoked to Mt. Mackay, head down left for 152 vertical metres (500 ft.) to a col. Then, regaining all the lost height, ascend Mackay's west ridge to the northernmost summit with cairn.

On topping out, look down the tempting north ridge to the left, the 4th edition's descent route, that ends "among the worst bushwhacking I have ever done," says Sonny. Turn your back on it and enjoy the view of the next two summits backdropped by a welter off higher peaks.

To Centre Peak 1.8 km
Aside from dodging a few little rockbands, it's a simple walk of 183 vertical metres (600 ft.) down to the north-centre col.

Not so simple is the 183+ vertical metre climb up centre peak via its northwest ridge. It's interesting, though, with its fragmented red cliffs and shiny sheets of black coal against which clumps of alpine cinquefoil dazzle. On coming up against a rockband, traverse left and then head back right to the cairned summit.

Opposite: Climbing the north ridge. Looking back to Mt. Kidd and Wedge Pond.

Below: On The Wedge traverse. Photo Alf Skrastins

To South Peak 1.1 km

The far-side descent of 152 vertical metres (500 ft.) to centre–south col is very easy and low down takes in a few larches spilling over from the northeast face. A sheep trail takes you partway, 61 vertical metres (200 ft.), up to the south peak. The lowest of the three summits is a smooth, grassy dome (no cairn) where you can spend a happy time identifying peaks and flowers before leaving the heights for the forest.

(Below this traverse line Prospect descends much more steeply, not to Rocky Creek Pass as many people hope but to halfway along the Shatto road. Possibly, the "black" trail starts from somewhere near the pass or even above it? Unfortunately, I ran out of time before I could check it out, so if anyone decides to give it a go by reversing Prospect trail, please contact me via our blog kananaskistrails. com. Thanks!)

GETTING OFF

There are two ways off the south peak onto Evan-Thomas Creek trail. See the map on page 138.

1. Via Prospect trail and Dead Horse Canyon 11.1 km

Shorter with one creek crossing, but with more height gain. Look for blazes.

From the top head down the steeper northeast ridge, a mix of meadow spruce and larch. At 347338 the high point of Prospect trail crosses the ridge. Turn left.

NOTE: For easier bushwhacking, drop off the ridge to the right farther back and pick up the trail on its traverse of the south-facing slope. Even farther back you will pick up a side trail shown as black on the map on page 138 that feeds into it. Either way, turn left and walk up to the high point on the northeast ridge.

From its high point the trail diagonals down the damp northeast face across the skirts of the three peaks you've just climbed, the trail alternating between dry rooty and soft boggy, the angle easy with a couple of steeper drops. Cross a side creek. Low down, cross the old bridge, pass between built-up walls of mossy boulders and only then cross side creek no. 2. On flat ground follow blazes (NOT flagging heading right) across a boggy area, beyond which a clear trail descends to clifftops above Dead Horse Canyon. (NOTE: If walking the trail in reverse, go straight on reaching flat ground. Do NOT follow flagging heading left.)

The finish is clearly exciting, the trail edging along the top of the cliffs, then winding down above the descending cliff line (safety fence at one bend) and into a gully. Turn right and descend a few stones to Evan-Thomas Creek in Dead Horse Canyon.

Top: The northwest ridge of centre peak from the north–centre col.

Opposite: Looking from the flowery south peak towards centre peak.

Bottom: View from centre peak of The Wedge (left) showing the traverse and the route to Mt. Mackay at right.

NOTE: On reaching Evan-Thomas Creek it is very tempting to just slosh back and forth down the creek to the Wedge Connector, and this you can do if water levels are really low. On the plus side there's no extra height gain, but kilometre-wise it saves only 500 metres.

Otherwise, wade the creek below a small two-tier waterfall and pick up the Dead Horse Canyon summer trail that heads left. Just a little way along, a picnic area with rock seats is the ideal place to replenish the body before tackling the 91 vertical metre (300 ft.) climb up to Evan-Thomas trail, which heads up the left side of a deeply incised side creek. Read #39 backwards. But once you're on it you should have no problem following it.

On reaching #37 Evan-Thomas Creek trail (exploration road) at 336371, turn left and follow it mostly downhill to the Wedge Connector junction 2.4 km distant.

Go straight and walk the Wedge Connector for 2.9 km back to the Wedge Pond parking area. See #40. Alternatively, turn right and walk 1.6 km to access 2 at Evan-Thomas Creek parking lot.

2. Via Rocky Creek Pass ~13 km
The longest return adds on 2 km to the total distance whichever ending you use, and comes with a minimum of three creek crossings.

Descend south-facing meadow, hopefully picking up the sheep trail that takes you through a belt of trees to Rocky Creek Pass. Turn left onto Shatto's grassy road that descends to the T-junction with Evan-Thomas Creek trail.

Turn left and follow #37 for 8 km to the Wedge Connector junction. Go straight on Wedge Connector, which leads in 2.9 km to Wedge Pond day-use parking lot.

Top: Prospect trail at the old bridge.

Bottom: The small two-tier waterfall in Dead Horse Canyon. Cross the creek just below it.

Opposite: #42 Old Baldy, showing the southwest ridge to left and the last section of the creek route up from the tarn. Photo Pete Irwin

42 Old Baldy, normal route   map 3

Long day hike
Unofficial trail, route
Distance 6.6 km to summit
from trailhead
Height gain 870 m (2855 ft.)
High point 2388 m (7835 ft.)
Map 82 J/14 Spray Lakes Reservoir

Access Hwy. 40 (Kananaskis Trail) at Evan-Thomas Creek parking lot. Via #37 Evan-Thomas Creek to Pass.

Comments Who would think this insignificant summit at 344410 would be such a fine viewpoint! However, getting there exacts a toll whichever of the two suggested routes you take. The original trail up the valley was damaged by flood water in 2013, leaving the southwest ridge the more popular choice. And apart from the nasty boulder field it's a pretty good route. Look for cairns. Some people make a 14.1 km loop, preferring the ridge as the ascent route and the creek as the descent route after a swim in the tarn.

About the trail Before K Country, we and a few others staggered up and down even more onerous routes: the northwest ridge from the ranger station and the west flank route up the front before Boundary Ranch turned the old access roads into horse trails.

In 1979 myself and a girlfriend went up the creek for the first time and down the southwest ridge, taking the boulder field straight and noting the lack of trails in the forest below it. Soon, most people were struggling up the valley route as described in the first edition of the KCTG. After the 4th edition in 2010 a firebreak was forged onto the southwest ridge in 2011 and a helicopter landing area cut out below the boulder field, to be used if prescribed fires down in Evan-Thomas Creek got out of control. (They did.) Of course, the public, especially trail runners, soon cottoned on to this and with trails improvements it is now the ascent route of choice.

Naming It is NOT Old Baldy Ridge, simply Old Baldy, a name coined over 60 years ago.

Follow Evan-Thomas Creek trail for 2.1 km. On a downhill, just before the first side creek crossing, turn left at a cairn onto a narrow trail.

To trail junction 180 m
The trail follows the left bank of the creek arising from the west slope of Mt. McDougall, the trail initially flat and easy despite being overrun by cobbles in one place. At the second split go left to a cairn at a junction. Turn left up a hill. (Trails to right carry on up the valley as #42A.)

To southwest ridge 370 m

After the initial climb, the trail turns right into a long ascending traverse above steep hillside. Uphills, one downhill and mini traverses lead to a left-hand bend signalling the relentlessly steep flog up the firebreak onto the ridge. On descent, this is a quad burner.

Southwest ridge to boulder field 1.5 km

The trail turns right, the gradient gradually easing as it follows the treed ridge past a couple of viewpoints for Volcano Peak and the burnt forest on its lower slopes. On reaching the helicopter landing site, it crosses the clearing, then descends through a few trees to a cairn at the bottom of the boulder field, which from this vantage point looks horribly steep and very high.

To the summit 2.6 km

Now for the crux, a 153-m-high (502 ft.) mix of boulders with snippets of trail. Look for cairns and orange-coloured rocks.

But first the trail turns right and gains height slowly twixt trees and rocks to a flat area. Giving a precarious-looking cairn a wide berth, cross boulders to the foot of the steep climbing. An unpleasant trail twists uphill then traverses right onto the ridge's south flank, where the going is no easier. Gear up for another three twisty climbs alternating with three boulder traverses, the last fading out among very much bigger boulders where there is no option but to clamber carefully up left to a big cairn on the ridgetop. Greeting you is an eerie forest of dead black trees,

On a stony trail, walk along the slowly rising ridge at the edge of a rockband. This gives way to a flat meadow with great views behind, ahead to the final rise and across McDougall Creek to Peak 357404. If you lose the trail, aim for a patch of fire-dead trees where a cairn marks the start of a trail traversing shale to a grassy slope beyond. Sans trail, climb grass to the summit ridge.

Walk along to the high point, finally enjoying the westerly view extending from Mt. Joffre, the white fang in the south, all the way north to Mt. Aylmer and the mountains of The Ghost. Naturally, the mountains about Ribbon Creek are pre-eminent.

Above: The route at the edge of the rockband. Photo Bob Spirko

Above: Looking towards the final rise to the summit ridge. The route crosses the shale low down, then climbs up the grass. Photo Bob Spirko

Opposite left: First view of the boulder field.

Opposite right: Near the top of the boulder field where the trail is about to give out.

Above: The beautiful meadows of the summit ridge. Old Baldy Peak ahead. Photo Alf Skrastins

Return

Many people return the same way. Others return via #42A, the valley route. If the latter, turn right (east), continuing to follow the ridge along to the col between Old Baldy and "Old Baldy Peak." From here descend a steepish grass slope with trail to the tarn seen below. Now read #42A.

OPTIONAL DESCENT/ASCENT ROUTE

42A via McDougall Creek

Distance 7.5 km from trailhead

Comments "Don't go the creek route ever" someone commented on AllTrails, someone descending blind with no idea about how to handle the dreaded banks after the 2013 flood. (Answer: From the top down, second and fourth banks are omitted by creek crossings.) On the other hand, Bob S wrote, "Good detours are in place and the trail runs nearly seamlessly."

Personally, I have no big gripes about the route (I love the meadow ending) and because it's the route to Peak 357404 and Mt. McDougall I've decided to describe it from the bottom up. Just know the two remaining bank crossings could be intimidating to

some and you need low water in the creek so you can hop across on rocks. Also watch for cairns and flagging. Luckily, the upper half of the trail is unaffected by the flood.

BOTTOM TO TOP

Follow the first section of the normal route to the cairn at 180 m. Turn right. Alternatively, keep right at the second split.

To the Forks 2.7 km

In the V-shaped section of the valley, the trail is less good. Initially there are two things to look for. First, stay low where a steep bypass trail climbs up and down the hillside. Second, just after clambering over some deadfall turn right on a bypass that follows the cobbles of the creekbed. Back on original trail, the going is straightforward to the start of the bank traverses.

Above: #42A Dicey traverse of a bank on the return trip. If in doubt cross and recross the creek. Photo Bob Spirko

Opposite top: #42A The cobalt tarn when full. Photo Pete Irwin

Opposite bottom: Peak 357404 from the ridge route. The ascent route more or less follows the right-hand ridge, the optional descent the left-hand ridge.

trail climbs steeply up the right (east) bank into a clump of spruce, then levels off again, passing below the optional descent route off peak 357404. Around the next corner is the seasonal tarn occupying a depression in scree.

Now take a look at the photo on page 145. From the near end of the tarn climb steeply-angled grass toward the col between Old Baldy and Old Baldy Peak. Hopefully, you will pick up the trail. Turn left. As you stroll toward your objective, the mountains rise up one by one until finally, from the summit, a breathtaking panorama to the west is revealed.

OPTION

42B Peak 357404

Height gain 487 m (1600 ft.) from forks, 991 m (3250 ft.) from trailhead
High point 2515 m (8250 ft.)

Comments The mountain between the forks at 358403 doesn't appear on the topo map as a separate peak, but it most assuredly is, with a definite col between it and Peak 362405. Mostly steep grass with some scrambling at the end.

On arriving at the first bank, cross the creek at cairns onto a reasonable bypass trail alongside a cascade. Recross and tootle along to the second bank, being careful not to go for a slide on that first steep hill. Just before third bank where crucial sections of the trail are missing, cross the creek. This time, the bypass trail is not obvious, so either stay close to the creek on flood debris or follow easier ground a little inland. Recross and walk cobbles past cairns, at the last one climbing up onto an intact portion of trail below a crag. On what is really the start to the fourth bank, climb hard-packed shale past a cairn and turn right, ambling across scree to the traverse. While the trail is good, again take care above steep, eroded slopes.

The terrain eases for the last 600-m-long stretch to the forks, the going very pleasant through grass and flowers. The main right-hand fork empties into the confluence in a chain of picturesque waterfalls and pools.

To the summit 2.5 km
Continue to follow the trail into the narrower left-hand fork, crossing a minuscule creek five times. After the last crossing the

To the summit

Follow #42A to the forks.

Take the right fork. Unless you want to potter about between waterfalls, follow a faint trail along a bench on the left bank. When the bench peters out transfer to the valley bottom. Around the bend barge through willows to the right bank and follow it to the valley head under Mt. McDougall, from here a foreshortened jumble of scree and slabs.

On the north side of the valley is an enticing grass slope, not too steep, leading all the way up to your objective. Scattered crags high up are easily avoided by heading straight up a draw, then leftish toward the top. From high up it appears less tiring to traverse right below the summit crags, then cut left *behind them*, only there is no behind and the jagged right-hand skyline is the east ridge rising up from a col. Oops! My excuse to a friend faithfully following along behind was that the resulting scramble made for a more sporting finish.

The summit is mainly turf, a perfect grandstand seat for Old Baldy down below, showing the route up from the tarn. To its right is Old Baldy Peak, named by Andrew and rated a moderate scramble up the left skyline from Old Baldy.

Your summit is connected to a ridge circling around to Mt. McDougall. According to Rienk, it's a moderate scramble with the crux, an exposed step, occurring between Peak 362405 and the col below the summit.

Optional return to the left-hand fork

A Jekyll and Hyde descent route down the northwest flank opens up a 3.6 km loop from the forks.

An easy grass slope (the Jekyll bit) lures you down to a squared-off plateau above a drop-off where it is essential you descend the boulder slope between crags. However, pussyfooting from one tippy rock to another is jaw-clenching when you have to concentrate every inch of the way. Arrive on #42B just downstream from the tarn.

Below: The summit of Peak 357404, looking north to Old Baldy Peak.

Opposite top: #43. The return leg in the trees.

Opposite bottom: #43. View across the Kananaskis River towards Mt. Kidd.

43 Eau Claire Interpretive Trail map 3

Hour hike
Official trail
Distance 1.5 km loop
Map 82 J/14 Spray Lakes Reservoir

Access Hwy. 40 (Kananaskis Trail) at Eau Claire campground. Day visitors should park outside the gate.

Comments A flat and easy forest loop with interpretive signs alongside the Kananaskis River.

ANTI-CLOCKWISE

From the gate, walk along the left-hand campground road. Just after sign no. 40, turn second left onto the start of the trail. Straight off, from near the first interpretive sign with memorial bench, you get the much-photographed view of Mt. Kidd south, or *Istimabi Iyarhe* as the Stoneys call it, meaning "where one slept mountain." From this direction it displays some terrific examples of anticline–syncline pairs—folds to you and me—which are the northern termination of the Lewis thrust fault according to my geologist friends. From the low point in the syncline plummets Mt. Kidd Falls.

Moving on, you follow the bank of the Kananaskis River below the steep east face of the Spoon Needle, or Aiguille de la Cuiller as scramblers call it, though no one person will take credit for what is actually an appropriate name. Along this stretch, crumbling banks, interpretive signs in isolation and trail realignments post 2013 tell you the river is on its way back to the east side of the valley.

At interpretive sign no. 5, the trail turns away from the river into mixed forest with much deadfall, some of the burnt timber dating back to the inferno of 1936. Trees in this part of the valley have always had a hard time of it, what with repeated wildfires and with logging by the Eau Claire Lumber Company, which in the 1880s ran a camp on the site of the campground.

On the return leg the trail runs parallel to the winding, willowy bed of an old river channel, then crosses it before reaching the campground road close to your outgoing trail. Turn right for the trailhead.

44 Opal Ridge South map 3

Day scramble
Unofficial trail, route
Distance 4 km to high point
11.3 km loop
Height gain 1020 m (3346 ft.)
High point 2605 m (8547 ft.)
Map 82 J/14 Spray Lakes Reservoir

Access Hwy. 40 (Kananaskis Trail) at Fortress Junction gas station.

Comments Driving up Hwy. 40, I had often wondered if this route went. Could you get through the cliffs to the ridgetop? So one day we climbed it and discovered the "gates." We also found out this was no new discovery, but a well-used route taken by paragliders who jump off the top. Nowadays, it's the descent route for scramblers doing Opal Ridge North.

As you might deduce from the distance and height gain, it's a demanding trudge up a rough terrain of grass and scree to the ridge. But despite its spectacular appearance from the gas station, there's nothing to the ridge itself and no exposure to worry about. Consider the optional return down #44A Grizzly Creek (11.3 km loop).

To the ridge 2.5 km
From the parking lot hike up a small creek a way, then follow the left bank to the powerline access road. Turn left and walk along the road. Cross a side creek. On your right and facing the highway is an open, triangle-shaped slope bounded on either side by ridges that meet at the apex. Both ridges go. The left-hand ridge is grassier. But naturally, the nearer ridge is more commonly climbed, so turn first right onto the paragliders's trail.

This ridge is broad and loosely terraced with small rockbands. Initially the trail winds upward on grass. Halfway up, the terrain changes to scree and the trail splits, the result of people searching for ways up between higher, wider rockbands. Take whichever route appeals and don't forget to look out for a geocache holding such handy things as nail clippers.

Arrive at the apex. Continue up the short scree slope behind to a grassy top with an airy feel of being far above the cares of the world. From here a rounded ridge connects to the grass slope below huge free-standing cliffs, which some call pinnacles. Can you

get through? A trail climbs the slope and in a magical bit of route-finding by sheep wends right and up through "gates" totally invisible from down below. You arrive at another meadow, separated from Opal Ridge by a small band of crags. This the trail avoids by traversing way out to the right on orange screes to the low point of the ridge at 315281 where another surprise awaits. While the ridge facing Hwy. 40 is plated in vertical cliffs, the east side rolls in a friendly convex curve down to the meadows of upper Rocky Creek and is mainly grass.

Opal Ridge South 1.5 km

Turn right. The trail continues up the rounded ridge to the south, where I was ecstatic to find clumps of woolly fleabanes. The two highest tops are rocky and the sheep elect to traverse the east flank. It's much more fun, though, to walk the crest, which is easy and has a buffer zone between you and the plunging cliffs so you never have to look down.

Look back along Opal Ridge north toward The Wedge. To the south is a magnificent view of Kananaskis Lakes and the Opal Range, named erroneously by George Dawson in 1883 after he found quartzite crystals in the limestone coated with films of "opal." On our first visit to this summit it was a day of sun and storm, and across the dark range a constantly moving spotlight was fanning back and forth, illuminating each spectacular peak in turn. Entranced, we sat and watched the theatrics for an hour.

You can follow the ridge in its entirety to a much lower top at 322262, then drop easily onto the watershed between Rocky and Grizzly creeks for a spot of meadow wandering. But check for grizzlies first.

Returns

The watershed puts you in position to descend Grizzly Creek. See #44A. A few explorer types head north and descend Rocky Creek, all meadows to begin with. Lower down where the creek turns northwest through the narrows you're into umpteen creek crossings. See #38B.2. Both routes require a second vehicle or bikes.

Opposite: Looking up at The Gates from the apex of ascent ridges. Photo Gillian Ford

Above: Opal Ridge South, looking down to Rocky/Grizzly watershed at left and across to the Opal Range. Photo Gillian Ford

44A Grizzly Creek

Unofficial trail, then route
Distance 2.7+ km from watershed
Height loss 740 m (2428 ft.)

Comments I knew I'd find a use for Grizzly Creek parking lot someday! Should you return this way, it requires two cars, stashed bikes or a 3.3-km walk along Hwy. 40 back to Fortress Junction.

This steep V-shaped valley is not for the vertigo-challenged. The willowy creekbed has an impassable canyon. The intermittent sheep trail of the north bank is for scramblers. The only reasonable route is "the grizzly trail" of the south bank.

GOING DOWN

From the watershed, head south down the luxuriantly grassy slopes of Upper Grizzly Creek Valley. There's a trail, if you can find it, leading to a flat below small waterfalls. Cross the creek to the far south bank and continue on trail, passing between two big boulders into forest.

The trail traverses a deepening, steepening side slope. Cross two side creeks and a bit of talus, with the canyon far below and out of sight. Suddenly emerge near the top of the huge scree slope below the northern cliffs of Grizzly Peak, which is climbed from the other side via Ripple Rock Creek. The trail traverses the scree high up and it's here where you meet my nemesis: cement till with a sprinkling of ball bearings on top. The tread has gone and without crampons or claws it's easy to go for a bit of a skid. On the far side of this slope the trail descends steeply, zigs right, then traverses back left not far above the creek. (At this point a side trail descends into the creekbed.)

The much-improved traversing trail heads back into spruce forest interspersed with narrow avalanche chutes. At the end of this section it turns left to get onto the west slope of Grizzly Peak. This requires descending diagonally left between rockbands to the head of a tributary, then climbing up onto a bench. Here ends the trail, the game dispersing in all directions across a wide, grassy slope.

Turn right and find two cairns on the bench. From here it's an easy jaunt of 213 vertical metres down a benched slope of grass and aspens. Low down keep right to avoid small rockbands and emerge on the powerline right-of-way. Turn left to reach the parking lot.

Grizzly Creek, showing the big scree slope and steep ground below Grizzly Peak crossed by the trail.

45 Fortress Mountain Ski Area maps 3, 4

Long day hikes, bike 'n' hikes,
Official trails, unofficial trails, routes
Map 82 J/14 Spray Lakes Reservoir

Access Hwy. 40 (Kananaskis Trail). At Fortress Junction turn west onto the Fortress Mountain ski area access road. Park at the side of the road before the gate. The other option is to park at the Fortress Junction service station.

Comments The two routes described here have been walked since the ski resort (then named Snowridge) first opened in 1967 and were first described in the first edition of the KCTG in 1979. Since then, under various ownerships and between bankruptcies and temporary closures the public could still drive up the access road. That all changed in 2007 when the bridge over the Kananaskis River was condemned.

Access problems Enter Warner Bros. in 2009 to make a movie. As part of the agreement, they made some improvements to the road, while the owners of the assets made repairs to the bridge over the Kananaskis River for the benefit of the film crew. So, we can all drive up the road now that the bridge has been approved by Stantec? Nope! The SRD is keeping the road closed, with exceptions made for cat skiers, park researchers and film and television crews. Want to hike up there? At present, White Mountain Adventures of Banff has exclusive use of the road for its clients. Incidentally, a short ATV-assisted walk along the easy part of Fortress Ridge will set you back $950.

Access now Because the public still can't drive up the access road, this means the two routes have turned into long-day marathons. You have to ask yourself, can I hack another 8 kilometres one way and another 518 metres (1700 ft.) in height gain just to get up to the trailhead? Biking is the only way to go. At least the run back down should be fun. The road is also the access to Mt. Lawson, but luckily the turnoff point is only 15 minutes beyond the bridge.

Future plans According to Fortress Mountain Holdings, which has held the lease since 2010 and run a cat skiing operation there since 2011, December 2023 is the opening date for the rejuvenated fully fledged ski resort, but more likely it will be 2024 or later. No one is sure what the summer plans will be at this time, so stay tuned to our website.

#45A The cat track to Fortress Ridge winds all around the head of Aussie Creek. To right is an unusual view of Fortress Mountain.

Facilities The Lodge and condos are boarded up. Eventually, a new lodge will be built and the condos refurbished

Movies Apart from numerous beer and car commercials for TV, movies made here include *The Claim*, *Jumanji*, *Inception* and *The Revenant*.

Water Tidbit The "ski area" is allocated just under 100 million litres of water per year from Aussie Creek that flows into Galatea Creek. About half of that amount is trucked away to be bottled and marketed as "pure glacier-fed water" (which it isn't).

45A Getting to Fortress Ridge

Distance 3.4 km, plus 8 km of access road
Height gain 273 m (896 ft.), plus 518 m (1700 ft.) up the access road
Height loss 60 m (197 ft.)
High point 2316 m (7600 ft.)

Fortress Ridge, on the outer rim of the ski area, is the prerequisite to ##45B and C. It lies two ridges away from the parking lot to the northwest and is accessible by bike.

The access road 8 km
After crossing the Kananaskis River, the access road winds uphill through forest (corner 7 being the infamous bend) to the ski resort parking lot. In early summer look for the big waterfall below the cirque just north of Mount Lawson, flowing not from an unmapped lake as we had hoped, but from melting snow.

First ridge 400 m
From the top of the upper parking lot walk up the cat track to the right of a T-bar which may or may not have been replaced. Turn first left, cross the T-bar and paralleling it, head to the ridgetop. All the way, you pass below ski runs dropping off Canadian Ridge — the site of the grim-looking tower in the $20-million sci-fi movie *Inception*. Apparently, it took four tries to blow it up so it would fall down Canadian Run.

Cross the ridge at a low point and continue ahead, curving left and down to a T-junction. Keep left on the cat track. (The steep track to right leads past the reservoir and pumphouse to the lower terminal of Farside double chair in Aussie Creek's valley bottom. This was the setting for the 2000 movie *The Claim*, the narrows crammed with "houses" mimicking the 1840s Californian goldrush town of Kingdom Come.)

To Fortress Ridge 3 km
The cat track makes a very gradual descent across ski runs to the lower terminal of Backside double chair at the head of Aussie Creek. En route keep straight. Still on the cat track, cross Aussie Creek downstream of a small seasonal tarn unmarked on any map. Then start the winding climb onto Fortress Ridge, keeping left through spruce and larch forest at the edge of ski runs scraped down to the ground. The whole hillside extending to Farside double chair must have been stunningly beautiful once, glacier lilies filling every forest glade.

You reach the wide, grassy ridge near its low point and are treated to a remarkable view of the Opal Range to the southeast. Stop here or continue on to the upper terminal of Farside double chair.

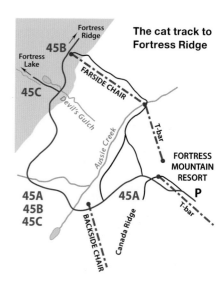

The cat track to Fortress Ridge

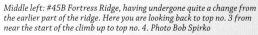

Top: #45B Fortress Ridge On top no. 1 "Baldy," looking down to the low point of the ridge and Fortress Lake in the cirque below The Fortress and Gusty Peak.

Middle left: #45B Fortress Ridge, having undergone quite a change from the earlier part of the ridge. Here you are looking back to top no. 3 from near the start of the climb up to top no. 4. Photo Bob Spirko

Middle right: ##45A and B The Mount Everest memorial cairn near the upper terminal of Farside double chair. Photo Jody Robbins

Right: ##45A and B Inscription on the cairn commemorating Sherpa Pasang Sona, who along with Sherpas Dawa Dorje and Ang Tsultim, lost his life in the Khumbu Icefall during the Canadian Mount Everest Expedition of 1982. On another facet of the cairn is a larger inscription dedicated to cameraman Blair Griffiths, who suffered the same fate a few days later. (See also #68.) Photo Jody Robbins

In the following two descriptions, distance, height loss and height gain are given from where you first reach Fortress Ridge.

45B Fortress Ridge

Scramble
Unofficial trail, route
Distance 5.4 km return from upper terminal of Farside double chair
Height gain/loss 244 m (800 ft.)
High point 2365 m (7760 ft.)

Comments The undulating ridge extending northeast from the upper terminal of Farside double chair ends at a superlative viewpoint overlooking the Kananaskis Valley at 264352. There is not much of a trail, nor is one needed, for the route over several tops is obvious and the going easy at first. Later, the ridge becomes steeper and rockier with the odd scramble step.

Follow the cat track to the upper terminal of Farside double chair. Nearby is a large memorial cairn commemorating Blair Griffiths and three Sherpas who lost their lives on Everest in 1982. Look closely. The cairn is built of wood, the "rocks" are styrofoam look-alikes glued to the wood, the whole most obviously a prop left over from the movies. Only the inscriptions are genuine.

Fortress Ridge from Hwy. 40, showing the fourth top at right. The Fortress appears above the ridge at left.

Heading northeast, walk along a broad, grassy ridge to top no. 1 — the highest — which the ski staff call "Baldy." Already there is a fabulous view of The Fortress and Fortress Lake below it.

After the next grassy hump (top no. 2), a rocky descent of 120 m brings you to the lowest point of the ridge, which is identified by larches spilling over from the east slope.

Climb a long, grassy slope to top no. 3. Suddenly, a change comes over the ridge: the ridge narrows and the slopes on either side steepen into cliff bands. A rock step immediately above the 3/4 col is avoided by a scramble down a grassy gully on the right (east) side. From the col it's a sometimes narrow but straightforward climb up black-lichened rocks to the fourth and final top.

Viewed from your island in the sky, the Kananaskis Country golf course is spread out below you like a screenshot from Google Earth. Look across to Mt. Kidd and up both forks of Galatea Creek. The trail climbing to Guinn's Pass is easily picked out. Of all the surrounding mountains none is more dramatic than The Fortress to the west. To the east and easily glossed over as you happily scan the higher mountains is the little peak across the valley at 27934. When you drive north up Hwy. 40 from Fortress Junction, though, this little peak assumes an awesome needle-like shape. Scramblers call it Spoon Needle, or Aiguille de la Cuiller, and rate the traverse as moderate with slightly exposed sections.

45C Fortress Lake

*Fortress Lake below The Fortress
(out of sight at far left) and Gusty Peak.*

Unofficial trail
Distance 3 km return from the ridge
Height loss/gain 122 m (400 ft.)
High point 2301 m (7550 ft.) on
Fortress Ridge

Comments An easy downhill hike with one steep hill to a lake tucked under the northern cliffs of The Fortress.

From Fortress Ridge, don't continue along the cat track to the upper terminal of Farside double chair. Cut off left to the low point in the ridge, which is occupied by a tarn feeding Devil's Gulch.

Dropping into the valley to the north (a south fork of Galatea Creek) is straightforward via a trail that starts from the far end of the tarn.

Initially it follows the right bank of a westbound creek to a fabulous viewpoint of your objective. Then entering trees, it zigs right and returns to the creek in one steep, shaley drop. The creek is crossed three times

en route to valley bottom meadows where the trail turns left and in less than half a kilometre reaches a junction with creel box. Go either way; both trails lead to the lakeshore.

This inky-blue lake has a spectacular setting under the shadowy north cliffs of The Fortress. If you want to get both the mountain and the lake in the same pic, make sure you have wide angle. And bring binoculars to look for goats wandering the ledges.

The mountain to the right of Fortress is Gusty Peak and in between the two is a col guarded by a vertical cliff. In a bravura piece of climbing in 1957, guide Hans Gmoser and two clients climbed the cliff en route to the first ascent of The Fortress — a route unlikely to be repeated when the southwest ridge is available as a walk-up. They called their mountain The Tower, a name later transposed to the peak above Rummel Pass.

46 King Creek Canyon

map 5

Half-day hike
Unofficial trail
Distance 1.6 km to forks,
2.1 km to religious site
Height gain to forks 122 m (400 ft.),
to religious site 229 m (750 ft.)
High point at forks 1814 m (5950 ft.),
at religious site 1905 m (6250 ft.)
Map 82 J/11 Kananaskis Lakes

Access Hwy. 40 (Kananaskis Trail) at King Creek day-use area.
Also accessible from #48 Opal traverse.

Comments Spectacular King Creek canyon leads to the forks and the beautiful country of the north fork hidden behind the outliers of the Opal Range — the domain of grizzlies and sheep. Part of the way is on old interpretive trail. When the bridges were demolished by the 1995 floods, the trail was demoted and the final interpretive sign about this trail being a grizzly highway was moved to Rawson Lake trail. Nevertheless, the route is still incredibly popular with adventurous hikers who more often than not are making the Stoney religious site their destination.

The many creek crossings have temporary log bridges of the tightrope variety. By late summer you can usually rock hop. Another good time to visit is winter when ice climbers have beaten down a trail.

King Creek accesses climber's routes in the Opals and the scrambler's route up Mt. Hood.

Naming "King's Creek" was named after Millarville rancher Willie King, who accompanied George Pocaterra and party on their quest for coal in the Pocaterra Creek area.

The Canyon to the Forks 1.6 km

The trail leaves the far end of the parking lot in good shape but gradually deteriorates after entering the canyon proper, where it is forced back and forth across the creek 10 times. The narrows is reached after crossing no. 9. This entails an easy scramble on polished rock along the left bank. One more crossing, then a longer stint along the right bank brings you to the forks. Thus far there have been tantalizing glimpses of Mt. Blane and The Blade. Now the Opal Range is more fully revealed from Mt. Hood to Mt. Jerram and is particularly spectacular at gaudy sunset.

To the Stoney religious site 500 m

Cross the south fork on logs to a junction. Ignore the trail to left. The trail ahead leads to the Stoney religious site, initially a steep flog up the high, grassy bank on eroded trail. This is where anyone who's worn flip-flops for the creek section will have a problem.

At the top, turn left and climb a little more into the forest to the left of the grassy slope. In a few minutes come to many trees wrapped with cloth, ribbons and socks. Often called prayer flags, they can signify any number of religious events, be it a vision quest or the giving and receiving of a blessing. The trail continuing on is the scrambler's access route to Mt. Blane.

GOING FARTHER OR NOT?

The trail heading left up the north fork to the col between King Creek Ridge and Mt. Hood quickly runs afoul of avalanche and flood debris. (See #47 King Creek Ridge and page 133 in the 4th edition.) Most of the mountain approaches use game trails crossing north slope meadows.

The longer route up the south fork to the Wintour/Jerram col has no trail at creek level and requires numerous creek crossings. (See #48 Opal Traverse.)

Opposite: The cliffs rising above the canyon.

Top: Scrambling around the narrows.

Bottom: Stoney prayer flags. They are never taken down, but are left to fade and rot in the elements. They should be shown "due respect, the same as any other religious object and left inviolate."

47 King Creek Ridge map 5

Day hike
Unofficial trail
Distance 3.5 km to summit
Height gain 742 m (2435 ft.)
High point 2434 m (7986 ft.)
Map 82 J/11 Kananaskis Lakes

Access Hwy. 40 (Kananaskis Trail) at King Creek day-use area.

Comments The ridge north of King Creek, also called *Kiska tha Iyarhe,* or "Goat Mountain" by the Stoneys, is a strenuous climb on trail to a fantastic viewpoint. Watch for flagging and cairns.

   Trail Update After the 2013 flood the return route via the north fork of King Creek is even worse than before and has therefore been omitted from this edition.

West flank to SSE ridge 2 km
Start from the segment of old highway on the north bank of King Creek. This is most easily accomplished by returning to the present highway, crossing the bridge and climbing the bank. At a survey marker go straight (segment of old road to the left) and

The ridge below the main summit.

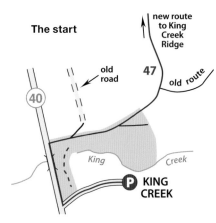

follow the grassy old road above King Creek. Very shortly, turn left on a trail that climbs into the trees. Keep left at the junction a little way in. (To right is the old route.) Now you're set for 564 m (1850 ft.) of height gain!

   The new trail starts by traversing to the north. Finally it decides to head up the west face and launches into a set of steep little zigs with stones underfoot. There's a brief respite after "the big step" where you cross a dell and enter flowery meadows. Resume zigzagging, and where the trail is crossed

by game trails go uphill at every option. The trail then heads up left into a traverse line with trees—a welcome relief on a hot day.

Enter a new meadow—the ridge crest seemingly as far away as ever. A few uphill zigs leads into a long, rising traverse to the right. After this ends, climb up the fall line in trees, the main trail again twisting its way uphill to the SSE ridge. Near the top you navigate past two cairns to the ridge trail. The junction is presently unmarked. Turn left (north). An "arrow" on the ground is something to look for on the descent.

SSE ridge to summit 1.5 km

Now for the payoff! Follow the ridge trail, keeping left at a split. Soon you're out of the trees and enjoying a curving, grassy ridge with cliffs down the left side. Look back down the ridge and across the gulf of King Creek canyon to the mountain shaped like whipped ice cream or the Matterhorn—take your pick. Mt. Wintour was named after the captain of the ill-fated HMS *Tipperary* that sank during the Battle of Jutland in 1916. Strangely, the ship is commemorated miles away across the other side of the Divide in B.C.

The main summit cairn. Looking back down the ridge toward Wintour at right. To left is Mt. Blane and through the gap of Opal–King Pass, Elpoca Mtn.

Reach a top with a few trees and a cairn. Descend slightly and then climb a broader grass ridge to the main summit cairn. Five minutes on there's a second rocky summit with drop-offs on three sides; not a place to drop your apple.

All the way up you've been ogling the Opals' hacksawed peaks. Virtually all the first ascents were made during the 1950s, one of the last to fall being The Blade, that impressive gendarme on the south ridge of Blane. The best view is reserved for the summits. Now you can look without obstructions to the north and southwest, where an immense ocean of conifers extends past Kananaskis Lakes to the mountains of the Elk.

Return

Returning the same way is much the easier option. If you really, really want to descend into the north fork of King Creek and return by that route see the 4th edition, page 133.

48 Opal Traverse map 5

Long day hike
Unofficial trails
Distance 12.6 km
Height gain S-N 960 m (3150 ft.)
Height loss S-N 1219 m (4000 ft.)
High point at Pocaterra-Elpoca Pass
2414 m (7920 ft.)
Map 82 J/11 Kananaskis Lakes

Access Hwy. 40 (Kananaskis Trail).
South Little Highwood Pass parking lot at the junction with Valleyview Trail the road.
North King Creek day-use area.
Middle Valleyview Trail the road at Elpoca day-use area.
NOTE: Hwy. 40 south of Kananaskis Lakes Trail is closed December 1–June 15. Valleyview Trail closes even earlier on Sept. 30. See Access note.

Comments That wild country of larches and meadows hidden behind the outliers of the Opal Range is only for experienced wilderness addicts who can navigate without trails if necessary. In fall when the larches are gaudy and the sky is blue, this is a hiker's heaven. At such times take care not to linger overlong or like us you'll be navigating King Creek canyon in the pitch black of night. If this is your plan take headlamps and Tevas for umpteen creek crossings. Most sensible people forgo the King Creek bit and exit by Opal Creek to Valleyview road.

Basically the route runs from Little Highwood Pass day-use area to King Creek parking lot on the line of the Lewis thrust fault, says Gord, so you will of course require two vehicles or bikes. If you escape down Opal Creek Valley expect a bit of road bashing to get to Elpoca day-use area.

A word on distance, height gain and height loss — those given under the main heading are the maximum and can be cut down by taking one of the options I give between cols. Even so, the whole outing is quite strenuous, because you can't avoid that first col, which is the scrambler's route to Gap Mountain and is by far the steepest pull of the day.

Access note Valleyview Trail the road is closed to vehicles between Elpoca day-use area and Little Highwood Pass parking lot. When roadkill is dumped on this stretch of road, it is closed to ALL users. Periodically, the whole road is closed. So before you set out it pays to check out its status.

Background For background on this fascinating area read *Kananaskis Ram* by Ernst Hanisch, a true story dating back to 1943 when the author was a POW at Camp 130 in the Kananaskis Valley. I am still waiting for this gut-wrenching story to be picked up by a film producer and set to the music of John Williams. The quieter section of *The Cowboys Overture* is perfect: you can easily imagine the progeny of Ernst's three-legged ram filing quietly along the old trails under the pale peaks of the Opals, the mist swirling about and ultimately hiding them from view just as the final credits roll. Just remember you read it here first, okay?

A very foreshortened view looking up the ascent gully to Pocaterra-Elpoca west col at left. One can also get onto the ridge at far right and follow that up to the high point between the west and east cols.

SOUTH TO NORTH
Pocaterra–Elpoca Col (38413)

Distance 1.7 km
Height gain 488 m (1600 ft.)
High point 2414 m (7920 ft.)

Above the parking lot is a steep slope seamed by three major gullies and you're going up the middle one. This is the scrambler's direct route to the ridge connecting Gap and Elpoca mountains, which is Pocaterra-Elpoca west col, and the highest point on the traverse at 2414 m. In these gullies George Pocaterra mined for coal from his cabin down in Pocaterra Creek.

From the parking lot head west along Valleyview Trail for about 200 m. Just past the road sign on the right turn right into the bush on a trail. Shortly the trail enters the middle gully that takes you all the way to the col. Keep right at a fork low down, then left higher up. Above the second fork the angle steepens to shale — great fun to run down but a pain in the calf muscles going up. NOTE: Just after passing the left fork there is the option of taking to the grass and tree ridge on the right.

Played out on Pocaterra-Elpoca Col below Gap Mtn after the big pull up from the highway.

Top out on the west side of the pass under Gap Mountain — a moderate scramble with a summit register.

While climbing the mountain called 'Gap,'
A fellow once took a big crap,
he said, "Holy cripes!
I didn't bring wipes!"
He now has a brown topo map!

Scramblers will know who the limerick writer is, so enough said!

Turn your back on Gap and head over a hump to the east side col under Elpoca Mountain (cairn). A coal outcrop halfway along is a fabulous place from which to view Highwood Pass and Pocaterra Ridge. From here Pocaterra took a photo of this same view sans the road. He called Gap Mountain "George" and Elpoca Mountain "Paul" after his Stoney blood brother Paul Amos, but nothing ever came of this self-indulgence. NOTE: To see the remains of Pocaterra's cabin in Pocaterra Creek turn to page 187.

The larch ridge en-route to Elpoca-Opal Col.

To Elpoca–Opal Col (378159)
High point 2362 m (7750 ft.)

This section crosses the head of Elpoca Creek below the magnificent west face of Elpoca Mountain.

From the cairn, head northeast on a trail that descends very steeply for a short while on shale. Arrive on a little ridge at 384135 dividing the east and south forks of Elpoca Creek. There are two routes onward. (Distance, height gain and height loss are given between cols.)

1. Ridge route 3.5 km, height loss 381 m (1250 ft.), height gain 320 m (1050 ft.) You are most tempted to follow the trail along the little ridge in the larches. The trail eventually drops off the end to the east fork (water). Rather than join the main valley of Elpoca Creek, which is close by at this point, cross the east fork and, using one of many game trails, traverse to gain the valley farther upstream past the confluence with its wee north fork, which arises from the col at 370155.

Continue along the right bank, later transferring to the left bank below a big grassy hill. Where the valley turns left return to the right bank. Not too far along, avalanche debris forces the trail up the right side of some scree to an intersection with a traversing trail — the east fork route. Turn left.

2. East Fork route 3 km, height loss 259 m (850 ft.), height gain 198 m (650 ft.) From where you gained the larch ridge at 384135, descend the right (northeast) side of it into the upper east fork, which is all meadow. Walk down valley. Where the east fork turns left through a gap, pick up the traversing trail heading straight for the next col. Cross two narrow scree fans. Keep straight at the junction where the ridge route joins in.

Routes united, the trail crosses more scree to a flat meadow at the base of the final rise. En route look up right to the ridgeline. Spot the window? A short climb up shale gains you the grassy col at 2362 m below the steep east face of Elpoca Creek Hill. Ahead lies the Kananaskis Ram country of Opal Creek.

Climbing to Elpoca-Opal Col.

To Opal–King Col (368170)
High point 2332 m (7650 ft.)

This section crosses the head of Opal Creek below Mt. Schlee to the col between Mt. Wintour and Cats Ears. There are two ways of tackling it: the direct and straightforward descent to Opal Creek Valley and ascent to the col; and the very much more convoluted traverse with its numerous game trails.

1. Direct route 1.6 km, height loss 183 m (600 ft.), height gain 152 m (500 ft.) Descend the trail to the head of the valley. Cross Opal Creek (water) and simply climb up the other side through meadows and larches to the col.

2. The traverse 1.9 km, height loss ~15 m (50 ft.), height gain ~30 m (100 ft.) Head right on a trail that traverses a gullied shale slope to the third, more deeply incised gully. Descend a little before crossing into larches. On the other side the trail starts heading uphill, so leave it and cross a scree fan. Come to the main fork with water.

Cross and climb uphill a little, then traverse left across meadow. In the trees pick up a trail crossing a shallow gully and climbing steeply up the left side of it. Shortly it cuts back left on a traverse line. Before a final gully, climb a shaley slope a short way, then again cut left above the gully to reach the grass and larch ridge that is the col. Walk down to the lowest point. Look back for a superb view of Elpoca Mountain through the gap.

South Fork of King Creek
Distance 3.9 km
Height loss 509 m (1670 ft.) to forks, 655 m (2150 ft.) to trailhead

The miserable forest section with no trail and innumerable creek crossings.

Head north down open larch forest to the infant south fork of King Creek, which comes in from the right off Mt. Jerram. Beyond the shale slope, cross to the right bank and for some time after cross back and forth across the creek in a dark forest.

On Opal-King Col, looking back to Elpoca-Opal Col and Elpoca Mountain. To right of the pass is the hill climbed in #49.

Opposite: #48A The fantastic rock scenery above the canyon of Opal Creek.

Progress slows with the start of crags along the left bank. Added to the creek crossings is avalanche debris, plain old deadfall, stones and willow bush. Conditions ease just before reaching the forks. Aim to be on the left bank because this puts you in position to hike the canyon section to King Creek parking lot. (See #46.) Only another 1.6 km and 10 creek crossings to go.

USUAL ESCAPE ROUTE
48A Opal Creek
Distance 3.5 km from Opal Creek

From Elpoca-Opal Col, use route 1 into the head of Opal Creek and turn left down valley, later using a trail on the right bank. What a beautiful place of meadows, larches and spruce. Lower down, though, a shadow falls over the valley. Not only is it narrowing but avalanche chutes follow one after the other all the way down to the drop-off place above Whiteman (Opal) Falls. After the trail crosses the creek to the left bank, either traverse avalanche slopes about 30 m up or muddle through the valley bottom to the death place of the Kananaskis Ram above the drop-off. Now what?

Trust the sheep, which have spent thousands of years perfecting routes around the impasse. Climb the sheep trail up the left (east) bank avalanche slope. The trail eventually cuts right to another avalanche slope, then descends low down, deking left through an unsuspected gap between cliffs into the head of a dry canyon — an awesome place of ruddy-hued cliffs thrust vertically into columns. Still the trail continues, climbing along the top edge of the left-hand cliff and around a slit to a tree blazed with a cross on the western rim.

This marks the spot where sheep and scramblers can slither down a stony gully to Elpoca day-use area. If you don't feel comfortable doing this, follow the rim trail in a southerly direction and lose height gradually. Low down beyond residual cliffs, circle left around a bog, then turn right and perhaps on elk trail descend to Valleyview Trail the road, reached about 300 m north of Elpoca Creek at a place impossible to pinpoint.

Turn right and walk the road to Elpoca day-use area. (Open June 15–Sept. 3).

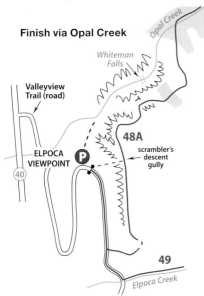

49 Elpoca Creek Hill

map 5

Day hike
Unofficial trails & route
Distance 4.3 km to summit
Height gain ~670 m (2200 ft.)
High point 2493 m (8180 ft.)
Map 82 J/11 Kananaskis Lakes

Access Valleyview Trail the road off Hwy. 40. Drive to Elpoca day-use area at the gate. NOTE: Valleyview Trail the road and Hwy. 40 south of Kananaskis Lakes Trail are closed December 1–June 15.

Comments Rough terrain with intermittent game trails make this trip up Elpoca Creek one for experienced wilderness hikers. While linking up with route #48 would seem an obvious thing to do, the big grassy hill that rises west of Elpoca-Opal Pass at 376167 is a far finer objective. Climbing the hill AND making a loop with Opal Creek is another possibility.

Access note Since the last edition the road has been closed to vehicles between Elpoca day-use area and Little Highwood Pass parking lot. When roadkill is dumped on this stretch of road, the road is closed to ALL users. It is worrying that even when it is open, grizzlies will have become so conditioned to meals on wheels they will be hotfooting it down there just for a look-see. Bring bear spray.

Walk or bike south along Valleyview Trail the road for 1 km to Elpoca Creek (crossed by a bridge above a fine waterfall). The trail starts from a small parking area on the near left (north) side of the bridge.

The good north bank trail heads east into the valley confines between Gap Mountain and the grey rocky ridge to the north. All too soon it descends to creek level where you become mired in willow brush. Either struggle through the valley bottom or climb the steep, grassy bank to left and pick up traversing game trails, keeping right and down as you near the confluence with a wee north fork that arises from a col.

The higher west top from near the saddle.

Cross the north fork and climb the hill's south ridge on grass to the saddle between the two tops. The east summit to right is narrow, a cairn balanced on top of a rockband overlooking Elpoca-Opal Col. The west summit to left is the higher. From both vantage points Gap and Elpoca mountains appear spectacular. Looking west between nearby heights, you can spot Mt. Abruzzi with Pass in the Clouds to its right.

Returns

From the west summit descend to the col at 370155. Turn left and descend to your ascent route. Alternatively, turn right and descend a much steeper, furrowed slope of larches to Opal Creek Valley and return via #48A.

50 Elbow Lake

map 6

Half day, day hike
Official trail
Distance 1.4 km to lake
Height gain 140 m (459 ft.) to lake
High point 2088 m (6850 ft.)
Maps 82 J/11 Kananaskis Lakes,
82 J/10 Mt. Rae

Access Hwy. 40 (Kananaskis Trail) at the greatly enlarged Elbow Pass parking lot. NOTE: This section of Hwy. 40 is closed December 1–June 15.

Comments This colourful lake is incredibly popular, in part because the access trail is so short. It is steep, though, and crowded. Be alert for such things as fishing rods, skis and poles, snowboards, horses, descending bikers and swinging Safeway bags packed with picnic lunches.

Officially, the access is part of Big Elbow trail (see Volume 2), but most visitors just go as far as the lake. Lose the crowds by heading to the Rae Glacier or down Big Elbow trail toward Tombstone backcountry campground. Farther away destinations off Big Elbow trail include Piper Creek described in Volume 2 and Lake Rae via the Elbow-Sheep Cutoff described in Volume 4, both of which are usually accessed from this trailhead as very long day trips or backpacks.

Facilities Elbow Lake backcountry campground. Lockers and separate cooking areas.

Straight from the parking lot it's a mostly steep uphill climb through forest and below talus slopes on a stony trail that was once a fire road. En route to a flat area under an avalanche slope falling from Little Arethusa, pass caution signs and a well-placed memorial bench.

Elbow Lake, looking from the west shore toward the Mt. Rae massif, which can be seen to better advantage from the end of the lake.

Starting uphill again, the trail turns left, then right, crossing over a ridge — Elbow Pass proper — to the lake's southwest corner. For the campground turn right. The high-tech Phoenix composting toilet is worth seeing and can shelter 10 people in a storm.

Otherwise, stay left and dawdle along the west shoreline to where scree slopes shelve into translucent blue-green water. The lake's colour was described on a 1931 Belmore Browne family painting trip as "much finer than Lake O'Hara," but has turned a little greener in recent years.

GOING FARTHER

50A Rae Glacier

Unofficial trail & route
Distance 5.7 km return from Elbow Lake,
8.4 km return from Hwy. 40
Height gain from lake 260 m (853 ft.),
400 m (1312 ft.) from Hwy. 40
High point 2316 m (7600 ft.)

Comments A very popular side trip with campers, and while the shorter of the two options, it involves a lot more effort and a lot of walking on cobbles and scree, even more so after the 2013 flood had a go at wrecking the trail. Interestingly, G G, an avid hiker and wine afficionado who believes in "matching wine with hikes," suggests taking along the full-bodied 2011 Chante Cigale from the Châteauneuf-du-Pape vineyards in France, because the cobbles there remind him of the stony creekbed approach!

The glacier I'm told the glacier has shrunk by 50% over the last century. There are even differences to be noted between editions of this book. Some may find this disappointing, because having once occupied the floor of the cirque, the glacier now clings to its back wall, the lower section of it covered in scree but betrayed on the surface by the dark slits of crevasses.

Start out on the east shore trail beyond campsite no. 15 on what is nowadays the main Rae Glacier trail. In an open area the trail turns right and heads northeast to the fledgling Elbow River issuing from Mt. Rae. The next stretch of trail has largely has been washed away by flood waters, the cobbles spread far and wide across the valley into the trees. Follow flagging and cairns on the right side. Where the valley pinches in at a mini-canyon, the resurrected trail climbs steeply up a rib to a fabulous viewpoint for mounts Elpoca, Tombstone and Rae.

Continue on grass through last trees into the stony upper creekbed, here enclosed by steep banks. The going gets a little slapdash where a new trail had to be forged after the flood along rocks at the water's edge.

Where the creek and trail divide at a flat, keep right (east cirque trail to left). Climb moraines below a crag, then zig up just left of the crag and across moraines to reach the glacier viewpoint.

Down below you is a muddy pond that dries by fall. Ahead, and still a little distance away, the back wall of the cirque holding the remnant of glacier rears up like the wave in *The Perfect Storm* to a col reached from the Ptarmigan Cirque side by scramblers bound for Mount Rae. It was here on August 1, 2018, that horrified hikers witnessed the fiery crash of a twin engine Piper into the side of the mountain.

SIDE TRIP TO EAST CIRQUE

Judging by the amount of water issuing from the east cirque, the névés below the summit of Mt. Rae are the main source of the Elbow River nowadays. At the creek and trail division go left and cross the wee stream issuing out of the moraines of the Rae Glacier cirque. Still on the flat, either cross the east fork to the left bank trail if you want a close-up of the falls, or if climbing into the cirque use the upper right bank trail which is a lot easier than the trail nearer the falls.

The cirque offers only scree and a foreshortened view of the summit, though I did stumble across an optimistic four-inch-high tree poking up between the rocks quite high up.

Plane crashed here out of sight

Bottom: The diminishing Rae Glacier from the viewpoint. Photo by Bill Rowe, who has marked on the crash site of the Piper aircraft just a few days after the incident.

Top left: Climbing out of the trees onto the moraines, Mt. Rae above.

Top right: People hanging out at the waterfalls below the east cirque. See SIDE TRIP.

Desolation Flat, looking north to Tombstone Mountain. Take the bypass trail to the left.

50B To Tombstone backcountry campground

Official trail
Distance 6.1 km from Elbow Lake,
7.4 km from Hwy. 40
Height loss from lake 229 m (750 ft.)
High point 2316 m (7600 ft.)

Comments The easiest of the options continues to follow the fire road down the valley of the upper Elbow between Elpoca Mountain and Mount Rae, and is the usual route in and out of Tombstone backcountry campground from Hwy. 40. En route are turnoffs to Piper Creek (Volume 2), Elbow-Sheep cut-off to Lake Rae and Sheep trail (Volume 4). Most people just go as far as Desolation Flat or Edworthy Falls.

To Sheep trail west 6.5 km

Use the west shore trail to reach the end of the lake. Cross a plank over the outlet and turn left onto Big Elbow trail.

After crossing a willowy flat, the fire road enters trees and starts descending. When you first enter grass meadows known as Desolation Flats, use the bypass trail to left. Other bypasses farther on are not worth taking, generally. Pass Elpoca Mountain and its tower, then look left through the valley of Piper Creek to Cats Ears. Tombstone Mountain lies ahead.

Once again, trees line the fire road. A cairn at 4.8 km from the highway signals Edworthy Falls to left. A smaller cairn to left at 5.2 km is the start to Piper Creek trail. Only 50 m on, a cairn to right is where you follow the Elbow-Sheep cutoff to Lake Rae.

Leaving Tombstone and all the peaks of Mount Rae behind, come to a T-junction with Sheep trail west on a banktop overlooking the flats of the Elbow River.

To campground 1 km

Turn left and descend off the bank. Zig right onto the flats and cross two channels of the Elbow on bridges. Then climb past the ranger cabin access road to the campground on the right. NOTE: A narrow trail heading right just before the cabin road takes you directly to the campsites.

Left: Edworthy Falls.

51 Ptarmigan Cirque map 6

Half day
Official trail
Distance 3.6 km return
Height gain 220 m (722 ft.)
High point 2420 m (7940 ft.)
Map 82 J/10 Mt. Rae

Access Hwy. 40 (Kananaskis Trail) at Highwood Pass parking lot.
NOTE: this section of Hwy. 40 is closed December 1–June 15.

Comments A short and very popular trail from Canada's highest navigable pass into alpine meadows below Mt. Rae. With most of the height gain occurring within the first kilometre, this trail is no pushover; there's a little uphill work to be done before you reap your reward.

Also the scrambler's access to Mt. Rae, the highest peak east of Hwy. 40.

To the high point 1.8 km

Follow the trail over the bridge into the meadows. Stay on the main trail. At a junction atop a rise, turn right and cross the highway. (The boardwalk ahead is the very short Highwood Meadows trail leading to interpretive signs.)

Soon start a zigzagging climb through fir and spruce forest. High up at 1.1 km is a T-junction with the return loop. Keep left.

After one more zig the gradient eases and you enter the cirque. As you wander across flowery meadows, Mt. Rae comes into view ahead, not the summit but the lower summit known as "The Pinnacle." Nearing the turnaround point, scramble up a step to a post at a 3-way. Go straight. (Left is #51A.)

Return 1.8 km

Descend above a small waterfall, then turn right and walk the top of a lateral moraine below the cliffs of Little Arethusa. Ahead is a new view across Highwood Pass of Highwood Ridge, Grizzly Peak, Mt. Tyrwhitt and Pocaterra Ridge. Under your feet keep an eye out for picas, marmots and ground squirrels scurrying about between rocks and pockets of grass and flowers.

Crossing the meadows of Ptarmigan Cirque, Kings Ridge in the background.

Above: Just after recrossing the creek, the trail descends last meadows back into forest.

Below: A hot day on the moraines.

The wonderfully camouflaged and unwary Ptarmigan are much harder to spot.

Descend and recross the creek above a mini canyon, then after further descending, come to a junction. The offshoot to left leads to a bench overlooking a vertical step in the creek—a waterfall early in the season. Return to the trail, and carry on downhill through last meadows into the trees. At the T-junction turn left and retrace your steps to the parking lot.

GOING HIGHER

51A The Moraines

Unofficial trail
Distance 600 m
Height gain 120 m (394 ft.)
High point 2540 m (8333 ft.)

Comments A very popular add-on along the first section of the Mt. Rae trail.

From the high point of the interpretive trail at the post, turn left on a trail heading farther into the cirque. The going is easy to the upper waterfall where a large percentage of people call it a day.

Continue up the steeper shale and scree trail to the left of the terminal moraine. When level with the moraine top take one of two side trails heading right that climb onto a rocky high point with cairn.

Stop here or wander even farther into the head of the cirque, meandering around a few sinks plugged with snow. The farther you go the better the view of the Mt. Rae scramble up to the col. The ridge ahead is Kings Ridge, named after High River's Don King who in the 1940s with a few friends traversed the ridge numerous times in an attempt to climb Mt. Rae from the Sheep River side. Each time they were thwarted by "The pinnacle." Today's route totally bypasses this impasse on the left side.

Day hike
Unofficial trail
Distance 8.8 km return
Height gain 620 m (2034 ft.)
High point 2674 m (8773 ft.)
Map 82 J/10 Mt. Rae

Access Hwy. 40 (Kananaskis Trail) at Highwood Pass parking lot.
NOTE: This section of Hwy. 40 is closed December 1–June 15.

Comments The trail into the beautiful head-waters of Pocaterra Creek is a popular one, particularly at larch time when a walk through one of K Country's premier larch forests has become an annual ritual. Some people just go as far as Pocaterra Tarn; many others go on to the highest summit of Pocaterra Ridge, described under #52A.

This trail also serves as a base trail for Highwood Ridge (#57), Little Highwood Pass (#54) and Grizzly Col (#55). It is also the scrambler's access to Mt. Tyrwhitt for people doing the "Kanes."

To Highwood Ridge junction 1 km

Follow the trail over the bridge into the meadows. A junction marked by a sign "Stay on the trail" is where you turn left onto a single track running through a grassy meltwater channel—the original pack horse route over Highwood Pass predating roads. At a boulder the trail heads left into the forest and meanders along to a 4-way. Turn left up the fall line. At the top of a very muddy hill is an important T-junction. Go straight. (The major-looking trail to left is the route to Highwood Ridge. It is also the original route into the cirque and no longer used as such except by ill-informed hikers.)

To Pocaterra Tarn 1.1 km

The latest best trail descends and rises a little, then descends at a reasonable gradient past the bottom junction with the original trail onto a lush avalanche slope bisected by a muddy creeklet, growing

Pocaterra Tarn in fall with Little Arethusa and Mt. Arethusa behind. At right is the north ridge of Highwood Ridge described under #57.

long-stemmed forget-me-nots, smelly cow parsley and large-leafed ragworts. The going is flat across meadow and a few rocks into larch forest, the trail ultimately twisting down to the south fork of Pocaterra Creek. Climb up its left bank, then cross to the right bank shortly before the creek is concealed by rubble. A few minutes later arrive at Pocaterra Tarn, located between larches and scree slopes. In the height of summer the scree is a riot of pink mountain fireweed.

To Grizzly Col junction in the upper cirque 610 m
The trail semicircles the tarn and climbs between scree and larches, eventually turning right into a big flat meadow with a view of Pocaterra Ridge's highest summit, from this direction a big grassy pudding of a hill. Likely you will see a procession of hikers strung out along the left-hand ridge.

Above: The highest summit of Pocaterra Ridge from the flat meadow in glorious summer. The ascent route follows the left-hand ridge.

Opposite top: The summit view in late fall. Looking across to Grizzly Col and Grizzly Peak.

Opposite bottom: #52A Coming up to the shoulder in late fall when the grass is brown, Little Highwood Pass to left. The south ridge is often snow free when everywhere else in snow covered.

52A Pocaterra Ridge Summit

Distance 4 km return from tarn
Height gain 430 m (81410 ft.) above tarn
High point 2678 m (8786 ft.)

Comments Many hikers continue along the trail to the highest summit of Pocaterra Ridge. While lacking any technical difficulties — the ascent route follows the grass and shale of the south ridge — there are enough steep stretches to give you a good workout.

Other than retrace your steps, you can continue on along Pocaterra Ridge via #53 in reverse. The distance is only 1 km longer, assuming you have a second vehicle at Little Highwood Pass day-use area or are willing to hitch a ride.

To Little Highwood Pass junction
At a Y-junction with cairn at 407063 you can choose between two ongoing trails. Left is the Grizzly Col trail.

1. Popular route 360 m Keep right, walking flat meadow to the left of the west fork of Pocaterra Creek. Cross a side creek emanating from rocks which appears to carry water seeping underground from

Grizzly Col. To avoid a problem area in the west fork up ahead, climb a steep, muddy hill up left into a bumpy area of rocks. Arriving in a flat strip of meadow below a terminal moraine, turn right. This is where route 2 joins in from the left, though very faintly in grass.

2. Lesser used route 470 m Go left, climbing Grizzly Col trail through a larch avenue. On reaching meadow, leave the trail and head right (no trail) below a high wall of terminal moraine. Thread a few rocks into a flat, longitudinal meadow which is traversed by a faint trail to its far end where route 1 joins in from the right.

After the two routes unite, the trail climbs to a junction on a ridge. Left leads to Little Highwood Pass (see #54). Go straight.

Almost at once the trail descends and crosses the west fork. This is where the serious climbing begins: a steep climb up the lower south ridge. Stay on the ridge crest. Don't be tempted by trails wandering off to the right. Easier going brings you to the shoulder, where a game trail traverses left across the west slope to Little Highwood Pass. Once again the ridge steepens, a calf muscle burner up a twisty dirt trail. Thank-

fully, the gradient eases for the final stroll to the south summit, which is of equal height to the next top along.

I especially like the summit view to the south. See the photo on page 188/189. It's even better when the peaks are plastered in snow and the larch forests are glowing orange as shown in the photo above.

53 Pocaterra Ridge Traverse   map 6

Day hike
Unofficial trail
Possible creek crossing
Distance 5.7 km to peak no. 4
Height gain N-S 1047 m (3436 ft.)
to peak no. 4
High point 2678 m (8786 ft.)
Map 82 J/11 Kananaskis Lakes

North access Hwy. 40 (Kananaskis Trail) at Little Highwood Pass day-use area at the south entrance to Valleyview Trail the road. **South access** Hwy. 40 (Kananaskis Trail) at Highwood Pass via #52 Pocaterra Cirque and #52A Pocaterra Ridge Summit. NOTE: for both accesses, this section of Hwy. 40 is closed December 1–June 15. **Also accessible** from #54 Little Highwood Pass. NOTE: This section of Hwy. 40 is closed December 1–June 15.

Comments The "Kootenay Ridge," as geologist John Allan called it in 1947, is a heavenly ridgewalk where it's possible to pick off four tops named even farther back in time: "the Pocaterra Peaks" by George Pocaterra. Scrambling is optional (except for the fourth top, the ridge is mainly grass), exposure is nil and you can escape from almost anywhere in the event of a thunderstorm. It is, though, a fairly strenuous flog with a substantial height gain. Making things easier since the previous edition is a trail that has replaced the initial bushwhack to peak no. 1. In fact, there's a trail all the way now!

The ridge is sometimes hiked in combination with Little Highwood Pass and Rockfall Valley to make a 11.9 km loop back to the parking lot. Much more popular is a one-way trip of 10.1 km to Highwood Pass using trails #52A and #52 through Pocaterra Cirque. It helps navigation if you have walked these trails beforehand. It will have occurred to you that by hiking the ridge in the N-S direction, a second vehicle is unnecessary as long as you have stashed a bike at the pass, because, readers, the highway is all downhill to where you started from.

Naming The creek you cross was named by a Dominion land surveyor who found a mining stake with George Pocaterra's name written on it on behalf of the Mackay & Dippie Coal Syndicate. The Stoneys were of the same mind: *Wasiju Wachi tusin ta Waptan Ze* means "Crazy mischievous white man creek" or "Where this Wasiju Wachi was taking a leak." What's left of Pocaterra's cabin lies downstream a way and is most easily reached by walking from Hwy. 40 into the trees 1.1 km north of the fire road.

NORTH TO SOUTH

To Rockfall Valley trail junction 400 m
Walk through to Hwy. 40 and cross. Almost opposite, a cairn indicates a trail heading down to Pocaterra Creek. Here the trail heads right along the bank. Either wade across at flagging or fight your way across a small logjam a little farther downstream. On the far bank, midway between the two crossing places, a trail climbs the bank and heads right. Shortly it turns inland between willow bushes and crosses a small ditch. Enter a meadow partially strewn with flood cobbles from Rockfall Creek. The unmarked fork at 383117 appears to lie under the rubble. Veer left past yellow flagging and in trees begin the climb up to top no. 1. (The trail up/down Rockfall Valley can be spotted on the left bank of Rockfall Creek.)

The ridge 5.3 km
The trail, though steep, is good and easy to follow as it twists uphill through menziesia bushes, which gradually thin out as you climb higher into the coal belt. Emerge from trees onto a wide, grassy ridge with rocky outcrops, the ridge narrowing and steepening as you approach the summit (cairn, surveyor's benchmark). In summer the west-facing slopes are packed with an incredible array of flowers.

From top no. 1 descend to a low point where larch trees spill over the gap. At this place an intersecting game trail offers an

The start/finish to Pocaterra Ridge Traverse and Little Highwood Pass

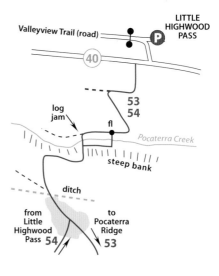

Above: Climbing to peak no. 1 is a steep grind, but at least there is a trail of sorts. Photo Bob Spirko

Top: View from descent off peak no. 1, looking ahead to peak no. 2. Down right is Rockfall Valley, showing the dried-up lake. Photo Maurice Gaucher

Top: On the 3-4 col, looking toward top 4. The high point lies at far right. Photo Dinah Kruze

Bottom: Looking back to tops 3 and 2 from the traverse beyond 3–4 col. Photo Tanya Koob

Opposite top: Crossing top no. 4.
Photo Bob Spirko

escape route into Rockfall Valley just down-
valley of the lake. (Don't aim for the lake; a
rockband gets in the way.)

After one sortie above treeline, the ridge
shakes off the last of the larches and climbs
a steepening, narrowing ridge to top no. 2
which is capped with an elegant cairn.

Drop to 2/3 gap. Top no. 3 is from either direction a very easy walk that one is
tempted to miss out altogether by traversing
to the 3/4 gap. Should you as a ridge walker
be guilty of such unnatural behaviour pre-
tend to be looking for instruments that for
a good many years measured creep along the
traverse line.

Top no. 4 with its three tops looks more
difficult. Start off by walking along the left
(east) side of a horizontal section, then
switch over to "The Sidewalk." The following cockscomb of rocks can be bypassed on
the left side by following a grey shale bench
that slants up to the ridge beyond the rock.
An orange shale slope leads to the first of
the three tops. As you cross from one top
to another on shale, scree and a little rock,
it becomes apparent that the formidable-

*The trail between the two highest summits that are of
equal height. From the far top most people descend the
south ridge to left.*

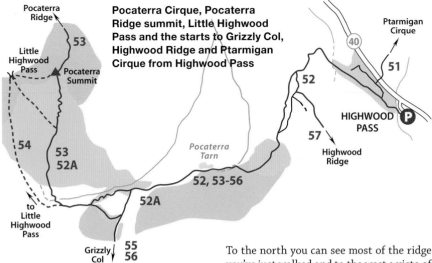

Pocaterra Ridge

Little Highwood Pass

53

Pocaterra Summit

Pocaterra Cirque, Pocaterra Ridge summit, Little Highwood Pass and the starts to Grizzly Col, Highwood Ridge and Ptarmigan Cirque from Highwood Pass

Ptarmigan Cirque

40

51

52

54

53
52A

Pocaterra Tarn

52, 53-56

52A

to Little Highwood Pass

Grizzly Col | **55 56**

HIGHWOOD PASS **P**

57

Highwood Ridge

looking rockbands seen from down below and that may have caused you some apprehension are merely north face facades. The middle top, the one with the cairn, is actually the exact same height as the south summit as measured by Gérard.

The south summit is where you leave the ridge. But first enjoy the fabulous view of Pocaterra Cirque down below and across to Mt. Tyrwhitt, Grizzly Col, Grizzly Peak and Highwood Ridge as seen on pages 188/189.

The anticline cave at Little Highwood Pass seen from GETTING OFF. Photo Gord Hurlburt

To the north you can see most of the ridge you've just walked and to the west a vista of peaks on either side of Elbow Lake. Views to the west are cut off by the high east wall of the Elk Range.

GETTING OFF

1. Via ##52A, 52 to Highwood Pass 4 km
This is your easiest option and all of it on good trail. Simply descend the easy south ridge to the west fork of Pocaterra Creek. Cross and go left. For a full description read ##52A and 52 and look at the sketchmap above. Just remember to keep left.

2. Via Little Highwood Pass 4.3 km
The loop back to the north trailhead via Little Highwood Pass and Rockfall Valley is the longer, harder option with scree, snow very often, and tricky trail-finding. There are two routes to the pass, no. 2 offering a good view of the cave.
1. The short and steep west ridge route is a steep drop of 122 m (400 ft.). When snow-free, it's a fairly simple descent with the benefit of a zigzagging trail on soft black shale near the bottom. When a cornice lingers on the ridge the going is more problematic.
2. The easier but longer route follows the trail down the south ridge. Halfway down at the shoulder a game trail traverses right into the pass.

54 Little Highwood Pass map 6

Day hike
Unofficial trails route,
possible creek crossings
Distance 9.7 km between parking lots
Height gain S-N 229 m (750 ft.),
472 m (1550 ft.) from trailhead
Height loss S-N 640 m (2100 ft.)
High point 2545 m (8350 ft.)

Access Hwy. 40 (Kananaskis Trail).
South at Highwood Pass. Via #49.
North Little Highwood Pass parking lot at the junction of Hwy. 40 and Valleyview Trail the road. NOTE: This section of Hwy. 40 is closed December 1–June 15 to both accesses.
Also accessible from #53 Pocaterra Ridge.

Comments The official name is puzzling, because Little Highwood Pass lies neither within nor on the boundary of the Highwood River drainage but between Pocaterra Creek and a south fork called Rockfall Valley, though Landslide is a more accurate name.

The main thing to know about this pass is that it lies in the cold shadow of a great rock wall and is usually snowbound until midsummer. So take poles just in case.

The southern approach from Pocaterra Cirque is straightforward with gentle gradients, though you could have a cornice to contend with at the end. The northern section in Rockfall Valley has extremely complex terrain with lots of scree but is redeemed by a seasonal lake, larches and a fascinating "valleys of the rocks." Since the previous edition a trail in the trees has cut out the bushwhacking. You just have to find it.

Many people combine the climb up to the pass with an ascent of Pocaterra's highest summit. Others, starting from north access combine the Rockfall Valley section on the north side of the pass with the ridgewalk along Pocaterra Ridge — a much more strenuous option with route-finding problems.

Little Highwood Pass from the south, showing a cornice. To right is the highest summit of Pocaterra Ridge.

SOUTH TO NORTH

Follow the first four sections of #52 Pocaterra Cirque (PC) trail and peruse the sketchmap on page 184.

To the pass 1.3 km

At the T-junction turn left along the ridge crest. When it seems you must stub your toes against the formidable wall of the Great Divide, descend easily to the creekbed. At this point the valley makes a right-angled turn to the north, disclosing a first view of the pass between steep walls.

It's a simple walk up the valley, following the line of the very obvious Lewis thrust fault on stones and patches of grass. Two-thirds of the way along, look up left to a cave at the bottom of an anticlinal fold. My friend Gord tells me its mouth makes a terrific frame for a picture of Grizzly Col and Mt. Tyrwhitt displaying its arch.

Cooling off in Rockfall Lake. Photo Alf Skrastins

As you draw closer to the pass, the gradient steepens and almost certainly you'll be tramping on snow and possibly kicking steps over a cornice. Often the cornice can be avoided by a detour up scree to the left. The pass is a narrow one. Nevertheless, little can be glimpsed of Rockfall Valley ahead. As mentioned, the best view is backwards. To your right a zigzagging trail climbs the steep west ridge to the highest summit of Pocaterra Ridge. Starting from the bench just below the col an easier trail traverses to the south ridge of the peak and is the route of preference when doing the pass/peak combo.

Rockfall Valley 5.9 km

Keeping right, descend into the south fork of Pocaterra Creek via the shallow gully at the demarcation of grey and brown rocks. Cross fans of névé/scree to the east bank of the emergent creek where a ribbon of meadow provides fast, easy going.

Halfway down the valley is Rockfall Lake, formed when a large portion of slope to the west slid and piled up in great mounds across the valley floor and halfway up Pocaterra Ridge opposite. In fall the lake dries, revealing the winding creek. Then you can hike across the lake bed. At other times pick your way along the left (west) shore. It's here where the water sinks and travels 2 km underground beneath the jumbled terrain.

From the end of the lake climb to the low point in the rubble pile. Descend stones at the base of the small ridge to the right, then round the end of the ridge to the east side of the valley. In larches pick up a trail that can be traced through a bumpy passageway of grass with boulders, which is the start of the east-side trough. (There is a parallel trough on the west side of the valley, a confusing number of cross-troughs and a small tarn in the middle of it all.)

At the top of a small rise is a cairn. This signals the start of a much clearer trail that straightaway descends a steep slope. The trail fades at the bottom. Look for a cairn and then head right into the trees where the

One of the more enjoyable stretches of lower Rockfall Valley. Photo Alf Skrastins

trail picks up. For the next long stretch you can either take the forest trail or continue down the open trough to left. On the forest trail follow cairns through runnels of rocks, keeping watch for where the trough trail joins in from the left. Shortly after this junction the trail heads across to the west-side trough at its last hurrah where rubble cascades into the old forest and the creek re-emerges for its brief fling in the daylight. In the rocks navigate from cairn to cairn, then follow the trail down the right bank of the creek into the trees.

There are reports the next section of trail was wiped out in the 2013 flood but that a new trail is developing. So keep on following the right bank of the creek into a meadow now partially covered with cobbles where you have to be alert for the junction with Pocaterra Ridge trail at 383117. Possibly the junction lies under rocks. Regardless, turn left.

Cross a ditch, keep straight (ignore trail to left) and head for Pocaterra Creek. The trail follows the banktop to the right a way, then descends the bank. There are two ways to cross. Either follow the trail to right and wade opposite some flagging on the far bank. Or go a little left and cross at the logjam which was unaffected by the flood. Either way, on the far bank turn right on a trail that winds its way through the forest to Hwy. 40. You emerge just slightly down road from the entrance to Little Highwood Pass parking lot at a small cairn. See the sketchmap on page 181.

SIDE TRIP TO POCATERRA'S CABIN

The ruins of George Pocaterra's cabin on Pocaterra Creek lie a little downstream of the crossing on the north bank. The best way of finding them is to drive 1.1 km west of the Kananaskis Loookout fire road parking lot and at a road sign on the right head right into the bush. The ruins lie in a willowy clearing back from the creek.

55 Grizzly Col

Day hike
Unofficial trail
Distance 4.2 km from parking
Height gain to col 507 m (1663 ft.)
High point at col 2595 m (8514 ft.)
Maps 82 J/10 Mt. Rae,
82 J/11 Kananaskis Lakes

Access Hwy. 40 (Kananaskis Trail) at Highwood Pass parking lot. NOTE: this section of Hwy. 40 is closed December 1–June 15.
Also accessible from #53 Pocaterra Ridge Traverse, #54 Little Highwood Pass and from the west fork of Storm Creek described in Volume 5.

Comments This is the col between Pocaterra Creek and the west fork of Storm Creek, which some call Tyrwhitt Col. Once reached by a horrible grovel up steep scree below the col, it now sports a cairned trail, which is nevertheless fairly rough and rocky and crosses snow tongues early in the season. Also the scrambler's access to Mt. Tyrwhitt.
The Grizzly Col mysteries In 2011, despite extensive searching, the disappearance of hiker Kevin Kennedy, who was bound for Grizzly Col and Highwood Ridge via Paradise Valley was never solved. A blue-striped button-up shirt found hanging on a branch just south of the col proved not to be his, nor did a set of human remains found south of Highwood Pass just off the old road.

Follow the first three sections of #52 Pocaterra Cirque (PC) trail and see the map on page 184. At the T-junction in a flat meadow at 407063 bear left

To Grizzly Col 1.1 km

The trail climbs a hill between larches, then traverses a grass slope below the high wall of the terminal moraine. Keep left. (Right is the alternative trail to Little Highwood Pass and Pocaterra Ridge Summit.)

The trail hugs the bottom of the moraine as it gradually ascends a draw into Tyrwhitt

Cirque. All the way up from the meadow is a side view of Mt. Tyrwhitt's east ridge displaying its Wishbone Arch two-thirds up the left-hand skyline ridge. Ahead rises Grizzly Col, a steep wall of scree and rock slung between Tyrwhitt and Grizzly Peak.

At a split go either way. The left-hand route seems more popular nowadays and has cairns to follow. The right-hand trail zigs into an upper draw, then partway along, climbs out of it onto grass (cairn), where it heads left across the flat to join the left-hand route.

Arriving at the foot of scree slopes, the trail climbs up the scree a way, then turns right and makes a slowly rising traverse to the col. Here and there rock and mud slides courtesy of the 2013 flood have wiped out bits of trail. Just below the col, the crossing of a rock rib is easy. As mentioned, some call this col Tyrwhitt. "Grizzly" is the older

name. While no one's yet met a griz face to face on the col, plenty of people have seen tracks in the snow.

To your right is the popular scrambler's route up Mt. Tyrwhitt, which is rated moderate with a helmet. To left is the west ridge of Grizzly Peak. Behind you is Little Highwood Pass and the highest summit of Pocaterra Ridge; in front a blinkered view of Storm Creek's west fork squashed between the southeast ridge of Grizzly Peak and the mighty east wall of the Great Divide.

ONGOING OPTIONS

Anyone with energy to spare can tack on Grizzly Peak or at least the west ridge bit for the view and then either return the same way or tack on the route to Highwood Ridge by which you can return to Highwood Pass parking lot. See ##56, 56A and 57. With two vehicles you can connect with the series of trails in Storm Creek via #56B. See also Storm Creek trails in Volume 5.

Top: Almost at Grizzly Col.

Left and above: The view from Pocaterra Ridge summit shows most of the route from the avalanche slope at bottom left, past Pocaterra Tarn into Tyrwhitt Cirque (right) and up to Grizzly Col, located between Grizzly Peak (centre) and Mt. Tyrwhitt (right). Note the arch about two-thirds of the way up the left-hand ridge of Tyrwhitt. At far left is Highwood Ridge, showing the ascent route up the left-hand ridge.

Above: Looking down on Grizzly Col from the climb up the west ridge to the southeast ridge of Grizzly Peak. Rising above the col is Mt. Tyrwhitt, showing the scramble route. Photo Bob Spirko

Opposite: Walking the southeast ridge of Grizzly Peak. Note the orange tower partway along.

56 Grizzly Peak

map 6

Day scramble
Unofficial trail, route
Distance 800 m from Grizzly Col
Height gain 165 m (540 ft.) from Grizzly Col, 677 m (2221 ft.) from trailhead
High point 2764 m (9068 ft.)
Maps 82 J/10 Mt. Rae,
82 J/11 Kananaskis Lakes

Access Hwy. 40 (Kananaskis Trail) at Highwood Pass parking lot. Via #55 at Grizzly Col. NOTE: this section of Hwy. 40 is closed December 1–June 15.

Comments The orange-coloured mountain on the east side of Grizzly Col at 413055 is an easier alternative to Mt. Tyrwhitt. Mostly it's a ridgewalk with one or two scrambly bits.

To Southeast ridge 300 m

On trail, head up the broad west ridge to the left (east), keeping an eye out for alpine poppies as you go. On rougher ground you zig right, back left, then head up steepish black-lichened boulders to the main southeast ridge. It's satisfying to look back to Mt. Tyrwhitt, where hardcore scramblers are having a much harder time of it labouring up high-angle scree and slabs.

To the summit 500 m

Turn left. Where the ridge turns northeast the black-lichened boulders give way to fine orange shales interspersed with a couple of rocky humps, the second of which has a slightly awkward descent on the right side. Farther on, turn the orange tower on the right side.

The ridge turns northwest and again changes character. The black lichen is back and you scrabble up broken rock on one side or the other of the ridge, finishing along the ridgeline to the summit.

There's a flat bit beyond the cairn where you can stretch out and look down on almost the entire route you came up from Pocaterra Creek, plus Little Highwood Pass, Pocaterra Ridge and Highwood Ridge. To the south, Paradise Valley is an amazing neon green colour. You can pick out the ramp leading down into it from lower down the southeast ridge.

Above: View of Paradise Valley from Grizzly Peak. To left is #57 Highwood Ridge extending to the southeast summit in the middle of the picture. In the background is the Misty Range, with Mist Mountain at far right, Storm Mountain at left.

To right of the photo is the southeast ridge of Grizzly Peak, showing the ascent route, the grassy ramp into the valley used by #56A and the easy climb up grass onto Highwood Ridge. Route #56B follows the southeast ridge of Grizzly Peak to its very end.

Left top: The suitably pointed summit.

Left bottom: #56A Hillsides of paintbrush above Paradise Valley.

56A to Highwood Ridge

Route
Distance from Grizzly Peak ~3.5 km
Height loss 393 m (1290 ft.) from peak
Height gain 259 m (850 ft.) to ridge

Comments A 10.5-km loop with Highwood Ridge (#57) is possible. Not the long, convoluted loop described in previous editions, but a tighter one that is no less strenuous on account of a substantial height gain coming late in the day. (Total height gain for loop is 942 m (3090 ft.)

Connecting the summit with Highwood Ridge is a serrated ridge. If you're a proficient scrambler and can handle moderate down-climbing on the far side of the serrations or are willing to circumvent them altogether on the right, give it a go.

For everyone else there is this route, which dips into the lovely head of Paradise Valley via the ramp route, a steepish grass slope with scree and the odd rockband.

Start off by returning down off the summit to where you first gained it from Grizzly Col. Continue on down the ridge for about 250 m onto some orange scree before the ridge turns grassy.

To Paradise Valley via the ramp 900 m

At about 413048 the steep slopes falling into Paradise Valley are replaced by a broad ramp of grass and scree offering a relatively straightforward descent on a slope only moderately steep. About halfway down, work your way between small, staggered rockbands, trending left. Lower down, keep left of another rockband, then right of rocky bluffs below which a dozen springs burst forth. At this level the well-watered hillside is crammed with flowers, most notably magenta paintbrushes and long-stemmed forget-me-nots.

To Highwood Ridge 1.2 km

It's a simple walk across the valley floor below the serrations of the ridge connecting the two summits. Underfoot is short grass, also crammed with flowers, which makes me suspect that the name "Paradise," which was popular before 1947, was coined by amateur botanists. Farther on there are rivulets to cross.

Reach the base of Highwood Ridge and look up a 300-m-high slope of orange shale and broken rock rising to the summit. My recommendation is to traverse MUCH farther right to less steep, grassy slopes.

After climbing about 200 m you arrive some way along the southeast ridge. Turn left and follow its broad back over a hump to the summit. Now read #57 backwards for the descent to Highwood Pass. Below treeline use the recommended descent trail.

POINT TO POINT

56B to Storm Creek

Route, unofficial trail
Distance 6.6 km to Hwy. 40, total distance between trailheads 11.4 km
Height loss from summit to Hwy. 40, 835 m (2740 ft.)

Comments A point to point between Grizzly Peak and Hwy. 40 south of Highwood Pass, via the entire southeast ridge. Apart from extending the ridgewalk, the other good thing about this option is that you don't finish with a bushwhack but with a worry-free 3.5-km walk on a trail which delivers you to Hwy. 40 some 750 m south of the Mt. Lipsett day-use area.

The southeast ridge 3.1 km
From the summit of Grizzly Peak return down the southeast ridge to where you first gained it from Grizzly Col.

Continue along the ridge for another 2.6 kilometres enjoying a slightly undulating ridgewalk with occasional rocky sections. On the right side the grass rolls tamely down into the west fork of Storm Creek. The left side is much steeper, offering no comfortable routes into Paradise Valley.

Descent 3.5 km
Drop off the gable end, a moderate slope of grass and first trees that lower down harbours some magnificent bushes of white rhododendron and bracted honeysuckle. Aim for the flat, treed ridge between the two forks of Storm Creek, specifically the point at 432024 where you can pick up the faint beginnings of the ridge trail.

Found it? Heading southeast all the way, follow the trail past a Y-junction (trail to right heads up Storm Creek) and on down to the promontory above the forks. Here the trail turns right and winds down to a hunter's camp. Continue to follow the trail alongside the west fork to a junction. Stay ahead. (The trail to right crossing the west fork is the west-side trail.)

On east-side trail, descend to the Paradise Valley fork just above the forks and wade across. The trail climbs up the opposite bank, then meanders (keep the faith) along the broad ridge and down to a T-junction. Turn left. The final stretch takes you out to Hwy. 40.

Descent off the southeast ridge to Hwy. 40 at Storm Creek

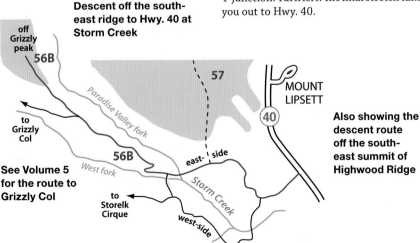

Also showing the descent route off the southeast summit of Highwood Ridge

57 Highwood Ridge

map 6

Short day scramble
Unofficial trails
Distance 5.5 km return
Height gain 515 m (1684 ft.)
High point 2709 m (8888 ft.)
Map 82 J/10 Mt. Rae

Access Hwy. 40 (Kananaskis Trail) at Highwood Pass parking lot. NOTE: This section of Hwy. 40 is closed December 1–June 15.

Comments Who can resist the summit overlooking Highwood Pass parking lot? Expect a steep trudge on trails with the worst of the scrambling avoidable.

While most people return the same way, with two vehicles you can carry on over the southeast summit and descend to Hwy. 40 via trails in Storm Creek. See also #56B and the sketchmap on the opposite page.

Route history It's known that the Boundary Survey used this summit as a camera station in 1916 called "Highwood Ridge North." And it's known from an undated photo that George Pocaterra was up there as well, though most likely just to the southeast summit from Storm Creek.

Looking up the north ascent ridge to the summit. The second rockband lies in shadow just above treeline.

Follow the first section of #52 Pocaterra Cirque (PC) and see the map on page 184.

To treeline 550 m
Turn left on the original Pocaterra Cirque trail, winding uphill for 120 metres to where the trail turns right and flattens at 418070. Either go straight on the narrow trail or walk a few more metres to the right where the main trail turns left. This is just before the original Pocaterra Cirque trail descends a little. Both trails climb steadily through forest and join a little way up.

Start a steeper climb, at the last stepping on a flat boulder en route to the base of the lower rockband. Turn left. (DO NOT cross a low point in the band to right). Follow the gently rising base past the first obvious go-up place to where the trail climbs a few easy steps to gain the top of the rockband at treeline. A few metres inland, pick up the better defined descent trail no. 1 and turn left to reach open ground.

To the north summit 1.2 km
Arrive on a grassy bench. To your right rises the second rockband, a grungy mess of rock and black Fernie shales with glintings of coal — the start of the north ridge proper.

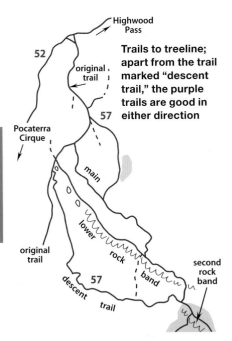

Highwood Pass

52

original trail

Pocaterra Cirque

main

lower
rock
57
band

original trail

descent trail

57

second rock band

Trails to treeline; apart from the trail marked "descent trail," the purple trails are good in either direction

right. High up, leave a black shale trail that is making a beeline for the summit tower (its looming blackness a thoroughly unappetizing sight) and head left to a grassy col. Here starts a dead easy bypass trail which traverses orange scree with cairns onto the broad, grassy southeast ridge beyond the rockbands. Swing back right and walk to the summit cairn.

This is a great viewpoint for the Misty Range: Mt. Rae looming above Ptarmigan Cirque, Mist Mountain at far right and in the middle the unclimbed west ridge of Storm Mountain, truly an awesome sight when mist swirls around its pinnacles.

You have to get to the top of this by one means or the other. People go all different ways, often looking for an easier way down. The two most popular routes are:

1. Scrambling Follow the upper trail along the grassy bench to WP 420067. Here starts a trail in black shale that zigs left, right, up and a long way left. Many people forgo the final corner of steep black shale and scramble up easy rocks to its left.

2. No scrambling Some people will have a happier time of it by plodding up the back side of the ridge. Just after leaving the trees, head right on a fainter trail that crosses the rock ridge in its infancy. On the far side, head diagonally upwards across easy scree to the tree edge where a trail heads uphill to the top of the trees. Traverse right and when rock and scree are behind you, climb a grassy slope to the ridge crest reached at the top of route 1.

Next up is the third scramble step, which is easily taken direct (NOT to the left), after which either keep to the ridge trail or follow a black shale trail just below it to the

OPTIONAL DESCENT ROUTES

See the sketchmap at top left.

1. Starting at treeline, a steep dirt trail gives a super-fast descent through forest criss-crossed by game trails. Nearing its end, the trail traverses right, descends left, again traverses right and drops onto the original PC trail to the left of boulders. Turn right.

2. Descend the ascent route below the lower rockband, only this time continue to follow a rather pleasant trail that stays below the gradually diminishing band and reaches the original PC trail to the right of boulders. Turn right.

GOING FARTHER
57A Southeast Summit

Distance 5.8 km to Storm Creek
Extra height gain 152 m (500 ft.)
Height loss 850 m (2800 ft.)
High point at southeast summit
2555 m (8385 ft.)

Comments The other end summit is 152 m (500 ft.) lower and reached by a 3.4-km-long grassy ridge. For this trip you need a second vehicle parked 750 m south of Mt. Lipsett day-use area on Hwy. 40. See also Volume 5, Storm Creek trails.

Head southeast along a remarkably wide, straight, grassy ridge, ambling up and over two minor bumps. Because your attention is not constantly on where to put your feet, you're free to admire the views. To the east you're treated to a parade of cirques, including Ptarmigan (showing the route up Mt. Rae) and Arethusa (showing the route over to Burns Lake).

Farther on, the ridge tapers to an elegant crest. There's one narrow bit (avoidable on the right), then a cairn where you too can take a photo almost identical to the one taken by George Pocaterra which archivists have inexplicably labelled "looking down the Elk Valley." A final climb gains you the southeast summit — a splendid viewpoint for Highwood Pass and the lovely country of the Highwood to the south.

Descend the south ridge, which gives you the chance to enjoy the myriad of alpines like roseroot that grow in the mix of grass and scree. After you enter forest, the gradient begins to ease and likely you will be following one faint trail or another farther down the ridge to an intersection in a flat area with east-side trail in the Storm Creek network of trails. This is not the first west-east trail you encounter, but the second, your trail unmistakable and blazed. Turn left. Now see the map on page 194.

Opposite: The second half of the easy third scramble step.

Above left: Heading left towards the bypass trail below the black summit tower.

Above right: #57A The southeast summit from halfway along the connecting ridge.

58 Lower Lake

map 5

Half-day hike
Official trail
Distance 4 km one way to Elkwood
Height gain N-S 30 m (100 ft.)
Map 82 J/11 Kananaskis Lakes

Access Kananaskis Lakes Trail (road).
North Canyon day-use area.
The trail starts by the boat ramp.
South William Watson Lodge or
East Elkwood parking lot.

Comments An easy stroll along the east
shore of Lower Kananaskis Lake Reservoir
between Canyon day-use area and William
Watson Lodge and on to Elkwood parking lot.
For views I prefer starting from Canyon and
walking the trail north to south. Low water reveals unattractive mud flats dotted here and
there with tree stumps. The trails around the
lodge are all wheelchair accessible.

Naming History The lake's original name
was Thorpe, after a director of Wisconsin's
Eau Claire Logging Company, which was siz-
ing up the timber berths back in 1883.

NORTH TO SOUTH

To junction 2.7 km
The trail heads west, passing through
a walk-in picnic area to the promontory marking the boundary of the sheltered
backwater near Canyon Dam. Turn the corner and travel south along the lakeshore in
the pines, making forays now and then to
the waterline (however far that is) for rather
stunning views of mounts Fox, Foch and
Sarrail and the cliffs of Indefatigable Outlier rising in front of Indefatigable North.

In 2.7 km come to a T-junction with
Lower Lake interpretive trail. Where you
go next depends on your final destination.

1. To William Watson Lodge 800 m
Keep straight past interpretive signs. In a
minute or two come to another T-junction.
Keep left on paved Bill Benson trail which
climbs the bank. (To right a trail dotted with
innumerable memorial benches heads out

*Lower Kananaskis Lake, looking south to mounts
Fox, Foch and Sarrail.*

The trail to Elkwood parking lot, which is gravelled low down for wheelchair users.

onto a man-made promontory.) Bill Benson trail climbs past his memorial bench, then zigs left with railings on both sides. At the next junction a minute or two later, turn right on a trail that wanders behind chalets H–A, giving access to them and to four parking lots before ending up at William Watson Lodge.

2. To Elkwood parking lot 1.3 km
Turn left inland. The interpretive trail climbs very gradually up a cool valley of old spruce, passing interpretive signs and crossing a bridge en route to a junction with a paved trail called Spruce Road.

Keep left. (Spruce Road to right leads to the camping area.) At the next junction it's worth detouring left to Marsh Viewpoint for a look, not at a mosquito-ridden bog as you might expect but at a large, mineral-encrusted flat with a view of far-off mountains. Such gleaming white flats are common in the Rockies and are formed by the slow evaporation of ponds. Watch where you are walking. Below some of the crust is water.

Back on Spruce Road, go left at the next junction and on paved bike trail cross the powerline right-of-way (Spruce Road to right leads to William Watson Lodge). On reaching Lodgepole bike trail, also the High Rockies Trail, go right and in a few minutes cross Kananaskis Lakes Trail (road) into Elkwood parking lot.

Trails to William Watson Lodge and Elkwood parking lot

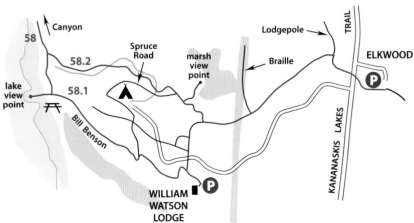

59   Marl Lake Interpretive Trail   map 5

Half-day hike
Official trail
Distance 3.4 km return
Height gain 15 m (50 ft.)
High point 1716 m (5630 ft.)
Map 82 J/11 Kananaskis Lakes

Access Kananaskis Lakes Trail (road) at Elkwood parking lot.
Also accessible by trails from Elkwood campground: from D loop between sites 114 and 115; from C loop between sites 78 and 79; and from A loop between sites 24 and 15. The interpretive trail crosses the B loop campground between sites 52 and 53, and 45 and 46.

Comments Easy forest walking on a wheelchair-accessible trail with plentiful benches leads to a lake. No biking allowed once you hit the loop. Nearly always trodden down for winter walking. See sketchmap on page 287.

Through the campground 1.1 km

Starting from the biffy in the parking lot, follow the paved bike trail Wheeler to the amphitheatre and turn left into it. (Trail from loop A comes in from the right.) The hiking trail starts from the right side.

As you head through the forest, keep left (trail from B loop ahead), then cross loop B access road twice. Stay left (trail from loop C to right), and left again (trail from loop D to right), the last junction coinciding with the official start at a trail sign. Go anticlockwise around the loop.

Marl Lake loop 1.2 km

Straightway pass a number of scenic fens to left and right. A downhill signals the approach to the lake. At a split definitely go left to the shoreline with its viewing platform and interpretive sign. Across the lake is a stunning lineup of high mountains: Mt. Fox through Mt. Foch to Mt. Sarrail. Close at hand, inspect the water for leeches and scuds, and feel the marl on the lake bottom. It may feel like sand, but it's actually a by-product of algae, which finds the calcium in the water indigestible.

After a memorial bench, the trail turns right and heads back to the trail sign past an interpretive sign bearing the current catchphrase "Keep exploring." Stay straight and return the way you came.

60 Boulton Creek Interpretive Trail map 5

Half-day hike
Official trail
Distance 3.2 km loop
Height gain 70 m (230 ft.)
Map 82 J/11 Kananaskis Lakes

Access Kananaskis Lakes Trail (road) at Boulton Bridge parking lot.
Also accessible from various sites in Boulton Creek campground.

Comments A forest walk about Boulton Creek with easy hills. See sketchmap on page 288.
   Trail update The 2013 flood did a number on the very best section alongside the creek, which was officially decommissioned and rerouted in 2015 to higher ground where it morphed into the 4-m-wide Boulton Creek ski trail. While great for skiers, it's a soulless trail to walk. Luckily, anyone with a shred of curiosity can still trace the creekside route.
   History En route you visit the historic Fish & Wildlife cabin that was relocated from the valley bottom prior to tree clearing for Lower Kananaskis Lake Reservoir in 1954/5. Lost were the original ranger cabin and several carvings on living trees made by Jack Fuller

Sr., who in the 1920s worked as a summer guide taking parties on trips to Kananaskis Lakes. All that remains of his most popular carving — a nude woman with "wanton eyes, blue-stained lips and nipples of a soft red" — are photos in the Glenbow Archives taken by such notables as Lizzie Rummel and George Edworthy. Or are they lost?
   By some fortuitous chance the nude resurfaced just a few years ago after residing for 50 years in a Calgary garden. Even more remarkably, it was a friend's husband's co-worker's father's garden, the co-worker's dad having rescued the carving while helping to clear the land back in 1955. Unfortunately, a list of names at the bottom of the carving is missing, namely of guides George Harrison and Guy Gano, of guests and 21 pack horses and two dogs.
   Naming Boulton's Creek (note the apostrophe) is an old name pre-1914 that appeared on a Department of the Interior sectional map. That it was named after an old-time rancher who lived in Willow Creek seems unlikely.

Opposite: #59 Marl Lake.

Below: The relocated historic Fish & Wildlife cabin.

To the bridge junction 1.8 km

From the near end of the parking lot cross the bridge over Boulton Creek. Immediately keep straight (left is the ski trail) and climb the bank to the old ranger cabin.

At the T-junction turn right. Heading south, the trail passes below what used to called Baseball Diamond Meadow, a once popular training ground for Jackrabbits that spawned not a few provincial and national X-C ski racers before there was the Canmore Nordic Centre.

As the trail undulates and winds along through the lodgepoles, keep right everywhere. Between signs nos. 2 and 3, the trail skirts the edge of the bank high above Boulton Creek. Rock flakes have been found all along here, pointing to the area's occupation some 8,000 years ago by Neolithic peoples of the Mummy Cave Complex. Lin-

"And glistening crag in sunlit sky,
'mid snowy clouds piled mountain high,
were joys to me"

Words on a memorial bench along this lovely section of trail between signs nos. 2 and 3.

ger awhile at three memorial benches and enjoy the mountain views.

The trail then turns away from the edge and zigs left up a longer uphill to sign no. 4, then up right to a higher terrace. Continue past signs nos. 5, 6 and 7 to a T-junction. Turn right and zig down the bank to Boulton Creek. Cross the new bridge to a T-junction with Boulton Creek ski trail at no. 8 sign and turn right.

Back to parking lot

Choose from one of the two return options.

1. Official trail 1.4 km Shortly turn left on the ski trail and climb a long, winding hill in pine forest with deadfall. From the high point, two long descents with a short uphill in between lead back to creek level and out to the parking lot. Overall, a hilly finish to the interpretive trail, boring for walkers but great for skiers.

2. Original creekside route 960 m Bypassing the blockade, continue ahead along the left bank of Boulton Creek. Almost straightaway, a bit of deadfall, some of it construction debris thrown down the bank from the official trail above, is easily dealt with. The major impasse occurs at old interpretive sign no. 9, where the trail is overrun by cobbles and the side creek is missing its bridge. Pick a route around to the right as you go taking a look for Boulton Creek flowing somewhere in the middle of all the flood debris.

A long good stretch past interpretive sign no. 10 at a muddy side creek leads to the stony overflow channel where the trail runs below a steep bank. Here you can expect a few metres of waterlogged trail at the far end just before the climb onto higher ground. Approaching the end, circumvent the downstream blockade to the left to gain the official trail for the final walk out to the parking lot.

61 Kananaskis Lookout   map 5

Day hike, bike 'n' hike
Official trails
Distance 6.7 km from Boulton Bridge parking lot, 4.7 km from Hwy. 40
Height gain 432 m (1417 ft.) from Boulton Bridge,
274 m (900 ft.) from Hwy. 40
High point 2118 m (6950 ft.)
Map 82 J/11 Kananaskis Lakes

Access Kananaskis Lakes Trail (road)
1a. Boulton Bridge parking lot.
1b. Boulton Creek Trading Post upper parking lot. From the southeast corner get onto a paved ski/bike trail and turn right. Follow it to a 4-way junction with biffies where the route from Boulton Bridge comes in from the right. Turn left.
1c. Boulton campground. The access road to loop A crosses the trail as does the access road between loops B and D.
2. Hwy. 40 (Kananaskis Trail). Park at the entrance to the fire road on the west side of the highway at 370118.

Comments There are two reasonable routes to Kananaskis Lookout. Both are wide forest trails, ski trails in winter, that join for the final steep pull to a fabulous viewpoint. If I'm on a bike I much prefer to zip along the fire road from Hwy. 40. But as this is a hiking guide I'd have to recommend starting from Kananaskis Lakes Trail at the Boulton area, which has campsites, some eats and lots of people looking for a walk. Starting from Boulton Creek Trading Post parking lot cuts out a little height gain.

History The present, second, lookout was built in 1976, the first in 1952, five years after Joe Kovach blazed a trail along what is now the fire road. Interestingly, he followed in part a secret Indian trail that crossed East Elk Pass into the country of the Elk. For enthusiastic readers of *The Buffalo Head*, this was the route George Pocaterra, Adolf Baumgart and R.M. Patterson took in 1931 to escape the watchful eye of the ranger McGregor!

Looking south from the lookout to the mountains of the Elk River.

FROM ACCESS 1A

To the fire road via Whiskey Jack ski trail 4.3 km

From the near end of the parking lot cross the bridge over Boulton Creek. Immediately keep straight (left is a ski trail) and climb the bank to the old Fish & Wildlife cabin. At the T-junction turn left past the garage. (To right is Boulton Creek interpretive trail.) At the following T-junction with Whiskey Jack ski trail, which is paved, turn right (the trading post can be seen to the left).

Climb a short hill to a 4-way junction with biffies where the trail from Access 1b joins in from the left. (To right is the amphitheatre.) Go straight on a wide, gravelled trail.

Climb a steep hill. At the top cross the campground access road to A loop (Access 1c). Climb alongside the campground road, then cross the road between B and D loops (Access 1c). All campground clutter left behind, continue on Whiskey Jack ski trail, which is uphill though undulating because you keep crossing Spotted Wolf Creek and all its tributaries. The most interesting part of all this is the name of the creek, which honours George Pocaterra's blood brother Paul Amos.

At 4.3 km come to the T-junction with the fire road that has come in from Hwy. 40 and is signed "Pocaterra."

Lookout trail 2.4 km

Under its various guises you're going to be following the fire road all the way to the lookout. Turn right on Pocaterra ski trail. In half a kilometre turn right onto Lookout trail. (Ahead is Tyrwhitt trail, which follows the secret trail over Tobermory Pass to the Elk. Nevertheless, I don't recommend it for summer hiking: boggy meadows and grizzlies just about sums it up.)

Coming up is the longest climb of the day, a steep grind up the north ridge of Lookout Hill, where total humiliation is to be passed by a mountain biker. The incline eases into a long straight, at the end of which you climb out of the trees to picnic tables. The hilltop has been shaved, a green meadow allowing a 360-degree view if you stand by the lookout. Look south to the mountains about Elk Lakes (that's mounts Cadorna and Swiderski through the gap), west to mounts Fox, Foch and Sarrail and Kananaskis Lakes, and north down the Kananaskis Valley to Mt. Kidd.

FROM ACCESS 2

The fire road is followed in its entirety. In detail, cross Pocaterra Creek by bridge (Lionel ski trail) to a junction with Pocaterra ski trail. Keep left and make a gradual climb to Whiskey Jack junction. Keep left and follow directions under subhead "Lookout trail."

62 West Elk Pass maps 5, 7

Day hike, bike 'n' hike
Official & unofficial trails
Distance 5 km to pass
Height gain 213 m (700 ft.) to pass
High point 1905 m (6250 ft.) at pass
Map 82 J/11 Kananaskis Lakes

Access Kananaskis Lakes Trail (road) at Elk Pass parking lot.
Also accessible from #63 at Elk Lakes Provincial Park entrance.

Comments Of the three Elk passes, this one is the nicest if you are travelling through to Elk Lakes. It shares 90% of the route with #79 along a Calgary Power powerline access road and a road built for a tram line that never came about. Only the final 10% follows the old trail, which is an easy plod through meadow and spruce forest.

Opposite: #61 Upper and Lower Kananaskis Lakes from the lookout.

Regulations Mountain biking is allowed on the road only. No biking on trails on the B.C. side.

History I can't imagine why all those early explorers and travellers insisted on going over North Kananaskis Pass when Elk Pass was so glaringly obvious. Although the editor of *Survival on a Westward Trek* surmised the John Jones Overlanders crossed North Kananaskis Pass en route to the gold fields of British Columbia in 1858, most people believe they went over the Elk. Myself, I'm convinced they crossed Highwood Pass. The mistake is understandable. In the days before photogrammetry and Google Earth, the fact that the Elk Valley and the Highwood Valley ran parallel but on either side of the Divide caused a lot of confusion, even to veteran mountain travellers like George Dawson and Walter Wilcox, and has resulted in mountains being misplaced. For instance, is Mt. Fox really Mt. Tyrwhitt?

Below: The long meadow at West Elk Pass.

But back to Elk Pass, which surveyor Arthur O. Wheeler named in 1915 after being astonished to find it was nameless. Elk Pass is actually three: East Elk, Elk and West Elk. East Elk harbours the secret trail through to Tobermory Creek. Elk Pass (the highest) is now followed by the powerline right-of-way. West Elk Pass (the lowest) was the usual route and was crossed by an old Indian trail headed to hunting grounds in *Nyahe-ya-Nibi*. Deadfall was always a torment. In 1901 it took Walter Wilcox's party six hours to travel between the pass and Kananaskis Lakes. And this was in the downward direction! Even 20 years later, in the days of early tourism, forest rangers were always hacking out the trail.

To Blueberry Hill junction 4.4 km
Set off up the powerline access road (also the GDT), in 500 m ignoring Boulton Creek ski trail on the left. The road climbs over a ridge at the powerlines, which sing in the wind, then descends into Fox Creek. Stay ahead (Fox Creek ski trail to left), in 500 m crossing Fox Creek to a junction on the far side. Keep right. (The trail zooming up the hill to left is Hydroline ski and snowshoe trail.)

For the next kilometre follow a new road that connects snippets of previous road badly damaged during the takeover by the creek in 2013. After two creek crossings, the second over the main west fork carrying the water, you are back on original road with the flood mess behind you. Enjoy walking the narrow valley of the tiny south fork between a grassy draw and a steep bank. At the Patterson ski trail junction go straight on the shortcut signed "Elk Pass," at the top of the hill turning left. Shortly after you rejoin the old road, Blueberry Hill ski trail turns off to the right at a picnic table.

To West Elk Pass 540 m
Continue along a straight to a Y-junction with sign "Elk Lakes." So you chain up your bikes here and turn right onto a narrow descending trail. (Road to left is #79.)

The trail crosses the draw, climbs up the far bank and wends left to West Elk Pass on the Great Divide. The Alberta/B.C. boundary (rightfully located at the purple hiking sign) is officially marked a little farther on by a kiosk, a map and a post giving distances to ongoing destinations. To your left is the start of a very long, longitudinal meadow of feathery marsh reed grass from where, with boots slowly sinking in the ooze, you get a tantalizing glimpse of the mountains of the Elk River rising up above the horizon.

The trails hereabouts are initially boardwalked. For Elk Lakes Provincial Park entrance and the cabin go straight. For Upper Elk Lake via Fox Lake and Frozen Lake turn right up the hill.

EXPLORING FARTHER
62A Frozen Lake
Unofficial trail
Distance 1.9 km from pass
Height gain 280 m (920 ft.)
High point 2185 m (7170 ft.)

Comments If you're just hiking to West Elk Pass, why not visit Frozen Lake, a truly worthy objective after the ice melts. True to its name, this gorgeous lake remains frozen for about

seven months of the year, so plan on visiting from late July on. The trail is quite clear and unremittingly steep. It is also the scrambler's access route to Mt. Fox.

History On the way you will pass a few "monuments." Designed by A.O. Wheeler, monuments were constructed during the boundary survey to delineate the Alberta/British Columbia boundary at important passes. Elk Pass was assigned the letter M, so with the pass being so wide there's a whole slate of monuments and cairns extending from Mt. Fox to Mt. Tyrwhitt, all with different numbers up to 23. The monument at the lowest point of a pass was always numbered 1. The Elk Pass bunch were constructed on the spot in 1916 using cement, and gravel gouged from a nearby creekbed, to make concrete. Unless a flat rock was handy, the concrete base generally extended a metre underground. The heavy zinc cover was painted bright red and filled with concrete, the whole weighing an incredible 2700 lbs.

Above: A wide-angle view of Frozen Lake below Mt. Fox. Photo Vern Dewit

One of the old monuments at West Elk Pass. If you head to Frozen Lake you'll pass a number of them. Photo taken before its restoration in 2015

From the kiosk head right (west) up the boundary cutline on boardwalk. Where #63B to Fox Lake turns off to the left just after '1M' monument, stay on the cutline. (Incidentally, 1M and other Elk Pass monuments were restored in 2015 and returned to their bright red colour.)

Cross a wet meadow (flagging both ends) and continue up the cutline that climbs very steeply to 2M monument. (Just before 2M a trail starting between two blazed trees on the left side descends to Fox Lake. Use it as a shortcut to trail #63B, should you be headed that way on returning from Frozen Lake.)

Another, longer climb brings you to the end of the cutline in the vicinity of 4M. Here the trail turns right, then left into another steep climb. The gradient eases at a newfangled metal boundary post that also marks the start of meadow and larch country. Traverse a grassy shelf between outcrops (view of Elk Pass and Fox Lake), then climb one final hill into the cirque.

Cradled in the precipitous arms of Mt. Fox, the deep blue water of Frozen Lake is an awesome sight, extremely hard to photograph unless you have a lens with a wider angle than 28 mm. The right (north) arm is the difficult scrambler's route up Mt. Fox.

When we were there last, a good hour's entertainment was provided by another party having an epic circumnavigation of the lake, which involved climbing up the little glacier below Mt. Fox (not marked on any map). Instead try Taiga Viewpoint.

GOING HIGHER

62B Taiga Viewpoint

Unofficial trail, route
Distance from lake 700 m
Height gain from lake 215 m (705 ft.)
High point 2360 m (7743 ft.)

Comments Rough trails lead to the col on the south arm of Mt. Fox at 348034 and up the outlier at 349035. But, to paraphrase a popular cosmetics ad, the view is worth it.

To the col 500 m

Starting from the lakeshore, head left on a trail that leads diagonally uphill, crossing two shale gullies into some trees. Climb the tree ribbon to below a rockband, then make an ascending traverse 'twixt rock and scree to the col.

To Taiga Viewpoint 200 m

From the col or before, transfer to other game trails that ascend Taiga Viewpoint, that heap of rubble on your left. The summit ridge is beautiful, though, being narrow, long and grassy and capped by a cairn built by the Boundary Survey, which used the outlier as a camera station in 1916.

You'll be thrilled by Frozen Lake, which from this vantage point looks more like a caldera lake than a lake in a cirque. Peeking over the top of the north arm are the Kananaskis Lakes. Less exciting is the forested expanse of all three Elk passes, their complexities made clear. To the south lies Lower Elk Lake backdropped by Mt. Aosta, and the sweep of the Elk Valley enclosed by the wall of the Elk Range.

Return the same way, or if headed for Elk Lakes via #63B try the following shortcut descent.

SHORTCUT DESCENT TO ROUTE #63B
Distance 1 km

Expect a prolonged steep drop of about 457 m (1500 ft.) Also, know the lush greenery of the route is a grizzly hot spot. Return to the col and turn left (southeast). Descend the grassy, flowery avalanche gully, which is not as easy as it looks, because lurking under the vegetation are rock snakes that roll under your feet. At a steepening a trail appears and takes you into the stony creekbed. Lower down where the incline eases, use the meadow on the left side. Intersect #63B about 1.2 km from Upper Elk Lake. Turn right to connect with Elk Lakes trail, left to return to West Elk Pass via Fox Lake.

Above: #62B Frozen Lake from Taiga Viewpoint. Upper Kananaskis Lake and Mt. Indefatigable (right) can be seen above the north arm of Mt. Fox.

Above: #62B Climbing up to Taiga Viewpoint from Frozen Lake. Photo Bob Spirko

Right: #62B Looking up the descent gully from trail #63B. Photo Brenda Everitt

63 Elk Lakes Provincial Park map 7

Official trails
Easy half day to strenuous long day
Map 82 J/11 Kananaskis Lakes

Trail access Via #63A or B from #62 West Elk Pass.

Road access Elk Lakes Provincial Park entrance is accessible by road if you have a few days to spare. Start from Hwy. 3 on the B.C. side of Crowsnest Pass. At Sparwood turn north on Hwy. 43 and drive 35 km to Elkford. Continue on the unpaved Elk River Road, another 67 km of very rough driving. At the end, keep left into the parking lot.

Comments A truly beautiful area that stuns all first time visitors and which is usually reached by backpacking in from Peter Lougheed Provincial Park over West Elk Pass. This volume describes only the more accessible core area of the park.

Trail update After the 2013 flood many trails have been rerouted, some of the info in the 4th edition now redundant.

Facilities and camping At the park entrance, Elk Lakes cabin operated by the Alpine Club of Canada was formerly a ranger cabin. Three campgrounds: 1. Park entrance camping area near the remains of the Bauer cabin. No water, no picnic tables. Nearest biffy is en route to Elk Lakes cabin. 2. Lower Elk Lake campground at the entrance to the lake has tent pads, biffy, lockers, eating areas. 3. Pétain Creek campground on Pétain Creek was decimated by the 2013 flood, leaving only two tent pads intact, though with a covering of mud. The eating area, lockers and biffy were untouched. There are bivouac sites above Pétain Falls.

Biking is not allowed, except on the trail to Lower Elk Lake campground. Bikers can reach the provincial park entrance from Elk Pass at the powerline (see pages 288/289) and bike down the Trans Canada Trail using the powerline access road.

History See the log cabin at the trailhead? There used to be two such cabins, built sometime before the Second World War by coal prospectors working for the CPR. In the

1930s they were used by hunting guide "Old Man" Frank Phillips and became known as the Phillips cabins. He in turn passed them on to guide Mike Baher, who had built a string of cabins up and down the Elk River and into Cadorna Creek. Later, the more habitable one, sleeping six, became the winter headquarters of the Elkford Snowmobile Club, according to their sign above the door, and while they may have looked after it, the cabin was generally "used and abused" by an ignorant public and was ultimately razed to the ground by three drunken snowmobilers who had sneaked in over Elk Pass.

The name Pétain As mentioned later under #66, people have been wanting a name change for a long time. Finally, in 2022, after lobbying by Geoffrey and Duncan Taylor, the B.C. and Alberta governments decided it was time to act. The name was rescinded on June 29, 2022, but the choosing of a new name is unlikely to happen soon — it could well be an Indigenous name — so stay tuned to our website.

Opposite: The kiosk at West Elk Pass. Photo Brenda Everitt   *Above: Lower Elk Lake and Mount Aosta.*

There are two hiking routes into the park from West Elk Pass. If heading for Lower Lake campground, the total distance via #63A is 4.8 km and for #63B 4.3 km. Often backpackers use one for going and the other for coming back.

63A via Elkan Creek

Short day from trailhead
Official trail
Distance 3.8 km from pass
Height loss 177 m (580 ft.)
High point 1865 m (6120 ft.) at pass

Comments An upgraded old Indian trail used by early explorers reaches Lower Elk Lake trail close to the Elk Lakes cabin. Expect one steep section and trail erosion.

    Naming In case you haven't twigged, the word "Elkan" is an acronym of Elk and Kananaskis.

From the kiosk, the trail keeps to the west edge of the longitudinal meadow. You cross the infant Elkan Creek trickling out of Fox Lake and about a kilometre farther on draw close to the bank of that creek, which by now has plunged into a deep valley labelled "Canon" on the boundary survey map of 1917. Wind steeply down a hill and at the bottom recross Elkan Creek on a log bridge. Upstream, the creekbed is filled with flood debris.

    On almost flat ground, walk through mature forest to a big damp meadow where I remember lurching from one tussock to another. It's now crossed by a tremendously long and very narrow boardwalk, so rather than have your eyes glued to the ground, you're free to admire many-buttressed Mt. Aosta, seen in all its Gothic splendour across the Elk Valley — the best (and only) view of the day. A final stretch of forest leads to the main park trail at a signpost. Turn right for Lower Elk Lake campground, 1 kilometre distant. Turn left for the park entrance 200 metres to the left and Elk Lakes cabin, located at the top of the hill.

Above: #63A Crossing boardwalk on the Elkan Creek route, with Mt. Aosta in the background.

Opposite: #63B Fox Lake. In the background is Taiga Viewpoint at left and Mt. Fox at centre. Photo Matt Clay

63B via Fox Lake

Short day from trailhead
Official trail
Distance 3.6 km from pass
Height gain 55 m (180 ft.)
Height loss 152 m (500 ft.)
High point 1980 m (6496 ft.)

Comments The most popular and scenic route used by the GDT reaches the main trail between Lower Lake and the new bridge over the Elk River. NOTE: Since the last edition, landslides have destroyed the final section of trail that used to cross the river near Upper Elk Lake. On the plus side, the reroute brings you within 660 metres of Lower Lake backcountry campground.

Before reaching the kiosk, head west for 200 metres up the boundary cutline toward Mt. Fox. A few metres beyond 1M monument, turn left at a signpost. The trail crosses bog on boardwalk and makes a gradual climb to the east shore of Fox Lake. While chiefly of interest as a watering hole for sasquatch (footprints 17.5 inches long recorded here in the summer of 1961), it does have a rather fine backdrop in Mt. Fox. You can distinguish the cirque holding Frozen Lake and to its left the large, grassy outlier known as Taiga Viewpoint.

Continue up the trail to its high point at the 1.5 kilometre mark, then start the descent. Glades allow fine views looking down the Elk Valley. Cross a creek with deliciously icy water, and lower down a wide, grassy avalanche track where the trail has been rebuilt following a thorough mashing by trees toppled in a 1991 avalanche. Grizzlies have been spotted here, so it's not a good place for a picnic. (It is, though, the optional descent route from Taiga Viewpoint.)

Nearing trail's end, turn sharp left on a new trail that delivers you to the main park trail in 360 metres. (Trail ahead with branches laid across it is the original trail to Upper Elk Lake. See SIDE TRIP below.)

Turn left for Lower Elk Lake backcountry campground and the park entrance, right for Upper Elk Lake, Pétain backcountry campground and Pétain Falls.

SIDE TRIP TO VIEWPOINT

Step over the branches and on original trail traverse forested hillside to the scree slopes, a distance of only 200 metres before the start of the landslips. The best view is of the Elk River backdropped by Mt. Aosta to the south. Of Upper Elk Lake there is only a glimpse.

64 Lower Elk Lake to Upper Elk Lake

map 7

Half day hike
Distance 2.9
Height gain 300 m (990 ft.)
High point 1756 m (5760 ft.)

Also accessible from #63A and B

Comments This is the main park trail between the park entrance and Upper Elk Lake. Easy and gravelled, it gives access to all other trails.

Park entrance to Lower Lake 1.2 km
Round the gate. At the junction with Elk Lakes Cabin go right and down a hill. Just after a wee creek crossing, #63A turns off to the right.

After crossing Elkan Creek, the trail climbs, then undulates, soon running alongside the rushing Elk River to its egress from Lower Elk Lake. On the right are entrances to Lower Elk Lake campground.

To Fox Lake trail 660 m
The trail follows the north shore of the lake, a tranquil body of water sheltered from westerly blasts by a high wall of forest, the highest bump with cliff being "The Viewpoint." Rising up above the forest wall are the peaks of the French Military Group. Across the lake to the south is the fabulous Mt. Aosta.

Beyond the lake, the trail climbs to the Y-junction with #63B Fox Lake trail. Turn left.

To the viewpoint trail 190 m
Zig down and along to the new fibreglass bridge crossing the Elk River, then zig up a hill to a T-junction. Turn right (trail to left is #65 to the Viewpoint).

To Upper Elk Lake 850 m
Taking a completely new line, the trail travels alongside ponds, then winds up over a ridge and down to Upper Elk Lake at a picnic table. Your attention is riveted on Mt. Fox across the water, from this direction an awesome precipice cleft by parallel gullies. Here ends the good trail. See #66 if carrying on into Pétain Creek valley.

Lower Elk Lake, looking toward The Viewpoint in the middle ground at centre.

65 The Viewpoint

map 7

Half day hike
Distance 3 km return to T-junction,
4.7 km return from Lower Lake
backcountry campground
Height gain 130 m (426 ft.)
from the T-junction
High point 1865 m (6120 ft.)

Access Via #63.

Comments The hill with cliffs on two sides
at 348012 is gained by a steady uphill climb.

Follow the main trail to the T-junction on
the west side of the Elk River. Turn left.

Shortly the trail turns right and slightly
downhill alongside the Elk River to the
original creek crossing, now a mess of many
channels. Continue on and when you reach
Lower Elk Lake head inland across boardwalk to a sign.

Here begins the uphill climb, following
a rooty trail up a lush draw between the two
tops. At the col the trail heads left along
the top of a drop-off — view to the west of
the McCuaig, Nivelle and Castelnau three-
some — eventually reaching the treed summit above the great east-facing cliff. Look
down on Lower Elk Lake and the Elk Valley
stretching away to the south.

On this last section from the col keep a
close eye on dogs and small kids.

Returning from the viewpoint.

**Elk Lakes between the entrance and
Upper Elk Lake, showing where the
accesses from West Elk Pass join in**

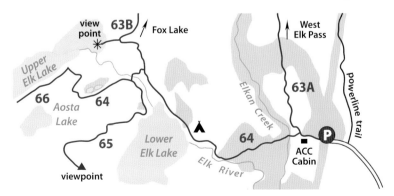

66 Upper Elk Lake to Pétain Falls map 7

Backpack to Pétain backcountry campground, long day hike from the park entrance and Lower Elk Lake backcountry campground
Official trails
Distance to Pétain Creek campground 6.1 km, to Pétain Falls 7.9 km
Height gain to falls 700 m (2300 ft.)
High point at falls 1865 m (6120 ft.)
Map 82 J/11 Kananaskis Lakes

Access Via #64 at Upper Elk Lake.

Comments Expect much rougher trails if you travel alongside Upper Elk Lake and beyond into Pétain Creek valley. The 2013 flood washed out some sections that have either been flagged and cairned or rerouted onto higher ground. Accesses Coral Pass and Pétain Basin.

Camping Pétain Creek backcountry campground with biffy.

To Coral Pass turnoff 3.6 km

A narrow trail follows the east shoreline of Upper Elk Lake. The lake is fjord-like, squeezed between the forest wall on the left and precipitous, slabby slopes on the right which rise over 1000 metres to the ridge between mounts Elkan and Foch. It's one of those places improved by rain. Layers of clouds trailing across the flanks hide the starting points of dozens of rills that burst into life and pour in parallel lines down the sodden slabs. Conversely, in hot fine weather, snow melting in the gullies of Mt. Fox produces spectacular free-fall waterfalls, including one that bursts out of a cave.

At 800 metres a side trail climbs to Upper Aosta Lake, a fishing tarn located 200 metres away over a ridge on a bench. The dark waters are entirely enclosed by forest.

Leaving Upper Elk Lake behind, you arrive at a signpost. Turn right and on plank bridges cross the outwash plain amid

Opposite: The easy trail alongside Upper Elk Lake.   *Below: A terrific view of Pétain Falls by Vern Dewit*

willow bushes. Strips of meadow are soon overrun by sand and stones from floodwaters. Navigate using flagging, cairns and footprints between black dead trees. (This is the site of the original Pétain backcountry campground. You can spot the remains of the Pétain Creek bridge on the bank.)

Look for the resurrected trail climbing into forest. In short order arrive at a signed T-junction with Coral Pass trail. Keep right.

To Pétain Creek backcountry campground 500 m
Descend and cross Pétain Creek on a fine bridge. Now on the right (west) bank, the trail crosses remnants of old trail as it follows the banktop in the trees to a 4-way. To your right is a biffy. Go straight if missing out the campground.

If camping turn left down the bank and cross two wee channels to the campground area.

To Pétain Falls 1.8 km
If camped at Pétain, do not follow the original trail up the flats. Return up the bank to the 4-way and turn left. Round the big bend to the west, the trail gradually moving away from the creek. At 1.7 kilometres you break out of the trees into a meadow and stand spellbound by the scene of not one but many falls plummeting down the cliffs from Pétain Basin.

At the T-junction go left to "Pétain Waterfalls" as the sign directs. (Pétain Basin trail to right.) Head toward Pétain Creek, but don't cross it, because poised above your head like the sword of Damocles is the snout of Castelnau Glacier. Pieces break off regularly with loud bangs that scare the hell out of you and can be heard from as far away as the park entrance. Stay on the trail marked by cairns, and at the end rock hop to the base of magnificent Pétain Falls, which, at a collective height of 375 metres (1230 ft.), is one of the highest falls in Canada.

You've noticed how almost everything else around here is called Pétain: the creek, the basin, the glacier and the mountain next to Mt. Joffre. Five too many Pétains, according to historian Donald Smith. He was not the first to wonder why Philippe Pétain, the "Hero of Verdun" in the First World War turned Nazi collaborator and traitor in the Second, should be so honoured. There's actually a precedent for replacing the name. In 1940 the station of Pétain on B.C.'s Kettle Valley line was changed at the CPR's urging to Odlum. For the latest news on this topic see page 210.

GOING HIGHER

66A Pétain Cirque

Day scramble from Pétain Creek backcountry campground
Unofficial trail & route
Distance 2+ km from Pétain Falls
Height gain 503+ m (1650+ ft.)
High point 2286+ m (7500+ ft.)
Map 82 J/11 Kananaskis Lakes

Access Via #66 at Pétain Falls first viewpoint.

Comments This is one tough climb: a relentlessly steep climber's access trail with easy scrambling to the basin below Mt. Joffre. Start really early if you want to explore. Alternatively, bivy at the camping area on the edge.

At the sign, fork right into trees. Cross a gully and start up the headwall, a torturous crawl up vertical bush on the left edge of the gully. In your desperation you'll be glad to haul yourself up with anything at hand — branches, roots, even gooseberry bushes. The terrain eases fractionally at some fallen trees, then continues as before.

Three-quarters of the height gain behind you, scramble up a grassy rib that leads into a narrow, stony channel between bushes. Ascend the channel for only a few metres before branching left toward a cairn marking the beginning of the traverse. (Some people go up the stony gully instead and then turn left at a cairn.)

What relief to traverse left on grass below talus slopes, then rockbands. The

trail descends slightly to the base of a two-tiered buttress that you climb to a cairn. Possibly easier routes can be found to the right; certainly harder variations exist to the left. Topping out into the basin, head left to where Pétain Creek shoots out into space. The bivy area is located across the creek in the trees and is more safely reached by a lengthy upstream detour.

Walk the flat below an encircling cliff for a closer look at Pétain Creek's middle waterfall. A little way on are easy ways up right into meadows with krumholtz and bedrock scored by rillenkarren. Maybe you'll find the spring dubbed "The Fountain of Youth" bubbling out of a hump of gravel. You can wander bedrock quite high to within 380 vertical metres of the summit of Mt. Foch. The higher you are, the more spectacular the view of Pétain Glacier with Mt. Joffre at its head. Alternatively, exploring the benches below the toe of the glacier reveals dozens of tarns, a few quite colourful.

Top: The lower meadows of Pétain Cirque showing just a glimpse of Pétain Glacier and Mt. Joffre. Photo Matt Clay

Above: The middle waterfall in Pétain Cirque. Note the size of the person. Photo Matt Clay

67 Coral Pass

map 7

Day hike or scramble from Pétain
Creek campground
Unofficial trail, route
Distance 6 km to pass
Height gain 780 m (2560 ft.)
High point 2515 m (8250 ft.)
Maps 82 J/11 Kananaskis Lakes,
82 J/6 Mt. Abruzzi

Access Via trail #66 between the old and new Pétain Creek campgrounds.

Comments Coral Pass is located between Pétain Creek and Cadorna Creek on the Great Divide at 318956. Of all the hikes I've had to do for this book, this was one of the most horrible because we didn't start from the campground at Pétain Creek and it was pelting with rain both going up and going down the headwall. The headwall is the steepest part of the route, which is otherwise fairly easy-angled. There's an alternative to the headwall, which is the avalanche slope of B.C. bush. But whichever route you take, getting to Coral Pass is for the experienced off-trail hiker who can hack B.C. bush, steep slopes, tricky route-finding, the odd creek crossing, snow, scree and a little easy scrambling. Last report is that some of the route in flagged. Nevertheless, a GPS receiver is useful for following the track log on the return.

The reward for all this trauma is wild, untrammelled uplands with glaciers, the most spectacular fossil beds you have ever seen (hence the name Coral), and a fantastic view of the Italian Group of mountains.

The scramble crux of the direct headwall route.

To Nivelle Cirque 3 km via direct route

From the trail junction, the trail is good to where it crosses a small side creek. Not far beyond this crossing the two routes up the headwall diverge:

1. The direct route entails one pitch of easy scrambling. First, cross the alluvial flat on a faint trail that follows an old river channel leading straight to Nivelle Creek. Cross and pick your way along the left bank (bushes, rotting logs) to the bend of the creek at 329982. Blocking the way ahead is the lower canyon. Don't even think of following it, especially if it's choked with snow. The safer route tackles the forested slope just left of the canyon, which appears quite innocuous with its staggered rockbands. The route may still be flagged, but don't depend on it. Rather, look for signs of struggle with the vegetation. Possibly a trail exists all the way by now?

In detail: Start from a small meadow to the left of the lower cliff. Wend left initially, then crawl straight up under menziesia bushes, the gradient and bushes easing as you approach the middle cliff band. Here, turn right, following the rising base of the rock. It gets quite steep and when the cliff ends it's a straight-up thrutch to a terrace for a brief respite.

Resume climbing, wending left below a small crag and up to a strip of meadow running below the top cliff band. At a T-junction, traverse right on a trail midway between the trees and the bottom of the cliff. This trail leads to the one place where you can break through the cliff at its lowest point between the north- and west-facing slopes. Climb the crux via a grungy, 5-metre-high groove, a bit difficult to start but handholds are good. Next up is the traverse high above the canyon. Just as the situation becomes airy, the trail turns uphill and fades away on easy ground. I need hardly tell you it's essential you hit this traverse line on the descent. The alternatives are the avalanche slope or a return via Cadorna Creek and the Elk River.

The final slope is easy going through forest, flats alternating with steps. The trail reappears at the top of the slope and heads slightly right and downhill through forest and meadow to Nivelle Creek, which is reached about 300 metres back from the lip of the lower canyon. Continue up the left bank of the creek.

2. Via the avalanche slope I'm told it's the easiest route, "which does not mean this is an easy route," says B.C. ranger Jack Paterson, who has struggled up it.

The final approach to the pass up the scree basin. In the background is the Elk Glacier below Mt. Nivelle.

In detail: Not too far along after the first side creek crossing, climb the avalanche slope to the left of the direct route for 300 vertical metres. Then traverse right between rockbands, following a game trail through the upper band onto treed benches. Continue to head southwest until you reach Nivelle Creek between canyons.

To the pass 3 km
Just below the right-angle bend at 327968, cross Nivelle Creek to the right (west) bank and follow a trail alongside the creek into larch and meadow country. Emanating from the upper canyon ahead is the thunder of waterfalls. The trail climbs above the first fall, then heads off up the hillside. Level with a crag on the left, keep left. Above the crag, turn left onto a good traversing trail that peters out in meadows. This is a heavenly spot, the bright-green grass and flowers a startling contrast to the glitter of glacier, névé and rushing stream.

Recross Nivelle Creek. As you climb out of meadows onto rock the lie of the land becomes clear. You're in a huge basin rimmed by a semicircle of ridges draped with permanent snow. To your right, Elk

Glacier sticks out a white tongue between mounts Gamelin, Nivelle and De Gaulle, the first and last names not official. Farthest away, the low point in the ridge is Coral Pass.

Ribbons of bedrock streaming toward you offer obvious ascent routes. However, crags immediately below the pass make a direct approach impossible. We gained the pass from the right.

At the pass you're looking into what George Pocaterra always referred to by its Stoney name, Nyahe-ya-Nibi, meaning "Go-up-into-the-mountains country": Cadorna Creek (the lake is out of sight) and the "three giants of Nyahe-ya-Nibi" — mounts Cadorna, Swiderski and Battisti. Walter Wilcox called them Goldwin Smith, Duchesnay and Steele.

Directly across the valley the mountain with horizontal cliffs is called Misty Mountain by old-timers. After crossing Pass in the Clouds in 1901, Walter Wilcox and Henry Bryant climbed Misty and looked across to Coral Pass. "Aha, a shortcut to Kananaskis Lakes," they thought. They returned to camp and the whole pack train moved down Abruzzi Creek and up Cadorna Creek. Wilcox carried on alone above Cadorna Lake and with field glasses pressed to his eyes, noted "no trail led up to the pass." So his party retreated down to the Elk River and crossed West Elk Pass instead. There may be no trail, but there is a reasonable route up it, writes Dustin in *Hiking Canada's Great Divide Trail*.

DESCENT VARIATION

Going down you can vary the route a bit by exiting the pass to skier's right via a scree ramp. Lower down you're sure to run into a huge fossil bed several kilometres square where horn coral is scattered all over the rock like grass seed. Just as exciting for me was the karst we encountered, which extends across to the meadows and down into the trees. Dropping into one sinkhole and popping out another gives you hours of childish fun.

The three giants of Nyahe-ya-Nibi (mounts Cadorna, Swiderski and Battisti) from the pass.

68 Canadian Mount Everest Expedition Interpretive Trail map 5

Half-day hike
Official trail
Distance 2.2 km loop
Height gain 104 m (340 ft.)
High point 1813 m (5950 ft.)
Map 82 J/11 Kananaskis Lakes

Access Kananaskis Lakes Trail (road) at White Spruce parking lot below Upper Lake Dam. In detail: drive past Upper Lake day-use area access road; then, at the 4-way with Mt. Sarrail campground access road, turn left.

Comments More strenuous than the usual interpretive trail, it loops over a hilltop between Upper and Lower Kananaskis Lakes. Make use of numerous benches, among them the Wendy Elekes memorial bench (same plaque, different bench), moved from its rightful place on Mount Indefatigable trail. Also plentiful are interpretive signs that cover mountain building, First Peoples, first explorers, first climbers and so on.

Naming In 1984 the trail was renamed the "Canadian Mount Everest Expedition Interpretive trail" to honour the 11 men of the expedition that made the first Canadian ascent of Mount Everest in 1982. (See also #45B.) Understandably, most people, including the Everesters, prefer the original name of "Interlakes," which is descriptive and dates back to 1916 when the Boundary Survey used a twin hilltop to the north as a camera station.

The trail starts at an interpretive sign and plaque on the right side of the parking lot and winds its undulating way through spruce forest to a Y-junction with the return leg. Keep straight.

The trail descends a little along the damp east side of the hill, all mosses and lichens, then starts climbing across a steeper slope, ultimately zigging and climbing tiers of steps onto the north ridge. Here it turns south and continues up more steps to a rocky summit with "viewing" platform, interpretive signs and memorial bench.

Steps on the way to the hilltop.

Trees have grown up all around the platform and it is no longer the all-around viewpoint of Upper and Lower Kananaskis Lakes that it once was. Still, it's a nice place to sit for awhile and look at mountain tops.

On the return leg, descend the south ridge, once open but now treed. Affixed to the next memorial bench down is the Wendy Elekes plaque. Down more steps is a less comfortable bench with a limited view of mountains plus an audio of Sarrail Falls across the upper lake.

Shortly after, the trail zigs back down into spruce forest and is flat. Climb a little to an unofficial junction of trails that can be confusing. (See NOTE.) Go first left up a hill and meander along to the Y-junction. Turn right to return the same way you came up.

NOTE: On the return, the side trail to right at the unofficial junction leads to Upper Lake trail in a few minutes. Turn left to return to the parking lot using the trail down the front of the dam.

69 Upper Kananaskis Lake Circuit map 5

Day hike
Official trail
Distance 16.2 km loop
Height gain ~61 m (200 ft.)
High point 1768 m (5800 ft.)
Map 82 J/11 Kananaskis Lakes

Access Kananaskis Lakes Trail (road).
1. North Interlakes parking lot. Walk down to the trailhead at the kiosk.
2. Upper Lake day-use area, a complicated collection of parking lots. Keep left (boat launch to right), keep right, turn next right into parking lots nearest the lake. For south shore trail, turn left and drive to the far end. For east shore trail turn right.
3. White Spruce parking lot. From the start of 1982 CMEE interpretive trail, a wide track climbs to the dam.
Also accessible from ##73, 75.

Comments Who can resist circumventing a lake, even if it is a reservoir? This easy trail offers mountain views, waterfalls and a unique spring considered by one awed person to be "one of the 7 wonders of the world."

Camping Point backcountry campground located on a peninsula reached by a spur trail.

History In 1883 the fledgling Eau Claire & Bow River Lumber Company hungered after the mature trees that grow around the lake, but stayed only long enough to name the lake "Ingram" after C.H. Ingram of C.H. Ingram Associates, who'd advanced capital for the trip from Wisconsin.

Walter Wilcox in 1901: "A revelation of beauty hardly equalled anywhere... has four large islands and several small islets, all densely wooded, which give an endless variety of views from various points." A.O. Wheeler in 1916: "One of the most beautiful, of a glorious blue, studded with little timbered islands. Nestling below the towering rock precipices of Mt. Sarrail, 10,400 feet in altitude, on a bright summer day it is a thing of beauty and of joy." The Canadian National Parks Association in 1931 after the lakes were removed from the national park to become

storage reservoirs: "People of future generations will curse us — or, we hope, bless us for what we are doing for them." R.M. Patterson post-reservoir: "A scene of wreckage to be shunned or hurriedly passed by. Nobody in their right mind would willingly visit the place now as an object of a trip."

So he was wrong, but knowing nothing better we continue to come to the heart of Kananaskis Country.

ANTI-CLOCKWISE

North shore to Point backcountry campground 3.6 km

Follow Three Isle Lake trail along the isthmus. You may have seen the cabin that was built here in 2007 for the German TV series set in 19th century Canada *Im Tal der wilden Rosen* (In the Valley of the Wild Roses).

Cross the intake pipe by bridge, noting North Interlakes power plant below at Lower Kananaskis Lake, then swing left onto the fire road. Almost straightaway the unsigned trail to Mount Indefatigable South turns off to the right between boulders (see #78).

A little farther on veer right as per the sign, then in 900 m from the trailhead turn left off the fire road onto a soft forest trail that descends to near shoreline within sound of the slap of waves. Offshore is Hawke Island, its few scraggy larch trees a mere remnant of those "small islets, all densely wooded."

The trail climbs out of the trees into the blinding glare of a vast boulder field known as the Palliser Slide. Continue climbing up craftily constructed steps to a signpost. Keep left. (Side trail to right climbs the edge of the slide to Three Isle Lake fire road.)

The trail undulates across the bumps and hollows of the boulder field and around the edge of an inlet. While still in the boulder field, now disguised by a sparse covering of vegetation and trees, come to a junction. Go right. (The spur trail to left leads to Point backcountry campground, its 20 sites scattered up and down the peninsula.

Above: Upper Kananaskis Lake from the north shore, Mt. Sarrail predominant.

Opposite: The trail in the Palliser Slide. The small corner on the right side of the big slab is the celebrated multi-pitch climb called Joy.

To the bridge 900 m

The main trail climbs and passes to the right of a large rocky basin sometimes filled with viridian-green water, so still and clear it looks like glass. A few minutes later, contour around the head of another inlet that looks very different at low water when the Kananaskis River is revealed winding between shores dotted with stumps. During this time watch for bears feeding on yummy shoreline vegetation.

Reach a Y-junction on the river's east bank. Go right.

SIDE TRIP TO LOWER KANANASKIS FALLS

Keep straight, following the old trail along the bank to the falls. At this spot was a bench in memory of Bernie Kathol, who was a district supervisor for Alberta Transportation. The trail beyond was washed out during the flood of 2013, so return the same way to the Y-junction and turn left.

The new trail built in 2014 climbs away from the river, then descends to the bridge above the falls. Immediately after, undesignated Lyautey trail (no signpost) turns off to the right. Stay on the main trail.

West shore to Aster Lake trail 1.7 km

The word "shore" is a misnomer here. The trail lies so deep in forest you're without views unless you count cliffs glimpsed from time to time above the treetops. The route is mostly uphill to the new Aster Lake trail junction. (See #71.) Stay ahead.

South shore to Access 2, 5.6 km

The trail continues to rise a little, then descends to the lakeshore. The roar you hear comes from Hidden Lake Springs, a great place to fill up the water bottles.

Gradually the trail curves to the east and travels close to the lake below steep, mossy slopes of spruce trees. Watch for bald eagles holding station on the tallest trees overlooking the lake. You may see a few loons on the water, but they won't nest here because of fluctuating water levels. In this section cross three avalanche paths, the first and widest sporting a huge variety of shrubs and small trees like mountain ash.

Next up is Rawson Creek bridge, appropriated from Sarrail Creek after the 2013 flood. A little farther on, the Rawson Lake trail takes off up the hillside to the right.

Lower Kananaskis Falls.

SIDE TRIP TO HIDDEN LAKE SPRINGS

A side trail leads down to them beyond the willow bushes. If coming from the opposite direction, look for the trail just after the boardwalk.

These are karst springs, the water coming from Hidden Lake, which dries up in fall to just an eddy spinning in a clockwise direction down a mudhole. There are two conventional springs and one very unusual one that erupts from the top of a high mound—an island at high water—and from the pool flows in opposite directions down to the lake. Pre-reservoir, the springs emptied into the Kananaskis River.

Keep straight and in an another 100 metres cross Sarrail Creek below a waterfall. As you will read, the newfangled fibreglass bridge was made necessary by the creek widening its banks during the flood. It's here where you'll meet lots of people hanging about both above the falls and on the lakeshore.

The final kilometre undulates in and out of every indent, the trend uphill on the final straight leading to the southernmost Upper Lake parking lot.

East shore 4.4 km

Walk through to the northernmost parking lot where the trail continues. Cross a bridge at interpretive signs, then cross the boat launch road onto Upper Lake Dam, the site of beautiful Twin Falls pre-reservoir. At dam's end, the track from access 3 joins in from the right and you wend left around a grassy bay. Cross a small ridge to gain the east shore.

Top: Hidden Lake Springs, showing the mound and a short-lived creek flowing from the pool in a cataract. The other creek flows down the far side of the mound into the lake more directly.

Bottom: Sarrail Falls.

SIDE TRIP TO GAHERTY POINT

At the top of the small ridge a 439-m-long side trail to left follows a promontory to the rocky point enclosing the inner bay. After a stint along the shoreline, you follow the treed spine of the promontory to a rock chimney and descend onto a finger of slabs. When the water's low you can walk farther along the shore to a second trail heading up into the trees.

You can idle away much time on the slabs, enjoying the view, watching kayakers and paddle boarders rounding the point between you and a small island, and listening to the roar of Sarrail Falls across the bay.

The trail, rebuilt since the first go-round, climbs in waves of uphills some distance above the lakeshore, which is character-ized by rocky headlands and the half-moon curve of bays. When strong west winds send waves racing across the lake to break with a thump on the shore, it's easy to imagine yourself by some inlet of the ocean. Height-ening that impression are terraces of shin-gle shaped by someone hitting a computer key. Across the water Mt. Sarrail and the Mt. Lyautey massif rise in great precipices, while farther away the distinctive shape of Mt. Putnik is revealed through the gap of the Kananaskis River.

But for all the fine scenery the east leg is a depressing section to walk. When the water's drained, the bones of the drowned forest are exposed and offshore islets are seen once again as headlands of the former shoreline. The deeply indented bay next to the treed "island" joined to the mainland by a causeway of stumps was once a lake. Near here archaeologists have recovered a few prehistoric flakes.

At the halfway point the trail comes close to the highway, then continues around what's left of a promontory, a splendid viewpoint 80 years ago for a half dozen islands that crowded this half of the lake. Schooner Island lay about half a kilometre out, a boat-shaped island whose few trees were so arranged to resemble the masts of a sail-ing ship. On windy days, the dash of spray against the rocks gave the illusion it was the island itself that was moving.

Turn the corner into the large artificial bay, thus completing the loop when you reach the kiosk at Three Isle Lake trailhead. Turn right for North Interlakes parking lot.

Top left: The chimney on Gaherty Point, all that's left of a large log cabin built for the president of Calgary Power as a honeymoon suite in 1933. From here the trail makes a steep descent to the slabs.

Top right: East shore bay, looking towards Mt. Sarrail. Rawson Lake lies hidden behind the forested ridge.

Opposite: #70 A first view of Rawson Lake and Mt. Sarrail from the outlet. Photo Bernie Nemeth

70 Rawson Lake

map 7

Short day hike
Official trail
Distance 3.9 km to lake from trailhead
Height gain 305 m (1000 ft.)
High point 2027 m (6650 ft.)
Map 82 J/11 Kananaskis Lakes

Access Kananaskis Lakes Trail (road) at Upper Lake parking lots. Via #69 Upper Kananaskis Lake circuit south shore section.

Comments The trail, steep enough to make you sweat, leads to a beautiful jade lake under Mt. Sarrail. Grizzlies den in the area — one good reason why camping is not allowed on the lakeshore. Check for bear closures before you set out.

Upper Kananaskis Lake trail 1.2 km
Follow Upper Kananaskis Lake trail clockwise along the south shore. Just beyond Sarrail Creek bridge at the waterfall, come to a Y-junction. Turn left onto Rawson Lake trail at the interpretive sign.

To Rawson Lake 2.7 km
Straightaway you're into a winding climb through musty old spruce forest with interpretive signs. The gradient eases half a kilometre before the lake and it's here where you encounter long stretches of single-track boardwalk. Near the outlet hop down to sign no. 6 for the classic view of the lake backdropped by the vertical east face of Mt. Sarrail.

The trail continues along the southeast shore below a line of cliffs, en route passing a green biffy up on a pedestal. Officially the trail ends halfway along the lake in a mix of meadow and rocks at the last interpretive sign "Constant Change."

All clear? Follow the ongoing trail on scree to the far end of the lake, from where you get a new perspective of this gorgeous piece of water. En route, flower aficionados should look for the elusive mist maiden growing on rocks near a small tarn.

The ongoing trail is the route to Rawson Ridge. See #70A.

70A Rawson Ridge

Unofficial trail, route
Distance 2 km to ridge
Height gain 366 m (1200 ft.) from lake
High point 2392 m (7850 ft.)

Comments The ridge at 301064 bounding the cirque to the northwest may not look up to much, and getting there is a steep, strenuous flog, but it's one fantastic viewpoint for Upper Kananaskis Lake. But first, with binoculars carefully scan the grassy slopes below the ridge for griz.

Top: #70A Looking down on Rawson Lake.

Bottom: #70A Upper and Lower Kananaskis Lakes from the ridge, Mt. Indefatigable South at centre.

The trail continues, making for the right side rib of the prominent gully immediately left of the forest edge. Not far up, break away right into a shallow draw that offers a more reasonable way upward. Just below the gully split, the trail heads back left onto the rib and after a second split climbs the right-hand gully.

At the top, head up right through lush flower meadows to a spectacular piece of ridge sandwiched between rock towers, so you can't walk too far in either direction. What you've come for is the bird's-eye view of Upper Kananaskis Lake and surrounding mountains. The colour of the water will have you drooling.

71 Aster Lake maps 5, 8

Long day scramble, backpack
Unofficial trail
Distance 11 km from trailhead
Height gain 570 m (1870 ft.)
from trailhead
High point 2292 m (7520 ft.)
Map 82 J/11 Kananaskis Lakes

Access Kananaskis Lakes Trail (road) at Upper Lake parking lots. Via #69 Upper Kananaskis Lake circuit. Follow the south shore section for 5.6 km to the signed junction for Aster Lake trail.

Comments Aster Lake and the high glacial valleys under Mt. Joffre aren't easy to get to. If you're hoping for an easy park trail with lots of zigs up the woody slopes of Foch Creek's west bank, you're out of luck, though I've known people who've given the slope a go, usually on the descent, like Henry Bryant did in 1901.

Unaccountably, the trail takes a thrilling line up the east bank, crossing scree slopes poised above cliffs that aren't for anyone whose legs turn to jelly in such places. And unless you're happy crossing steep snow, wait until August. Mid-August to mid-September is the prime time for exploring this area.

Obviously, this is no trail for novices. The trail is mostly used by experienced backpackers doing a three-day trip incorporating Northover Ridge and Three Isle Lake. Scramblers/climbers use it as access to mounts Joffre, Sarrail, Northover and Cordonnier as well as Warrior Mountain. Waterfall lovers can visit Fossil Falls without climbing the second headwall. Campers can explore amazing options B and C from the campground, or just roam around at random.

Route update I am happy to report that since the fourth edition a new trail has been built around Hidden Lake and up the first headwall.

Camping A backcountry campground located alongside Aster Creek just below Aster Lake. (Biffy, food lockers.) The oft-seen grizzly doesn't seem to bother anyone.

First view of Aster Lake, with Warrior Mountain reflected in its still waters. Photo Sonny Bou

Trail history Before Joe Kovach cut out a trail on October 12, 1945, access from Upper Kananaskis Lake to Hidden Lake was described by Walter Wilcox as "an hour of the most difficult bush work I have ever seen." Of course, he started from the shore of the original lake, which was a lot lower down in 1901. At the time, he and Henry Bryant were on their way to discovering Aster Lake by way of Fossil Falls.

For the last few decades, getting to Hidden was easy, but getting past it was always a problem. It belongs to the bathtub class of lakes, so you never knew what to expect. When the water was circling clockwise down the drain, you could walk dry mud flats blotchy with scarlet copepods. When the water reached the trees you were forced into a painfully slow bushwhack along a rustic "trail" with copious deadfall.

Then a few years ago James C and his crew not only cleared out the trail around the lake but also made zigs up the first headwall, so eliminating the "otter slide" as James called it. A future project is to put a chain down the crux gully.

First follow the south shore section of Upper Kananaskis Lake Circuit for 5.6 km.

Hidden Lake and lower headwall 2.5 km
At the signpost on Upper Lake trail turn left. Shortly the trail descends to join the old trail beyond the meadow. Go left and wander through bushes to Hidden Lake, where a side trail leads to the lakeshore. There are two ways on, depending on water levels.

1. Via trail Keep left and meander up and down and across the hillside above the lake. At 285072 the route from the lake joins in.

2. Via Hidden Lake At little or no water simply walk the mud flats. Just before the end of the lake look for a swath of stones in the trees to the left (flagging) and walk up them to intersect the trail at 285072 Turn right.

This signals the start of the lower headwall. After the initial uphill diagonal, three zigs with high rock steps at bends take you to treeline. The trail continues at the demarcation of scree, meadow and trees and includes three easy forays on the rocks. On arriving at the top of the lower headwall, look back to Hidden Lake and forward to your first view of Fossil Falls.

Upper headwall 1.3 km
From here the "goat trail," as Wilcox called it, climbs diagonally across low-angle scree to a gully with water. Stagger up the right bank a way, then continue the diagonal traverse across a bigger, steeper scree slope. Easier going leads to the crossing of two hanging scree slopes where cliffs peel off immediately below the trail. It's here, going down, where the exposure grabs you by the throat.

The trail continues its amazing line, traversing slightly less vertiginous ground to a small boulder field. When snow free the upward traverse below a high waterfall is no problem, but under snow it has its perils. Most obviously, you don't want to go for a slide. Secondly, when snow covering the creek below the fall melts out from underneath, it leaves a very fragile snow bridge

Opposite: On the zigs of the lower headwall.

Above: Descending the upper headwall at hanging scree slope no. 2. Since this photo was taken, the trail has improved a lot.

Below: The crux gully which after erosion is more difficult than it looks. Luckily, it can be circumvented.
Photo Matt Clay

Above: Looking back down to the trail crossing the second hanging scree slope.

at this point. So if the slope looks at all iffy, cross a shelf of boulders below the snow and scramble up rocks on the far side.

Up next is the technical crux, a gully with no good holds after erosion unveiled a vertical step. (Matt C says the gully can be avoided by heading up left on a grassy ramp and cutting across the top of the crag.)

But first, anyone interested in hydrology should visit the "confluence" at a pool and stand on the shingle. Far beneath your feet is the rumble of a waterfall, the subterranean waters of Marlborough Tarn passing *beneath* those of Aster Creek.

Looking across Aster Lake from the north shore trail to mounts Sarrail and Foch.

To Aster Lake 1.6 km

Suddenly the trail dips into trees. The contrast is astonishing, the savagery of the headwall replaced by the beauty of alpine meadows with flowers, larch and spruce, a hugely complicated terrain of miniature ribs and valleys all sloping in a northwesterly direction. The first feature you come to is Foch Pond, with its dazzling glacial backdrop of Mt. Marlborough. The trail heads along the right bank, then crosses a meadow down the centre of which dribbles a fork of Foch Creek, a tiddly little thing you can step over. In 1916 the Boundary Survey made a blunder compounded ever since by every other mapmaker. They named what is really boisterous Aster Creek after a trifling tributary.

Shortly start a long descent, en route passing the patrol cabin/weather station side trail at left. The trail wends its way down a miniature rockband and across a miniature creek running through one of the miniature valleys, then enters a parallel valley which is dry at this point and marked by two cairns. Turn right. (Left heads toward Marlborough Tarn.) Descend the dry valley toward Aster Creek and at three cairns turn left uphill.

The winding climb up the left bank of Aster Creek is alternately flat and scrambly. If you're a sucker for pools and waterfalls, like me, you'll be continually rushing over to the creek to see what it's doing. A green biffy is the first sighting of Aster Lake backcountry campground, located on a flat below Aster Lake and sheltered somewhat from katabatic winds that blow nightly off the Mangin Glacier.

Climb a little higher to Aster Lake with its surround of meadows. Disappointingly, the water is grey from glacial silt, but the mountain scenery is superb — Sarrail, Foch, Lyautey and Warrior, all first climbed in July 1930 by Katie Gardiner with guide Walter Feuz.

But back to Walter Wilcox. While Wilcox was getting off a few photos of Fossil Falls, Bryant wandered off and climbed a gully to join today's access trail. Wilcox followed later and independently of each other they roamed all over the meadows, although only Wilcox ventured up to the lake "half a mile long at the base of a long glacier." So Wilcox was the first discoverer.

#71A Fossil Falls in midsummer is an awesome sight.

71A Fossil Falls

Route mainly
Distance 2 km return to col,
18.2 km return from trailhead
Height gain ~76 m (250 ft.) return to col
High point ~2012 m (6600 ft.)

Comments Although K Country's premier waterfall lies close to the beaten track, few people have time to make it a side trip. Why not consider it a day trip from the trailhead? A paddle 'n' hike works even better.

Leave Aster Lake trail at the cairn above the lower headwall. Walk straight through a gap between the scree and a treed knoll on the right. Descend a little, then traverse a wide scree slope, keeping just above a patch of tall trees, to a perpendicular band of thick vegetation on either side of a side creek. Push through to a small meadow

Below: #71B Marlborough Tarn below Mt. Marlborough. Photo Alf Skrastins

Opposite top: #71C The lower tarn in the hanging valley. In the background are Onslow Mtn. and the Royal Group. The tarns, being in B.C., are good places to random camp.

Opposite bottom: #71C Waka Nambé. Photo Alf Skrastins

below a crag. Cross diagonally upwards to some flagging which signals the crux — a much longer, harder push through head-high bushes on a slant. This gets you to easy ground below "Alberta Falls" as Wilcox called them.

Return the same way. Don't emulate Wilcox and Henry Bryant by trying to rejoin the "goat trail" from the falls. The gully, sadly, was the scene of a recent fatality.

71B Marlborough Tarn

Unofficial trail, route
Distance 2.1 km
Height gain 168 m (550 ft.) via 1.
High point 2393 m (7850 ft.)

Leave Aster Lake trail two cairns before the climb alongside Aster Creek to the campsite. Turn left up-valley into meadows. Water is now running lively in the creekbed with lots of small waterfalls to delight in before you reach the spring at the foot of the moraine. Climb the terminal moraine and continue on to an overlook for the bright-blue lake tucked under the glaciers of Mt. Marlborough.

71C Hanging Valley and Waka Nambé Viewpoint

Unofficial trail, routes
Distance 3.2 km to tarns, 2.9 km to viewpoint, 7.6 km round trip
Height gain 317 m (1040 ft.) to tarns,
460 m (1510 ft.) to viewpoint
Height loss 91 m (300 ft.) to tarns
High point for tarns 2588 m (8490 ft.) at
pass, high point for viewpoint 2731 m
(8960 ft.)

FROM ASTER LAKE

Follow the Northover Ridge trail (read the
first two sections of #72) to the high pass
at 252041 between Warrior Mountain and
Mt. Northover. Leave the trail here and
stroll down scree and grass into the hanging
valley on the B.C. side of the Divide, which
harbours two tarns first visited by George
Pocaterra and his dog MacDuff in 1911. A
few metres from the lower tarn the ground
drops away in a repulsive downfall of screes
and crags streaked yellow and black. In
the valley far below, Giorgio did some gold
panning, but he got there via Joffre Creek.

Return to the pass, then head southwest
up scree, grass and likely snow for 152
metres (500 ft.) to the flat-topped hill at
247037. There is the option of going farther

up the north ridge of Warrior for a closer-
in view of Waka Nambé, which overhangs
Joffre Creek 1200 metres below. The "Great
Spirit Thumb" or "Hand of God" was named
by Pocaterra, who photographed it from
the lower south ridge of Northover. While
it looks spectacular from this direction, it
looks even more surreal when seen from the
opposite side in Joffre Creek.

Scramble, backpack
Unofficial trails & route,
creek crossings
Distance 11.9 km
Height gain 820 m (2690 ft.)
Height loss 905 m (2930 ft.)
High point 2800 m (9190 ft.)
Map 82 J/11 Kananaskis Lakes

Access from the south via #71 Aster Lake at Aster Lake.
Access from the north via #73 Three Isle Lake & South Kananaskis Pass at Three Isle Lake.

Comments Northover Ridge is to Jasper's celebrated Skyline trail what Smirnoff is to any other vodka, or so the ad goes. It's a sublime ridgewalk! Don't thank me for telling you about it; thank Alf Skrastins, who first traversed the ridge in 1979 and brought it to everyone's attention in the *Foothills Wilderness Journal*. (As far as I can ascertain, the Boundary Survey in 1916 just visited the northwest tip to set up a camera station.) Combine #72 with routes #71 and 73 (and even with routes #74 and 75) to experience the best backpacking trip in K Country.

Amazing to me, the ridge plus access trails is being promoted as a one-day 35-km trip for mountain runners. While it is true that between editions of this book a trail has developed that sometimes travels below the crest, does it make it THAT easy? As one runner put it, "Staying alive is the main goal." The thing is, there's no actual scrambling where you can cling to comforting rocks. In places the ridge is as narrow and airy as it ever was. Don't go if you're a klutz with two left feet or are bothered by heights. Poles are a good idea, and wear footwear suitable for snow. Lastly, wait for good conditions. Serious accidents have happened to physically fit people slipping on snow on the Aster Lake headwall and losing their footing on the narrowest part of the ridge during stormy weather, blown off by strong wind gusts.

SOUTH TO NORTH FROM ASTER LAKE

Around the lake ~2 km

There are trails round both sides.

1. The slightly shorter **north shore trail** involves a shallow wading of the outlet right at the start. Walk below the many summits of Mt. Lyautey and cross the mouth of the glaciated pass east of Mt. Northover, which looks terrifyingly sharp from this direction. The trail takes you onto the grassy knoll to the west of the lake.

2. Being averse to an icy creek crossing right after breakfast, many people take the slightly longer **south shore trail**. At the steep side hill it's easier to tiptoe along the edge of the lake on rocks. On reaching gravel flats and a braided stream (the outwash from the north glaciers of Mt. Joffre), make for the grassy knoll ahead, where you will pick up the trail. But first you will likely have to wade the stream.

To first pass 1 km

The trail aims for a scree gully at 256037, where cairns mark the start of a good trail up its right bank. A short way up the gully, the trail turns right up a more confined draw toward the pass at 252041 between Warrior and Northover. High up, the trail traverses some cement shale which can be avoided by a simple walk up the draw bottom on scree and then snow to the pass. A sign reads "Height of the Rockies." Down left is a hanging valley with two tarns which make a pleasant side trip from the campground. Of course, a pass implies you can travel through to Joffre Creek, and while I know someone who's done it, I can guarantee you'll be petrified.

To Northover Col 1.7 km

Continue along the trail that traverses the west face of Mt. Northover on scree. Enter a scree scoop with permanent snow patches and plod up to the col immediately west of Mt. Northover at 242054.

What a fantastic viewpoint for Mt. Joffre, which sticks up like a white tooth with a distinct lean to the right. In 1901 Wilcox suggested it be named Mt. Walcott after the director of the US Geological Survey, but it got shot down and is named instead after a French general. To its left a glacier can be seen snaking through a gap from Pétain Glacier. Down below are the twin tarns.

Northover Ridge 2.7 km

Follow the ridge to the left. A rocky 10-m-long stretch is a taste of the ridge to come: an almost 3-km-long tightrope of scree poised between the névé of Northover Glacier and scree slopes plunging over 1200 m, or nearly 4,000 ft., into Joffre Creek ("Fury Stream" to Wilcox). At first, though, the rolling, rounded ridge and the thickness of the ice buffer the drops on both sides.

The ridge narrows, rising elegantly to the northernmost high point. Where névé is replaced by cliffs you run into vertigo-inducing places where careful footing is required and, at the crux, a bum shuffle if the pack is heavy and the wind is blowing cross-wise. This is the place where you might encounter a traffic jam.

On the far side either take the trail to the left or continue the excitement by walking the crest to the high point. Look out if you dare across the gulf of the Palliser River Valley to the Royal Group framed between Onslow and Defender mountains (Battle of Jutland destroyers nicknamed "the Cripple and the Paralytic" by Rudyard Kipling). To the north, Sir Douglas rises above Three Isle Lake. To the south, the spectacular wall of the Great Divide is seen continuing past Mt. Joffre to the White River.

View from just beyond the pass at 252041 toward the scree scoop leading to the col between Northover Ridge to left and Mt. Northover to right.

The easy stretch ends at 232062. WARNING! Don't think for one minute you can exit the ridge before the col at 221065. Enticed by a first view of Three Isle Lake or perhaps intimidated by the ridge ahead, some people have rushed off down the alluring side ridge at 232062, which traps you in its fatal embrace. Slips on ice lower down have resulted in injuries and one fatality. I don't want this to happen to you. So ignoring the false trail, *keep left at 232062, following a line of cairns* built in 1994.

All too soon the glorious ridge comes to an end and you drop about 183 vertical metres (600 ft.) to the col at 221065.

To Three Isle Lake 4.4 km to campground

Turn right (north) and on glissadable scree, descend to meadows and finally to the flat valley floor of an unnamed stream arising from the glaciers of Northover Ridge. A trail takes you out to Three Isle Lake (where you might just discover that third isle) and along the south shore past the patrol cabin to the campground.

Top: Northover Ridge. At first the ridge has a rounded crest and is easy. Mt. Northover and col to left.
Photo Alf Skrastins

Bottom: Northover Ridge, looking out towards Mt. Joffre, Warrior Mtn. and Waka Nambé.
Photo Sonny Bou

Top: *The final section, showing the escape col at lower right. The Royal Group is framed between Onslow Mtn. (left) and Defender Mtn. Photo Clive Cordery*

Bottom: *Looking back along the crux narrows where a steady foot is essential. Photo Verne Dewit*

73 Three Isle Lake and South Kananaskis Pass
maps 5, 8

Long day hike, backpack, bike 'n' hike
Official trail
Distance 7.9 km to forks, 11.7 km to lake
Height gain to lake 487 m (1600 ft.)
High point before lake 2200 m (7215 ft.)
Map 82 J/11 Kananaskis Lakes

Access Kananaskis Lakes Trail (road) at North Interlakes parking lot. Walk down to the trailhead at the kiosk.
Also accessible from trail ##68, 69, 72, 74 and 73.

Comments Three Isle Lake is the most popular overnight destination of all the trails radiating out from Upper Kananaskis Lake. Although you can hike there and back in one very long day, it is far better to backpack in to the campground for a long weekend and spend time looking around some fantastic high country. Alternatively, camp at The Forks below the headwall.

Consider biking the fire road section to Invincible Creek. The trail remains easy to the forks, then climbs steeply over a ridge to the lake. Despite improvements and realignments (the latest after a washout in 1993), the headwall still exacts its pound of sweat.

Trail update In 2014 the trail between Lyautey and Forks campground was tweaked and realigned after the original was lost to the Kananaskis River widening its banks.

Camping Backcountry campgrounds at The Forks, Three Isle Lake and Three Isle Creek.

History Unlike North Kananaskis Pass, South Kananaskis Pass is thought to be a pass of no historical significance. Precipitous slopes on both sides would seem to preclude it as a logical route to Oregon, or even as a good trading route to the west. Nevertheless, a legend persists that 50 years ago hunting guide Jim Tegart found Sinclair's abandoned wagon wheels in the bush on the east side of the pass. And R.M. Patterson DID get a pack train up the headwall to Three Isle Lake in 1938. And they were carrying not only camping gear but also a faltboat.

To Invincible Creek 4.1 km
Head north across the isthmus, stopping en route to read three bronze plaques on a boulder paying tribute to Lt. Col. Donald G. Worthington and Lt. Col. William Hart-McHarg, both commanders in the British Columbia Regiment, Duke of Connaught's Own, though they died in different world wars. The dedication ceremony was held on August 13, 2006, by members of their regiment, "The Dukes." You'll be seeing mounts Worthington and McHarg later.

Moving on, cross the intake pipe by bridge and swing left onto the fire road, an undulating, often stony track that gives you sore feet. If someone were to start a ferry service across Upper Kananaskis Lake, I'd be the first to get in line.

Just after the bend, keep straight. (To right the unsigned trail to Mt. Indefatigable South takes off between boulders.)

Shortly fork right as per the sign and in 900 metres from the trailhead keep right at the top of an uphill. (The descending trail to left is Upper Kananaskis Lake trail.)

At the next unsigned junction, at km 2.3, stay on the fire road. (To left a stony trail descends to meet Upper Kananaskis Lake trail in the boulder field.) This junction occurs at the Palliser Slide where two big chunks of Mt. Indefatigable collapsed at different time periods and flowed to the north shore as catastrophic sturzstroms. What's left is a big slab with a couple of routes on it. Geologists tell us we're in for more bedding plane failures someday, so best not to linger.

A little farther on, a rock slide careering down a gully in 2019 nearly did away with the memorial bench, one boulder as big as a semi landing in the lake, where it still remains. Plod stonily on, back into denser bush, ultimately descending to Invincible Creek at bike locks, which is where you leave the fire road.

To Forks campground 4 km
Cross Invincible Creek on a new footbridge. After what's gone before, walking a soft forest trail under the cool canopy of mature forest is heaven. Somewhere among the spruce is a stand of Alberta's oldest lodgepole pines, which sprang from seed after a fire in 1586. To put it into perspective, this occurred during the reign of England's Elizabeth I.

Descend to the Kananaskis River and cross it by a fine log bridge above Upper Kananaskis Falls. In about 300 m the trail bends right. (At the bend the undesignated Lyautey trail turns left and as a deterrent is strewn with logs. So you're thinking "what is to stop me from taking this shortcut to Upper Lake trail?" Nothing, as long as you're carrying chest-high fishing waders.)

The resurgence of Three Isle Creek below the headwall.
Opposite: Mt. Putnik from the talus slope.

The headwall steps.

After crossing a side creek, the trail stays within earshot of the noisy Kananaskis River. At one point it rounds the bottom of a talus slope offering a view of Mt. Putnik and a more distant one of the headwall below Three Isle Lake with Mt. Worthington peeping over the top. To your left is a bewildering array of cliffs and towering peaks that are all part and parcel of Mt. Lyautey. A wonderfully clear spring bridged by the trail is the best place to fill up the water bottles.

The next section of trail has been completely rebuilt. You cross Dead Horse Gulch, as James calls it, and the wide flood plain of Three Isle Creek with its numerous streamlets, in all requiring eight assorted new bridges and one very long boardwalk. After the last bridge the trail meets the old trail and travels through trees to a Y-junction at 3.8 km with Forks campground. To access campsites, food lockers and eating areas go straight. A picnic table area 'twixt trail and river is the logical place for refuelling.

If giving the campground a miss, turn left at the Y-junction. In about 200 metres is a major junction. Go straight. (Trail to right leads to Turbine Canyon campground and North Kananaskis Pass.)

Headwall to Three Isle Lake 3.8 km

After a flat stretch the trail climbs through an area of monster Engelmann spruce, then drops down to Three Isle Creek. Shortly the main valley turns a right-angle to the SSE, aiming for the glacial pass east of Mt. Northover. The trail, however, continues due west, climbing toward the headwall. The gradient eases momentarily and the resurgences of Three Isle Lake come bursting out of hillside to your left.

Climbing again, the trail twists up a bushy avalanche slope turning to scree. Keep right where the old trail went left and arrive at the lowest rockband, which is equipped with wooden steps and chain handrails — the whole assembled in a factory by people seven feet tall with correspondingly long legs.

At the top, walk a narrow ledge between rockbands, at the end of it scrabbling uphill to join the old route on the traverse below the long rockband. Turn right. At the end of the traverse, climb a set of small zigs, traverse up left, then traverse up right to the summit of the ridge. Through all of this, you wonder what route did Patterson's horses take?

Drop 30 vertical metres down a draw to the east tip of Three Isle Lake. I don't find the lake particularly beautiful. The shoreline reminds me too much of a reservoir. And where is the third isle? The setting is undeniably grand, though, with Mt. Worthington presiding at the head.

The trail to left leads along the south shore past the patrol cabin (built in 2000 "to improve security of staff and visitors") and on into the valley below Northover Ridge. Trails to right lead to backcountry campgrounds. The first is "Three Isle Lake" and the second, 500 metres on, is "Three Isle Creek," which lies beyond a small creek on a promontory and has lake view lots available. The same trail continues on to South Kananaskis Pass.

GOING FARTHER

You're settled in and looking for places to go. South Kananaskis Pass is the obvious place to make for, from where other options present themselves.

Opposite: Three Isle Lake and the unnamed peak at 229086. Photo Leon Kubbernus

Above: The meadows of South Kananaskis Pass, Northover Ridge in the background at centre. Photo Wendy Devent

73A South Kananaskis Pass

Half-day walk
Distance 2.2 km
Height gain 122 m (400 ft.)
High point 2301 m (7550 ft.)

Comments An easy walk through meadow and forest to a pass on the Great Divide — the jumping-off point for peak 193107, Beatty Lake and the backpacker's traverse to North Kananaskis Pass.

From the far campground the official trail continues along the north side of Three Isle Lake, at times following the shoreline of bays. Looking across the lake, ridge walkers will be motivated by an end-to-end view of Northover Ridge showing its glaciated aspect.

Ahead rises the bulwark of Mount Worthington and to its right the little scree summit 193107 climbed by #73B. From this viewpoint Mt. McHarg is hidden behind Worthington. Both are basically rubble plods from the col at 204081. So it is baffling that a team of nine soldiers from the Duke of Connaught's Own Regiment failed to get up the peaks on the 10th of

August, 2006, three days before the big ceremony down at the trailhead. Or maybe not, because the September 2006 issue of *The Duke* shows a photo of the unnamed peak at 229086 as being Mt. Worthington! So until some scrambler finds their high point cairn containing the summit register, which peak the soldiers succeeded in climbing is likely to remain one of K Country's enduring mysteries.

But back to the trail. From the west end of the lake it turns right, the lake quickly lost to view as you climb steadily through trees to South Kananaskis Pass at the demarcation of meadow. A signpost marks the Great Divide. A trail through meadows lures you on. In fact, if the Three Isle Lake campsites are fully booked, consider camping at Beatty Lake in B.C. (See #74.)

OPTION
73B Peak 193107

Day scramble
Distance 3.8 km to summit, 6.4 km loop
Height gain ~558 m (1830 ft.)
High point 2798 m (9180 ft.)

Comments Although the peak at 193107 is a modest summit compared to everything else around it, you'll be ecstatic at the views it reveals of the Royal Group. While the recommended loop can be done in a half day by starting before dawn, why return to the parking lot at North Interlakes looking like a dropout from the Iron Man triathlon? Reserve a whole day from the campground.

Expect oceans of scree, some snow, some easy scrambling and mild exposure. Missing out the first part of the ridge does away with the exposure. Regardless, you've got to be familiar with loose rock and adept at route-finding.

History It was from this very peak that George Pocaterra discovered the Royal Group in 1911. I have never understood why, when Walter Wilcox's party went down the Palliser River from Palliser Pass in 1901, he made no mention of this fabulous group of mountains. I can only assume they were

so intent on finding the trail up to North Kananaskis Pass, they never looked to see what was to the right.

Anyway, Pocaterra was so impressed with this "country of burnt timber and hanging glaciers" that he immediately contacted the Geographer General about his discovery and sent photos. In 1913 the Boundary Survey were sent into the area (Wheeler, of course, claiming first discovery) and on their return, the Geographer General wrote Pocaterra asking him to give the group an Indian name. Because he knew an "Indian name would be cruelly mutilated," GP wrote back suggesting they choose an English name instead.

As luck would have it the number of peaks coincided with the members of Britain's Royal Family. Though if I'd been Prince George I'd have complained at being given a substandard peak you can walk up. To sort out the various summits you need to carry the Gem Trek map of Kananaskis Lakes.

FROM SOUTH KANANASKIS PASS
To the second draw 1.2 km

Head up steepening meadows on the west side of the pass. The aim is to gain the cirque north of Mt. Worthington, which means that at some point high up on the grass you're going to have to traverse left. When you hit a draw follow it up to the lip. The feeling is one of total astonishment at the scene in front of you. Once again the topo map is wildly wrong and any idea you may have of a simple scramble to the top of Worthington from this direction is shattered by glaciers plastering the entire north face. Due west beyond a bewildering mess of moraines, your summit rises in an ungainly heap of scree and bedrock.

When the draw you're in starts to go downhill, haul yourself out of it onto the moraine to its left and head off in the direction of the col at 196095, keeping the draw to your right. When this particular moraine ends tackle the low rock step above. Bypass a second step by a weakness farther to the right. Enter a second draw, likely covered by névé. This second draw is where the descent route comes back in.

To Col 196095 1.3 km

Straightaway climb onto the sharp-edged moraine to the left of the draw. Follow it to its end below a higher, steeper step. Luckily, a diagonal R–L scree ramp offers a way into the basin above. Watch out for some tottery boulders en route. On gaining the basin, walk up left on low-angle névé to the col between McHarg and Peak 193107.

Perhaps you'll be thinking tuna salad sandwiches and a sit down and be totally unprepared for the stunning view. Unlike other Royal Group viewpoints, this lofty col is perfectly located for looking straight down the Palliser River Valley. Bounded on

Top: View from Beatty Col (see #74) of peak 193107 at right. The optional descent follows the right-hand skyline ridge. To left are mounts Worthington and McHarg. Photo Eric Coulthard

Middle: The ridge which is followed between the col, seen at upper left, and Peak 193107.

Bottom: The summit taken from the same place as the middle photo.

the left by the great wall of the Divide and on the right by the superb Royal Group, it is a scene as sacred to view specialists as Mt. Assiniboine.

Traverse to summit, 1.3 km

From the col the entire ridge to 193107 is revealed. Névé reaches almost to the ridgeline of the first section, which is occasionally scrambly and narrow. If necessary, it can be omitted by crossing the basin lower down and rejoining the ridge at 195099.

After this the going is easy, though the final approach to the summit requires some desperate grovelling up fine scree. Top out at two cairns.

Some of the new things you can see are the Royal Valley, Tipperary Lake, Mt. Assiniboine, Palliser Pass slung between Mt. King Albert and Mt. Sir Douglas, and farther to the right the pocket handkerchief of the Haig Icefield. Some might say the best view is of Three Isle Lake.

Descent to second draw 1.4 km

From the summit head down the rubble of the broad east ridge. At ~198107 descend off the right side, heading diagonally right on whatever line appeals between slabs. Arrive in the second draw. Turn left and follow it out to your ascent route.

OPTIONAL DESCENT TO BEATTY LAKE

A tricky descent off the north ridge from the route-finding point of view.

To avoid some steep névé, head down the broad east ridge initially, then cut back left onto the equally broad north ridge. Lower down, curve right with the strata into the bottom of a basin. At this point you're 300 vertical m above Beatty Lake and stymied by cliffs.

Traverse right until stopped by a line of perpendicular cliffs. It's a little worrying, but all is well. From here a ridge drops toward the lake, unravelling beautifully in little rock steps and grassy platforms.

Low down, drop off into the small valley on the right and head north on game trail into spruce forest to — another dropoff. Far below is a glimpse of blue water. By walking right you'll find obstacle-free grassy slopes descending to the east shore of Beatty Lake. Now for that swim!

Return to South Kananaskis Pass via #74, a distance of only 2.1 km.

Above: Cooling off in Beatty Lake. Photo Bob Spirko

Opposite: The meadow between South Kananaskis Pass and Beatty Lake. In the background is Beatty Col, which is easy from this direction. Photo Eric Coulthard

74 South Kananaskis Pass to North Kananaskis Pass   map 8

Backpack
Unofficial trails, creek crossings
Distance 10.5 km
Height gain S-N 738 m (2420 ft.) via
route 1; add 213 m (700 ft.) for route 2
Height loss S-N 655 m (2150 ft.)
High point 2362 m (7750 ft.) via route 1
Map 82 J/11 Kananaskis Lakes

South access Via #73 Three Isle Lake &
South Kananaskis Pass at the pass.
North access Via #75 Turbine Canyon &
North Kananaskis Pass trail at the pass.

Comments On the B.C. side it's possible to
traverse from one Kananaskis pass to the
other without dropping all the way down to
the Palliser River. Except for one missing
section, the old trail is in fairly good shape,
much better than when A.O. Wheeler did
the trip in 1916 during the Boundary Survey.
Nevertheless, this is still a strenuous trip, in
parts rocky, bushy and very steep, with a
humongous height gain coming at the end
of the day.

This is the key section of a four-day backpack
starting from Upper Kananaskis Lake that
takes in Aster Lake, Northover Ridge, Three
Isle Lake, South Kananaskis Pass, Leroy
Creek, North Kananaskis Pass and Turbine
Canyon.

Camping Free backcountry campsite at
Beatty Lake with tent pads, pit toilet, one
picnic table and food lockers.

To Beatty Lake 2.1 km

From South Kananaskis Pass the ongoing
trail through meadows makes you yearn
to carry on, the walking easy and slightly
downhill to a gem of a lake rimmed by
spruce and larch and enclosed on the south
side by a high, craggy wall.

To LeRoy Creek 4.3 km

There are two ways downward into the valley of LeRoy Creek, neither of them easy.

1. Via the shoulder The easier route
attempts to follow the old trail. Cross the
lake's outlet and turn right with the creek,
entering a dry canyon bed, Beatty Creek

having sunk underground in the meantime. The nice, safe canyon ends cold turkey above a steep rockslide down which the trail picks a tenuous line toward the wild middle reaches of Beatty Creek. Here, rockfall has created a miniature "valley of rocks," a cataclysmic mix of trees, boulders, sinks and tiny blue tarns. Amongst the chaos Beatty Creek resurges into the light of day. Drop-off number two is supposedly unassailable, although I did hear of a mad mountain biker downclimbing the route with the bike wrapped around his neck.

The "trail" avoids both these impasses by heading right (north). Traverse the scree low down and climb across hillside onto the flat shoulder at 177133 of the mountain above Beatty Lake. The terrain funnels you to the escarpment edge for views of Palliser Pass and your objective.

The final zigzag descent to LeRoy Creek has been lost in some horrible over-the-head willow bush and deadfall. Luckily, another "trail," some of it blue-flagged, has developed over the years, one that traverses

right to an avalanche slope offering a more reasonable descent. Cross LeRoy Creek and on the far (northwest) bank pick up an excellent trail come up from the Palliser River. Turn right.

2. Via Beatty Col The crossing of the col requires skill with scree on the other side, so is reserved for scramblers. It may cut the corner off but it's no shortcut.

But like R.M. and Marigold Patterson in 1938, you too will be lured by the grassy slope rising to the col on the southwest ridge of Mt. Beatty at 201137. At 2484 metres (8150 ft.) it is amazingly easy to get to. From low down you get classic views of Beatty Lake backdropped by the Royal Group. Nearly 300 metres higher up, the col gives bird's-eye views of the trail seen snaking up both passes. Mt. Joffre has come into view as well as the Haig Icefield, out of which flows LeRoy Creek.

The north slope is very steep initially, the obvious scree chute a mix of atrociously loose rock and cement shale where it's easy to go for a skid. Early and late in the season

this stuff is covered by snow, which is a whole new ball game.

After the gradient eases there's miles of scree to pick your way over before you reach the vegetation. The best thing here is to just head on down the forest to LeRoy Creek. Most likely you'll pick up the trail from the Palliser River on the near east bank.

To North Kananaskis Pass 4.2 km
The trail on the left bank of LeRoy Creek crosses to the right (east) bank at 188148 and begins a gradual climb away from the valley. (That it issues from the Haig Glacier is surely further scope for exploration.)

As soon as you cross the tributary arising from North Kananaskis Pass, the trail steepens dramatically and climbs straight up the tributary's left bank on a mix of grass and scree. Behind you the scenery is growing in magnificence and no excuse is needed for frequent stops to admire the Royal Group framed between the canyon-like walls of the valley. Near the top the trail crosses to the right bank. Nowadays the creekbed carries hardly more than a trickle, but before landslides blocked Maude Lake's exit to the west, the white rushing water must have been a fine sight.

Unlike the south pass, North Kananaskis Pass is a bleak ridge of tundra connecting mounts Beatty and Maude. Where once there was nothing, it now sports an array of signs and cairns marking the various boundaries.

If making for the backcountry campground at Turbine Canyon, keep right of Maude Lake. If that campground is full, consider random camping on the B.C. side of the pass.

Opposite: Beatty Lake, backdropped by the peaks of the Royal Group. Left to right: mounts Prince Edward, Prince Henry and Queen Mary. Photo Alf Skrastins

Top left: View from the shoulder of Palliser Pass below Mt. Queen Elizabeth.

Top right: The north side of Beatty Col. The route descends the obvious chute. Photo Eric Coulthard

75 Turbine Canyon and North Kananaskis Pass   map 8

Backpack
Official trail
Distance 8.3 km to Turbine Canyon backcountry campground from the forks, 15.8 km from trailhead
Height gain 427 m (1400 ft.) to campground from the forks, 518 m (1700 ft.) from trailhead
High point 2240 m (7350 ft.) on bench
Map 82 J/11 Kananaskis Lakes

Access Kananaskis Lakes Trail (road) at North Interlakes parking lot. Via #73 Three Isle Lake & South Kananaskis Pass just beyond the forks.
Also accessible from #74.

Comments A moderately strenuous trail with one long climb to a pass in that gorgeous country above treeline. The pass is a historic one and you'll be following in the footsteps of many a famous explorer and surveyor.
  Camping Backcountry campgrounds at The Forks and Turbine Canyon.

Trail history It all started in October, 1854, when some 100 men, women and children struggled over Mackipictoon's secret pass, walking their horses and stumbling over boulders made treacherous by a heavy fall of snow. This new route for Red River immigrants under the Oregon Emigrating Scheme elicited such comments as "our rascally guide took us by a pass over the mountains (known only by himself), which he represented as the best and the shortest (10 days instead of the usual 30)," and "altogether it is the worst road I ever travelled."
  Mackipictoon (or Mas-ke-pe-toon), known as Broken Arm because of a conspicuous infirmity, was a very great Cree warrior of ungovernable temper. Miffed because Hudson's Bay boss Sir George Simpson had not engaged him to lead his party over Simpson Pass, he inveigled chief trader James Sinclair into trying a new route over the Rockies, faster even than the White Man Pass he had shown him a few years earlier. Unfortunately, when they got to Kananaskis

Lakes the Cree admitted he was lost and Sinclair was forced to take over the role of guide, so who knows where they really went?

Incidentally, if any filmmaker is reading this, Sinclair (Brad Pitt) was "brave, restless, ambitious" and constantly at odds with the rather pompous Simpson (Anthony Hopkins). Only two years later, in the Columbia River Valley, he was killed while trying to save a party of American settlers besieged by Snake Indians. The survivors were about to take a boat into the rapids and perish together rather than under the cruel hand of the Indians when, like in all good westerns, help arrived in the nick of time. Too late for Sinclair, though, who was finally thinking of settling down with his family to farm.

If it hadn't been for this trip it's unlikely the Palliser Expedition would ever have travelled up the Kananaskis Valley and the place would be called something completely different.

Anyway, in 1858 Capt. John Palliser and party crossed what they thought was the same pass in search of a southern trade route across the Rockies. I say "apparently" because there's a move afoot, spearheaded by Longview's Larry Boyd, to show that Palliser took another route entirely. Some of the description fits North Kananaskis Pass,

Opposite: Approaching Lawson Lake on the bench. In the distance are the two summits of Mt. Maude, the Haig Glacier and mounts French and Jellicoe.

Above: North Kananaskis Pass with its various cairns and signs. Looking west to Mt. LeRoy at right.

but there are glaring discrepancies. Other parts of the description fit South Kananaskis Pass and Highwood Pass. Interestingly, the altimeter reading of 5,985 feet at the pass correlates with none of the above. This was borne out by George Dawson, who in his "Preliminary Report of the Physical and Geological Features of that portion of the Rocky Mountains between latitudes 49° and 51° 30'" corrected Palliser's reading to 6,200 feet, the almost exact height of Elk Pass. A year later the John Jones Overlanders intended going over North Kananaskis Pass using the map given them by James Hector, but most historians are agreed they went over Elk Pass (although I'm convinced it was neighbouring Highwood Pass, an understandable error). If only all these people had taken an artist along with them!

In 1901 Walter Wilcox couldn't even find North Kananaskis Pass from the Palliser River end and finally arrived at Kananaskis Lakes via Pass in the Clouds and Elk Pass.

He decided to pay the missed pass a one-day flying visit and fell prey to one of Palliser's discrepancies, as you'll read. In July 1916 the Boundary Commission's Richard Cautley, alone and on snowshoes, reached the pass after many attempts and determined once and for all that it was absolutely useless as a route through the mountains. Since then the old trail has seen sporadic use, a faint revival occurring in the 1960s and '70s with the growth of a new breed called backpackers.

When K Country took over, the trail was upgraded and realigned at the avalanche slope, destined to be trodden by a torrent of grateful hikers and skiers clad in GoreTex and Spandex. You are guaranteed to make the pass every time. More recently, in 2022, an adjustment was made to the start of the trail to sidestep the eroding river bank.

Top: #75A North Kananaskis Pass from the lower slopes of Mt. Maude. To left is Maude Lake below glaciated Mt. Beatty. To right, LeRoy Creek and the Royal Group rising above the Palliser River Valley.

To Turbine Canyon campground 8.3 km
Follow #73 for 8 kilometres to the turnoff about 200 m *beyond* Forks campground.

Turn right on a 2022 reroute built to avoid the continually eroding left bank of the Kananaskis River. It climbs gently up a side hill, crosses a stony bench, then back in trees joins the original route near the bottom of the first avalanche slope.

Level with a waterfall, start a tedious climb up and across wide, steep avalanche slopes covered in head-high willows and alders with a permanent downhill lean from the weight of the winter snowpack. Reenter forest and climb some more to the stream exiting the cirque between Mount Putnik and "Razor Flakes." Cross and drag yourself up a final set of switchbacks to treeline.

The payoff for all the hard work is kilometres of joyous wandering along an almost level bench through meadows and larches. The Haig Glacier comes into view ahead, enclosed by mountains shaped like battleships. A tarn is where Walter Wilcox and packer Jim Wood lunched in 1901 and where Wilcox went on alone and on foot,

telling Wood he'd be back in an hour. Wood probably said, "Oh sure." A little farther on, the trail undulates across a boulder field, then descends through larches to Lawson Lake, named by Wilcox, who thought at first it was the lake at the pass.

Follow the west shore, the trail then descending farther past the patrol cabin to Maude Brook. Cross the bridge to an important T-junction. Go right for Turbine Canyon campground, left for the pass.

Back at Lawson Lake in 1901, a perplexed Wilcox, though realizing his hour was up, was determined to find the wretched pass, and after divesting himself of his field glasses and later his jacket, then his camera on various "scrubby spruces," broke into a run down the hill "splashing through an icy stream" with no time to see what lay downstream.

The trail through the campground leads to the dizzying brink of Turbine Canyon. Supposedly it can be jumped across in one or two places as it twists its way down 330 metres (1000 ft.) of hillside to the Upper Kananaskis River.

Turbine Canyon.

75A North Kananaskis Pass

Official trail
Distance 2.2 km from campground
Height gain 152 m (500 ft.)
from campground
High point 2362 m (7750 ft.)

Comments A fairly easy walk into alpine meadows about the pass. This is also the backpacker's route to South Kananaskis Pass (see #74).

Return to the T-junction on the north bank of Maude Brook and go straight.

The trail gains height slowly through alternating meadow and forest, passing to the right of huge morainal mounds hiding South Maude Lake. What's left of Beatty Glacier is still a thrilling sight below the shapely peak of Mt. Beatty. A steeper pull onto a forested knoll reveals the classic view of Maude Lake and North Kananaskis Pass backdropped by mounts LeRoy and Monro, "a desolate lake surrounded by bare cliffs and the awful solitude of that halfway belt, which has neither the beauty of the green valleys nor the grandeur of the great snowfields," said Wilcox. Palliser called it "our little tea-kettle lake," though nobody knows which lake he was referring to. The Stoneys know it as Îyârhe Apadahâ Îyabize, or "lake by the pass." It's a popular playground for grizzlies, which have been seen rolling down the steep east shore to go splash in the water.

The trail follows the west shore past a spate of prohibitory notices to the northwest corner, where a line of cairns leads you into the windswept passage between mounts Beatty and Maude. Here are more notices held up by cairns.

Back in 1901 Wilcox was still running, along the muddy shore and over snowbanks, finally gaining the pass at the mind-boggling hour of 4 in the afternoon! I bet he rued not bringing his camera.

75B Haig Glacier

Day hike
Unofficial trail
Distance ~3.2 km from campground
Height gain ~533 m (1750 ft.)
Height loss 30 m (100 ft.)
High point ~2713 m (8900 ft.)

Comments The skier's access trail to the Haig Glacier via the Beckie Scott High Performance Training Centre is a fairly strenuous slog on moraines with the odd patch of bedrock where the trail is less obvious. Luckily the way is well cairned and there's a bridge over Haig Creek.

To Beckie Scott High Performance Centre 1.4 km

From the campground follow the trail to Turbine Canyon that starts at the junction of Maude Brook and a small creek issuing from moraines.

The trail crosses the small creek and turns left up a forested rib right (east) of the creek. There's a steep bit in the middle of this section, then the trail eases off to treeline.

Climb left of a big heap of moraine and enjoy your first view of the glacier and three shiny white Quonset-style huts perched on the ridge below Mt. Jellicoe. Not far now.

Descend right to Haig Creek, which is crossed by a metal bridge. The glacier snout has retreated and is now locked behind high rock walls penetrated by a gorge cut by the glacial stream. Below the gorge the water slows down and makes plaited patterns across a flat, then below the bridge gathers together and, picking up speed, passes through a cave with four entrances and shoots out into space over a 300-m-high cliff. The water then re-enters the darkness and drops 40 vertical metres (130 ft.) down a vertical shaft before once again seeing daylight. Some of this exciting stuff can be seen from Option C. See also Chas Y's article in *Canadian Caver, no. 71.*

Pick your way up a ridge of bedrock to the helipad and the huts (at 218176), a Winsport training facility for Canada's national and provincial X-C ski racers. To left is the swim hole down on the flat.

Opposite: #75B Skiers returning down the Haig Glacier access trail below the gully.

To the Haig Glacier ~1.8 km

Continue up the bedrock ridge above the huts, then turn left and traverse scree slopes sandwiched between the southeast ridge of Mt. Jellicoe and cliffs falling to the glacier. (I have never climbed Jellicoe but I'm told it's an easy scree scramble from the trail.) At one point there's a steep climb up a bit of a gully, and later on a steep descent on the final approach to the ice.

While the Haig appears safe compared to such crevassed horrors as the Athabasca, casual wandering can be dangerous. I know someone who almost disappeared down a moulin near this spot. And on no account follow ski tracks, as you're liable to be set upon by irate skiers. So unless you're properly equipped for crossing the glacier to either the French or the Robertson glaciers, end the walk on the moraines. From the high point of the trail there are astonishing views back to Lawson Lake on the bench and ahead to mounts Sir Douglas, Robertson and French towering over the icefield.

Below: #75B The Beckie Scott High Performance Centre from the approach. Beyond are the Haig Glacier and Mt. Jellicoe. To right, the big drop-off.

#75C The view from near Jellicoe Shoulder of the Kananaskis River Valley, the Lyautey massif, Mt. Joffre and Mt. Putnik above Lawson Lake.

75C Kananaskis Glacier

Day scramble
Unofficial trail, route
Distance ~4.3 km from campground
Height gain ~366 m (1200 ft.)
Height loss 213 m (700 ft.)
High point 2454 m (8050 ft.)

Comments Getting to the glacial birthplace of the Kananaskis River requires easy scrambling and finicky route-finding. But what a valley! Hidden away and not easy to get into, it possesses an aura of wildness quite unlike that of other valleys in the area. Mid summer is best for waterfall viewing.

To Jellicoe shoulder 1.1 km

Follow #75B to the training centre.

First off, you're going to hop over the cliff below the huts! It's easy if you know where to go; it takes humans about 20 minutes, grizzlies about three. First thing is to reach the broad ledge below the initial drop-off. This is most easily gained by walking along the top of the drop-off in a southeasterly direction to where a stony draw heads down left. Below it, some easy slabs deposit you on the ledge. Turn left. There's a narrow bit, then the ledge broadens out and slants downwards, eventually merging with easy-angled slabs. Walk down the slabs to the scree.

Follow the grizzly trail that climbs diagonally across the scree slope onto the verdant shoulder of Mt. Jellicoe. Take time to detour onto the rib to the right and walk south a bit for a spectacular view of the Kananaskis River Valley. It has to be one of my favourite viewpoints — on the left the great west wall of the Spray Mountains, on the right Mt. Beatty and its glacier, Lawson Lake on the bench, and nearer at hand the cliff down which tumbles the waterfall. And blocking the end of the valley is the massif of Mt. Lyautey, behind which rises the white tooth of Joffre.

To head of the valley 1.8 km

But back to the grizzly trail that heads north below the eastern cliffs of Mt. Jellicoe. From the route's high point is a first view into the upper valley; a mix of meadow and scree with a winding stream. Presiding over the scene is Mt. Smith-Dorrien at the valley head.

From the shoulder a grassy rib leads almost but not quite into the valley bottom. Low down, the rib ends at a small step. Continue down scree or use an easy gully in the rock to the left. Hereabouts is a sizeable marmot colony.

There is much to explore. Ahead and left you discover a green tarn fed by twin waterfalls pouring off Kananaskis Glacier between mounts Jellicoe, Smith-Dorrien and French. Farther along and on the oppo-

site side of the valley are little morainal hills covered in dryas — exceptional viewpoints for looking back down the valley to Mt. Joffre. Above them rears the west wall of Leaning Mountain and its hugely impressive rock tower. Yet another option is to flog up scree to the col between Smith-Dorrien and Leaning Mountain to take a peek at Hero Knob a thousand feet below.

Top: #75C View from near Jellicoe Shoulder showing the descent route from the training centre. The route traverses the top ledge from left to right then descends the area of lighter coloured slabs below the shadow.

Bottom: #75C Kananaskis Glacier below Mt. French.

76 Upper Kananaskis River Viewpoint

maps 5, 8

Day hike
Unofficial trail, route
Distance 7.1 km from trailhead
Height gain 500 m (1640 ft.)
from trailhead
High point 2225 m (7300 ft.)
Map 82 J/11 Kananaskis Lakes

Access Kananaskis Lakes Trail (road) at North Interlakes parking lot. Via #73 Three Isle Lake & South Kananaskis Pass at Invincible Creek at 4 km.

Comments The promontory overlooking the forks of Upper Kananaskis River at 256114 is one of the very best vantage points in the park, discovered back in 1916 by the Boundary Survey, who set up a camera station called "Lyautey N" on the point. Getting there requires careful route-finding in rough and complicated terrain, a challenge to anyone who's just completed Map Reading Level 1. Sorry, AllTrails users, there's no app for this little bushwhacking beauty.

Trail update Since the last edition, deadfall across the fire road and infilling by millions of little trees has made travel even more difficult! But as my friend says, the view is well worth getting scratched up for. Wear long pants and take binoculars.

Follow the Three Isle Lake trail for 4 km and cross the bridge over Invincible Creek.

Fire road section 1.8 km
Turn immediately right and follow a narrow trail alongside the creek back to the continuation of the fire road on the west bank. It takes just a few minutes. Turn left and follow the main fire road through old forest to its end at the bottom of a firebreak zooming up the hillside. En route ignore an obvious side trail with cairn zooming up the hillside to Invincible Lake. (See #77.) What you can't ignore is some particularly dreadful deadfall before this point that requires a chain saw and an army of volunteers. It's

Top: *The historic cairn on the point was built by the Boundary Survey in 1916.*

Bottom: *Unearthing the small cairn at the top left-hand corner of the "small meadow." Photo Gillian Ford*

here where Tony declares it a shitty trail. "You're not putting this in the book again are you?" Despite requests from hikers, Parks has constantly refused to upgrade the fire road, so only the determined will arrive at the bottom of the firebreak built to contain the Invincible Creek fire. This is at 267121.

View of the Mt. Lyautey massif and its numerous summits.
Photo Gillian Ford

To the viewpoint 1.3 km

Climb the break on single-track trail to what was once a small meadow, now in-grown with spruce. Search for a cairn amid the greenery at the top left-hand corner.

From the cairn a trail heads left to the edge of a steep bank — cairn and blazes — then turns uphill and ends near treeline on an avalanche slope. Note this spot for the return journey.

Using fragmented game trails, traverse left across a rough mix of talus, grass and shrub until you are able to drop a little into the head of a tiny creek. Ahead rises the promontory, a complexity of knolls and sinks best handled by heading west up the draw of the creek, aiming for the low point between the promontory and the slope of the mountain to the right. Only then head

south along a ridge to the camera station cairn at 256114 out on the point.

To anyone plodding along Three Isle Lake trail, Mt. Lyautey appears a hugely compli-cated massif, but from this viewpoint you're finally able to sort out which top is the true summit. The creek draining the glaciers is the base of a syncline with intense folding at its core where waterfalls plummet over the cliffs. As my geologist neighbour pointed out, it's worth a side trip from #73.

Another highlight is a rare view of Upper Kananaskis Lake backdropped by Elk Pass and the Elk Range. Best of all, you can follow route #75 from start to finish as it climbs onto the bench to Lawson Lake, then slips through the gap between mounts Beatty and Maude to North Kananaskis Pass. With binoculars you can even follow the route onto the Haig Glacier and over Jellicoe shoulder to the glacier at the head of the Upper Kananaskis River.

All this and larches, too.

77 Invincible Lake

Long day hike
Official, unofficial trails, route
Distance 15 km return
Height gain 707 m (2320 ft.)
from trailhead
Height loss 107 m (350 ft.)
High point 2370 m (7775 ft.) at ridge
Map 82 J/11 Kananaskis Lakes

Access Kananaskis Lakes Trail (road) at North Interlakes parking lot. Via #73 Three Isle Lake & South Kananaskis Pass at Invincible Creek at 4 km.

Comments This is a strenuous haul up over a ridge into the secluded valley west of Mt. Invincible, which has no easy way in. The main objective is a gorgeous blue lake, but just as exciting are the alpine meadows under Mt. Warspite and a traverse of little Mt. Nomad. To give yourself time to look around, start early. The old days are gone and you can no longer camp there.

Trail update Since the previous edition, more deadfall across the fire road and infilling by millions of little spruce trees has made travel even more difficult for the first kilometre after Invincible Creek crossing. On the plus side, there is nowadays only one trail to follow up onto the ridge.

Walk Three Isle Lake trail for 4 km to Invincible Creek crossing.

The fire road 1.3 km
Start by crossing the bridge over Invincible Creek. Then turn immediately right and follow a narrow trail back to the continuation of the fire road on the west bank. It takes only a few minutes.

Progress along the fire road is painfully slow in places where you have to crawl under and climb over big fallen trees and push through all those little spruce trees. I decided not to show you a pic!

In 1.3 km, a large cairn on the right side of the road indicates the start of your trail up fairly open hillside.

Up to the ridge 1 km
Follow this trail up the south face of the ridge, a steep direct line that climbs about 457 metres (1500 ft.) in just over a kilometre High up, where the trail fades away, continue climbing through the ruins of a forest extending all across the hillside to the left and even up the west slopes of Mt. Indefatigable across Invincible's canyon to your right. A strong wind blowing out of the west makes eerie flute music among their white, dead branches.

The grassy ridge is one of the finest vantage points for Upper Kananaskis Lake and its surrounding mountains. And you finally get a look into Invincible valley. Unfortunately, the lake remains hidden by Mt. Nomad — the mountain that stands alone in the angle of the two forks.

On trail, walk up the ridge crest for about 300 m. In an area of larches, at a second notch marked by a cairn at ~268129 the trail hops over onto the north flank. (If calling it a day, its worth walking higher up the ridge for a view of Invincible Lake far below.)

Down to Invincible Lake 1.2 km
Unlike the people trail of the south face, the game trail down the even steeper north slope into the west fork takes a sensible diagonal line from right to left, lower down crossing a shale slope, then a wider scree slope before fading out on grass near the valley bottom. Jump the creek and walk up easy-angled grass to the lake.

Long and blue, Invincible is bounded on the west by a line of sombre cliffs and on the east side by a grassy terrace under little Mt. Nomad. Crossing the low ridge beyond the lake gives access to the head of the north fork, where you can spend an hour of pleasurable wandering in the meadows below Mt. Warspite and the so-called "Hermione Peak." "Keep an eye out for grizzlies. Likely this is why no camping is allowed anywhere in the valley.

Top left: Climbing up to the ridge after the trail ends. As you can see, the forest is slowly making a comeback. Photo Bob Spirko

Top right: On the ridge at the point where the trail descends the north slope. Walking higher up the ridge to the foot of the rocks is another option.

Below: Invincible Lake. Photo Alf Skrastins

Mt. Nomad, showing the usual ascent route up the left-hand slope. Mt. Warspite to right.

Summit of Mt. Nomad. Photo Sonny Bou

OPTION

77A Mount Nomad

Scramble
Distance 600 m from Invincible Lake
Height gain 229 m (750 ft.)
High point 2543 m (8343 ft.)

Comments The little summit between the forks is an uncomplicated scree scramble via its south ridge.

Naming It was named as recently as 1995 by "The Grand Fleet Expedition" (alias Calgary's 144th Lake Bonavista Sea Venturer Company), which in 1991 climbed a few of the ship mountains to commemorate the 75th anniversary of the Battle of Jutland. It is, of course, named after a destroyer sunk in the battle.

From the south end of Invincible Lake walk up the grassy south ridge, then up a steeper slope of scree. You may find it easier (less scree) to head right to the gap between two crags before tackling the final bit of scree to the summit ridge. From the cairn look down on Invincible Lake and back to a snippet of Upper Kananaskis Lake seen through Invincible Creek canyon.

Return the same way or descend the northwest ridge to the low ridge between the two forks of Invincible Creek, then work your way back along the terrace above the lake.

Now for that climb back onto the ridge. I can assure you, it's far less onerous than trying to shortcut down the canyon.

78 Mount Indefatigable South map 5

Day scramble
Unofficial trail
Distance 3.6 km from trailhead
Height gain 938 m (3080 ft.)
from trailhead
High point 2646 m (8680 ft.)
Map 82 J/11 Kananaskis Lakes

Access Kananaskis Lakes Trail (road) at North Interlakes parking lot.

Comments Did you know Walter Wilcox made the first ascent in 1901 after lunch? The fact is Indefatigable's south summit is little more than a strenuous walk up steep slopes with some rubble. Nowadays a trail takes you almost to the south ridge. There's nothing to be scared of unless you count the final 200 metres of ridge which is optional.

This is also the scramblers route to Indefatigable's north peak and the way over to Gypsum Tarns.

Upper Kananaskis Lake from the Wendy Elekes Viewpoint minus the memorial bench.

About the access trail "If you had to choose only one trail in the Kananaskis Lakes area, this should be the one" so I wrote in an earlier edition. It was disappointing, then, that in 2006 the "glorious" trail was without public consultation demoted to unofficial status and is no longer being promoted by park officials. Citing the trail could "no longer be maintained to safe standards," conservation officers promptly removed all signage and memorial benches and put them into storage. Large white boulders were dumped across the entrance, thus ensuring that even without a signpost the trail is easily identifiable. So how bad is this "erosional nightmare?" Just wear hiking boots with good traction. As Dave Hanna puts it, "Don't be hiking it in your oxfords."

Naming Walter Wilcox suggested the mountain be named Mt. Merriam after Dr. C. Hart Merriam of the US Agriculture Bureau, but luckily the name was not approved. Instead,it was named after a battle cruiser in 1922. Not a good name for the ship either. During the very first foray in the Battle of Jutland it was sunk with the loss of 955 crew.

The escarpment trail 2.3 km

Head north across the isthmus on Three Isle Lake/Upper Kananaskis Lake trail (fire road) and cross the intake dam and spillway via the bridge. Shortly after the fire road swings left, at precisely 320 metres from the parking lot, turn right onto an unsigned trail with white boulders at the entrance.

Initially, the trail winds gradually uphill through old forest. A rising traverse up left leads to the start of a moderately steep climb up the left side of a rib and onto the top of the eastern escarpment. En route, the main trail is fairly obvious amid a wide range of variations—a hot, powdery treadmill with occasional easy scramble steps. This section doesn't last long and soon the trail swings right onto a promontory. This is the superb Wendy Elekes Viewpoint with or without the memorial bench. Look across Upper Kananaskis Lake to the mountains of the Elk.

Descending rubble off the south ridge.

Descend a little, then continue climbing less steeply between a gully on the left and the edge of the eastern escarpment on the right. As Upper Kananaskis Lake falls astern, so Lower Kananaskis Lake comes into prominence along with the whole of the Opal Range.

At 2.3 km the trail reaches its high point and levels off. The first trail junction is where you turn off the trail to the left. There may be flagging.

To the summit 1.3 km

Head uphill towards your objective through an open forest of spruce, larch and heather. At a junction in a levelling keep left. (Right is another route to the outlier.)

Carry on through dwindling trees and up a broad grassy rib. Initially the trail veers right, but after the gully on the left peters out, it swings left onto another broad grassy rib and follows that up to the rock zone below the south ridge of the mountain. Here the trail enters a shallow scoop on the left and climbs diagonally right to left up the scoop on good, firm rubble. Top out on the south ridge at a large cairn.

Ahead is a view to die for: Upper Kananaskis Lake with a backdrop of blue mountain shapes receding into the distance. When the sun is west of south it puts a glitter on the water and a shine on the icefields and névés about Mt. Joffre. Farther to the right you can pick out the routes to Aster Lake, Three Isle Lake and Invincible Lake, and identify such notable peaks as Sir Douglas and King George in the Royal Group.

Turn right and plod up low-angle scree to a summit with cairn. Into view comes the summit ridge and Firenet's VHF repeater station #103, consisting of solar panel, antennae, a large square green container and a large round red container the "size of a newborn calf shelter" according to Dave M. (And yes, people do use it as a shelter in bad weather.) It may have been replaced by a newer white version.

High up on the rib trail, not far from the high point.

Above: The south ridge gives a fabulous view of Upper Kananaskis Lake. Shows the route to Aster Lake beyond Hidden Lake. Photo Matt Hobbs

Either call it a day or carry on past the repeater station to the true summit, treading warily across Wilcox's "several hundred yards of knife edge." It gives you a taste of the moderately difficult scramble between the south summit and Mt. Indefatigable proper — a dramatic narrowing, a drop on the right, scree and slabs on the left, a sudden feeling of exposure. After setting up his tripod Wilcox found no room to stand behind his camera and "had to focus and expose plates by a method adapted to such emergencies."

The red box on the summit looks extraordinarily out of place.
Photo Dave MacDonald

78A Indefatigable Col and Outlier

Day hike
Unofficial trail
Distance 1.6 km from Mt. Indefatigable trail junction, 4.3 km from trailhead
Height gain 777 m (2550 ft.)
from trailhead
High point 2484 m (8150 ft.)

Comments The easier option takes you through flower meadows and larch forests to Indefatigable's eastern outlier, at 298132 the high point of the eastern escarpment. This is, likewise, a very popular trail, probably because it's the scrambler's access to Mt. Indefatigable North. It is also the cross-country route to Gypsum Tarns. (See #106A.)

With demotion, K Country is no longer issuing bear warnings and closures for the area. And yes, people hiking this trail do occasionally spot the male grizzly crossing back and forth from Gypsum Creek to munch on the corms of glacier lillies, but usually he is seen from afar minding his own business. There has never been an incident. Nevertheless, take the usual precautions and turn back if necessary. We want him to stay on his home turf.

To the col 1.4 km from junction
Start from the high point of the access trail. In only 4 m after the turnoff to Mt. Indefatigable South turn left onto a narrower trail that climbs gradually up hillside into the larch and glacier lily belt. Keep straight at the next T-junction. (The trail to left joins with Mt. Indefatigable South trail.)

The trail then traverses steep hillside to a hanging valley crammed with Indian paintbrushes all the colours of nail varnish. En route a side trail to right heads down to a spring. The trail continues along the right side of a seasonal pond and crosses the outlet. Climb through larch meadows to a junction. Keep left. (Trail ahead is the optional descent route from the outlier.)

Climb a grassy, shaley trail to the left of a shallow gully direct to the col at 297329 between the outlier and Indefatigable North. From its broad neck in the orange scree zone look across to Mount Invincible and down on Gypsum Tarns

To the outlier 200 m
Turn right and walk up to the summit of the outlier, the high point marked by three cairns and a branch occupying an airy spot

The summit of Indefatigable Outlier above Lower Kananaskis Lake.

on the edge of the eastern escarpment, a place to watch your step while taking selfies. From this higher vantage point, the whole of route #106A from the col to Gypsum Tarns and across to the gypsum quarry is visible. New is a view up the Smith-Dorrien valley and an almost complete panorama of Opal Range peaks.

OPTIONAL DESCENT

The southeast ridge is a beautiful route to descend, the edge of cliffs sharply etched against the blue waters of Lower Kananaskis Lake. In scree a trail develops, eventually leaving the southeast ridge for the grassy south ridge dotted with krum-

holz. It's here you'll find long-stemmed flea-banes blurring to a purple haze on hillsides dropping away to the lower escarpment edge way down to your left — an unforgettable sight for those lucky enough to be here at the right time.

The trail turns right twisting more steeply downhill to the Y junction with the col trail. Turn left.

Top: In the hanging valley looking towards the col and Indefatigable Outlier to its right. It's late summer, the pond is drying up and the fireweeds are now the dominant flower.

Bottom: Initially, the optional descent follows this southeast ridge.

79 High Rockies Trail – Buller Mountain to Elk Pass
maps 9, 4, 5

Backpack, long day hikes
Official trail
Total distance 50 km
Height gain N-S 1590 m (5217 ft.)
Height loss N-S 1410 m (4626 ft.)
High point 2065 m (6775 ft.)
Maps 82 J/14 Spray Lakes Reservoir, 82 J/11 Kananaskis Lakes

North Access Hwy. 742 (Smith-Dorrien/Spray Trail) in 8 locations.
1. Buller Mountain day-use area. Use the first parking area on the right. If the gate is closed, park in front of it. Then walk Buller Pass trail for 560 m.
2. Engadine Burn. 1.4 km north of Mt. Shark Road park off road. Follow the trail up the burn right-of-way for 700 m. (See #83 Rummel Ridge for details.)
3. Rummel Lake trail. Park off road opposite the Mt. Shark Road. Follow Rummel Lake trail for 2 km.
4. Chester Lake trailhead. Going north, follow Chester Lake trail. Going south, start from the south side of the parking lot on what is also Frost Heave snowshoe trail.
5. Sawmill trailhead. The trail runs through the picnic area below the parking lot.
6. Black Prince day-use area. Walk up the access road for 300 m to the highway, or park on the verge opposite the day-use area access road. Either way, follow the winding access trail for 500 m up the hillside to the T-junction.
7. Blackshale Creek at 289178. Park off road. Trails up both sides of the creek join the HRT on either side of the suspension bridge.
8. Pocaterra Dam road. 200 m north of Peninsula day-use area, park on the west side of the highway at the entrance to a gated TransAlta Road heading north (route to the South End of Lawson). Across the highway, the gated TransAlta road heading south to Pocaterra Dam is the southerly continuation of the HRT.

South Access Kananaskis Lakes Trail in 11 locations.
9. Canyon day-use area at the end of Canyon Road.
10. Canyon campground from all loops.
11. Peter Lougheed Discovery Centre. A 700 m-long paved bike trail leaves the parking lots access road and heads west across Kananaskis Lakes Trail (road). Follow it down across the powerline right-of-way and up a hill to Canyon campground loop C at site no. 34.
12. William Watson Lodge. A paved trail called Spruce Road heads north from the cottages access road between D and E cottages to a T-junction. Keep right (Spruce Road goes left) and join the HRT (Lodgepole bike trail) close to Kananaskis Lakes Trail (road).
13. Elkwood parking lot.
14. Elkwood campground. Roads and trails from all loops
15. Boulton Creek upper parking lot.
16. Boulton Creek campground. Loop A gives the nearest access to the HRT.
17. Boulton Creek Trading Post from lower Boulton Creek parking lot.
18. Boulton Bridge parking lot. Follow the interpretive trail over the bridge and up the hill to the ranger cabin.
19. Elk Pass parking lot. Walk Elk Pass trail for 1.5 km to the junction with Fox Creek

Comments In K Country, the High Rockies Trail (HRT) section of the Trans Canada Trail runs between Goat Creek and Elk Pass. Volume 3 describes the section between Goat Creek parking lot and Buller Mountain day-use area via the Spray. The section south to Elk Pass and over into B.C. via the Smith-Dorrien valley is described here in Volume 1. Other sections of the Trans Canada Trail are described separately under different trail names.

It's intended for day hikers, backpackers and bikers. In winter it is popular with winter walkers, snowshoers, fat-tire bikers and even skiers. A few people will travel right through, most will use portions of the trail, perhaps in combination with other trails.

Contrary to its name, this section keeps to the valley bottoms, hardly "the Jewell in the Trans Canada Trail Crown" as touted; surely that moniker must go to the section over Cox Hill described in Volume 2. So much of the trail lies within forest. However, much to the planners' credit, they searched out every conceivable viewpoint and waterfall along the way. Overall, the trail is undulating with bridges across the many creeks.

Camping Off Kananaskis Lakes Trail (road) Canyon, Elkwood, Boulton Creek, Mount Sarrail Camping areas specifically for backpackers and bikepackers at Buller Mountain and Sawmill on Hwy. 742 and Pocaterra overflow off Kananaskis Lake Trail. No one is turned away.

Facilities Hwy. 742: Day-use areas at Buller Mountain (open May 15–Nov. 1) Chester Lake (open year round), Sawmill (open year round), Black Prince (open year round), Peninsula (open May 1–Nov 1). Mount Engadine Lodge on the Mt. Shark Road offers accommodation and Sunday brunch to non residents. Book in advance.

Kananaskis Lakes Trail: Day-use areas at Boulton Bridge (open year round), Canyon (open year round), Elk Pass (open year round Pocaterra (open year round). The Discovery Centre dispenses information. Boulton Creek Trading Post sells groceries, snack food and icecream between mid May and mid September. William Watson Lodge is open all year for seniors and people with disabilities.

Trail history Alberta TrailNet, had been planning the Trans Canada Trail through Alberta for 13 years. Finally in 2014 they hired McElhanny Consulting Services, and under engineer Darin Langhorst, and trail designer Matt Hadley (avid mountain biker) split this section into four phases, each to be built by a different trail construction company from across Canada. Most of the work was done in 2016, a few bridges carried over to 2017. As usual, fine turning was carried out by Friends of K Country.

Camping sites for through travellers were finally approved in 2020 thanks to the persistent efforts of Jeff Grutz.

Buller Mountain day-use to Rummel Lake trail

Distance 5.9 km
Height gain N-S 310 m (1017 ft.)
Height loss N-S 100 m (328 ft.)
High point 2060 m (6759 ft.)

Highway access 1, 2, 3

Comments The first two sections are undulating forest walks taking in viewpoints and crossings of Engadine and Rummel creeks en route to Rummel Lake trail.

To Engadine Burn 3.1 km

The trail leaves #81 Buller Pass trail 560 metres in from the parking lot (430 m from Hwy. 742). If coming from the north, it's 550 metres from the junction with Buller Pass trail.

Turn right onto the HRT. After a flat stretch, the trail climbs through spruce forest across the west flank of Mt. Engadine. Pass a stand of magnificent spruce just before crossing four fingers of burnt forest.

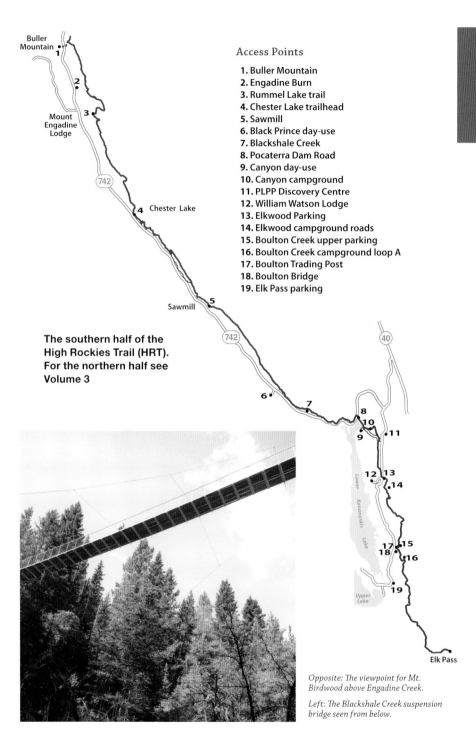

Access Points

1. Buller Mountain
2. Engadine Burn
3. Rummel Lake trail
4. Chester Lake trailhead
5. Sawmill
6. Black Prince day-use
7. Blackshale Creek
8. Pocaterra Dam Road
9. Canyon day-use
10. Canyon campground
11. PLPP Discovery Centre
12. William Watson Lodge
13. Elkwood Parking
14. Elkwood campground roads
15. Boulton Creek upper parking
16. Boulton Creek campground loop A
17. Boulton Trading Post
18. Boulton Bridge
19. Elk Pass parking

The southern half of the High Rockies Trail (HRT). For the northern half see Volume 3

Opposite: The viewpoint for Mt. Birdwood above Engadine Creek.

Left: The Blackshale Creek suspension bridge seen from below.

Not sure what a cairn indicates on burn no. 3, but burn no. 4 appears to be the trail's high point. Between blackened trees are views of Spray Lakes Reservoir, Cone Mountain, Tent Ridge and best of all Mt. Assiniboine.

On the descent, traverse steeper slopes to another wider burn. A short distance on, cross the Engadine Burn right-of-way. (Downhill leads to Hwy. 742 in 700 metres. Uphill leads to Engadine Cirque and #83 Rummel Ridge Viewpoint.)

To Rummel Lake trail lower junction 2.8 km

On the banktop above Engadine Creek's narrow valley first visit the viewpoint bench for first views of Birdwood and Commonwealth, then head down left to Engadine Creek bridge.

Climb up the other side of the valley, at the top wending across to the Rummel Creek drainage at a far more gentle gradient featuring banked corners for bikers coming the other way. Look down on the forested valley of Rummel Creek. Descend and cross Rummel Creek on a bridge. A long climb up the far side ends on the fairly open ridge to the west.

There join #84 Rummel Lake trail at the upper T-junction and turn right. (Trail to left heads along the ridge to Rummel Lake.) Going downhill, there are new views to enjoy of Sir Douglas, Commonwealth Ridge, Commonwealth Peak and Mounts Birdwood and Smuts. In 330 metres reach the lower T-junction where a bench gives views of Spray Lakes Reservoir and Tent Ridge. Turn left. (Right is Rummel Lake trail descending to Hwy. 742 at access 3, 2 km distant.)

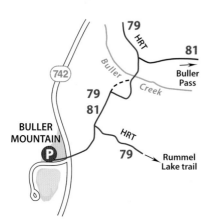

Left: Magnificent spruce forest between Buller Pass trail and the Engadine Burn.

Opposite top: Walking the Engadine Burn in winter gives better views of Spray Lakes Reservoir and Mt. Assiniboine.

Opposite bottom: On the small section shared with Rummel Lake trail, Sir Douglas, Commonwealth Ridge and Commonwealth Peak come into sight.

The High Rockies Trail, access from Buller Mountain day-use area and the route to Buller Pass

Rummel Lake trail to Chester Lake trailhead

Distance 6.7 km
Height gain 140 m (460 ft.)
Height loss 250 m (820 ft.)
High point 2080 m (6824 ft.)

Highway access 3, 4

Comments A hilly forest trail with occasional good views. Joins Chester Lake logging roads and ski trails for the last lap. In winter, fat-tire bikers and winter walkers take a different line into the parking lot.

To Three Lakes Valley bridge 4.5 km

The trail continues through once-logged forest with occasional views west to Mt. Birdwood. In mature trees dip in and out of a seasonal creek. Then it's back to once-logged forest, climbing past old skid trails to a flat, perhaps once a sawmill site, which is the start for a much longer uphill to the trail's high point. Alas, there aint no view.

The trail descends, climbs a little more, then descends stony ground. Partway down the hill the side slope steepens markedly. This the best part, big gaps in the trees allowing views of Mt. Smuts, Birdwood again, Commonwealth Creek between them, and the upcoming great peaks of Robertson, French and Sir Douglas as you progress. Hwy. 742 looks incredibly far down at the foot of Commonwealth Ridge. Have we really climbed this high up?

The side slope lessens as the trail climbs another hill, the ground flattening as you wend left to the bridge over Three Lakes Valley creek.

To Chester Lake parking lot 2.2 km

The trail climbs out of the valley and joins a logging road. Turn left. A long straight leads to a junction with a gravel road which is #97 Chester Lake trail. Keep right.

As you descend the Chester Lake trail, into view comes the north outlier of Mt. French which climbers know as Prairie Lookout — a seemingly inappropriate name for such a gorgeous looking peak though I'm told you can spot a bit of prairie off to the east from the summit. Arriving at a T-junction with Chester Lake alternate route, keep right.

At the next junction turn right and make the final descent to Chester Creek where you cross the bridge and pass through a gate into Chester Lake parking lot. (NOTE: In reverse direction, the trail starts to the LEFT of the kiosk as you face it.)

NOTE: In winter the HRT avoids Chester Lake trails which are ski trails. See the blue trail on the sketchmap on page 278.

In a nutshell: Turn off left before coming to the first Chester Lake trail, cross that trail at a 4-way, follow a long logging road, finally descending off right to the Chester Lake alternative route at a 4-way. Cross, go left, then right onto the Chester Lake snowshoe trail. At a T-junction on a logging road turn left and cross Chester Creek to Snowdrift snowshoe trail. Turn right to return to the parking lot.

Opposite: On the descent to Chester Lake parking lot, the north outlier of Mt. French called Prairie Lookout comes into view.

Above: Rummel to Chester. At the halfway point, new mountains to the southwest are coming into view, Mt. Robertson on the left.

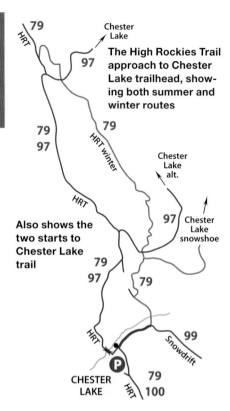

The High Rockies Trail approach to Chester Lake trailhead, showing both summer and winter routes

79
HRT

Chester Lake
97

79
97
79
HRT winter

Chester Lake alt.

HRT

Also shows the two starts to Chester Lake trail

97 Chester Lake snowshoe

79
97
79

HRT
99
Snowdrift

79
100
HRT

CHESTER
LAKE
P

The 9-foot-high signpost at Frost Heave/Graupel junction, for which you need binoculars.

Chester Lake trailhead to Sawmill trailhead

Distance 7.4 km
Height gain 230 m (755 ft.)
Height loss 150 m (492 ft.)
High point 1960 m (6430 ft.)
Highway access 4, 5

Comments For the main part this section follows snowshoe trails along logging roads. At Headwall Creek crossing view the destructive aftermath of the 2013 flood.

To Graupel north junction 1.4 km
Either cut across the top of the parking lot, or pick up the trail on the southeast corner, then follow Frost Heave snowshoe trail (née Blue ski trail) through a gate and down to a side creek crossing. Turn left up a hill into a lovely S-bend below some magnificent Engleman spruce. Descend slightly.

NOTE: At the left-hand bend a 70 m-long, slightly overgrown logging road leads out to Hwy. 742 reached 800 m south of Chester Lake parking lot. It's often used as a shortcut to Headwall Lakes.

In another 120 metres come to a major T-junction with a map sitting atop a 9 foot-high post. Turn right on Graupel snowshoe trail (yellow ski trail). (Left is Frost Heave leading to Snowdrift.)

To Graupel middle junction 2 km
In 430 metres, at the second bend, a second 130-foot-long little-used logging road heads out to Hwy. 742 reached 1.4 km south of Chester Lake parking lot. Wind uphill and into a very long flat straight. A downhill deposits you on the cobble flats of Headwall Creek where you can ogle the mess left behind after the 2013 flood. Cross Headwall Creek on a wide bridge.

Easy slightly uphill going leads to a T-junction. Turn left. (Graupel turns right down a hill.)

To Graupel south junction 2.3 km
Deviating from Graupel, the HRT climbs up the logging road, at the top turning right and resuming its southeasterly direction. Come to a 3-way junction. Keep right. (Uphill road zigging back left is Whiteout snowshoe trail that joins with Snowdrift much higher up the hillside. Slightly uphill trail to left is snowshoe trail Sun Cups that connects to the Sawmill Snowshoe Loops above James Walker Creek.)

Your narrower road called Wind Chill by snowshoers remains flat for a while then descends a very long hill to the Y-junction with Graupel.

Go left on the HRT. (Graupel to right has dipsy doodled along close to Hwy. 742.)

To Sawmill trailhead 1.7 km
The wider road descends a few slight hills then flattens out and crosses James Walker Creek on a bridge. Not long after, climb into the big open meadow that is Sawmill. Go left, then right into the parking lot.

If heading south on the HRT, go straight through a picnic area and cross the Sawmill access road.

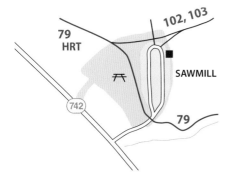

The High Rockies Trail through Sawmill day-use area

Top: Luckily, there's a bridge over Headwall Creek.
Bottom: The logging road after leaving Graupel.

Sawmill trailhead to Black Prince

Distance 6.2 km
Height gain 220 m (722 ft.)
Height loss 180 m (6759 ft.)
High point 1950 m (590 ft.)

Highway access 5, 6

Comments A forest trail see-saws across the west flank of Mt. Kent, giving fine views at the north end and crossing some interesting bridges and side creeks. N-S direction has many more downhills.

To the high point 2 km

The trail runs through the grassy picnic area below the parking lot, then crosses the parking lot access road back into trees.

The trail climbs gradually to a T-junction with an old logging road. Turn right, then in a few metres left up another logging road that climbs a long hill. At the top it veers right along a straight into a bushy meadow with a view of Cegnfs, Mt. Murray, the north peak of Mt. French and Mt. Smith-Dorrien.

Keep left, following the left edge of the meadow below a bank, and into a long climb with relief sections ending just before side creek crossing no. 1. The view from the bridge looking downstream was positively vertigo inducing before the handrails went in. Trail designer Matt's excitement at having discovered such an amazing crossing place explains why the trail leading to it is uphill from both directions. See the photo on the next page. (Not without reason, Alf calls the HRT the High Bridges trail.)

To Black Prince 4.2 km

A long downhill leads to no. 2 creek crossing. More downhill and undulations leads to side creek no. 3, a rather pretty stream between mossy banks crossed on rocks. Continue undulating and downhilling to creek no. 4 that is crossed between a welter of slabs. For some scramblers, this creekbed is a direct route up Mt. Kent from the highway.

More undulations bring you into a sunnier area of smaller trees, after which it's all slightly downhill to a T-junction. Go straight to continue on the HRT.

NOTE: For Black Prince trailhead go right and descend a 500-m-long side trail to Hwy. 742 reached opposite the access road to Black Prince day-use area.

Sawmill to Black Prince: View from the bushy meadow to Mt. Murray, Cegnfs to its right.

Sawmill to Black Prince: Looking up at the first bridge south of Sawmill day-use area.

To get to this viewpoint descend steep ground just beyond the bridge A trail starts you off. Alternatively, take the lower loop of the South Sawmill snowshoe trail and at the bend where it starts climbing up left, head off right on a game trail following the bottom of the steep slopes to the side creek. There is a reason this segment of the HRT is called the High Bridges trail.

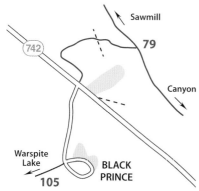

Black Prince day-use area and its access to the High Rockies Trail

Black Prince to Canyon day-use area

Distance 7 km
Height gain 140 m (459 ft.)
Height loss 280 m (919 ft.)
High point 1830 m (6004 ft.)

Highway access 6–9

Comments Staying close above Hwy. 742, this section calls in at access 8, then crosses the highway and Pocaterra Dam to Canyon day-use area. While there are several pleasant viewpoints, the biggest attraction by far is the suspension bridge across Blackshale Creek, the most remarkable engineering feat along the whole of the HRT.

To Blackshale Creek 2.3 km

The trail traverses steeper hillside to a creek crossing. Soon after cross an alder filled cutline and make the trail's first foray to the banktop above the highway. Back on the cutline, the trail follows it a short way, then peels off to the left. After this, you're climbing most of the way to Blackshale Creek drop off at a Y-junction.

Ahead is the trail of "high bridges" crowning achievement, a 73 m (240 foot-long) suspension bridge finally finished on Wednesday August 23, 2017. After an official opening was not forthcoming, the bridge builders took it upon themselves to string some flagging across the entrance and let the first biker across cut the ribbon. As you go be sure to look up from the mid point to the summit of Blackshale Creek.

For anyone who feels wobbly on such things, know the bridge is tethered by anti sway/wind brace cables connected to each side of the bridge. Nevertheless, the bridge can be avoided by turning right and descending the 500 m-long access trail to Hwy. 742, from where another trail climbs 540 m up the far bank. As you can tell by the vehicles parked on the highway at the creek, this is a super popular tourist attraction, which, incidentally, is closed in winter for safety reasons.

Above: Looking southeast to Elpoca and Gap mountains at the tail end of the Opal Range.

Below: The red-brown trail through subalpine fir forest close to access 8.

To access 8, 3.8 km

Straight off the bridge, keep ahead at the junction. (Right is the 540-m-long access trail down to Hwy. 742.) A few metres farther along, a faint trail climbing the hillside to left is the start of the steep flog up South Kent. From the top is an amazing top to bottom view of Blackshale Creek.

Descend steeply at times, then more gradually down to the banktop above Hwy. 742. Further stints above grassy banks give views across the valley to mounts Warspite and Invincible and ahead to the pale grey peaks of the Opal Range.

Back in trees, a built-up trail undulates across boggy ground, the frequent gaps filled with rocks which enable the water to keep on moving. After crossing a footbridge, enter a lovely forest of subalpine fir and a change in the colour scheme, the soil and trail now an attractive reddish brown. After two more brief visits to the banktop, the last disclosing a view of Lower Kananaskis Lake, begin the long descent to access 8.

Above and bottom right: Black Prince to Canyon: Two views of Blackshale Creek suspension bridge. A couple of regulations to know about: Only 20 people are allowed on the bridge at one time and the bridge is closed when snow-covered winter.

Left: Blackshale Creek from Gypsum Mine trail. Note the bridge at the bottom of the photo.

Arrive on Hwy. 742 at the junction with TransAlta's diversion canal taking Kent Creek into Lower Kananaskis Lake.

To Canyon day-use area 880 m
Cross Hwy. 742 and follow the dam road through a gate. At a Y-junction keep right. (Left is Penstock snowshoe trail) and cross Pocaterra Dam built in 1956 to hold back the waters of Lower Kananaskis Lake. At the far end, descend left, cross the penstock via the bridge, then climb right onto the Canyon day-use area access road.

Where you go next depends on your destination. For Canyon day-use area parking lot turn right uphill, following the road around to the right past the biffy into the parking lot.

For Canyon campgrounds and the next section of the HRT turn left down the hill, staying straight and downhill at the next junction.

Canyon day-use to Elkwood

Distance 3.8 trail km
Height gain 30 m (98 ft.)
Height loss 30 m (98 ft.)
High point 1720 m

Highway access 8–12

Comments The route is paved throughout, as it follows campground roads and Lodgepole bike trail. Not good news for hikers.

Through Canyon campground 1.6 km
From Canyon parking lot follow Canyon Road around and down past Pocaterra Dam. Keep straight and downhill at the next junction onto the gated Canyon campground access road,

Pass A Loop on the right, then B Loop on the left. Just after the entrance to the now defunct Canyon interpretive trail, the road bends right and climbs through C Loop to the loop at road's end. En route, opposite site no. 34, the connector trail from Peter Lougheed Discovery Centre comes in from the left. See access #11.

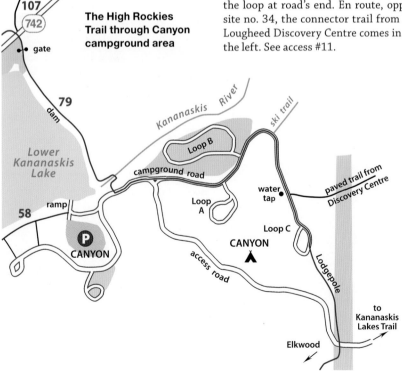

The High Rockies Trail through Canyon campground area

**Canyon campground to
Elkwood parking 2.2 km**
Leaving the far end of the loop road, Lodgepole bike trail continues on in the same line. On a powerline right-of-way it crosses Canyon Road, then after a short stint up the right-of-way turns right into the trees. Higher up, at a T-junction with grassy, boggy Lodgepole ski trail it bends back left onto the right-of-way. From this vantage point are views back to the Opal Range, mounts Blane, Brock and Wintour predominant.

As you cross over the height of land, the great wall of mounts Sarrail and Foch rises up ahead. Descend, at the bottom turning left into the forest. Arrive at a T-junction. Keep left. Right is the access to William Watson Lodge and Lower Lake trail.

Shortly cross Kananaskis Lake Trail (the road). In a couple of minutes turn left into Elkwood parking lot. Ahead is Wheeler bike trail and the continuation of the HRT.

Lodgepole bike trail along the powerline. Mt. Sarrail up ahead.

Elkwood to Boulton Creek

Distance 4.8 km
Height gain 210 m (689 ft.)
Height loss 270 m (886 ft.)
High point 1755 m (5758 ft.)

Highway access 12–14

Comments Again the route is all on paved bike trail. In winter you can substitute Elkwood and Frozen Toad snowshoe trails.

Through Elkwood campground 1 km
From Elkwood parking lot follow Wheeler bike and ski trail past the amphitheatre. Keep right. (Left is #59 Marl Lake trail.) At a biffy, cross a campground access road between A Loop (right) and B loop (left). Then cross the main campground access road. (Left leads to C and D loops.)

Straight off, the bike trail turns sharp left along a bench, running parallel with the campground road past a picnic table. Two shortcuts come in from opposite the entrance to C Loop, then D Loop. See the sketchmap on the next page.

Above: Fox Creek.

Opposite: Marl Ponds, looking toward Gap Mountain at right and the higher summits of Elpoca Mountain behind.

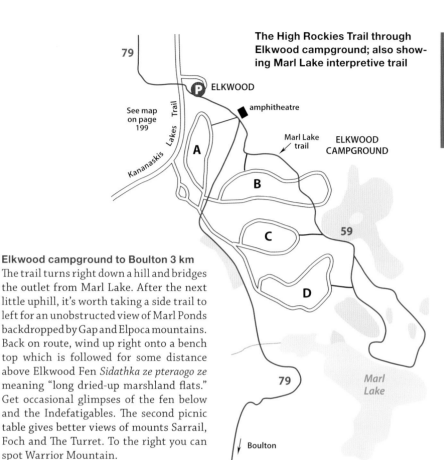

The High Rockies Trail through Elkwood campground; also showing Marl Lake interpretive trail

79

ELKWOOD

P

See map on page 199

Kananaskis Lakes Trail

amphitheatre

Marl Lake trail

ELKWOOD CAMPGROUND

A

B

C

D

59

79

Boulton

Marl Lake

Elkwood campground to Boulton 3 km

The trail turns right down a hill and bridges the outlet from Marl Lake. After the next little uphill, it's worth taking a side trail to left for an unobstructed view of Marl Ponds backdropped by Gap and Elpoca mountains. Back on route, wind up right onto a bench top which is followed for some distance above Elkwood Fen *Sidathka ze pteraogo ze* meaning "long dried-up marshland flats." Get occasional glimpses of the fen below and the Indefatigables. The second picnic table gives better views of mounts Sarrail, Foch and The Turret. To the right you can spot Warrior Mountain.

Leaving the bench, the trail climbs to the junction with Amos ski trail, then meanders on. On nearing Boulton Creek campground access road, the HRT turns first right. (Should you be camping at Boulton Creek, going straight here is a shortcut to the campground access road.)

Through Boulton Creek 800 m

The HRT descends alongside the campground access road, then crosses it, and runs topside of the upper Boulton Creek parking lot from where you can access the parking lots and Boulton Creek Trading Post at a Trans Canada Trail sign.

Otherwise, continue on the bike trail. At a 4-way turn right down a paved hill. Turn next left onto Boulton Creek interpretive trail which is not paved.

Boulton Creek to Elk Pass

Distance 8.3 km
Height gain 310 m (1017 ft.)
Height loss 150 m (492 ft.)
High point 1950 (6398 ft.)

Highway access 15–19

Comments The HRT follows Boulton Creek interpretive trail, a couple of ski trails, then various reworkings of the cutline access road to Elk Pass on the B.C. boundary.

To Fox Creek 4.2 km

The trail leads to a T-junction at the old ranger cabin. Keep straight. (Down right is access 16 at Boulton Bridge parking lot.) A winding section of Boulton Creek interpretive trail along the banktop above Boulton Creek melds into Moraine ski trail. Just after post no. 7, keep straight at a T-junction and descend into Boulton Creek valley. At the next T-junction with Boulton Creek ski trail, turn left up Fox Creek.

Fox Creek 1.5 km

Throughout, enjoy a narrow trail in dark forest festooned with lichens. Cross Boulton Creek, then Fox Creek, the trail then widening as it runs creekside. This section ends with a climb onto Elk Pass trail. Turn left. (#62 comes in from the right.)

To West Elk Pass junction 2.6 km

In 500 metres the access road crosses Fox Creek to a T-junction on the far side. Keep right. (The trail zooming up the hill to left is Hydroline ski and snowshoe trail.)

For the next kilometre follow a new road that connects snippets of previous road badly damaged during the takeover by the creek in 2013. After two creek crossings, the second over the main west fork carrying the water, you are back on original road with the flood mess behind you. Enjoy walking the narrow valley of the tiny south fork between a grassy draw and a steep bank. At the Patterson ski trail junction, shortcut on a trail signed "Elk Pass," at the top of the hill

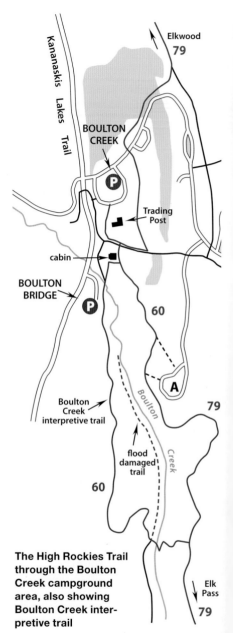

The High Rockies Trail through the Boulton Creek campground area, also showing Boulton Creek interpretive trail

turning left. Shortly after you rejoin the old road, Bluberry Hill ski trail turns off to the right at a picnic table.

Continue along a straight to a Y-junction with sign "Elk Lakes." Stay ahead on the road. (Narrow trail to right leads to West Elk Pass and Elk Lakes Provincial Park. See ##62, 63.)

To Elk Pass 1.4 km

A long, steep climb with one relief section leads to Elk Pass on the powerline right-of-way with picnic table. The road turns right just before the right-of-way and passes under a cedar portal into B.C. "Welcome to the Elk Valley," reads the crosspiece. Initiated by educator Stephen Larsen, designed by the students from Sparwood, Elkford and Fernie secondary schools and sculpted by artist Michael Penny, the two poles represent the animals and the human activity in the valley. Students then hauled the logs up the 5 kilometres from Elk Lakes Provincial Park—which took them 2.5 hours—and with help from Clarkson Contracting installed the arch on June 27, 2017.

To reach Elk River Road simply follow the powerline access road down the hill.

Above: Cedar portal on Elk Pass on the day it was erected by students from Sparwood, Elkford and Fernie secondary schools who worked with the artist to create the arch. Photo Nikita Paskiewich, courtesy of Stephen Larsen

Below: Elk Pass trail picnic table near Blueberry Hill ski trail junction.

80 Red Basin

map 4

Day to long day
Official, unofficial trails, route
Distance 4.9 km one way to basin
Height gain 686 m (2250 ft.)
Height loss 107 m (350 ft.)
High point 2286 m (7500 ft.)
Map 82 J/14 Spray Lakes Reservoir

Access Hwy. 742 (Smith-Dorrien/Spray Trail) at Spray Lakes day-use area.
Also accessible from #82 Red Peak.

Comments Red Basin Creek lies opposite Spray Lakes day-use area and to the south of Red Ridge, the main fork of it curving into a basin between Red Peak and Mt. Buller.

Access is not via the creek, but by way of an intermittent hunter's trail up the north ridge of Mt. Buller. In 2009 the lower section of trail was still flagged with pink and white

One of the boulders in the forest.

tape decorated with mushrooms and pine beetles and bearing the words "pest mgmt. zone." After this you are on your own, so only experienced off-trail hikers should even consider this hike.

From the basin, hiker/scramblers who start early from the trailhead can climb onto the south ridge of Red Peak to join the normal route up the mountain. For more proficient rubble scramblers, peak 210395 is also accessible.

Geology This is one of the most geologically fascinating valleys off Hwy. 742. Its attractions include the two best examples of rock glaciers in K Country, possible tension gashes (see explanation in the text) and a boulder field to make boulderers drool. Pity it requires so much effort to get up there.

To the HRT 600 m
Walk out to Hwy. 762 and turn right. In a few metres turn left onto a twisty trail that connects to the High Rockies trail. Turn right and cross the bridge over Red Basin Creek. In a very short distance your route turns left up a forested ridge. Possibly a cairn still marks the spot.

Basin viewpoint 2.7 km
On varying bits and pieces of trail, climb up the ridge nearest the creek, steep bits alternating with easier sections. Gradually, the ridge turns south and it's here, higher

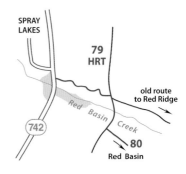

The start to Red Basin trail

up, where you run into an oddity: a series of massive gashes filled with spruce that slice across the ridge and are clearly seen on Google Earth. My friend the geologist thinks they might *possibly* be sigmoidal tension gashes arranged *en échelon*, i.e., stress fractures caused by a large-scale change in orientation right around Mt. Buller. All except the last one can be avoided by staying right.

After one last steep uphill push you emerge on open ridge at 192407 and look down on Spray Lakes Reservoir. Ahead rises Mt. Buller, its northern cirque chockablock with boulders, some so huge they show up on the topo map as little circles of contour lines. To the east rises Red Ridge, the source of two tongue-like rock glaciers creeping down its west flank to the south fork. The multiple lobes (also seen beautifully on Google Earth) are what distinguish rock glaciers from regular rock slides.

If not going up Red Peak, it's worth either carrying on up the north ridge of Buller to where you feel uncomfortable, or exploring the boulder field for the one with the hole through the middle.

Top: Red Basin from the Basin viewpoint. Note two rock glaciers flowing down the west face of Red Peak at left and centre.

Bottom: From the same viewpoint, Spray Lake Reservoir during the pine beetle burn of 2009.

Photo showing the route to Red Peak from the basin. The route climbs a grass slope onto the bench at far left, then heads diagonally right, finally climbing the rib to the left of the gully below the low point. After this it's an easy walk along the ridge to the summit at left.

Into the basin 1.6 km

Descend to the larch col between your ridge and the north ridge of Buller proper, then head down left through trees at the edge of the boulder field. Rather than traverse into the basin, it's easier to descend the whole 100 m (300 ft.) to the flat above a small tributary of Red Basin Creek (camping spot), then follow one of the trails down the steep little bank into the tributary valley. There always seems to be water flowing just downstream of this point. (This tributary is shown on the topo map as a split in the south fork. Not so, as you'll find out.)

Turn right and walk UP the valley to where it unfolds. Continue on and look DOWN on the main creekbed far below you, an arid, stony swath below the steep end wall of the bigger rock glacier. Descend into the bed at a comfortable place, which may mean following the banktop to the right for a way, then simply walk up it into the basin. Below the headwall is an island of meadow and trees, which makes a logical turnaround point.

GOING HIGHER

80A To Red Peak

Route, unofficial trail
Distance 1.1 km to col, 1.6 km to peak
Height gain 320 m (1050 ft.) to ridge, 503 m (1650 ft.) to peak, 1189 m (3900 ft.) from trailhead
High point at peak 2758 m (9050 ft.)

The following is based in part on Alf Skrastins's description.

From the end of the meadow, climb up the grass slope on the left to a bench, and from there follow a game trail all the way to the ridge between peak 210395 and the Red Peak. In detail: from the bench the trail climbs to the last patch of vegetation, then enters a gully (snow early and late in the season) leading through some small rockbands. It then heads right onto a scree rib and follows it straight up to the ridge. While the footing is firm on ascent, on descent the scree is a little too large to descend easily and you'll probably want to make a few zigs.

On gaining the ridge, turn left. In a short distance you meet up with the normal route up the mountain. Now read #82.

81 Buller Pass

Backpack, long day hikes
Official trail
7.4 km to pass, 10.2 km to Ribbon Lake
Height gain 670 m (2200 ft.)
High point 2484 m (8150 ft.)
Map 82 J/14 Spray Lakes Reservoir

Access Hwy. 742 (Smith-Dorrien/Spray Trail) at Buller Mountain day-use area. Use the first parking area on the right.
Also accessible from #26 Ribbon Falls and #35 Guinn's Pass.

Comments The moderately strenuous Buller Pass trail was conceived as a backpacker's trail to the backcountry campground at Ribbon Lake. It's a varied trail taking in forest, flower meadows and a high rocky pass with a fabulous view.

Options People with two vehicles can make a one- or two-day trip to Hwy. 40, either via Ribbon Creek (21.4 km) or via Guinn's Pass and Galatea Creek trails (16.7 km). Day hikers usually head to the pass and back. The more experienced can make a loop with #81A North Buller Pass on a much rougher trail.

There are a few relatively easy mountains within reach of the passes such as Red Peak at 214404 and its neighbour 210395 (see #82) and the big grey peak at 217373.

Facilities Backcountry campground at Ribbon Lake.

Be Aware The verdant area before Ribbon Lake is a grizzly hangout. Campers have never been bothered, so it's all the more reason to keep a clean campsite.

To HRT south junction 560 m

Walk down the access road to the highway. The trail starts from the far side at a myriad of signs and after crossing a footbridge makes a beeline for Buller Creek. At the top of a long, gentle uphill is a T-junction. Go straight. (Trail to right is High Rockies Trail heading south across Engadine Creek to Rummel Lake trail.)

To HRT north junction 550 m

After flat going, the trail zigs right and descends to Buller Creek bridge, rebuilt in 2014. Cross the bridge. At the next junction turn right up a steep hill. (Trail to left is High Rockies Trail heading north.)

To the forks 3.2 km

For the next few kilometres the trail climbs steadily along the north bank of Buller Creek valley at the edge of a burn set in 2010 to combat pine beetle. In early summer the blackened forest contrasts strangely with its understorey of bright yellow arnicas.

Arrive at Engelmann Spruce Flat and a bridged crossing of the creek just upstream of the confluence with a "side creek." Here you discover most of the water comes from the side creek, which has its source below Mt. Engadine.

The trail then winds up a step in the valley floor. At the top is a long traverse left to North Buller Creek. En route, round a

The waterfall and bowl, a favourite rest stop.

buttress below a scree slope and return to the creek at the waterfall and bowl—the usual rest stop. The creek above is where you should fill up the water bottles, 'cos the next guaranteed water is over the pass at Ribbon Creek springs.

Soon after, the trail crosses the usually dry south fork to a T-junction. Turn right. (To left is the north fork that carries water. See #81A.)

Buller Pass 3 km

Walk the uppermost reaches of burnt-black trees into the larch zone. In an amazingly short time the landscape changes to a wide, flat valley floor hemmed in by ridges of grey scree. Underfoot are flowery meadows with a sprinkling of last trees. The going is easy and in no time at all, it seems, you reach the foot of the headwall.

The second big climb of the day is 168 vertical metres up scree. The trail climbs up the left side, then make a long traverse right above a slabby area, finally turning left into the pass. Marking the high point is a large cairn. Ahead is the million-dollar view of Ribbon Lake backdropped by the two summits of Mt. Kidd.

To North Buller Pass cut-off 400 m

The east side of the pass is much steeper. Luckily a good trail zigs down the boulder slope, then traverses left to gain a grassy rib taking you all the way down to a draw. Just before the drop-off, cut left at a large cairn if heading for North Buller Pass. Otherwise keep straight.

To Guinn's Pass trail 1 km

The trail drops into the draw, crosses it and turns right, continuing through meadows to another steepening, where you'll spot an unofficial trail shortcutting along a bench to Guinn's Pass trail. Partway down the descent, just after Ribbon Creek bursts out of the hillside in great spouts (Ribbon Springs), is a T-junction with sign. Turn left. (Straight on is #35 Guinn's Pass trail to Galatea Creek.)

To Ribbon Lake 1.4 km

The trail descends the right bank of boisterous Ribbon Creek and on reaching flat ground crosses a bridge to the left bank. Walk through alternating spruce forest and smelly flower meadows (it's the valerian) to the west shore of Ribbon Lake and its backcountry campground. En route, a side trail to left leads to the patrol cabin.

Opposite: Buller Pass and the dry south fork.

Above: The first view of Ribbon Lake from Buller Pass. Rising above is Mt. Kidd to left and its south peak to right.

81A North Buller Pass

Unofficial trail, route
Distance 5 km, 16.9 km return trip
Height gain 183+ m (600+ ft.), 853+ m
(2800+ ft.) return trip
High point 2484 m (8150 ft.)

Comments This route circles around the peak between the two passes, crosses North Buller Pass (the original route to the lake) and descends the north fork to join Buller Pass trail at the forks.

It's a hugely popular option for a day trip, which should always be taken in the anti-clockwise direction. Should you be seen toiling UP the north pass from the north fork, people will stop you and tell you you're crazy. Simply say you are heading left at the pass to Red Peak.

The trail is intermittent and the going enjoyable, mostly on grass, EXCEPT on the west side of the pass, which is steep and unpleasant. On the east side a cornice and snow persist into mid-July.

Geology Fossil lovers should check out the Devonian reef located high in the north fork valley.

Buller Pass to North Buller Pass 1.5 km
Leave Buller Pass trail at a cairn above the drop-off into the draw and head left across a few rocks to grass. Ascend the left side of the upper draw to a gap at 217388 between peak 213385 and a grassy knoll to the right. Descend slightly towards the grassy basin under the north pass.

If you can hack climbing another 100 vertical metres, I recommend taking in the knoll for a superb view of Ribbon Lake and the upper Ribbon Creek valley, which features one sizeable tarn and lots of little ones.

Next up is the climb to North Buller Pass itself, which is around the corner to the left. I am happy to report there is now a reasonable trail heading across the scree directly to the cairn. Early in the season you could be crossing a snow slope.

The view just misses seven-star status — the pointy peak far to the west *not* being Mt. Assiniboine, which is hidden behind Mt. Buller, but the infamous Mt. Eon. In the other direction the view is largely blocked by nearby ridges. It pays to wander a way up the ridge to the north, the south ridge of peak 210395, which is more easily climbed from the other side.

To Buller Pass trail 2.8 km

The west side of the pass is a steep, rubbishy mess where scree has been shuffled about on hard underlying shale. (See the pic above right.) Slither down the first 30 metres, then on reasonable trail traverse right to the top of a grassy strip. The trail corkscrews down the strip, the angle gradually easing as you near the flat valley floor.

The trail more or less continues to the right of the dry creek, then along the sandy creekbed. Just after passing the large patch of trees, use either the creekbed or bits of trail in the meadow to right.

As you go, look up right to cliffs and hoodoos of black Devonian limestone with plentiful fossils, including amphipora that once grew in back-reef lagoons. Stagger up scree to observe numerous windows and fossils in situ. But if it's fossils you're looking for, there's no need to climb high. The scree low down and even the creekbed is loaded with them.

Come to the waterfall at the head of a tiny box canyon. This signals the start of a good trail taking you all the way out to the forks. It follows the right banktop, then descends to the creekbed below the canyon at a cairn. Walk the creekbed into meadow where the trail continues into some trees. At cairns the trail crosses the creek to the grassy left bank.

Shortly it climbs into open forest with magnificent trees where it makes an ambling descent with some step-over deadfall to the forks. A sharp left turn precedes the junction with Buller Pass trail at the bridge. Turn right and return the same way you came up.

Opposite: View from the draw looking up the east side of Buller Pass to peak 217373. You can just make out the trail descending from the pass.

Top left: Cliffs and hoodoos of Devonian limestone in the north fork.

Top right: Climbing up the west side of North Buller Pass. The reasonable trail is about to end some distance below the pass.

82 Red Peak

map 4

Long day scramble
Unofficial trail, route
Distance 1.8 km from North Buller Pass, 8.9 km from trailhead
Height gain 366 m (1200 ft.) from North Buller Pass, 1036 m (3400 ft.) from trailhead
High point 2758 m (9050 ft.)
Map 82 J/14 Spray Lakes Reservoir

Access Via #81 Buller Pass at the forks. **Also accessible** from #80 Red Basin.

Comments This is the brightly coloured peak at 214404 overlooking Sparrowhawk Creek Tarns and Red Ridge. In optimum conditions, meaning after August, it's a very easy climb from North Buller Pass, which is far harder than anything on the ascent route. Earlier in the season, getting through the cornice that fringes the summit ridge could be a problem. Regardless, it all makes for a very long day.

Returning the same way is easiest. For something more challenging try #80 Red Basin (15.6 km road to road), which requires two vehicles or bikes or a walk of 6.9 km along High Rockies Trail.

Warning Grizzlies dig the grassy rib.

North Fork to North Buller Pass 3 km
Rather than requiring you to read the last entry backwards, here is the description from the forks for North Buller Pass.

At the forks turn left and on trail begin an ambling ascent through open forest with step-over deadfall. Descend to the grassy right bank of the north fork and at cairns cross it into trees. The trail continues along the left bank into a meadow, then climbs above a tiny box canyon. Look down on a waterfall at the canyon's head.

Right: View from the grassy rib, looking down on the meadows and tarns towards Ribbon Lake. To right the route from Buller Pass is shown crossing the grassy saddle to North Buller Pass at far right. Along the skyline: Mt. Kidd South, peak 237374, Guinn's Pass, peak 217373, Mt. Galatea.

Opposite: Red Peak from the summit ridge.

The good trail ends here, Follow either the now dry creekbed or remnant trails in the meadow on the left side to the foot of the headwall — a wide band of orange scree and rubble. En route, check out the fossils strewn about under crags and hoodoos of Devonian limestone.

On trail, corkscrew up a strip of grass just left of centre. From its top the trail traverses right, then disintegrates, leaving you to pick your own way up 30 vertical metres of scree and rubble shuffled about on a slippery layer of hard shale. Reach North Buller Pass at a cairn.

Climbing the Red Peak 1.8 km
There is no need to descend the east side of the pass. From the cairn follow a game trail diagonally down left to a finger of grass. Then, descending slightly as you go, traverse the lower grass slopes of peak 210395 to a fork of Ribbon Creek — a wide, stony gully with water. Cross and climb onto the rib beyond.

Turn left (north) and walk up the broad, easy-angled grassy rib to the right of the

gully, making for the wide band of permanent snow you can see on the skyline. Where the gully turns left, continue ahead on the rib where grass is slowly being replaced by scree. High up, the rib steepens a little and narrows, delineating the right end of the snow bank. At the last, grovel up a few metres of steep scree (or snow) to gain the connecting ridge between peak 210395 and Red Peak.

Turn right and walk along the broad easy-angled ridge. At an unexpected glitch use a bypass trail on the right side. One last uphill burst on reddish-orange screes sees you at the summit. A small cairn with canister is perched on the edge of tottery red crags falling to the north and east. Even the soil nurturing tiny cushion plants is red.

The view to the west is panoramic: thunderstorms can be seen approaching from 100 kilometres away. Of course, Mt. Assiniboine is pre-eminent. The view east is blocked by lofty Mt. Bogart, which from the prairies is often mistaken for Assiniboine. To the south, The Tower and mounts Galatea and Buller are standouts in a welter of lower peaks. To the north the main features are Spray Lakes Reservoir, the grey, sprawling mass of Mt. Sparrowhawk, the high point of

Red Ridge and below you the Sparrowhawk Creek Tarns, the complexity of the cirque and its tarns made clear from this high vantage point.

NOTE: A few experienced scramblers descend the north ridge to access Red Ridge or Sparrowhawk Tarns as described in Volume 3. The rock is said to be "extraordinarily crappy."

83 Rummel Ridge Viewpoint   maps 9, 4

Day hike
Unofficial trails, route
Distance 3.4 km to high point
Height gain 640 m (2100 ft.)
High point 2455 m (8050 ft.)
Maps 82 J/14 Spray Lakes Reservoir

Access Hwy. 742 (Smith-Dorrien/Spray Trail). Park on the northeast side of the highway 1.4 km north of Mt. Shark Road (access road to Mount Shark and Mount Engadine Lodge).

Comments Rummel Ridge is really the south outlier of The Tower that overlooks Rummel Creek and the lake. Though barely rising above treeline, it offers larches and a fantastic panorama to the west reserved for people who can hack 305 metres (1000 ft) of sustained climbing up the Engadine firebreak. Technically, it's very easy and is often climbed in winter when you might be in the company of backcountry skiers enjoying the deep powder.

To High Rockies trail 700 m
Follow a wide right-of-way with narrow trail into a black forest called the Engadine Burn. On coming to a steepening, use the zigging trail on the right side of the fire-break. Thereafter, it's a steady climb above the left bank of Engadine Creek to the intersection with the High Rockies Trail (left and right). Go straight.

To top of burn 950 m
Continue climbing, steeply at times, up the right-of-way. In early summer the black forest is ablaze with arnica. In fall the colour changes to the wine red of fireweed leaves. After the right-of-way turns right and descends a little, turn off it to the right at 181343. (NOTE to explorers: The right-of-way continues into the mouth of the V-shaped valley between Mt. Engadine and The Tower.)

From the summit, a nearby view of Mt. Galatea with Rummel Lake at its foot. I chose not to show the amazing vista to the west so you can discover it for yourself.

To Rummel Ridge 1.7 m

Walk down grass to flagging indicating the trail down the bank to Engadine Creek. It's an easy crossing on stones. The trail continues on the far bank, climbing up right onto the banktop, where it joins another trail. Go right, following the trail around to the left through a few menziesia bushes onto the lower slope of the northwest ridge.

At first, the gradient is barely perceptible, the trail disintegrating into multiple bits and pieces in an open larch and spruce forest with frilly grouseberry underfoot. As the ridge becomes more defined and steeper, the strands gather into one trail climbing out of trees to the grassy summit.

Mt. Galatea with Rummel Lake at its foot comes into view, but what stuns is the amazing vista of peaks to the west, including such notables as Sir Douglas, the Royal Group, Assiniboine and Eon. Beyond Spray Lakes Reservoir, the eye is caught by flat-topped Mt. Turbulent, an easy scramble with a long approach.

OPTIONAL RETURN

83A Via Rummel Lake trail and the HRT

Distance 7.8 km

Comments At the top there is a decision to be made: return the same way or descend to Rummel Lake trail. NOTE: Under snow, the open descent slopes are prime avalanche terrain, the scene of one fatality.

Descend the short east ridge on grass and shale to the col between the ridge and The Tower. Turn right and drop down a moderately steep grassy draw into the forest, aiming to intersect Rummel Lake trail in about 1.2 km. Turn right and follow it to High Rockies Trail. (See #84.) Turn right on the HRT, which crosses Rummel Creek, traverses the west flank of Rummel Ridge, then crosses Engadine Creek back to Engadine Burn. (For this section read #79 at pages 272 and 274.) Turn left and return the same way you came up.

Top: Looking down the ascent ridge towards Spray Lakes Reservoir.

Bottom: #83A Rummel Ridge from the col below The Tower, showing the easy descent ridge.

84 Rummel Lake

Day hike
Official trail, unofficial trail
Distance 5.5 km
Height gain 396 m (1300 ft.)
High point at lake 2210 m (7250 ft.)
Map 82 J/14 Spray Lakes Reservoir

Access Hwy. 742 (Smith-Dorrien/Spray Trail). Park off-highway opposite the access road to Mount Engadine Lodge and Mount Shark ski trails.
Also accessible from #98 and #36.

Comments To some people, this little lake, named after Baroness Elizabeth "Lizzie" Rummel, surpasses Chester Lake in colour, setting and number of larches. It is one of the few trails with a biffy at its destination. The going is fairly easy with no creek crossings if you take the usual finish.

Facilities and Regulations A biffy near the lake on the usual finish. Only winter camping is allowed.

Trail update In 2016, the first 2.4 kilometres was conscripted into the High Rockies Trail (HRT) as official access and the rest as part of the trail itself, the whole of this section improved and lengthened by 500 metres. Also note there are two finishes: the 2007/8 reroute through avalanche-safe forest and the old trail along the south bank of Rummel Creek.

Lakes near timberline are often a stepping stone to the alpine above, in this case Rummel Pass and the opportunity to go right through to Hwy. 40.

To HRT lower junction 2 km

The trail starts from the east side of the highway and follows the line of an old logging road heading southeast. Turning left, it climbs a passageway of young trees between mature forest into more open terrain (née cutblock) where it turns right and taking a new line, meanders along to the lower junction with High Rockies Trail. Look back for a glimpse of Spray Lakes Reservoir.

Turn left onto the HRT heading north towards Buller Creek via Engadine Creek. (Straight on is the HRT heading south to Chester Lake parking lot.)

To HRT upper junction 330 m

Your trail and the HRT combined climb to a T-junction with inukshuk on a ridge high above Rummel Creek. Turn right uphill. (Trail to left is the northbound HRT.)

To bridge junction 2 km

At an arrow, the trail enters forest, following the broad, gently inclined ridge in a southeasterly direction, soon slipping into a wonderfully open mature forest with grouseberry and red heather underfoot. After three major dips, the trail turns sharp left. (The faint trail ahead with a stump laid across it is the "wrong" route but the "right route" if you're taking the grizzly trail to Chester Lake. See #98.)

The trail descends a little, then veers right running parallel to Rummel Creek, finally zigging down the bank to a T-junction.

To Rummel Lake 1.1 km

Choose from two ongoing routes.

1. via usual finish Now there is a trail, the meandering and official winter route through the trees with yellow markers has come into favour as the summer route as well. Most people use it.

Go straight and cross the bridge over Rummel Creek. The trail winds its way through open forest, climbing here and there, finally descending to the gleam of aqua that is the southwest corner of the lake. Across the outlet is a forest of larches.

Before you can say "Who's got the lunch?" it's mandatory to read the latest signs and check out the trail to the biffy. Then wander the grassy left shore of the lake, which is lovely, its translucent turquoise waters overlooked by Mt. Galatea and its southwest outlier which throws down cliffs and screes to the water's edge.

2. via original finish The original route along the southeast bank is interesting but slower going.

Go right past the yellow "avalanche area do not enter" sign. The trail climbs a bit, then runs alongside Rummel Creek. Just after a small meadow the trail turns sharp right onto the rocky bank above a cascade. The ledge traverse has got slicker with time, so much so that hikers have taken it into

their own hands to develop a bypass trail. It starts back in the meadow at a small cairn and heads right, cutting up and over a little ridge to rejoin the main trail just above the cascade. Continued on the next page...

Top: Rummel Lake below Mt. Galatea. Photo Matt Clay

Bottom: #84A The first tarn below the scree slopes of The Tower. The route to Rummel Pass goes through the gap.

Continue between a steep scree slope and shoreline willows to a tributary—often dry—issuing from the cirque to the right. After another stony stint you enter a small meadow distinguished by the "flag tree" that, sadly, keeled over in the winter of 1990. It must have been a quite magnificent tree in its time, but it's now a recumbent trunk of incredible girth, festooned with fluorescent wolf lichen and sheltering all kinds of creepy-crawlies within its rotting heartwood.

From here the trail climbs into the trees and back down again to Rummel Creek at the crossing place. Cross via logs. Now on the left bank, the trail climbs without pause to the lake.

GOING FARTHER
84A Rummel Pass

Unofficial trail, route with cairns
Distance 2.4 km from lake, 4.3 km to Lost Lake
Height gain 192 m (630 ft.) from lake
Height loss 375 m (1230 ft.) to Lost Lake
High point 2402 m (7880 ft.)

Comments Getting to Rummel Pass, located between The Tower and Mt. Galatea, is fairly easy on grass and scree with no steep slopes to contend with. Most people return the same way or just go to the first tarn and back. To view the tarns before the water sinks underground, visit during the first half of July.

Going farther to Lost Lake in the southwest fork of Galatea Creek ups the difficulty a couple of notches and requires accurate route-finding. However, if you've got two vehicles and a willing party who can hack steep slopes and a little bushwhacking, why not continue on to Hwy. 40 via ##36 and 34. The total distance is 16.1 km.

Opposite top: #84A The second tarn below Mt. Galatea. The trail can be seen running along the left shore. Photo Matt Clay

Opposite bottom: #84A Grassy Rummel Pass, looking toward Mt. Galatea. At left you can spot The Fortress.

To Rummel Pass 2.4 km
Follow the trail along the meadows of the northwest shore. Not too far along it turns left and climbs open forest to a bench. Turn right and continue through last trees into a big expanse of flat meadow. Make for the obvious gap between Mt. Galatea and The Tower, a name transposed from The Fortress. Around a big rock the trail peters out, and rather than tromp over scree, it's easier to cross the valley to the right side and pick up a cairned trail in grass that leads directly to the first tarn. From this direction The Tower is considered a walk-up, if 777 vertical metres of steep scree appeals. Personally, I would rather loll by the tarn and through binoculars watch someone else's struggle while slurping nectarines. In fall this tarn dries to a long swath of soft white sand that is a pleasure to walk on.

A second tarn lies beyond the upcoming scree field, one that in midsummer is still rimmed by snowbanks and has mini ice floes wafting about its surface. A trail develops in the scree of the left shore and continues beyond the tarn up a short scree rise to cairns. Walk through a stony defile. At the far end the trail reappears in grass and winds around left onto the pass at the edge of a drop-off.

There is something in the configuration of the mountains at this spot that squeezes the air and sends it battering like a wild thing on the walls of The Tower. So you hunker down behind a small crag and look ahead to a new, dark landscape holding Alvin Guinn's lost lake.

GOING FARTHER
To Lost Lake and beyond 1.9 km
The same trail continues down left over rubbly ledges and across a big scree slope. Before reaching a ridge, cut down a ribbon of grass into the bowl. Exit to the next level down via a sheep trail on the left side of a cement-hard slope littered with ball bearings. Boulders, dribbled down the slope, have fanned out across the flat at the bottom into the trees.

On the flat make for the grassy draw ahead. A trail develops on the right side of the fledgling stream that without warning plunges over a cliff. Now what? The trail crosses a side creek to right, descends to the lip of the drop-off for a look-see, climbs to an overlook farther to the right, then drops over the edge. While there's no cliff at this point, it's a branch-clinging slither for about 35 vertical metres.

End up just west of the lake. The question now is which way around the lake to go?

Right The right (southeast) shore lures until dense thickets and cliffs drive you up onto grassy bluffs. Follow a bit of a game trail along a bench and at lake's end drop down to the outlet. Pick up the valley trail at the forest edge.

Left My preference is to follow the game trail around the left (northwest) shore. Just beyond the lake proper, cross the creek on a beaver dam to the southeast bank and continue to a junction with the main trail. Turn left. Now read ##36 and 34.

85 Watridge Lake

map 9

Short day hike, bike 'n' hike
Official trails
Distance 3.7 km to lake
Height gain 60 m (200 ft.)
High point 1798 m (5900 ft.)
Map 82 J/14 Spray Lakes Reservoir

Access Hwy. 742 (Smith-Dorrien/Spray Trail). Turn west onto Mt. Shark Road, signed Mt. Engadine Lodge, Mt. Shark trailhead. Keep right at all intersections until you come to the end of the navigable road at Mt. Shark day-use area in 5.3 km. (The road ahead is gated and known as the Watridge Lake trail.)

Comments An easy walk on ski trails and logging roads through the Mount Shark X-C ski area to Watridge Lake, one of "the finest cutthroat lakes in Alberta." It is usually combined with a steeper slog to one of "the largest karst springs in North America."

Access note This is the official access to Bryant Creek, the Spray River Valley and Mount Assiniboine Provincial Park. Also the scrambler's access to Mt. Shark.

To Watridge Lake turnoff 3.3 km
Straight off you can see the tip of Mt. Assiniboine from the parking lot, which bodes well. Start from the kiosk and short-cut through to Watridge Lake trail (old logging road) beyond the gate. Turn left. The old road is obvious as it winds through the convolutions of the Mt. Shark X-C ski loops, recently renamed after the constellations. In 600 metres Ursa Major takes off to the right. Cross Marushka Creek in a dip. At the top of the hill Ursa Major comes back in. In 400 metres cross Virgo at junctions 13 and 12. Enjoy fine views of Tent Ridge, Mt. Shark, Mt. Turner, Cone Mountain and Mt. Nestor from all along this stretch. In another kilometre Hercules joins the road for 200 metres in order to cross Watridge Creek bridge. Note that this important tributary of the Spray River is wide and rushing.

Turn left up a hill. Just before leaving the ski trails, you are seamlessly transferred from logging road to a four-person-wide trail built in 1988/89. Before then we followed the old trail to Watridge Lake and

Watridge Lake and Cone Mountain.

Bryant Creek that ran below the bank to the left. The present trail rises gradually to an important junction with signpost. Turn left. (The trail ahead shortly enters Banff National Park and is the main access to the Spray River Valley, Bryant Creek and Mount Assiniboine Provincial Park.)

To Watridge Lake 300 m

The trail drops to the line of the old trail and turns right. At the T-junction with Karst Spring trail, keep straight and reach the pale green waters of Watridge Lake in a minute or two. You are looking northwest to Cone Mountain, a "sharp, symmetrical peak, with a conspicuous, oblique fissure on the south side" according to George Dawson in 1884. Around your feet the bog flowers are beautiful, particularly the white bog orchids.

If you have time, walk along the north shore a way. Breaking the mountain silence is a continual roar emanating from somewhere in the forest to the south of the lake. You'd have to be a pretty dull person not to wonder what the hell is going on up there.

So on to Karst Spring!

GOING FARTHER
85A Karst Spring
Official trail with interpretive signs
Distance 800 m
Height gain ~122 m (400 ft.)
High point 1870 m (6135 ft.)

Comments A narrower, steeper trail leads to K Country's largest karst spring.

History Nowadays there's an official trail, but 45 years ago when Harry Connolly led us to Grotto Spring, as he called it, there was no trail and the thrill of discovery was still burning bright.

The first person to set eyes on the spring was Dean Marshall, then foreman of Spray Lakes Sawmills. While making a preliminary study west of Marushka Lake prior to logging in 1967, he stumbled across a creek "so unique" he returned the following day, approaching on a higher line to find the source of the noise.

Hydrogeology We now know a lot more since the previous edition, thanks to researchers at the University of Calgary. Back in 1979 we were speculating that the water came from Birdwood Lakes, a far-fetched idea according to some. Turns out the answer is even more amazing.

Since 2016, Sara Lilley and Masaki Hayashi, using hydrochemical monitoring and dye tracing methods, have finally established the catchment area, which is far greater than anyone had imagined. On August 30, 2022, tracer dye injected into a sink below the west glaciers of Mt. Sir Douglas showed the glacial meltwater headed north via a "karst aquifer in fractured Devonian Carbonates," taking only 53 hours (2.2 days) to cover the 14 kilometres to the spring, en route collecting waters from sinks and pots in the Burstall Pass area and to a lesser extent from Lower Birdwood Lake. Tracer dye injected into snowmelt water in Burstall Pots at South Burstall Pass in July of 2022 took a mere 21.5 hours to travel 11 km.

Meanwhile, cave divers entering the spring in winter have so far reached a depth of 40 metres.

Return to the last junction, turn right and cross the outlet from Watridge Lake on boardwalk. The trickle gives you a clue that this Watridge Creek as marked on the topo map (Gem Trek has it right) cannot possibly be the same as the one you crossed earlier. Ergo, Watridge Lake is not the source of Watridge Creek.

The trail enters the humidity of old-growth spruce forest and heads across to a creek, which is racing pell-mell down the hillside. As you climb along the right bank the trail steepens and zigs to its ending at a bench, viewing platform and interpretive sign. The mystery is solved! The *real* Watridge Creek glides out of a gloomy grotto on Mt. Shark and thunders down the mountainside in great waves as Elizabeth Falls. It's at its most spectacular during early summer after snowmelt and spring rains. In fall and winter the rate of flow slackens and reveals boulders carpeted in bright green moss.

Top: #85A Watridge Creek below Karst Spring.

Bottom: #86A Lower Kirsten Tarn backdropped by Mt. Smuts to left and Mt. Marushka to right.

86 Marushka (Shark) Lake map 9

Short day hike
Unofficial trail
Distance 3.7 km to lake
Height gain 36 m (120 ft.)
Height loss 68 m (225 ft.)
High point 1920 m (6300 ft.)
Map 82 J/14 Spray Lakes Reservoir

Access Hwy. 742 (Smith-Dorrien/Spray Trail). Turn west onto Mt. Shark Road. In 1.8 km park in a small parking area on the right side of the road.

Comments This silky sheet of blue-green water, which I persist in calling Marushka, lies in that strange valley between Tent Ridge and Mt. Shark. A revegetating logging road, then an easy to follow trail give easy access.
  Naming The name Marushka (not named after the vodka) came about donkey's years ago when the guru of the Spray, Harry Connolly, took Terry Beck, his cousin Myra Willey from England, and Jozef Turcan (a doctor of engineering and hydraulics at the Czech Academy of Sciences) to view the then unnamed lake. "Is Myra the same as Mary?"

Jozef asked, then suggested they use the lovely Czech name Marushka.

To Tent Ridge junction 700 m
About 100 metres farther along the road beyond Monica Brook, turn first left onto the grassy Marushka Lake logging road that we used to drive by car. It starts off with an uphill, then flattens off to the junction with a secondary logging road to left that climbs. (This is route #87 to Tent Ridge.) Continue straight on the flat road.

To Marushka Lake 3 km
On rounding a bend to the left, the road climbs to its high point at Y-junction 146347. Keep right, following flagging to a cairn. (Do NOT go left as some people do. This road climbs to a high point and ends at a gully far above where you should be. From here really good trail lures you into the gully, then the trap sprung, abandons you in a difficult forest of head-high menziesia bushes and downed trees.)

Marushka Lake and Mt. Shark.

The correct right-hand road makes a long, gradual descent that is easy. After crossing a spring it narrows to single track giving pleasant walking to a gravelled area at the end of 1970s cutblocks. Continue ahead into mature forest, the trail crossed by much step-over deadfall before arriving at the lake's east shore not far from the outlet.

The colours of this lake will have you drooling; emerald green shot with azure, and delicate shades of orange and cream in the shallows. Later in the year the colour changes to turquoise.

Anyone headed across the outlet to Johnny Musco's historic cabin, Tony's Place, will be in for a disappointment. It's been burned down between editions.

He did. Walking farther into the upper valley is a fascinating business; no creek, no trail and heaps of recessional moraines. But in two places the water surfaces in two lovely azure pools at the bottom of sinks called collectively Kirsten Tarns.

A trail more or less follows the shoreline around to the south shore. Jump the short-lived inlet and turn left. Climb the hill strewn with boulders via its right side. At the top descend off left into a sunken valley, one of a good many. Open and sprinkled with boulders, these intermittent valleys tend to follow the line of the underground stream, but not always. They also occur at right-angles to it.

Upper Kirsten Tarn

GOING FARTHER
86A Kirsten Tarns

Distance ~2 km
Height gain 100+ m (330+ ft.)

History Back to Harry Connolly. Anticipating widespread logging in the area, Harry, starting in 1967, spent over 20 years of his life looking into and promoting Tent Ridge as a ski area. His company's proposal for "Assiniboine" was used in Calgary's successful bid for the 1988 Winter Olympics but was then unceremoniously dropped. I won't go into that here. But during the early days when Bob Niven was president of CODA and Frank King was chairman, Niven's daughter sadly succumbed to a rare heart condition at age 12. Harry suggested to Bob that "it would be nice to name a little lake after your daughter."

Luckily the route to the tarns is straightforward. Just continue up the valley ahead, slip through a gap to the left of another hill and descend to the sink containing the largest Kirsten tarn. The scene is fairy-tale, the clear, blue-green waters backdropped by mounts Smuts and Marushka.

Continue up the main valley, here and there listening to the stream gurgling under your feet. A short piece of creek emerging from rocks and disappearing into rocks precedes Upper Kirsten Tarn, which is much smaller and shallower and completely enclosed by boulders.

It's a good place to stop. Going farther to the valley head entails complex navigating around steep morainal walls and all you see is more moraines and more sunken valleys minus trees, grass and tarns. You've seen the best the valley has to offer.

87 Tent Ridge

map 9

Day hike
Unofficial trail
Distance 3.7 km
Height gain 630 m (2067 ft.)
High point 2503 m (8212 ft.)
Map 82 J/14 Spray Lakes Reservoir

Access Hwy. 742 (Smith-Dorrien/Spray Trail). Turn west onto Mt. Shark Road. In 1.8 km park in a small parking area on the right side of the road.
Also accessible from #88.

Comments If yearning for larches and a great view that includes Mt. Assiniboine, take the trail up Tent Ridge. After an easy start, expect a relentless uphill trudge with scree to the north top. Since the previous edition the trail has become clear and features a reroute onto the north ridge.

   Warning In winter, don't go beyond Gawby Gulch. Avalanche accidents, a few fatal, testify to its notorious reputation.

   Naming and history Tent Ridge was named, very aptly I think, by Harry Connolly and for a while was destined to be plastered with ski lifts, a gondola and the Fir Tree Day Lodge with restaurant. Snow depth indicator stations were scattered all around the ridge, including one at the head of Gawby Gulch, and recordings taken for over 20 years. In the end, Assiniboia was abandoned in favour of Nakiska.

To Marushka Lake junction 650 m
About 100 metres farther along the road, just beyond "Monica Brook" (unofficially named after Monica Prociuk by Harry and Terry Beck), turn left up the Marushka Lake logging road. It undulates a little to a junction of logging roads. Turn left. (Logging road ahead leads to Marushka Lake.)

To Gawby Gulch 1.1 km
Your new logging road climbs and winds to the left, levelling out below what was once cutblock no. 23 reaching far up the slope. It is now completely infilled.

At a cairn the trail leaves the logging road (which carries on into cutblock no. 26) and climbs easily up the left edge of the "cutblock" to the top left-hand corner. Here it turns left and enters old forest at flagging. Descend a rooty trail into Gawby Gulch and turn right.

Top: A steep bit of trail to the left of the ascent gully.

Bottom: The ascending traverse onto the north ridge showing the split where the trail steepens.

Looking up the north ridge to the north point.

To open slopes 1 km

Walk up the easy-angled gulch to a flat area in a bit of meadow, site of a snow depth indicator station in the 1970s. In a direct line with Gawby Gulch is your ascent gully, one of several parallel gullies scoring the lower slope of trees bent and snapped in half by the weight of snow and avalanches.

The trail heads up the gully, then climbs out of it to the left, twice more visiting the gully bed, the second time at a prominent white boulder. A final push gains you open slopes below the steep east face of the ridge. No meadows here, just scree and scanty vegetation.

To Tent Ridge 950 m

The best trail heads up left on scree and leads into a diagonal L-R uphill traverse across the east face to the north ridge. Ignore the first game trail crossing it. At the steepening the trail splits. Take the middle trail, which is a shade easier than the upper trail. (NOTE: On descent, a rock arrow on the ridge points to the upper trail. You can

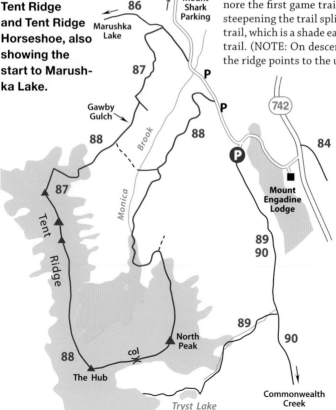

Tent Ridge and Tent Ridge Horseshoe, also showing the start to Marushka Lake.

Marushka Lake

Mount Shark Parking

86

87

742

Gawby Gulch

Brook

88

88

P

P

P

84

87

Monica

Mount Engadine Lodge

Tent Ridge

89
90

89

North Peak

90

88

col

The Hub

Commonwealth Creek

Tryst Lake

follow it a way, then when you see the middle trail below you transfer onto it quite easily.)

Turn left and follow a scree and rubble trail up the north ridge to the north point of Tent Ridge— a magnificent viewpoint for Spray Lakes Reservoir. To its left you can trace the route from Mt. Shark trailhead up Bryant Creek to Assiniboine, the great peak itself peeping over the top of Mt. Turner. Glittering like jewels in the dark forest are the lakes of Marushka and Watridge.

An easy walk on grass leads to the high point (no cairn now), where you can have a fine time identifying the upwelling of shapely peaks suddenly disclosed to the south.

The ongoing trail is Tent Ridge Horseshoe described under #88.

Top: View from the top looking back to the north point and Spray Lakes Reservoir.

Bottom: From the top looking toward Tent Ridge Horseshoe; the north peak at left, the Hub at centre right in front of The Fist and Mt. Birdwood.

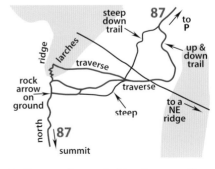

Trails onto the north ridge from treeline

88 Tent Ridge Horseshoe map 9

Day scramble
Unofficial trails
Distance for circuit 10.1 km
Height gain 807 m (2648 ft.)
High point 2538 m (8327 ft.)
Map 82 J/14 Spray Lakes Reservoir

Access Hwy. 742 (Smith-Dorrien/Spray Trail). Turn west onto Mt. Shark Road. In 1.8 km park in a small parking area on the right side of the road.
Also accessible from #87 Tent Ridge.

Comments "This is one of the most enjoyable ridge walks you'll ever do." Since I made this comment in the last edition, this loop has become a five-star must-do scramble, seeing hundreds of people each day during COVID. It takes in three summits — the north peak, the Hub and Tent Ridge grouped around Monica Basin — and though occasionally steep and narrowish with a few easy scramble steps, most people don't consider it exposed. Clockwise is the usual way round.

Getting to the ridge and back is easy on well-travelled trails.

CLOCKWISE

To Monica Basin 2.8 km
From the parking area walk back along the road a short distance, then turn right (west) up a logging road. Round a bend into what used to be cutblock no. 27. At a cairn turn right onto a narrow trail that climbs through young trees toward old forest at the top of the "cutblock." En route keep left at a split.

In old forest the gradient is easy to a T-junction at kilometre 1.6. Turn left. (The trail to right almost connects to the Tent Ridge trail but is little used nowadays.)

Very shortly keep right. (Faint trail ahead appears to head for the north ridge of your objective.) The trail climbs a little, then runs above Monica Brook, soon descending into its valley and criss-crossing the small creek. Arrive in a large meadow at the valley head called Monica Basin.

To North Peak 2483 m (8146 ft.), 1.3 km
The trail heads into the trees to your left and climbs onto the north ridge at last larches. Turn right and start up the delectable north ridge of the north peak, the route unravelling beautifully with long promontories alternating with scrambly rock steps.

First off is a zigzagging climb up step no. 1 that leads to a narrow rock ridge. Walk past a pinnacle to the base of scramble step no. 2. Either tackle it direct up the groove, then left on ledges, or avoid it altogether by taking to the right-hand slope, all loose scree and rubble. This involves descending from the narrows on a trail which then

Left: First alarming view for some of the north ridge of the north peak showing the first, second and third steps.

Opposite top: The second step from the narrows. Either climb solid rock up and left or descend a scree trail down right (out of the picture) and climb rubble up the right edge of the rock.

Opposite centre: Looking down the third step to a queue.

Opposite bottom: Coming up to the third step.
Photo Dinah Kruze

climbs to the right of the solid rock and into an upward traverse heading right. Follow it all the way, or step up onto the crest at a point of your choosing.

Continue along the ridge to step 3, which may look alarming but goes easily up the front on good, firm rock. Some people with dogs go left here on a bit of a trail. Step 4 is surmounted via ledges on the left side. Little step 5 can be avoided by a trail on the right side.

This exciting form of progress stops short of the summit, which is the size of a tennis court with red Firenet repeater station #108 dumped on top of it. But it would be hard to ruin such a great viewpoint completely. The view south is particularly fabulous: Tryst Lake far below and all of K Country's shapeliest peaks grouped together in one frame: Robertson, French, Sir Douglas, Commonwealth, Birdwood, Smuts and The Fist.

To the Hub at 146308, 800 m

On twisting trail descend the broad west ridge to a col touched by fingers of spruce reaching up from the left side. (This is where with a thunderstorm brewing you can escape to Tryst Lake, a steep, slip-sliding 244-vertical-m (800 ft.) descent through larches and spruce with a permanent lean from the weight of the winter snowpack to

Top: The ridge between third step and the summit of the north peak at right. Halfway along is the 4th step.

Bottom: Looking towards the Hub from the easy descent off the north peak. Down left is Tryst Lake.

Opposite top: Leaving the Hub for Tent Ridge. Unseen is a considerable drop between the two summits.

Opposite bottom: Looking back to the steep descent off the Hub (top left) onto Tent Ridge. Photo Vern Dewit

the scree basin where a trail connects to the lake. Otherwise I don't recommend it.)

The upcoming climb to the Hub of the horseshoe is not as steep as it looks, the ascent helped in its upper stage by a winding trail in the scree.

At the summit a fresh view opens up of nearby connecting ridges to The Fist and Mt. Smuts. Down below you to the west are the sinks of upper Marushka Creek.

To Tent Ridge 1.6 km

Turn right (north). Not far along, vertigo sufferers may prefer to follow a trail below the ridgeline on the left (west) side. While this connecting ridge to Tent appears level, it's anything but. Unseen are two drops on well-scratched, tippy rocks where it's easy to come a cropper.

The final pull up colourful Tent Ridge is a long, easy walk on rocks and grass, with several false tops to plod over before you reach the last summit of the day. How satisfying to view the whole ridgewalk you've almost completed. The start to the north peak certainly looks hard.

Descend the broad ridge to the lower summit on the north point (see the top photo on page 313)—a superlative viewpoint for Spray Lakes Reservoir.

GETTING OFF

Via #87 Tent Ridge 3.6 km

Turn right and descend the rubbly north ridge on bits of trail to a flattening where you turn right and make a diagonal descent across the north face to treeline. After this there is only one good trail to follow. Read #87 and view the sketchmap on page 312.

89 Tryst Lake

map 9

Short day hike, bike 'n' hike
Unofficial trail
Distance 3.3 km one way
Height gain 260 m (853 ft.)
High point 2149 m (7050 ft.)
Map 82 J/14 Spray Lakes Reservoir

Access Hwy. 742 (Smith-Dorrien/Spray Trail). Turn west onto Mt. Shark Road. In 1 km turn left onto a side road and park a little way in.

Comments A steepish climb up a narrow valley to a cirque lake. Fall is the busiest season with a procession of larch lovers coming and going. Not recommended in winter when the valley is the runout zone for avalanches.

Naming Tryst is another of those lakes formerly called "Lost" until Harry Connolly arranged a lover's meeting there some 50 years ago. Though June, the lake was still frozen when Harry guided Elizabeth Willey (Marushka Mary's sister) and her fiancé, Jim Springer, to the lake. Enamoured of the wonderful scene, Elizabeth and Jim embraced and Harry took a photo for posterity.

Walk south along the flat grassy logging road for 1.9 kilometres to where a cairn and flagging indicate the start of the Tryst Lake trail to the right.

After a temporary sharing of the trail with Tryst Creek, you head up its right bank. Shortly cross to the left bank on avalanche debris and continue easily up the valley alongside the creek (last water). Note the start of broad avalanche slopes on the right. This is where the valley begins to rise up in steep steps, the willow bushes of the runout zones lower down giving way to clumpy white heathers. After a final zigzag climb, the trail levels, with larches signalling your arrival at lakeshore meadows.

Tryst is wonderfully situated between a peak shaped like a clenched fist and the Tent Ridge Horseshoe, the whole scene becoming magical in fall when larches on both sides of the basin turn colour.

The trail continues around the right side of the lake and beyond to the scree bowl.

Tryst Lake backdropped by The Fist (left) and the Hub of the Tent Ridge horseshoe at right.

90 Birdwood Lakes map 9

Long day hike, bike 'n' hike
Unofficial trail
Distance 7.7 km via 1; 6.6 km via 2
Height gain 438 m (1437 ft.) to lake,
538 m (1765 ft.) to Smutwood Pass
High point at lake 2296 m (7533 ft.),
Smutwood Pass 2396 m (7861 ft.)
Map 82 J/14 Spray Lakes Reservoir

Access Hwy. 742 (Smith-Dorrien/Spray Trail).
1. Usual Turn west onto Mt. Shark Road. In 1 km turn left onto a side road and park a little way in.
2. Shortcut Park at the side of the hwy. 2.2 km south of Mt. Shark Road opposite the mouth of Commonwealth Creek.
Also accessible from #93 Burstall Pass.

Comments Accessing some wonderful country above treeline is a Jekyll and Hyde route that starts with a long, flat walk up Commonwealth Creek Valley and ends with a steep grunt up a headwall to Smuts Col. Either spend time exploring the lakes or continue up to High Col where hiker/ scramblers can climb Smutwood Peak for the most "jaw-dropping" view you'll ever get of Mt. Birdwood. For details see Andrew's *More Scrambles in the Canadian Rockies.*

From High Col there is another option: crossing over Birdwood Pass to Burstall Pass trail and even to Birdwood Pass, which requires two vehicles. (See Option A.) Very experienced scramblers (climbers) use the trail to access Mt. Smuts and The Fist. But whatever you do, start early and carry bear spray; the route is a well-known grizzly thoroughfare.

Trail Changes Since the last edition the route up the headwall takes a different line.

There are two starts. The usual route is uncomplicated with no creek crossings. The shortcut, while reducing the two-way trip by at least 2.2 km, has two creek crossings minimum and a little more height gain, so time-wise there may not be a lot in it. See the sketchmaps on pages 312 and 327.

FROM ACCESS 1

Usual 2.4 km Walk or bike the grassy N-S logging road heading south. In 1.9 km Tryst Lake trail (cairn) takes off to the right. Shortly enter a more open area with a breathtaking view of Commonwealth Peak and Pig's Back up ahead. At a T-junction turn right onto a flagged secondary logging road. Park the bikes here. (Logging road ahead is route 2.)

Commonwealth Creek Falls in spate.
Photo Roy Millar

Top: On the easy scree traverse, the most enjoyable part of the headwall. Smuts Peak to right.

Bottom: Lower Birdwood Lake and Smutwood Peak from Smuts Col. Photo Andrew Nugara

FROM ACCESS 2

The Shortcut 1.3 km After changing into Tevas, descend the bank on a faint flagged trail through the grass and slosh through Smuts Creek that is usually shallow at this point. The trail continues across the flat valley floor, crossing the odd channel en route to the grassy avenue on the far side. Keep the Tevas on until you reach the trees at a white diamond, where a really good trail starts up. Follow it to an open area, née sawmill site at 171310 with cairn and flagging.

runouts of large avalanche slopes falling from The Fist, in season colourful fields of ragwort and cow parsnip which the bears crave. Come to a wide stony creek bed where the latest route diverges from the old one.

The latest trail crosses the stony area, then straightaway climbs a long hill in the trees to avoid a mishmash of debris in the valley bottom. Descend a less steep avalanche slope of snapped-off trees back to the valley bottom at a rather magnificent spruce tree.

The flat meadows of the valley where Mt. Birdwood is reflected in the still waters of Commonwealth Creek.

Stay right with the main trail, once a logging road, that descends to Commonwealth Creek and crosses it — likely another wade — and climbs up the far side to a T-junction. Turn left on a flagged secondary logging road. (The road ahead is start 1.)

Commonwealth Creek valley 3.8 km
Follow the road, soon infilling to a winding trail, to the forest edge, where a very rooty trail takes over and descends to Commonwealth Creek at a waterfall. The next stretch through the narrows is slow going, a roller coaster across steep banks superseded by flatter areas of mud requiring detours.

Enter flat meadows where the creek flows lazily over gravel beds in great meanders. To your left is Pig's Back, while ahead rises the north face of Mt. Birdwood. Fast time can be made along the trail in the trees at the meadow edge. Farther on, you cross the

Shortly arrive at the toe of scree slopes below Birdwood's north face, which sports two small remnant glaciers. Not surprisingly, the huge tabletop boulder is a big attraction for boulderers.

Headwall to Smuts Col 1.1 km
Coming up is the hard climb of the day: 350 vertical metres (1148 ft.) to Smuts Col. Initially the trail zooms up the very steep hillside of bushes and small trees to your right. It can be mitigated at the start by taking the *second* trail to the right. Some people, going both up *and* down, take to the grass and stones at its left edge near the scree slope and at the top of this variation turn right on a side trail that joins the main trail after its unnecessarily steep beginning. Have the instigators of this trail ever heard of zigs?

Mt. Birdwood reflected in the tarn. Photo Andrew Nugara

Opposite top left: Upper Birdwood Lake tucked under Smutwood Peak.

Top right: #90A The low point in the flower meadows en route to Birdwood Pass. The trail has descended the treed slope in the background from High Col. Photo Alf Skrastins

Bottom: Birdwood Pass, looking across to South Burstall Pass. Mountains along the skyline from left to right: Prairie Lookout, Mt. French, Mt. Robertson, Whistling Ridge and Sir Douglas. Photo Alf Skrastins

Traverse right, then climb easily to a large cairn. Turn sharp left and climb more steeply to the start of the very enjoyable scree traverse. This leads to a flat grassy area below Mt. Smuts from where it's just a short climb onto Smuts Col between mounts Birdwood and Smuts, which is NOT the Banff Park boundary as shown on the topo map. Look down on lower Birdwood Lake and up to Smutwood Peak behind it.

Exploring Birdwood Lakes

From Smuts Col a trail descends to the west shore of the lower lake, which geoscientists surmise drains rather slowly at 2 litres per second to join the underground aquifer. From its southwest corner another trail climbs left of a seasonal ribbon of white water to the upper lake. Located under the shadowy east wall of Smutwood Peak, it melts out later in the summer, only then seeing a few people fishing along its deeper west shore for cutthroat trout.

I like wandering the bench between the lakes to where it abuts against the brown screes of Sepia Ridge, en route stopping at the small tarn that reflects the spectacular image of Mt. Birdwood. From Sepia Ridge itself, the view is only secondary to that of Smutwood.

GOING FARTHER
90A Birdwood Pass

Unofficial trails, route
Distance 1.9 km to pass,
19.7 km trailhead to trailhead
Height gain 167 m (550 ft.)
Height loss 107 m (350 ft.)
High point at Birdwood Pass
2454 m (8050 ft.)

Comments Making a point to point with Burstall Pass trailhead is a long day's hike on intermittent trail. The terrain varies from steep slopes to wastelands of stones and snow patches that make navigation a nightmare in a whiteout. Throw in a bit of scrambling and bushwhacking at the end and you've got a route that only hard-core hikers will enjoy.

To High Col 500 m

From Smuts Col the main trail makes a rising traverse across scree and dirt slopes direct to the meadows of the higher col which is the true pass between Alberta and B.C. It's a very fine vantage point for Snow Peak, looking its most dramatic, and the west face of Mt. Birdwood.

To Birdwood Pass 2.4 km

Start from High Col. Without losing height, head southeast across meadow to the trees on the skyline. Find the game trail that drops steeply through the trees for 10 vertical metres, then cuts left through a diagonal rockband into a long, slightly descending traverse. Between forested ribs you cross steep avalanche chutes crammed with flowers, the gorgeous scenes looking remarkably like a Neo-impressionist painting by Georges Seurat.

At black shale the trail drops sharply to a flat meadow nowhere near Birdwood Creek (which is farther down the slope in a mini-canyon). This is the low point, a delightful area with tiny pools and flowers in abundance.

Restart the climb to Birdwood Pass between Mt. Birdwood and the precipitous northeast face of Snow Peak. Use the draw immediately under the west face of Birdwood, a simple walk up grass, much scree and often snow leading directly to the pass at 146264.

This is a bleak spot, wide open to bad weather. Somehow I can't seem to get here without a thunderstorm gathering. But the view is stupendous, not only of where you've come from but looking ahead to the fabulous karst country of South Burstall Pass, the smooth slabs of Whistling Ridge leading the eye toward the great peak of Mt. Sir Douglas.

To Burstall Pass trail 2.2 km

The far side is a two-step scree slope dropping to a grassy bench. Gain a lower, narrower bench sited above the high cliff defending the pass from the Burstall Creek side. It was here, just as a storm was imminent, where we came upon a couple of climbing acquaintances with a tent. Unfortunately, we couldn't cram another six people into a tent made for two and had to leave. This means walking to the far left end of the bench (as you look out), where a "trail" in scree leads down to a 4-m-high rock step that can be managed holding an umbrella in one hand. After this you descend under the cliff, heading a long way right to grass where the trail, its duty done, vanishes. Descend where you fancy. The end result is always the same: some bush-bashing to gain the Burstall Pass trail in the big meadow above the headwall. Turn left and follow it out to Burstall Pass parking lot.

GOING FARTHER STILL
90B Burstall Pass
Distance 1.7 km
Height gain 91 m (300 ft.)

Comments At Birdwood Pass you decide whether or not to carry on to Burstall Pass and grab three passes in one day. The key section is a traverse of the east face of Snow Peak. You want as little snow as possible on this traverse. Check conditions by viewing Snow Peak from the east shore of Mud Lake near the Burstall Pass parking lot.

Start from the lower bench on the southeast side of Birdwood Pass and head south, at the obvious place transferring to a higher bench of varying width and slant. This too peters out and you must climb steep broken ground to gain the broad south ridge of Snow Peak above. This means passing below, then scrambling up the LEFT side of a permanent snow patch. The danger comes early in the season when a more extensive snowfield forces you farther left onto ledges above a drop-off. On reaching the ridge, turn left and descend to Burstall Pass.

Top: #90A Doing Birdwood Pass in reverse direction, the hiker is climbing up the trail to the 4-m-high step giving access to a narrow grassy bench. Photo Alf Skrastins

Bottom: #90B If you go up the RIGHT side of the permanent snow patch, you have this problem getting across the top of it. Photo Carl Potter

91 Commonwealth Lake map 9

Day hike, bike 'n' hike via start 1
Unofficial trails
Distance 4.5 km via start 1,
2.2 km from start 2
Height gain 198 m (650 ft.)
High point 2042 m (6700 ft.)
Map 82 J/14 Spray Lakes Reservoir

Access Hwy. 742 (Smith-Dorrien/Spray Trail).
1. Long way Turn west onto Mt. Shark Road. In 1 km turn left onto a side road and park a little way in.
2. Shortcut Park at the side of the hwy. 2.2 m south of Mt. Shark Road at 176312.

Comments After an easy logging-road start, a moderately steep forest trail, cleared by Rudi Kranabitter, takes you to a body of water formerly called Jeanette, then Lost and now, officially, Commonwealth — a pretentious name for a small green gem. Both starts have creek crossings.

There are two starts to this trail. No 2, though reducing the return distance by a whopping 4.4 km, is soggy underfoot. Take Tevas. See the sketchmaps on pages 312 and 327.

FROM ACCESS 1
Long way 2.9 km Walk or bike the grassy N-S logging road heading south. In 1.9 km Tryst Lake trail (cairn) takes off to the right. Cross Tryst Creek and enter a large cutblock/plantation with a breathtaking view of Commonwealth Peak and Pig's Back up ahead. At a Y-junction keep left. (Secondary logging road to right is the normal route to Birdwood Lakes.)

Descend and cross Commonwealth Creek, hopefully on logs. At the top of the hill at waypoint 171310 in a clearing turn right onto a trail with small cairns.

Commonwealth Lake backdropped by Commonwealth Peak and Pig's Back. Photo Bob Spirko

FROM ACCESS 2

Shortcut 750 m After changing into Tevas, descend the bank on a faint flagged trail through the grass and slosh across Smuts Creek that is usually shallow at this point. The trail continues across the flat valley floor, crossing the odd channel en route to the grassy avenue on the far side. Keep the Tevas on until you reach the trees at a white diamond. Here starts a really good trail leading to an open area (née sawmill site) at 171310 with cairns. Cross an old logging road that is not obvious as a road at this point. (Logging road coming in from the right is start 1.)

To Commonwealth Lake 1.6 km

A trail waymarked with small cairns heads southwest into a young, bushy forest (née cutblock). Flat, easy going ends when the trail climbs up left, traverses right, then after crossing a draw climbs very much more steeply through mature fir forest. At one point crawl under a fallen tree.

After passing a cairn at 166300 (see #91A) the trail moderates and makes a beeline for the lakeshore.

The lake is beautifully situated in the forest below Commonwealth Peak, and as I've mentioned, it's green, the colour of unripe Granny Smith apples.

The shortcut at Smuts Creek, really the combined water of French and Burstall creeks. At centre left is Commonwealth Ridge, with Commonwealth Peak, Pig's Tail and Mt. Birdwood to its right.

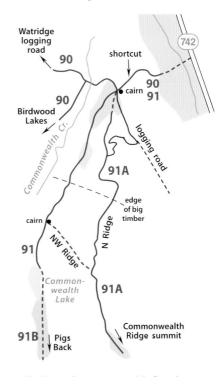

Trails to Commonwealth Creek, Lake and Ridge

91A Commonwealth Ridge

Day scramble
Unofficial trail, route
Distance 2.2 km from #90, 4.1 km from start 2, 6.2 km from start 1
Height gain 709 m (2326 ft.)
High point 2553 m (8376 ft.)

Comments The high rock ridge looming above Hwy. 742 is most often visited in winter, at least to treeline. In summer it's an easy scramble to the summits. Go at the turn of the larches, or in midsummer when the larch meadows are chock full of flowers. See the sketchmap on the previous page.

Lower ridge 540 m

There are two starts onto the northwest ridge. Route 1 is steeper with bushwhacking. Route 2, despite flagging, requires expertise in finding the trail. If the bushes were pruned back and deadfall removed, this would definitely be the route of choice.

1. Direct Leave Commonwealth Lake trail at cairn 166300 near the top of the climbing. Bushwhack up the northwest ridge, initially steep, then moderating with menziesia and some deadfall to skirt around. Aim for 169297 where you'll pick up a trail come up the north ridge. Turn right.

2. From the north Leave Commonwealth Lake trail at the open area (née sawmill site) at 171310. Cross a logging road that is not obvious and walk across open ground to the start of the trees, Flagging starts here.

You'll be following an old logging road in-filled with shrubs and small trees. The angle is easy, even flat where it zigs to the left. At an opening the road heads up right to the edge of mature forest. A trail takes over, the angle mostly easy with the occasional steep hill between menziesia bushes. Continue on past WP 169297.

To north summit 1.7 km

Easy walking on trail brings you to larch meadows on the east side of the ridge. From the last meadow the trail climbs onto the ridge crest, which by now towers over 250 ft. above you. In detail: climb steeply up right through a gap in a small rockband, continue uphill to the left of a creeklet, traverse right across shale and finish up left.

Walk up the ridge to a saddle where the fun begins, the rock ridge rising in small steps ahead of you, each requiring easy scrambling and care with loose rubble. Here and there a trail can be traced along the west flank.

To your right rise the big, shadowy peaks of Commonwealth and Birdwood, and above the aptly named Pig's Back, the bulk of Mt. Smuts. Down below in the valley, Commonwealth Lake gleams like a green gem. To left, look down on muddy Mud Lake and colorful Hogarth Lakes and across the highway to all the peaks of the Kananaskis Range. You can even trace the HRT.

But best is reserved for last. As you gain the north summit cairn, the fabulous peaks of Sir Douglas and its satellites, Robertson and French et al burst into view as well as the Burstall Lakes. Most people stop here.

The south summit (2566 m, 8419 ft.)

Continue along the ridge to where the pinnacle, blocking up the way ahead, forces you to descend loose scree down right for a mind-blowing 100 feet before climbing rubble back up behind the pinnacle to the top. Otherwise you're in for a rock climb.

Opposite: Higher up, the north summit comes into view at centre left. The south summit to its right lurks behind the pinnacle.

Above Looking back along the ridge.

Below: The slightly higher south summit from north summit. Getting there is blocked from a direct assault by the pinnacle.

GOING HIGHER
91B Pig's Back

Day scramble
Unofficial trails, route
Distance 2.5 km from lake
Height gain 427 m (1400 ft.) from lake
High point 2454 m (8050 ft.)

Comments The fit hiker can extend the trip to the col between Commonwealth Peak and peak 163287, called Pig's Back, and from there climb Pig's Back for the view. Interestingly, the name was coined by K Country employees to be in keeping with the nearby peaks of Pig's Tail and Piggy Plus.

From the col there is the option of making a loop with Commonwealth Creek trail, which involves wading Commonwealth Creek. Whatever you decide, all options travel through rough terrain with steep slopes and likely snow until mid-summer.

To col 163281, 1.9 km

Continue up-valley through forest with flowery glades. Some people follow the trail that heads up right, then ends, having lured you into a most unpleasant traverse across acres of scree too high up the slope. I much prefer to continue to the larch and boulder zone in a meadow and take the direct route

up steep grass, threading between a mishmash of small slabs and scree patches and along a larch bench to easy-angled talus sweeping down from the col.

When we arrived at the col on our first visit a fierce rainstorm had just passed, the clouds parting theatrically to reveal the black steaming rocks of Commonwealth Peak glittering in the sun like anthracite. Andrew Lloyd Webber couldn't have stage-managed it better.

Up Pig's Back 600 m

Anyone arriving at the col and not heeding the siren call of the little pointy summit to the north is missing out on a fabulous viewpoint. So, set out on grass, promising not to turn around until I say. After scree begins, the ridge steepens and narrows dramatically, with cliffs on the left side pulling away from the ridge and on the right side a convenient sheep trail running below the crest to the summit. Ahead stretches a wide, flat pig's back clothed in high altitude grass. Walk to its end and look back. What a place to view the north faces of Commonwealth Peak and Mt. Birdwood! In early July, winter's snow still lies heavy on the peaks, but here is green grass and flowers and picas running about between your feet.

LOOP RETURN
Distance plus peak 13.6 km

Starting from the col between Pig's Back and Commonwealth Peak a faint trail descends scree into the barren valley on the west side. Follow this drainage down to the first drop-off via a game trail on the left side of the creek. Where a side creek comes in from the left, cross to the right bank. Above the second, steeper drop-off a trail traverses right across scree into forest, then plummets to valley bottom. Matt C reports some avalanche debris you need to detour around.

Push through bushes to Commonwealth Creek and wade across to Commonwealth Creek trail on the northwest bank. Turn right and follow it along to the main logging road you started out on. Turn left for Mt. Shark Road, or right across Commonwealth Creek for the shortcut.

Opposite: Pig's Back from Commonwealth Ridge, showing the preferred ascent route starting from the patch of sunlight in the valley bottom.

Below: Ascending Pig's Back sheep trail to the summit. Photo Bob Spirko

Bottom: Loop Return, looking down the barren valley on the west side of the col. Photo Dinah Kruze

Top: #91B *The summit of Pig's Back, looking back along the promontory to Commonwealth Peak.*

Bottom: #92A *First Hogarth Lake, looking toward the Kananaskis Range.*

92 Hogarth Lakes

map 9

Half-day hikes
Map 82 J/14 Spray Lakes Reservoir

Access Hwy. 742 (Smith-Dorrien/Spray Trail) at Burstall Pass parking lot.
Also accessible from #93 Burstall Pass trail in two places.

92A Hogarth Lakes Loop

Distance 5 km
Official trail, unofficial trails
Height gain 18 m (60 ft.)
High point 1914 m (6280 ft.)

Comments A flattish forest walk around a string of coloured fishing lakes named after ranger Jock Hogarth. So while the walking is easy, in summer you may be thwarted by the boisterous Burstall Creek crossing if logs aren't in place. Just in case they're not, carry Tevas and hiking poles.

The red markers you see indicate the Hogarth Lakes snowshoe route, which more often than not follows a different line, like crossing the lakes. If well trodden, it can be walked in the winter.

To First Burstall Lake turnoff 2 km
Forgoing the gated gravel access road, cross Mud Lake Dam on trail. Join the road briefly, then swing right at the hiking sign onto Burstall Creek trail (logging road). Cross the French Creek pipeline. Just before the road turns left and starts up a hill with hiking sign, go straight on the flat Hogarth Lakes logging road (red snowshoe sign).

The road swings right into forest and after one flat kilometre crosses Burstall Creek. Keep left (return leg to right), then right, always staying on the most well-used road that leads straight to First Hogarth Lake. Likely, someone will be floating around in a blow-up boat. (We once tried looping around the lakes in our Canadian Tire cheapie, but swampy shorelines, difficult bush and getting punctured from deadfall lurking under muddy Mud Lake decided us this was a one-time adventure.)

The road runs along the west shorelines of first and second lakes under the cliffs of a knoll. Unlike Mud Lake, these lakes are remarkable for their translucent green colour shading to cream in the shallows, the shorelines rimmed by picturesque Tom Thomson trees. Halfway along the deeper second lake a side trail leads down to the water. At the following Y-junction stay ahead. (The uphill logging road to left is First Burstall Lake loop.)

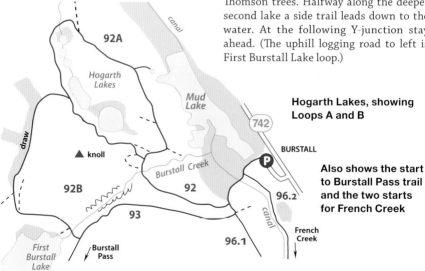

Hogarth Lakes, showing Loops A and B

Also shows the start to Burstall Pass trail and the two starts for French Creek

Above: First Burstall Lake from the east shore, looking toward Whistling Ridge at left and Snow Peak at right.

Return leg 3 km

Carry on past the smaller third lake comprised of three circular pools. If heading for the shoreline be aware of sucking mud surrounding the last pool. The trail rounds the end of it and after crossing its tiny outlet starts back on the return leg, which is almost totally enclosed in old forest amid a complexity of secondary roads infilling with small spruce. The snowshoe trail comes in from the right off Third Hogarth Lake and is followed (red markers) to a T-junction near Burstall Creek. Here turn right. (DO NOT follow the snowshoe trail to left unless you want to swim.) Keep left and arrive back on your outgoing trail. Turn left and retrace your steps over Burstall Creek back to the trailhead.

92B First Burstall Lake Loop

Official & unofficial trails
Distance 5.2 km
Height gain 91 m (300 ft.)
High point 1975 m (6480 ft.)

Comments A scenic loop with hills that takes in two Hogarth lakes, first Burstall Lake and the Burstall Pass trail. Two crossings of Burstall Creek can be problematical, so carry Tevas and poles.

To lake 3.5 km
Follow Hogarth Lakes loop to the Y-junction at Second Hogarth Lake.

Turn left up the hill and keeping left on a trail climb into a draw between the knoll and the east slope of Commonwealth Ridge, notable for its ice smears in winter.

The trail follows the grassy draw to a small meadow, then enters a spruce avenue. Ignoring a track to right, continue straight up a hill to an open area where the trail is vague. Go left a bit and pick up a grassy logging road that is followed down right through what once was a huge cutblock covering the entire southwest slope of the knoll. Now it's infilled with young pines and offers no view.

Not long before the road crosses Burstall Creek, push through a few trees to the east shore of first Burstall Lake. With luck you'll hit the meadow with a fallen tree to sit on. Unusual for the Rockies, the lake is almost colourless, flanked by Mt. Burstall on the left and Commonwealth Peak on the right. Straight ahead is Burstall Pass.

Return to the road and wade Burstall Creek. Climb a short hill to a T-junction with Burstall Pass trail (logging road).

Return leg 1.7 km
Turn left and follow the Burstall Pass trail down a long hill. At French Creek trail intersection the road curves left and down to the T-junction with the Hogarth Lakes logging road. Keep right and return over the dam to the parking lot.

93 Burstall Pass

map 9

Long day hike, bike 'n' hike
Official trail
Distance 7.8 km
Height gain 472 m (1550 ft.)
High point 2362 m (7750 ft.)
Maps 82 J/14 Spray Lakes Reservoir,
82 J/11 Kananaskis Lakes

Access Hwy. 742 (Smith-Dorrien/Spray Trail) at Burstall Pass parking lot.
Also accessible from #90A and #90B, Birdwood Lakes.

Comments The Burstall Pass trail takes you into that cheerful green and white karst country above treeline. Once you are up high, there are many enticing opportunities for off-trail exploration: See options and #94 Snow Peak.

Not all of this route is scenic trail. It kicks off with 3.3 km of tedious old logging road that we used to drive pre K Country. Now you can bike it to a bike rack. This cuts down the hiking to 4.5 km one way. Okay, so you may be walking your bike up some hills, but coming down is a blast.

Creek crossings on the flats are unavoidable, but after the cool down in October you can generally cross dryshod.

As Joe Kovach and Bill Balmer noted on October 6, 1948, the pass can easily be crossed to the Spray River. Nowadays there is a trail that deposits you close to Burstall backcountry campground, so anyone aiming for Leman Lake or Palliser Pass can come this way in preference to slogging all the way up the Spray River trail.

This is also the access for #94 Snow Peak, Mt. Burstall, Piggy Plus and #95 Piggy Plus Col.

To Piggy Plus Col junction and bike rack 3.3 km

Forgoing the gated gravel access road, cross Mud Lake Dam on trail. Join the road briefly, then swing right at the hiking sign onto Burstall Creek trail (logging road). To left is French Creek canal, the water feeding into a pipeline to be deposited into Mud

Burstall Pass. In the background are Mt. Birdwood, Pig's Tail and Commonwealth Peak.

Lake, a receptacle for all the muck carried down from the Robertson and French glaciers. At the next hiking sign curve left up a hill. (Ahead is the Hogarth Lakes logging road.) At the top, the road turns sharp right. (Ahead is the lesser used French Creek logging road start no. 1.)

Continue to follow the Burstall Pass logging road, which climbs on and off past numerous revegetating logging roads and skid trails, the end result of Balmer's visit to look over the timber. Down to your right at the big left-hand bend, Burstall Creek is closeted in a canyon.

After the road descends a little, keep straight at km 1.7. (To right, a secondary road reduced to trail heads downhill and crosses Burstall Creek. See #92B.)

Below the avalanche slopes of Mt. Burstall, the going is mainly flat or slightly undulating with a few small uphills. Pass a massive boulder and down to the right the three drab-coloured Burstall Lakes, which lie out of sight from the road, though not out of earshot. On a left-hand bend the roar you hear comes from the cascade at the outlet of the second lake. A short distance on, a short side trail to right leads to waterlogged meadows surrounding second lake. (See OPTION 93A Avalanche Impact Pool.)

The next point of interest is a cairn on the left side which indicates the access trail to Mt. Burstall, a difficult scramble. The second short side trail to right leads to third Burstall Lake, a side trip worth taking for the view of Mt. Birdwood and Commonwealth Peak rising steeply above the water. The third side trail to right descends to the flats above the lakes.

At 3.3 km, route #95 to Piggy Plus and Piggy Plus Col turns off to the left from a small meadow, a former sawmill site. The road continues a wee bit farther to a bike rack where it reverts to trail.

To the pass 4.3 km

From the rack, a rooty trail descends gradually to the valley bottom and runs alongside Burstall Creek to a bridge. Cross and navigate a large, willowy alluvial flat extending from Robertson Glacier moraines to third Burstall Lake. This entails following foot-

prints in gravel and signs on posts. Wading continually shifting braided streams is the norm. As you cross the bend in the valley, look left for a view of Robertson Glacier slung between the vertical strata of Mt. Robertson and lordly Sir Douglas.

Above: Burstall Pass (centre) from the lower south ridge of Snow Peak. To left is South Burstall Pass below Sir Douglas. Ridge 147230 at centre shows both ascent and descent routes. To the right is Leman Lake between mounts Leman and Leval. The pointy peak is Talon Peak above Talus Lodge.

Below: Mt. Robertson, Robertson Glacier and Mt. Sir Douglas from the flats.

Entering forest again, climb the timbered headwall, which is a bit of a grunt with overnight gear and a six-pack if bound for B.C. Some 120 vertical metres later you reach the long, flat meadow below Birdwood Pass and Mt. Birdwood's Lizzie Ridge. This is where route 90A comes in.

Cross the meadow and climb steadily through open forest to a flattening where the trail turns right at a signpost. (The less worn trail ahead is #93B.)

The trail heads up right, zigs back left below a rockband into meadows, then right again, ultimately approaching the pass from the south. A national parks signpost marks the spot.

When the cloud's down, Burstall Pass is a hugely complicated terrain of barren ridges, confounded by a deep sinkhole on the west side. In fine weather it's a marvellous place to be. Mountains encircle you, Mt. Birdwood to the northeast, Sir Douglas pre-eminent to the south, while to the west, Assiniboine lords it over a welter of lesser peaks. Bounding the pass to the south is the unnamed ridge 147230 (#93C) and to the north the oddly named Snow Peak (#94).

Top left: Crossing one of numerous runouts from Robertson Glacier in August. Photo Alf Skrastins

Top right: #93A The avalanche impact pool and mound above third Burstall Lake, Mt. Burstall in the background.

Above: #93B South Burstall Pass, looking into Burstall Pots. Photo Sara Lilley

To Leman Lake Viewpoint 700 m
It's worth carrying on into Banff National Park. Traverse the left side of the sink, then instead of turning right for the Spray River valley, continue ahead to a grassy shoulder. Keep walking until the peacock colours of historic Leman Lake come into view. In 1901 Walter Wilcox named it Lake Castelleia after the wild flower observed on its banks, i.e. the Indian paintbrush.

OPTIONS

93A Avalanche Impact Pool

Half-day
Route
Distance 600 m from Burstall Pass trail, 3.2 km one way from trailhead

Comments A flat, wet walk to a small pond lying close to the northeast end of third Burstall Lake and shown on the topo map at 173272. As ponds go it's rather unusual.

Geology Its full name is "snow-avalanche impact pool" because it's been excavated by climax avalanches shooting down the 580-m-high gully from the ridge above. The ejected material piled up in a mound on the downhill side and the hole filled up with water.

Start from Burstall Pass trail at 2.6 km from the trailhead. Head right on a narrow trail leading to a waterlogged meadow about second Burstall Lake. Put on the Tevas and make your way around the left shore to Burstall Creek between lakes. While in the vicinity take a gander at the cascade downstream, then follow the creek up to third Burstall Lake where it's an easy wade.

Walk a short way along the northwest shore of the third lake. Ahead is a grassy mound and behind it a green pool about 9 metres deep. The best viewpoint is from a little way up the avalanche gully as shown in the photo on the page opposite.

It's hard to think of a better lunch spot than the back side of the mound that slopes down to the lake at sun-bathing angle and gives fine views across the water to Mt.

Burstall and Whistling Ridge. Closer to the lakeshore are some cleverly constructed seats made out of large rocks and deadfall.

93B South Burstall Pass

Long day hike
Unofficial trail then route
Distance from main trail 1.7+ km
Height gain from main trail 168+ m (550+ ft.)
High point 2454 m (8050 ft.)

Comments The broad and slightly higher pass at 155226 is really the culmination of the Burstall Creek valley between Whistling Ridge to the east and Ridge 147230 to the west. Much of it is a rough walk on rock, but an exciting one for karst lovers.

Many hikers combine this trip with Ridge 147230. A few make a circuit with the Spray River valley and the Burstall Pass trails, the off-trail section much easier than you might suppose.

Leave Burstall Pass trail at the signpost at 150245 where a fainter trail heads south. After it peters out, do your own exploring, perhaps keeping right under Ridge 147230 to a flat area of fissured pavement which is the high point. At a cairn look back at four mountains: Smuts, Birdwood, Pig's Tail, and Commonwealth Peak that have lined up four abreast. In the opposite direction is a close-up view of Mt. Sir Douglas, its north and west faces mantled with glaciers.

If you have time, hop into B.C. to investigate an area of "shattered karst full of depressions and blocked shafts" and "two vadose caves along the axis of a syncline."

On your way back under Whistling Ridge, pause to admire Burstall Slabs, "one of North America's finest friction climbing areas," then search for South Burstall's showpiece, located not too far away, "where streams plunge into beautifully sculptured elliptical shafts," wrote caver Jon Rollins describing Burstall Pot. He even surmised that the water may rise again at Karst Spring. See page 307 for the answer.

93C Ridge 147230

#93C Sir Douglas and its west glaciers, source of Karst Spring and the Spray River.

Day hike
Route, unofficial trail
Distance 2.3 km to South Burstall Pass
Height gain 244 m (800 ft.)
High point 2606 m (8550 ft.)

Comments If motivated by fabulous views, traversing the unnamed ridge between the two passes is something you can't pass up. Most often it is combined with #93B.

Getting onto the ridge is not as straightforward as you might expect, though possibly there is a trail by now. From the signpost at Burstall Pass head southwest onto the big grassy rise 145239 through a break in the rockband. Steer south and gain a smaller rise by the left edge. Ahead lies the main body of the ridge. Sneak through the obvious draw on its left side, cut back right on steep grass, and finish with a simple scree plod on sheep trail.

Except for one short climb before the second cairn, the summit ridge is broad and flat, the right side falling away in cliffs to the Spray River valley. You'll revel in the

view that takes in the whole of the Spray Valley from Bryant Creek to Palliser Pass, plus Mt. Assiniboine and all the peaks you could see from Burstall Pass. Look *down* on blue-tinted Belgium Lake and across the pass to Mt. King Albert, named after the King of the Belgians who died in a climbing accident. Carry on to the very end, dropping slightly to a spectacular grassy promontory that gives you the best view of the day — the classic shot of Sir Douglas.

To regain the Burstall Pass trail
Most hikers drop off the left (east) side of the ridge onto South Burstall Pass. From the end point this is a fairly simple descent of alternating scree steps (the second is the steepest) and grassy terraces. Then turn left and wander back north through the valley karst.

Alternatively, keep heading left along the lowest terrace. Where the terrace slips a notch at midpoint, descend to the flat meadow and pick up the Burstall Pass trail just below the pass.

94 Snow Peak

map 9

Long day scramble
Unofficial trails & route
Distance 19.8 km return from trailhead,
4.3 km return from Burstall Pass
Height gain 430 m (1410 ft.) from pass
High point 2789 m (9160 ft.)
Map 82 J/14 Spray Lakes Reservoir

Access Via #93 Burstall Pass trail at pass.

Comments An easy scree scramble via the south ridge with variations lower down. Expect intermittent trails and a couple of hands-on steps near the top. While it can be climbed on a whim from Burstall Pass, most people should plan for this trip by starting early from the trailhead (it IS a nearly 20-km round trip!), and by waiting until the peak is snow free from mid-July on. And anyway,

Snow Peak from Ridge 147230. The route follows the right-hand ridge with the option of taking the grassy gully to the left of the big step. Photo Alf Skrastins

you're going to be spending a long time on the summit taking in the tremendous view.

Naming Not exactly a glaciated peak, it was named after the extremely large cornice which overhangs the east and northeast faces for half the year.

Start at Burstall Pass and head north along the very broad, undulating ridge of grass, slabs and last trees. On the left side are a series of depressions and holes. At the base of the mountain proper, below a small cliff and in line with the depressions, are the 3 D Caves, which are really two caves with three entrances. Don't even try venturing in. According to Jon, the bouldery passageways suddenly end in vertical ice. More obviously dangerous is the entrance to the elliptical pot.

Starting to the left of the elliptical pot, climb up alternating grass and scree to a wider, higher, sloping grass bench.

Above is the big step leading to a shoulder. Some scramblers head right on scree toward the ridgeline with the very much steeper east face, then make their way up rubble between small bands just to the left of the ridge and to the right of a crag. I like to traverse left, and when past the crag slog up the obvious swath of grass turning to scree at the top. (This is just left of the scree run descent.) Your choice.

Above: Scramble up the second rockband.

Above the shoulder the ridge narrows and is crossed by rockbands. A twisty trail in scree avoids the first band by keeping to the left. The next band requires a scramble up its right edge above the northeast face. The third two-tier band is taken on the left side. All that remains now is a simple walk along the summit ridge above the cornice, perhaps to the top (cairn, register). Some people carry on to a lower summit.

Of course you have been ogling the stupendous view all the way up. It's hard to imagine a more magnificent viewpoint for the Burstall/Palliser Pass area than this one. The standout peaks include Sir Douglas to the south, Talon Peak to the west and Assiniboine to the northwest. Down below you to the east you can trace the route from High Col to Birdwood Pass below the massive cliffs of Mt. Birdwood. By the time you tear yourself away from the summit, perhaps Leman Lake will be glittering in the late afternoon sunlight.

DESCENT NOTE: Return to the shoulder above the big step. From here a scree run is available at skier's right. Various trails lead into it.

Below: The summit ridge. To right is the lower summit below Mt. Assiniboine.

95 Piggy Plus Col

map 9

Day hike
Unofficial trail, route
Distance 13.2 km return from trailhead,
6.6 km return from Burstall Pass trail
Height gain 630 m (2070 ft.)
from trailhead
High point 2515 m (8250 ft.)
Map 82 J/14 Spray Lakes Reservoir

Access Via #93 Burstall Pass at 3.3 km at 171264.

Comments A straightforward but initially steep trail follows a side valley to the col between Mount Burstall and Piggy Plus — one of K Country's most dramatic viewpoints. Snow patches early in the season aid travel, but then you would miss the turn of the larches at the end of September.

The view from Piggy Plus Col toward the French Glacier and Mt. Robertson. Photo Alf Skrastins

To Piggy Plus Col 3.3 km

Follow the first section of #93 Burstall Pass trail to the 3.3 km mark at the sawmill site (171264). If you reach the bike rack you've gone too far.

Turn left up a well-used trail that climbs relentlessly, finally easing off half a kilometre before reaching a narrow side valley. Cross the creek.

Turn left, following the easy trail upstream through meadows and over bits of scree. It's only at the steeper-angled narrows between a cliff and a scree slope where one would wish for a snow patch to bridge the gap. On the flat above is a cairn.

This is where the latest trail leaves the creekbed and climbs up right between crags into a grassy ramp lined with larches. Keep left where the much less obvious sinkhole trail turns right up a steep hill.

What follows is a long ascending traverse below a crag. Top out on a small ridge and

follow it along to a small cairn. Descend into a series of flat draws leading to scree slopes at the head of the valley. A cairn marks the start of a really good trail winding easily up the middle of the headwall to the col.

The col is a narrow balcony poised above a precipice with a view across French Creek to mounts Murray, French and Robertson and the French Glacier. To left the easy south ridge of Mt. Burstall is worth walking up for a more expansive view. To right is the scrambler's Piggy Plus, named along with Pig's Tail in 1972 during a High Horizons Camp for teenagers.

OPTION

95A Piggy Plus Bluffs

Comments When the larches turn and the day is sunny, this viewpoint is a little bit of heaven.

Either head directly up the sinkhole trail, or cut across on your return from the col onto the wide bench of larches. This is karst country, an area so complex you need an easily recognizable starting/finishing point for getting to/from the bluffs. The

On the bluffs at larch time. Piggy Plus Col is to left. Then going right, Piggy Plus, Robertson Glacier and Sir Douglas. Down right and a thousand feet below is the deep valley of Burstall Creek.

large, flat, green sinkhole in the middle of the rocks fits the bill perfectly. Not really flat, it is filled with enormously high frost humps. Jumping from top to top, aim for the broad north ridge of Piggy Plus and turn right, following the ridge to the highest of the bluffs with cairn. (The steep bit at the end can be avoided by going around to the right.) Short-cropped grass is perfect for a siesta. Just be aware of the yawning drop-off on the left side.

From its top another superlative view has opened up, the deep, shadowy gulf of Burstall Creek valley rising to Robertson Glacier slung between mounts Robertson and Sir Douglas.

Return via the Sinkhole trail

Return cross-country to the sink, which is easier said than done. On its northeast corner is a bit of a gap with a game trail leading through it. Soon it wends left and down a steep hill to your ascent ramp. Turn left for the creekbed.

96 French Glacier

map 9

Long day hike
Unofficial trail, one creek crossing that
is avoidable via start 2
Distance 7.7 km to high point
Height gain ~670 m (2200 ft.)
High point 2530 m (8300 ft.)
Maps 82 J/14 Spray Lakes Reservoir,
82 J/11 Kananaskis Lakes

Access Hwy. 742 (Smith-Dorrien/Spray Trail) at Burstall Pass parking lot.

Comments The trail up French Creek leads to larch meadows and moraines at the foot of the French Glacier. Getting there is not a whole lot of fun, so you've got to be a dedicated adventurer who enjoys a long forest trudge. Skiing up this valley is a lot simpler.

During its years of tramping by provincial and national team x-country skiers en route to summer training camps on the Haig Glacier, the old trail was improved and in places carefully rerouted to miss out the waterfalls. Now that skiers either helicopter in or walk up North Kananaskis Pass trail to a more permanent camp, the trail is again falling into disuse. Nevertheless it is still followable with more variations than one would wish for. I would be surprised if your up route is exactly the same as your down route.

Going farther from the end of the trail through the French/Robertson Col to the Haig Icefield and on down the Haig Glacier to meet up with route #75B requires all the paraphernalia of glacier travel. In summer those innocent-looking snowfields have snared quite a few people, including a ranger fortuitously accompanied by two search and rescue experts.

The alternative to the long trudge is a visit to first waterfall, or sorties to second and third waterfalls that often get missed out in the rush to get to the glacier.

This trail is also used by scramblers after Cegnfs and Mt. Murray and as faster access to Mt. Jellicoe over the pass.

Warning The valley is a grizzly hot spot, so carry deterrents.

Nowadays there are two starts. The original involves a crossing of French Creek which can be avoided by using alternative start 2.

1. Original 1.8 km The original route uses good logging roads but entails an extra hill climb and a crossing of French Creek. Use if just going to the first waterfall.

Looking up the French Glacier to the Robertson–French Col, which is still a long way off.

Moss campion at the toe of the French Glacier.
Up right is Mt. Robertson.

Forgoing the gated gravel access road, cross Mud Lake Dam on trail. Join the road briefly, then swing right at the hiking sign onto Burstall Pass trail (logging road). To left is French Creek canal, its water feeding into a pipeline to be deposited into Mud Lake, a receptacle for all the muck carried down from the Robertson and French glaciers.

At the next hiking sign curve left up a hill (Hogarth Lakes logging road ahead). At the top, leave the Burstall Pass road, which turns right, and continue ahead. The unsigned French Creek logging road is more like a trail at this point as it climbs a hill, en route passing a side road to right. From the top it's a long, drawn-out descent into French Creek Valley. Amid vegetated side roads the main logging road is always obvious. Come to a T-junction on the bank of French Creek with cairn. Ahead rises the lower summit of Cegnfs. The name derives from the initials of the first ascent party: F, F, G, N, P and S (surnames), or C, P, M, J, P and B (first names). Not only is the name unpronounceable, it is also unfathomable.

Go straight (the logging road to right is #96A to the first waterfall) and wade French Creek. Since the previous edition the remains of the bridge have departed downstream, replaced by a few logs that are overwhelmed at high water.

Keep following the logging road, which shortly intersects another logging road. The flagged road to left is the alternative start. (To right the much less obvious "road" leads to an old camping spot with collapsible picnic table.) Continue ahead. Skip the next section of text and go to the section headed "To end of logging road."

2. Alternative start 2.1 km I like this route because there is no creek crossing, less climbing and you can easily bike the first 1.2 kilometres, thereby reducing the return trip by 45 minutes or so.

Cross Mud Lake Dam on trail. On joining the gravel road, simply follow it to its end. It takes 20 minutes on foot or five minutes by bike. Accompanying you on your right

for most of the way is the French Creek diversion canal built in 1959. The road ends at French Creek Dam, which stops the water from following its natural course down Smith-Dorrien Creek Valley. Instead it enters Mud Lake, then via the Mud Lake canal flows north as Smuts Creek.

Cross the overflow channel and continue on the obvious logging road that wends rightish and becomes single track as it enters the forest of French Creek Valley. Near the creek, deadfall makes a bypass necessary, so on the flagged trail climb up the bank to left, turn right at the top and descend back down to the logging road at flagging. Turn left. Shortly the logging road turns right and intersects the original route (logging road) at flagging. Turn left.

To end of logging road 600 m
The logging road gains height up the left (east) bank of French Creek between Cegnfs and Mt. Burstall. Shortly beyond the road's high point at the narrows, you reach French Creek. The road crosses to the west bank above first waterfall. Do NOT cross. The route stays on the east bank throughout.

To Cegnfs/Mt. Murray turnoff 900 m
Transfer to a trail which climbs steeply up the bank into trees, then shortly descends back down to the creekbed — an annoying pattern to be repeated numerous times over the length of the valley. Make another uphill foray and descent toward the creekbed, only this time keep left everywhere on the forest bypass trail.

At a piece of red flagging the trail starts a longer, more gradual climb through dim, old-growth forest smelling like a newly opened bag of peat moss. En route cross two side creeks. Then listen for the roar of Second Waterfall below you. A little farther on descend and cross a side creek with grassy banks. To view the second waterfall, head down the side creek to its confluence with French Creek. If climbing Cegnfs and Mt. Murray, head up the side creek. For French Glacier continue along the trail.

To the headwall 1.4 km

After a flat with flowery glades, make a gradual return to the creek. Again, watch for where the trail climbs steeply up the bank for a longer inland stretch with much deadfall.

Back down at creek level, round a right-hand bend on steep hillside with one awkward step at high water. For some distance beyond this, the trail follows the creek and is hard to spot on stony ground. Look for it climbing once again into forest, soon arriving at a small meadow with a view ahead of a summit north of Mt. French that is officially nameless despite being prominent in all views. (I don't like to call it Prairie View.) Soon after, the trail is blocked by deadfall and you must detour right (trail, flagging), then back left (no trail, no flagging). A flat leads to the foot of the forested headwall down which falls the spectacular third waterfall in two steps.

Below left: The second waterfall.

Below right: The third waterfall at the headwall.

To the French Glacier 3 km

To get above the headwall, the old trail made a lengthy arc to the left. The newer version stamped out by athletes with superior VO_2 max, zigs straight up the steepest part of the headwall. Two-thirds up, go either straight or right at a split.

A relief section follows above a mini-canyon, ultimately returning you to creekside for an enjoyable stint alongside the creek. Up ahead you can spot Sir Douglas poking up above the Robertson–Piggy Plus Col.

Opposite avalanche slopes falling from Piggy Plus the trail turns away from the creek, cutting off the corner as it alternately climbs and traverses through meadows at treeline. A short descent leads into larch country below a complexity of hills and ridges of snow-streaked moraines. It's a gorgeous spot, but where is the French Glacier, you ask?

The trail carries on, turning left and leaving the meadows behind, follows a ridge of lateral moraine on the left side of the valley to its high point, where it fades out. Still no view of the glacier. Descend a little, then climb the obvious snow-filled

trough — rather longer and steeper than it appears — to last scree, the taking off point for the Robertson–French Col. Finally, you've reached the toe of the French Glacier, a little bit of the Haig Icefield spilling through the gap between mounts French and Robertson, which have to be two of the most spectacular mountains in K Country. Incredibly, the col is still 2 kilometres away. (See the photo on page 345.)

On the return, drop skier's left to the stony flat at the foot of the glacier, where you will likely experience the glacier wind, a giant cooling fan on a stinking hot day. It's not as barren as you might suppose; dotting the flat are mounds of intensely coloured moss campions and springs bubbling up into small pools fringed with grasses.

Unless you are crossing the ridge between Mt. Robertson and Piggy Plus to the Robertson Glacier, work your way back over the moraines to the trail and return more or less the same way you came up.

The low ridge between Piggy Plus and Mt. Robertson is a scramblers route over to the Robertson Glacier which I have never done. Note the pools fringed with grasses at the bottom of the photo.

SHORTER OPTION

96A First Waterfall

Half day
Distance 1 km return, 4.3 km return to trailhead via route 1

Comments First waterfall is usually missed in the haste to get to the glacier. Why not make it the destination of a leisurely half-day trip? Could also be combined with the alternative start to make a 4.6 km loop for those interested in river diversion infrastructure.

Hike the regular route, and at the T-junction on the bank of French Creek turn right up another logging road that follows the right (west) bank of the creek. The road soon turns to single track. At a large fallen tree the trail climbs the bank to some flagging. Rather than carry on to another piece of flagging (beyond which all descents to the creek are STEEP), descend easily down left to the creek while the going is good. Turn right and edge your way along the bottom of the bank into a cliff-girt recess bisected by the two-tier waterfall.

First waterfall.

97 Chester Lake

map 4

Day hike
Official trail with signs
Distance 4.3 km one way
Height gain 305 m (1000 ft.)
High point 2210 m (7250 ft.) at lake
Map 82 J/14 Spray Lakes Reservoir

Access Hwy. 742 (Smith-Dorrien/Spray Trail) at Chester Lake parking lot.
Also accessible from ##79 and 84 via 98.

Comments This jade-coloured lake is a year-round popular destination and you are unlikely to be alone. In addition to the hiking crowd, scramblers use the trail to access mounts Chester and Galatea and Gusty Peak, and boulderers to access Elephant Rocks.

The start up steeply inclined logging roads is less than aesthetic, but after that it's a pleasant, easy walk though alternating forest and flowery meadow. Biking is only allowed on the shared section of the High Rockies trail. Nevertheless, it reduces the hiking distance to 2.7 km.

In Winter walkers and snowshoers do not follow the summer trails; they're reserved for skiers. Start off on Snowdrift, the trail to the right of the kiosk, and follow HRT's winter route across Chester Creek as shown in blue on the map on page 278. Just before hitting the alternate route to Chester Lake turn right.

Closures After decades of traditional camping by the lake, backcountry camping is no longer allowed. Grizzlies think of it as their own private swimming pool according to some photos I've seen. Note also that the trail is closed between May 1 and June 29 to protect fragile vegetation. Ironically, grizzlies make an awful mess tearing up the ground after lily corms and ground squirrels. The trail is often closed after grizzly sightings, so check the KC advisories.

To end of logging roads 2.1 km
The trail, also shared with the High Rockies trail, leaves the parking lot to the left of

the kiosk and straightaway crosses Chester Creek on a bridge. A series of uphills lead to a T-junction with a logging road. Turn left. At the next T-junction with signs you have a choice of routes: left is signed "Chester Lake"; right is signed "Alternate Route."

1. **Left** Still on High Rockies trail, easy uphill going leads to a signposted junction at 1.6 km from the parking lot where you leave the bikes. Turn right off the HRT. The 4-way crossing with HRT's winter route signals the start of steepish zigs and one relief section before the final pull up to the 3-way at the high point of logging roads. Turn left.

2. **Right** After a downhill and the 4-way crossing with HRT's winter route, the alternative trail climbs in earnest, then settles into flattish sections alternating with steep zigs. At the end of the last straight, come to a 3-way at the high point of logging roads. Turn right.

To Chester Lake 2.2 km
A steep start soon eases into a pleasant trail winding through spruce and fir forest and two meadows with frost humps. The third and biggest meadow extends right across the valley floor to Mt. Chester. Near at hand, Chester Creek is bubbling away to your right. This meadow is the place of departure for route #98 to Rummel Lake trail.

A biffy on the left precedes your arrival at Chester Lake. At the outlet, the trail forks, the main trail carrying on along the meadows of the west shore. The trail bridging the creek leads to a larch area and pica rockpile where marmots do sentry duty atop large boulders.

Around the lake 1 km loop
The latter trail continues on, crossing the scree slopes of the east shore. At the northeast corner note the avalanche impact pool. Carrying on along the north shore, you pass below an intermittent waterfall step — the recently resurrected Chester Creek — and farther along straddle a greasy white slab. The trail improves after you join #97A and gets even better when you join #97B, which takes you back to your starting point.

GOING HIGHER

97A Upper Chester Creek

Unofficial trail, route
Distance 2.1 km to tarn
Height gain 259 m (850 ft.) to tarn
High point 2454 m (8050 ft.) at tarn

Comments The alternative route to/from the Fortress–Chester col.

Follow the west shore trail past the turnoff to Three Lakes Valley. Keep left and climb into a grassy draw below Gusty Peak, following the edge of the left-hand scree slope to the lip of a hanging valley.

The upper Chester Creek valley between Gusty Peak and The Fortress is filled with rocks of all sizes and shapes, piled up in great heaps like unwashed dishes. Going farther is unpleasant if you're aiming for the blue tarn at the valley head. Just before the tarn, the shale slope to right leads to the Fortress–Chester col. Nearer at hand, meadows as immaculate as city lawns border the infant creek, which sees daylight for perhaps 50 metres before sinking into the ground below a permanent snowbank and resurging at a waterfall lower down.

Opposite: Chester Lake below Mt. Chester.

Above: #97A Lawns in upper Chester Creek.
Photo Roy Millar

Top: #97B *The second tarn in Three Lakes valley, looking out to mounts French, Robertson and Sir Douglas. Photo Annette Le Faive*

Below: #97B *Elephant Rocks. Photo Rachel Oggy*

GOING FARTHER

97B Three Lakes Valley

Unofficial trail, route
Distance 2.2 km to third tarn
Height gain 244 m (800 ft.)
High point 2454 m (8050 ft.)

Comments The picturesque valley to the north of Chester Creek holds three small tarns. It's the scrambler's route to Mt. Galatea.

From the west shore trail, turn left onto a well-used trail that climbs over the intervening ridge of larches and jumbo-sized boulders (Elephant Rocks) to the valley north of Chester Creek.

The trail continues upstream to the first tarn, whose damp shores are beautified by clouds of silky white cotton grass. Climb the grassy headwall above, noting tufts of goat hair snagged on knobbly boulders. The finger valley between Mt. Galatea and Gusty Peak is a goat hot spot, and if you're lucky you can spot them feeding on delicacies in damp, slanting gullies high up to the right. Tarn no. 3 is a sink lake, often disappointing. Tarn no. 2, sited picturesquely on the headwall's brink, is a place to linger by.

98 Chester Lake to Rummel Lake   map 4

Day hike
Unofficial trail, route
Distance 3.6 km
Height gain and loss south to north
61 m (200 ft.)
High point 2277 m (7470 ft.)
Map 82 J/14 Spray Lakes Reservoir

Access Hwy. 742 (Smith-Dorrien/Spray Trail).
1. Via #97 Chester Lake.
2. Via #84 Rummel Lake.

Comments Though a fairly easy traverse with one creek crossing, you need to be a good navigator.

Bears Nearly every time I've been to Rummel Lake I've always met a hiker who's come in from the Chester Lake trail. They are usually found recuperating at the junction and talking in a quivering voice about "the grizzlies." Don't let this deter you from following this route; there's never been a close encounter and the route between the two lakes, or to be scrupulously correct, between the two access trails, is surprisingly scenic. But with all those grizzlies around, it's best to be a group.

Leave Chester Lake trail at the third (last) meadow before the lake. Strike up-meadow to the left and through a few token trees on the watershed to a brown-coloured pond marking the southeast edge of a large, flat meadow, which is the middle portion of Three Lakes Valley. Pass left of the pond, following the left (south) edge of the meadow to Three Lakes Valley Creek. Cross the creek.

Indistinct at first, a good trail materializes in the grass of the far bank and climbs diagonally from right to left across steep, flowery slopes. As it turns northwest into the trees the gradient eases and red flagging appears. Cross over the watershed and emerge (red flagging marking the spot) in a draw filled by an extremely lengthy longitudinal meadow between larches. Through the V are blue mountain shapes. To your right rise steep, grassy slopes that I like to check for furry brown shapes.

The trail continues down the centre of the draw, which seems endless. But there comes a point when the meadow fills up with bushes and it's here (flagging) where the trail climbs the bank on the right past a large dead tree into spruce forest. The final stretch is slightly downhill and straightforward to the junction with Rummel Lake trail.

Easy meadow-walking in the draw.

99 Mount Murray Viewpoint map 4

Half Day hike
Official trails
Distance of loop 5.5 km
Height gain 230 m (750 ft.)
High point 2110 m (6920 ft.)
Map 82 J/14 Spray Lakes Reservoir

Access Hwy. 742 (Smith-Dorrien/Spray Trail) at Chester Lake parking lot.

Comments While a designated snowshoe trail, as are all the Sawmill trails (née ski trails, logging roads), this little forest loop is walked year round.

Mt. Murray appears as a steep wedge to the left of Cegnfs.

To Viewpoint 3.1 km

At the kiosk as you face it go right through a gate and up a track named Snowdrift. Keep right around a bend, ignoring the HRT and Chester Lake winter routes crossing Chester Creek. Climb gradually across a forested hillside. In 470 m Sinter snowshoe trail takes off to the right and comes back in at the top of a hill. A short distance on, the return leg of your loop enters from the left. Stay ahead and descend to the junction with Frost Heave.

Turn left on Snowdrift, which is also the route to Headwall Lakes, and climb a long hill. After turning the corner to the left, turn left onto Mount Murray Viewpoint trail.

The trail climbs to a high point, en route giving views of Mt. Chester. The high point itself, lacking a viewing tower, is viewless now the trees have grown up. But if you walk left into an open area, the top wedge of Mt. Murray appears to the left of Cegnfs.

Return 2.4 km

The trail meanders on through open forest, eventually turning left and descending a series of steep hills back to Snowdrift. Turn right to return the same way you came up. In winter you can add on Sinter snowshoe trail. In summer, DON'T even try. The longitudinal meadow is one big swamp.

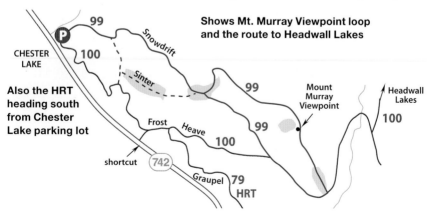

100 Headwall Lakes   map 4

Day hike, bike 'n' hike
Official & unofficial trails, cairns
Distance 7.3 km from usual access,
6.2 km from shortcut access.
Height gain 457 m (1500 ft.) to upper
lake from usual access
High point 2341 m (7680 ft.)
Map 82 J/14 Spray Lakes Reservoir

Usual access Hwy. 742 (Smith-Dorrien/
Spray Trail) at Chester Lake parking lot.
Shortcut access Park 800 m south of
Chester Lake parking lot by the side of the
highway. The trail is marked by flagging and
a cairn atop the bank.

Comments This has to be the most delectable valley on the east side of the highway, containing within its boundaries all the finest components of mountain scenery: blue lakes, springs, meadows, a karst pavement.

The prerequisite to heaven is a plod through a network of snowshoeing and mountain-biking trails (née logging roads). See the map on the previous page. After this you follow an occasionally steep and well-used trail to the upper lake (also the scrambler's access to The Fortress). NOTE: Flood damage in 2013 has forced reroutes, but the way is still obvious. Less easy is the steep climb below the lower lake, the torrential rains having scoured the trail down to bedrock.

Pedal or push bikes to the end of logging roads and enjoy a fabulous run down at the end of the day.

FROM USUAL ACCESS

To Graupel junction 1.4 km

If you want to be officially correct and add 2.2 km to the trip it's up to you. At least your vehicle won't be covered in dust when you return.

Follow the HRT (Frost Heave snowshoe trail) from the southeast edge of the parking lot. It descends slightly, then turns sharp left and climbs a hill. At the top, the trail turns right and meanders along past

Looking down on Lower Headwall Lake from the top of the headwall leading to Upper Headwall Lake.

Top: The steep climb up from the valley has been eroded down to bedrock.

Bottom: The spring below the upper lake.
Photo Alf Skrastins

the shortcut to a T-junction with map atop a 9-foot-high post. Go left on Frost Heave. (Right is HRT/Graupel snowshoe trail.)

FROM SHORTCUT

To Graupel junction 300 m

The trail soon widens into a recognizable logging road with sign "No open fires. Camp stove only." In 170 m join the official access and turn right. In 120 m come to a T-junction with Graupel snowshoe trail. Turn left on Frost Heave.

To end of logging roads 2.6 km

Wind steadily uphill to a T-junction. Turn right on Snowdrift snowshoe trail. (Snowdrift to left takes you back to Chester Lake parking lot.)

A long uphill traverse ends with a left turn to a T-junction. Go straight. (Left is Mt. Murray Viewpoint trail.) For a long way the route is flat and straight, eventually descending right and following a new 2016 road along to a new bridge over Rummel Creek. Climb a hill. At the top the road turns left. It's here at a cairn where the single-track Headwall Lakes trail takes off to the left.

To Lower Headwall Lake 2.9 km

The trail delves into the forest and down to Headwall Creek valley bottom at flood debris. The next section with reroutes is a mix of steep ups and downs alternating with easy stretches through willow and spruce and two forays along the stony creek bed. Watch for cairns.

Following on from a forest section is a flat meadow strip below a huge scree slope. This is where I wish for a nice zigzag trail up the scree to treeline. Instead the trail re-enters trees and climbs straight up the fall line on scree and bedrock.

Nearing treeline it turns left and meanders along with a few uphill steps and an easy scree slope crossing. At 234289 side trails lead to the lower springs, the waters commingling in a pool before dashing over a rock step, the creek's first waterfall.

On arriving at the lower headwall — a gleaming white wall of slabs — the trail climbs up the right side of it on scree to a karst pavement scraped by a passing glacier. Just ahead is Lower Headwall Lake occupying a rock-girt bowl.

To Upper Headwall Lake 500 m
The trail descends slightly past a creel survey box, then splits to cross the big scree slope. Take the high line. The trail then climbs the upper headwall, brief scrambles alternating with an easy trail to the right of the tumbling stream that springs out of the hillside at three-quarter height. Just over the top lies the beautiful blue upper lake, its setting austere amid screes and crags. At the head of the valley rises The Fortress.

Going farther? Keeping high, make your way above the east shore, looking across the lake to a waterfall tumbling down a cliff into the water. The upper valley beyond the lake is greener than you expect and there are many small waterfalls to delight in. Alternatively, explore the meadows at the top of the headwall, perhaps making a beeline for the last larch.

Above: Waterfall on the west side of the upper lake.
Photo Alf Skrastins

Below: Upper Headwall Lake. In the background is
The Fortress showing the route up the left-hand ridge.

101 The Fortress

map 4

Long day scramble
Unofficial trail & route
Distance 9.6 km from trailhead,
2.7 km from Upper Headwall Lake
Height gain 685 m (2246 ft.) from Upper Headwall Lake,
1142 m (3746 ft.) from trailhead
High point 3016 m (9895 ft.)
Map 82 J/14 Spray Lakes Reservoir

Access Hwy. 742 (Smith-Dorrien/Spray Trail). Via #100 Headwall Lakes at the upper lake.

Comments The Fortress, which appears impregnable from Hwy. 40, is a walk-up from the back, accessible to hikers who can handle scree and a few metres of easy scrambling. There's even an intermittent trail. For vertigo sufferers there's certainly not much to be scared of. However, don't think of it as just a detour from Headwall Lakes; plan an early start from the parking lot and pick a fine day. In late October of 1997 two descending hikers went off route in thick mist, resulting in injury and a difficult helicopter rescue.

To Fortress–Chester col 2 km

Follow the east shore of Upper Headwall Lake into the upper valley. At a pool, start up low-angle scree, aiming for the low point on the ridge to the left (northwest), which is the col between The Fortress and Mt. Chester. The slope steepens below the col, which you discover is not one but two cols separated by splinters of rock with a cairn. What a situation! Apart from being able to look into two valleys at once, Mt. Chester, which from most angles resembles a sponge pudding, displays an east ridge built like a ripsaw.

To the summit 600 m

At the col turn right and follow the scree trail up the southwest ridge. The first rise is the crux, scree on top of slab. That done with, the ridge broadens and the gradient eases slightly. Higher up, after you pass a couple of cairns, the angle eases even further as the ridge tapers and you become conscious of the drop on the right and then on the left.

Opposite: Looking down on the The Fortress–Chester col from the easy-angled ascent ridge. To left of the northeast ridge of Mt. Chester are Headwall Lakes and to the right, Chester Lake. Photo Matt Clay

Top: Approaching the summit rampart which is easily climbed. Photo Matt Clay

Left: The scramble through the summit crags to the top. Photo Roy Millar

OPTIONAL DESCENT
101A to Chester Lake

Comments Chester and Headwall creeks share the same trailhead, so why not make a 17.2 km loop by descending from the Fortress–Chester col into upper Chester Creek? Not often used as an ascent route.

Approaching the summit rampart, the trail cunningly turns left, traversing below the cliff band on broken ground. As you're about to drop off the edge of the world, scramble diagonally to the right up big blocks to a tilted platform of scree and walk to the summit (cairn, rock shelter).

The view is superb, taking in Mt. Assiniboine, of course, and the white fang of Joffre farther south, the whole of the Opal Range, Guinn's Pass and Fortress Mountain ski area, to name just some of the features. With care, Fortress Lake can be spotted 823 vertical metres below the eastern abyss.

Return to the Fortress–Chester col. From the low point farthest south, drop down the concave west slope, 230 vertical metres (~750 ft.) of black shale, that's not as easy as it once was, having become hardpacked over the years. On arriving in upper Chester Creek Valley, boulder-hop to the sink and pick up the trail taking you down to Chester Lake. See ##97A and 97.

102 James Walker Creek   map 4

Day hike, bike 'n' hike
Official trail with signposts & coloured
markers, unofficial trail
Distance 1.6 km to lake
Height gain 259 m (850 ft.) to lake
High point 2118 m (6950 ft.) at lake
Map 82 J/14 Spray Lakes Reservoir,
82 J/11 Kananaskis Lakes

Access Hwy. 742 (Smith-Dorrien/Spray
Trail) at Sawmill day-use area.

Comments Like Headwall Lakes, this geologically fascinating valley is accessed via the
Sawmill snowshoeing, skiing and mountain-
biking network of logging roads. So it's a
fairly easy walk to the lake. Once there, you're
within reach of twin upper valleys divided by
Mt. James Walker. This trail also accesses
the easy scramble route up the mountain.

Snowdrift trail 2 km

Start up the single track to the left of the
biffy. On reaching a stony logging road, turn
right. After the gate is a Y-junction with
a 9-foot-high sign. Go left on Snowdrift
snowshoe trail. Waves of uphills end at a
signed junction with Sawmill Snowshoe
Loop. Go left on Snowdrift, which is almost
flat for the next 320 metres. At a Y-junction
with cairn turn right onto what used to be
the James Walker Creek logging road but is
now reduced to a trail.

To lake 2.5 km

The trail curves around into the spruce-
filled valley of James Walker Creek, here
and there gaining height. The final half
kilometre undulates at the edge of larch
meadows strewn with boulders, then descends to the lake, which is quite attractive
at high water with a touch of deep azure, one
tiny island and a surround of grass. In the
background is Mt. James Walker, named
in 1975 after Calgary's "Citizen of the Century." To your right rises the 2,000-foot-
high north face of North Kent, a textbook
example of an anticlinal mountain. You get
a foreshortened view of it from the opposite
side of the lake, the best view being from the
top of the headwall.

*Approaching the lake below the headwall. In the
background is the south ridge of Mt. James Walker.*

102A Upper Valleys

Unofficial trail, routes
Distance 1.5 km plus
Height gain 320+ m (1050+ ft.)
High point 2438+ m (8000+ ft.)

Comments A more strenuous trip up a headwall to the upper valleys. Anyone willing to sweat a bit is rewarded with meadows, waterfalls, tarns, karst pavement, the amazing Grotto Spring and the last remaining glacier in the Kananaskis Range.

The Headwall 1.5 km

At low water follow the trail along the right (east) side of the lake through giant ragworts. Past the lake, jump a wee side creek. On coming to a barrier of tall willow bushes, go right into the trees, and walk up the side creek for a few stony metres before stepping off left onto cobbles with cairns. Follow the cairned cobble trail to James Walker Creek at a waterfall. Alternatively, after the side creek crossing, head left at the edge of the willows to James Walker Creek where a trail pushes through willows to the cairns on the cobbles.

The climbing starts straightaway, then moderates, the trail following the right bank of the creek past many waterfalls. There's an increase in step-over deadfall prior to the forks trail junction where the creeks from their respective cirques meet in parallel waterfalls. To get a good view, descend the steep trail to the left. Otherwise, turn right up an equally steep hill. (A traversing shortcut above the junction omits some of the uphill.)

Up next are the zigs which lead into a long, leftward traverse at the base of scree slopes topped by a high rockband. After crossing the right-hand fork, which can be seen pouring out of a cave in the rockband, the scree trail steepens. A little way up, be sure to take the easy side trip to Grotto Spring as some people call it.

Continue up scree to the alpine meadows where the good trail peters out.

Top: #102A The waterfalls at the forks.

Bottom: #102A Grotto Spring from below.

Top left: #102A Meadows in line with the left-hand valley. Photo Angélique and Allan Mandel

Bottom left: #102A The austere head of the left-hand valley, showing the glacier tongue and the tarn below it. Photo Gord Hurlburt

Top right: #102A First tarn in the right-hand valley.

side and above the tarn hidden under debris. It has retreated hardly at all since 2007; is still hanging in there, the last of the glaciers in the Kananaskis Range.

North (left-hand) valley 2.7 km

Trail's end is in line for the left-hand finger valley, meadow and limestone pavement soon giving way to a long, stony wasteland pitted with small tarns ringed with moss. If you can persevere to the very end, and very few people do, there is much to be curious about, starting with mammoth mounds of black terminal moraine which can be sidestepped on the left side. Down the middle of the flat valley beyond, runs what Gord believes is a kame moraine, a sinuous ridge with a very narrow crest and very steep sides composed of super-soft deposits. He compares it to a monster snake with a bulge 150 ft. high marking the location of a meal.

Your turnaround point is a wee tarn under the tongue of a glacier which is steeper and wider than you think, the ice on either

Northeast (right-hand) valley 1.5 km

The shorter valley between mounts Inflexible and James Walker is the more attractive. To get there either climb over the large, grassy hill, use the gap to its left or traverse around the hill to the right into a large area of meadow where innumerable tiny creeks from melting snow gather together, then sink, following some underground passage to the creek's resurgence below the headwall cliffs at Grotto Spring.

This right-hand branch holds a particularly beautiful tarn in a green and white setting of grass and limestone pavement. A string of shallow tarns can be followed up-valley to a deeper pool hidden within the moraines of the valley head. From here easy scree slopes lead to the summit of Mt. James Walker.

103 North Kent

map 4

Day hike
Unofficial trail, route
Distance 3.9 km one way
Height gain 1106 m (3630 ft.)
High point 2904 m (9530 ft.)
Maps 82 J/11 Kananaskis Lakes,
82 J/14 Spray Lakes Reservoir

Access Hwy. 742 (Smith-Dorrien/Spray Trail) at Sawmill day-use area.

Comments The unnamed peak at 254256 anchors the north end of Kent Ridge and is the highest point along it, nearly 300 metres (1000 ft.) higher than Mt. Kent itself, which I have always considered a mere bump along the ridge. Despite its height and ease of ascent, it's been a rarely climbed peak to date, with few entries in the summit register.

The Smith-Dorrien skiing, snowshoeing and mountain-biking network of logging roads gives access to open slopes, after which you're in for a relentless uphill slog, with no scrambling. The one absolute es-sential is finding an overgrown logging road dating back to the 1970s.

Despite its prized summit views of the James Walker glacier and the head of Kent Creek, its western outlier is actually the more interesting trip! Combining the two is another option.

Geology North Kent is one of the best examples of an anticlinal mountain in the Rockies. View its remarkable structure from #102 James Walker Creek.

Logging road section 1.6 km
Start up the single track to the left of the biffy. On reaching a stony logging road, turn right. After the gate is a Y-junction with a 9-foot-high sign. Keep straight (Snowdrift to left) and straight again on Sawmill Snowshoe Loop with red marker. (Track to right is South Sawmill Snowshoe Loop.)

North Kent from Hero Knob, showing almost the whole ascent route, plus the ridge route up the west outlier at bottom left.

Shortly the logging road starts climbing and heads right, then left and up the fall line to a junction with Sawmill Snowshoe Loop, which veers left towards James Walker Creek. You zig right.

At the next bend and junction zig left (cairn). The road is becoming ingrown with mini-spruce. Zig right and follow single tracks one side or the other of the roadbed, being careful to stay left and uphill. Finally, the road curves left and up the ridgeline — the south ridge of the west outlier.

Coming up at 1.3 km (about 244240), is a difficult piece of navigation where the road forks. Only the ridgeline road can be guessed at. There is absolutely no trace of your road to the right. What you do is this. Continue a little higher up the ridgeline road to a divergence of flagging at a wee cairn. Follow the flagging to the right along a narrow trail that joins the right-hand "road" in a minute or two. Go leftish following flagging through the trees. The roadbed is flat and becomes obvious as it traverses a steep slope to the right of the ridgeline. After passing a crag on the left

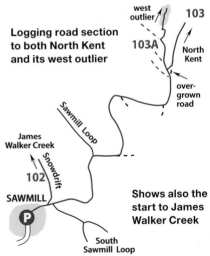

Logging road section to both North Kent and its west outlier

Shows also the start to James Walker Creek

side, it sheds itself of trees and DESCENDS into the head of Sawmill Creek Valley. It ends a little way up from the creekbed below meadows sweeping down from the west outlier. Ahead you can see the next part of the route up the north fork gully between the west outlier and North Kent. It doesn't look too far.

To Col 246254 1.3 km

Continue on trail to where it peters out. Then either follow strips of meadow in the valley bottom, veering left at the forks into the north fork, or make a slightly rising traverse of the meadow to the left just above tree ribbons, and on trail descend into the north fork.

Follow the north fork gully to the col, which is much higher and much farther away than it looks — all of 335 vertical metres (1100 vertical ft.). Alternate between the stones of the creekbed and the banks to either side, wherever you find remnants of game trails.

At 2484 metres (8150 ft.) the col is cushiony with convenient hollows to sink into for a break. To left, the west outlier rises steeply with rockbands. Ahead are weather instruments, though what they are doing just here is one of K Country's mysteries.

To the summit 1 km

Turn right, up the billowy west ridge of the mountain. Dryas and heather with a few scattered larches give way to an endless scree slope, grossly foreshortened. After 424 vertical metres (1390 ft.) of putting one step in front of another you arrive at the summit cairn perched above drop-offs.

Early in the season be wary of a cornice on the east side.

Naturally the view is 7-star, with mounts Assiniboine, Sir Douglas, Joffre and King George all in one frame. Mt. Inflexible is the big yellow heap immediately to the east. To its left is James Walker Creek, its upper valleys separated by the ghostly pale peak of James Walker, which from this direction has an elegant bent to it. In fall, the glacier in the left-hand valley shows up really well.

What you have come for, though, is the bird's-eye view into the head of Kent Creek. Enjoy its meadows, larches and tarns vicariously, because getting to the valley head is something hikers rarely aspire to. Bounding the valley to the east is Mt. Lawson, its incredibly long southeast ridge ending at #107, which looks "bloody miles away."

Return the same way unless you're a really proficient scrambler, in which case another 11 km of Kent Ridge is available. Just bear in mind that while everyone else will be stuffing their faces at the Georgetown Pub in Canmore, you will still be somewhere on the ridge.

Opposite: The col at 246254. At left rises the west outlier (see #103A). In the background is Mt. Birdwood.

Below: The summit cairn. Mt. Inflexible at centre, Mt. James Walker at far left with a smidgen of the glacier showing at the left edge of the photo.

103A West Outlier 244254

Unofficial trail
Distance 2.9 km one way
Height gain 676 m (2220 ft.)
High point 2536 m (8320 ft.)

Comments A short, rather beautiful ridge that is bound to become more popular than the trudge up North Kent. And it comes with a trail.

The trail follows the top of the eastern cliff.

To the open slopes 1.8 km
At the flagged junction near 244240 continue uphill on the ridgeline road. Look for flagging at points of infiltration. After the gradient eases off and the road turns leftish, come to a place where the road is blocked by branches. On the right bank is a cairn atop a stump and some flagging on a tree beyond. This is where you leave the road and take to the forested south ridge.

At first the trail is minimal. After you climb over two fallen trees, it picks up and follows the right side of the ridge above steep slopes. Squirm under a fallen tree onto open slopes.

The ridge 1.1 km
The ridge rises fairly gradually with steeper steps here and there, the grass of lower down giving way to slaty orange rocks harbouring a wide variety of alpines including roseroot and two types of yellow draba. Most spectacular are the big bunches of alpine cinquefoil. The ridge's main feature, though, is the vertical (even overhanging) cliff lining the east side.

The summit is capped with soft, tufty grass ideal for view gazing. Should the west wind be cold and blustery you can hunker down below the rockband that fortuitously peters out at the summit. Of course, the view to the east is blocked by the sprawling mass of North Kent. But to the west the whole of the Spray Mountains are displayed, from Tent Ridge to Indefatigable and across to Hero Knob.

OPTIONAL DESCENT
Possibly you'll want to climb North Kent on the same day, or return via the north fork gully for a change. So, first you have to descend to the col at 246254. (See the photo on page 364.)

This is not as easy as it looks from above, and if there's snow on it, forget it. The photo in *More Scrambles in the Canadian Rockies* should do the trick. To find ways through two rockbands, go right at the first one and left at the second.

104 Hero Knob
map 8

Day scramble
Unofficial trail, route, creek crossing
Distance 4.3 km
Height gain 710 m (2330 ft.)
High point 2524 m (8280 ft.)
Map 82 J/11 Kananaskis Lakes

Access Hwy. 742 (Smith-Dorrien/Spray Trail). Park by the west side of the highway at 240228, 540 metres south of Sawmill access road.

Comments Hero Knob is an eastern outlier of Mt. Smith-Dorrien at 228216. Extreme skiers doing the Black Prince traverse pass below it at the second col, which I hesitate to call a pass. K Country features it in their avalanche report, but spells it "Heros nob." The consensus of people asked about the name think it immortalizes not a Greek god's head, nor the Health & Education Research Operative Services, but some skier with a death wish — Sean from Canmore? — who was the first to ski one of those horrendously steep and narrow gullies off the summit.

In summer there is no need to be a hero. The approach is fast and easy via a logging road and trail up the unnamed valley between Warspite Creek and Murray Creek. The headwall offers up some scree, and while the summit ridge is decidedly knobbly, most of it can be avoided. Take Tevas.

Hero Knob (left) and Mt. Smith-Dorrien as seen from Hwy. 742 .

The valley 2.4 km
Head down the west bank into the forest, where the old logging road is obvious. It trends downhill to Smith-Dorrien Creek and crosses it — an easy crossing. Some way before the crossing, put on the Tevas to slosh through marshy ground near a small pond.

On the west bank, the road is in remarkably good shape as it climbs gradually through spruce forest, then turns right, into the valley confines. Almost at once it narrows to trail width where it passes through a logged area (go either way at a split). As a road it crosses a band of old forest with a fallen giant you skirt around. The line of it can then be traced across a grassy avalanche slope and into a final band of forest where the road ends close to the creek. A trail continues along the right bank, en route crossing a wash of stones to a long, flat, willowy meadow at the valley head. Many trails lead through to the bottom of the headwall.

The headwall 600 m
The direct route works best. Starting you off is a trail climbing diagonally up the right-hand slope of a small knoll. From behind the knoll, continue ahead through a grassy avenue and up the prominent grass slope where the gradient steepens. You can hear the sound of water to your left.

Below a rockband, a bit of trail heads left to the centre creek. Don't cross. It's easier just to clamber straight up the rocks of the bed and through the gap into the bottom of a steep fan of scree where the creek runs underground. During its brief re-emergence as a cascade, stay to its left, then traverse to the right above it out of the fan and onto easier ground. Head left up a scree rib to the top.

The summit 1.3 km

You find yourself in a hanging valley below the formidable black walls of Leaning Mountain, a name coined by first ascentionist John Martin to describe the cornice-like profile of the summit rock ridge. The black chute to left is the skier's descent route from the first col!

Turn right and walk up the scree and meadow of the trough towards the second col. Higher up, climb onto the south ridge of the knob to your right. A trail of sorts winds through dense subalpine scrub harbouring masses of a snowy-white lousewort called parrot's beak (*Pedicularis racemosa*). The going is faster when the ridge turns to grass.

Arriving below the first knob on the summit ridge, you make a decision. Hardcore scramblers can tackle the knobs, which are exposed to a deepening drop on the left.

People who get the wobblies in such places can traverse the right (east) slope on a scree/grass mix between the crest and a rockband, and at the obvious place work their way back up to the ridge not far from the summit. The actual top is quite narrow. Interestingly, the knobs carry on down the far side a way and somewhere between them is the kamikaze ski gully.

This higher vantage point gives a superb view of Leaning Mountain. Close at hand, the great northern cliffs of Mt. Smith-Dorrien make Mt. Murray and Cegnfs look like pygmies. Across the valley rises North Kent and the whole of Kent Ridge.

Return

Return to the ridge below the knobs. Turn west and descend the easy west ridge towards second col. En route, look back at Hero Knob to view the vertiginous northwest flank you were walking above!

Before reaching the col proper, run black shale into the head of the trough, revelling in the many flowers dotting the slope. At the bottom keep left and eventually join up with your ascent route.

Above: One of the summit knobs, with Leaning Mountain in the background.

Opposite: #105 Warspite Lake. Trail to Black Prince Lake goes through the gap at centre.

105 Warspite Lake

map 8

Half day hike
Official trail
Distance to lake 4.2 km return
Height gain 122 m (400 ft.) return
High point 1820 m (5970 ft.)
Map 82 J/11 Kananaskis Lakes

Access Hwy. 742 (Smith-Dorrien/Spray Trail) at Black Prince day-use area.

Comments A somewhat strenuous interpretive trail with a loop on the end leads to little Warspite Lake in a boulder field below Mount Black Prince. To interpret trail stop numbers, refer to the online brochure.

    Naming After the legendary battleship HMS Warspite that refused to be broken up in a scrap yard. The memorial above Prussia Cove in Cornwall, UK, tells you all about it.

To the loop 1.4 km

The route starts at the kiosk and heads west to a 2016 bridge over Smith-Dorrien Creek. After doubling back, it follows a logging road up an endlessly long hill. At the top is trail stop 4 and a well-placed bench. Now on trail, descend to a T-junction with the return trail between trail stops 5 and 6. Go straight

The loop anti-clockwise 2.3 km

After crossing the creek the trail meanders along through a thinning forest into a boulder field at trail stop 8. In the midst of the boulders lies Warspite Lake, its astonishing emerald-green colour caused by algae activated by strong sunlight. The water sinks underground. You can hear it gurgling deep down beneath the trail around stops 9 and 10. (The hydrology of this whole area is quite fascinating.) In the background is Mt. Black Prince. The gleam of white seen just above the trees surrounding the lake is Warspite Cascade, visited by #105A en route to Black Prince Lake.

    At trail stop 10 the trail winds its way back through the boulder field and then crosses a deep and dry mossy creekbed below a reflecting pool. Climb a little, cross a running side creek and descend to join your outgoing trail at the T-junction.

    Turn right and plod up the hill to trail stop 4, after which it's all downhill.

Above: #105A Warspite Cascades.

Below: #105A Black Prince Lake from the southeast rib of Mount Black Prince. Photo Alf Skrastins

105A Black Prince Lake

Unofficial trail with cairns, flagging
Distance from Warspite Lake 2.9 km,
4.9 km from trailhead
Height gain 503 m (1650 ft.)
from Warspite Lake,
663 m (2174 ft.) from trailhead
High point 2323 m (7620 ft.)

Comments Following the line of an ages-old elk trail, you climb into a cirque below the north face of Mt. Warspite. If the steep grind up the headwall isn't enough, you can carry on climbing to Black Prince Lake. This trail is the scrambler's approach to both mounts Warspite and Black Prince.

Note When Warspite Lake dries up in fall, you can miss out the trail around the lake by simply crossing the dry bed to pick up the trail on the west shore. However, there are disadvantages to going at this time of year: Warspite Cascades will be dry and Black Prince Lake reduced to three puddles.

Bear note Watch for griz on the lush, flowery, willowy hillsides, possibly the same one that frequents the slopes of Indefatigable and Gypsum Creek but keeps to himself and troubles no one.

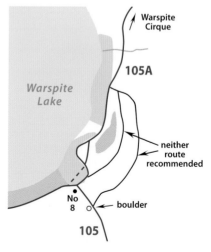

The trail leaving Warspite Lake for Black Prince Lake

To Warspite cirque 1.6 km

First, go around the lake anti-clockwise. At trail stop 8 step right off the interpretive trail onto a smaller trail. Go left straightaway, then right at a split. Turn right, then keep straight as per the flagging. Now you're set, just one good trail to follow. Cross four wee creeks with water, the last drinkable water until you hit Warspite Cascades. Near the inlet the trail turns right through a belt of spruce.

A soft trail through grass and high willow in the runout zones of avalanche slopes leads onto a boulder field. Cross with the help of many big cairns. Shortly after, enter the lower, gentler slopes of the headwall where the trail heads straight into avalanche snow and debris. Follow a fainter trail to its right and eventually up the left side of a gully. Be alert for a faint trail cutting left to a big cairn and follow it.

Back on the original trail turn right. Soon enough it climbs very much more steeply alongside the gully, then turns left and climbs on the diagonal (still a few steep hills) through lush meadows and bush to Warspite Creek at the cascades.

#105A Mt. Warspite from the cirque below it, which deserves more than a passing glance.

Up next is the hard part: climbing the headwall to the right of the cascades, the eroded trail steep and slippery with no trees to hang on to. But finally the gradient eases off and it's a pleasant, undulating amble into the beautiful meadows under Mt. Warspite sprinkled with boulders, flowers and elk droppings.

To Black Prince Lake 800 m

Continue on flagged trail well into the cirque until past the trees on the right side. Then turn right and on an obvious flagged and well-cairned trail climb another 122 vertical metres (400 ft.) up a grass and boulder slope to the top of a terminal moraine. Look down on inky blue/black Black Prince Lake in a basin.

Those with energy to spare can wander up the grassy southeast rib of Mt. Black Prince to rockline. It's a great viewpoint for the cirque and for Warspite Lake a few thousand feet below your feet.

106 Gypsum Quarry

map 5

Day hike to quarry
Unofficial trail, creek crossing
Distance 7.4 to end of quarry
Height gain 457 m (1500 ft.)
High point 2133 m (7000 ft.)
Map 82 J/11 Kananaskis Lakes

Access Hwy. 742 (Smith-Dorrien/Spray Trail) at Peninsula day-use area, far parking lots.
Also accessible from #78A at the col between Indefatigable Outlier and the north summit of Mt. Indefatigable.

Comments This is a long, easy and scenic walk up an exploration road to a gypsum quarry on the north ridge of Mt. Invincible. From this trail a couple of options present themselves. The shorter is Gypsum Ridge Viewpoint. The longer, for the more adventurous, leaves the quarry for Gypsum Tarns from where you make a point to point with #78A. If doing that trip in reverse, it's essential you check the water level in Smith-Dorrien Creek first, or you too can spend the night out on the west bank of Lower Kananaskis Lake and be forced to hail a passing boat in the morning. So, the very big problem hikers have is the creek crossing 750 metres in from the start.

How and when to cross Smith-Dorrien Creek In summer the creek can be thigh-deep. You might think fall is the best crossing time, but at such times the water in Lower Kananaskis Lake rises and mingles with that of the creek and then you'll be swimming. Another fall option is to wade the creek upstream of the bridge site, then backtrack along the flood-eroded south bank, a truly awful time-consuming endeavour.

Best, then, to buy a cheap blow-up boat from Canadian Tire and paddle across from the trailhead. Just know the old put-in bay facing the creek is blocked in by driftwood. So you'll be paddling all around the peninsula and landing on the flat, grassy promontory to the left of a raft of floating flood debris. From its far end a trail leads up the bank onto the quarry road. Alternatively, carry the boat the 750 metres to the bridge site near the picnic table and cross to the promontory between the raft of floating flood debris and the creek.

About the quarry This particular gypsum outcrop was reported by the Geological Survey in 1964 (Report 65-1), and resulted in a 21-year lease being issued to CP Oil & Gas, who transferred it several times over to the Alberta Gypsum Company. After all the trouble in getting a road to the area — your road is the second attempt — they operated for just a few years until August 1970 when the lease was cancelled, the company having failed to make a cash deposit to cover land restoration costs. By 2000 the quarry face was slipping down the hillside and in 2007 reclamation was carried out by A.M. MacKay Contractors Ltd. of Cochrane in partnership with Interior Reforestation Co. Ltd. It is they who have improved the access aside from removing the bridge over Smith-Dorrien Creek.

To the creek crossing by trail 700 m

If walking with or without boat, transfer to the old quarry road (gated track) from the loop road. Keep left and descend to Smith-Dorrien Creek/Lower Kananaskis Lake at a meadow with picnic table near the bridge site. Maybe you'll meet people out on the guided hike "Cut the Bull," which informs about Smith-Dorrien Creek's role as an important spawning bed for bull trout that live in Lower Kananaskis Lake.

Getting to the start

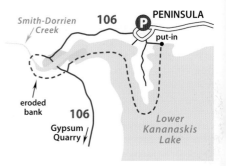

The road rises slowly across avalanche paths below Gypsum Ridge. Nearing the big bend, be sure to look across the valley to Blackshale Creek where you can spot the celebrated suspension bridge way down at the bottom. Higher up still, keep alert for where the better road zigs left at a split. The following right-hand bend up the fall line is where the route to #106B Gypsum Ridge Viewpoint takes off to the left. This is also the start of a lightly treed area crammed with bushes of menziesia and white flowering rhododendrons.

To Quarry 2.8 km

After leaving Gypsum Ridge behind, the road zigs up the north ridge of Invincible. At a higher step, it runs in a straight line along the right side of the ridge toward the face of the mountain, at the last minute deking left through a gap to the quarry.

Walk a bench halfway up the face to the far end of the quarry, en route checking out the methods used to restore this vast slope, which include the use of jute blankets to stabilize the soil, and straw and willow-weave wattles, which "take the energy out of the water during runoff, and promote a platform for growth to establish naturally."

To Gypsum Ridge turnoff 3.9 km

So you've crossed the creek/lake in some fashion and are now on the continuation of the quarry road/first road on the south bank of Smith-Dorrien Creek. At the hairpin bend your road turns right. (The "trail" ahead, thoroughly obscured by spruce at the junction, was the first attempt at getting a road to the gypsum deposit via Gypsum Creek, but came a cropper when it hit a series of rocky gullies.)

Top: The quarry road and Mt. Warspite.

Below: The gypsum quarry during reclamation.

be followed through the next tree ribbon to a shallow scree gully beyond. Rising and falling, but mostly falling, the trail crosses alternating tree ribs and stony gullies all the way to first gypsum quarry road. There are a few tricky metres where the trail disappears on a steep side slope, then reappearing, circles around a wider than usual gully manufactured from cement shale. But eventually you arrive on the first gypsum quarry road, which starts (or rather ends) on the far bank of the last gully.

The flat, easy road crosses below a humongous avalanche slope divided by a stream leaping down the headwall. Cross the stream (not marked on the topo map despite supplying 90% of the water to Gypsum Creek), then in trees cross the very much smaller creek from Gypsum Tarns. Just after the latter crossing, exit the road and turn right onto a small trail near the forest edge.

GOING FARTHER

106A Gypsum Tarns

Unofficial trails
Distance 2.1 km from quarry
Height loss 91 m (300 ft.)
Height gain 152 m (500 ft.)
High point 2179 m (7150 ft.)

Comments Although the distance is relatively short, this cross-country jaunt from the quarry to the tarns in the cirque between mounts Invincible and Indefatigable is only for the experienced finder of game trails. Expect a rough, steep hillside to the first gypsum quarry road.

To first Gypsum Quarry road 1.4 km
From the far end of the quarry, follow hoofprints up a dirt ridge, then cut up left and through one or two trees to a gravel slope. Here pick up a definite trail that can

Above: The largest Gypsum Tarn. In the background are Indefatigable Outlier at left and the col at centre. Photo Alf Skrastins

Opposite: Carrying the boat back along the trail to the parking lot.

Shows quarry road and routes to Gypsum Tarns and Gypsum Ridge Viewpoint

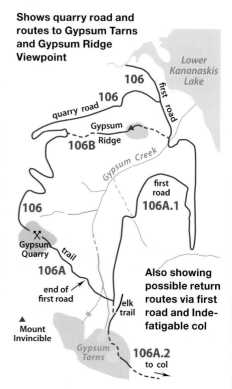

To Gypsum Tarns 630 m
The trail heads upwards to the bottom of a boulder slope. Here intercept an excellent elk trail and follow it rightward back into trees. At a division climb either way to the lip of the cirque — a not too onerous task in larch and glacier lily country. Cupped in grass at the bottom of scree slopes are three small green tarns.

OPTIONAL RETURNS

1. Via the first gypsum quarry road
Distance 7.5 km to trailhead
The dreadful thing is that from this direction the first couple of kilometres lures with a clearish path through trees. Then, at the point where the road turns away from the valley, you hit a wall of prickly spruce, gooseberry bushes, 6-metre-high alders and deadfall. After crossing Gypsum Creek the road improves somewhat and is built up across steep hillside. The last push through spruce to the quarry road can be avoided by detouring to the right. Regardless, you'll emerge looking like an escapee from the polar bear complex at the Calgary Zoo.

2. Via Indefatigable Col 5.1 km
Distance to col 900 m,
extra height gain 304 m (1000 ft.),
high point at col 2484 m (8150 ft.)
Having made it to the tarns, it's definitely shorter to carry on through to North Interlakes parking lot via the Indefatigable trails, which of course requires that you have two vehicles. The question is: can you hack another 300 metres of steep climbing?

First, check the slope for the resident male grizzly. All clear? From the larger tarn a very convenient trail heads southeast up the left bank of the inlet creek to treeline. While it's possible to climb direct to Indefatigable Outlier via its stony west ridge, the more attractive grizzly route tackles the grassy, shaley slope farther to the right. It leads straight to the col at 297329 between the outlier and Mt. Indefatigable North. Now read #78A Indefatigable Col and Outlier, descending via the ascent route.

OPTION

106B Gypsum Ridge Viewpoint
Unofficial trails & routes
Distance 6.6 km from trailhead
High point 2100 m (6889 ft.)
Height gain 420 m (1378 ft.)
from trailhead

Comments Gypsum Ridge Viewpoint is a popular snowshoe destination when Smith-Dorrien Creek is frozen and the menziesia bushes are covered by snow. At such times the route avoids the quarry road because of avalanche danger by shortcutting up steep, forested hillside direct from Hwy. 742 near Blackshale Creek. Far fewer people visit in summer. A pity, it's worth bashing through a few bushes, because like many a small height, this is one really fine viewpoint.

Follow the quarry road to the third zig after the creek crossing. Just beyond the bend note flagging on the left (4.7 kilometres from the creek crossing).

To summit 1.2 km
Leave the road and heading off in a southeasterly direction, plow through 680 metres of menziesia bushes, searching out bit trails and narrow avenues of grass as you climb gently upwards on the shapeless east end of the ridge. The idea is to hit waypoint 298162, where you'll pick up a good trail taking you all the way to the summit.

The bushes lessen and the ridge becomes more sharply defined as you follow the left edge. A final section of grass (likely the high point) leads to rocky knobs above crags. The lone pine viewpoint gives the best view of Lower Kananaskis Lake backdropped by the Opal Range and the Elk Range beyond the Highwood Pass gap. Looking south you can trace all the route from the quarry to Gypsum Tarns.

Above: #106B Gypsum Ridge Viewpoint, looking back at the high point from the end viewpoint.

Below: #106B Lower Kananaskis Lake from trail's end.

OPTIONAL RETURN
Loop 9.6 km
From the lone pine nubbin descend the indeterminate and forested southeast ridge, losing 360 metres (1181 ft.) in only 800 metres. Game trails help initially, then comes deadfall and a steepening toward the bottom. But, hey, descending is a lot easier than climbing up this slope! Be careful to recognize the first Gypsum Mine road, here a flat, built-up trail with occasional jungly bits on the north side of Gypsum Creek. Turn left and follow it for 590 metres to the quarry road.

107 The South End of Lawson   map 5

Day hike, scramble, bike 'n' hike
Unofficial trail, route
Distance 4 km
Height gain 762 m (2500 ft.)
High point 2393 m (7850 ft.)
Map 82 J/11 Kananaskis Lakes

Access Hwy. 742 (Smith-Dorrien/Spray Trail). About 200 m north of Peninsula day-use area access road, park at the intersection of gated TransAlta roads. The road heading south leads to Canyon Dam, the road heading north leads to Kent Creek.

Comments This refers to the southernmost tip of the ridge extending SSE from Mt. Lawson at 306209. Driving Hwy. 40 from Fortress Junction into Peter Lougheed Park, you see it as the last high point before the ridge drops to Hwy. 742.

I'm betting this route up the south ridge will become enormously popular with experienced hikers; there's a rudimentary trail most of the way, the gradient is gentle with occasional steep steps, a rock ridge at the top adds spice, the summit is an unusual viewpoint, and lastly, hard-core scramblers can go a little farther.

Biking The first 700 metres along the TransAlta road can be biked.

Kent Creek section 1.2 km

Head north on the TransAlta road alongside a diversion ditch built in 1956 to redirect water from Kent Creek to Lower Kananaskis Lake. This is also a part of Penstock Loop snowshoe trail. Around a bend the pointy lower summit of your objective comes into view, the ascent ridge looking very foreshortened. Then several things happen within a short distance. The ditch is replaced by a metal flume, and at a red sign the snowshoe trail turns off to the right across the real Kent Creek (no bridge) opposite a bridge over the flume. Kent Creek pours out of a pipe and the water issuing from the canyon is swallowed up by an intake structure.

NOTE: The road ends at the canyon's mouth. Farther in is a waterfall only attainable by wading. The canyon and the cliffs on both hillsides are the reasons why entering Kent Creek valley is so difficult.

To Kent Creek junction 400 m

Just before the intake, cross boulders in the dry bed to the far bank and turn right. After the slope on the left loses its crags, look for a trail climbing steeply onto the lower south ridge.

The south end of Mt. Lawson from Hwy. 40, showing the two tops and the gap in between.

The gradient eases right off, the trail keeping mostly to the right side of the ridge crest. Just past a boulder it steepens again, zigging up easy ground between the big cliff on the left and the escarpment on the right. At the top is an unmarked Y-junction. Go straight up the fall line. (The easier-angled trail to Kent Creek forks left at 10 o'clock.)

To lower top 1.8 km

The ridge trail continues to climb moderately steeply, but then the angle eases with a capital E and for a kilometre you stride along above the eastern escarpment in pines with almost no understorey. Down right you can spot unsuspected ponds amid the forest and buildings that were once a minimum-security work camp (Kananaskis Correctional Centre) whose inmates helped build the Mount Shark ski trails back in 1984.

So easy is the going that the trail is almost redundant, and in fact it disappears temporarily just before a very small dip. After this the pattern is short steepish climbs alternating with long easy stretches. A longer-sustained uphill, where you must look harder for the trail, leads to a grass ridge and a narrowing. Look back for a first thrilling view of Lower Kananaskis Lake glinting in the noonday sun. At the top of the slope a lower summit is decked out in larches.

To summit 600 m

The trail heads gently down at the edge of a big rock gully to a col.

Coming up is the day's steepest climb, along the rim of the gully and onto a wide, flat ridge of scree and grass. The knob of scree at the end of it is not the summit, merely the lead-in to an entertaining rock ridge where for a few metres you traverse the left side while hanging onto the ridge crest. After this the ridge broadens to grass and you walk through a few trees to the true summit (cairn).

What a place to view the Opals! Scramblers can pick out the route up Mt. Hood and hikers the route up King Creek Ridge opposite. To the west is the incredibly long Kent Ridge anchored by North Kent at the head of Kent Creek Valley. Looking down into the valley's dark forest reminds you that hiking the ridges is much more fun.

GOING FARTHER

The next section of open ridge — another nameless bump on the way to Mt. Lawson — is a come-on if you don't mind losing nearly 100 metres (328 ft.) in height and plodding through a lot more trees. Initially the ridge is broad, but it soon narrows and undulates, becoming the realm of the scrambler–climber.

OPTION
107A Kent Creek

Long day hike, backpack
Unofficial trail, then route
Distance to end of trail from trailhead
1.8 km, to valley head 11 km
Height gain 808 m (2650 ft.)
to valley head
High point 2484 m (8150 ft.)

Comments Meadows and tarns at the head of this long, straight, dead-end valley are extraordinarily hard to get to. Climbers can drop in from the heights, but the rest of us must bushwhack. Because of the canyon's cliffs, the access trail described here starts from some distance up the south ridge of

Lawson and drops in from above. NOTE: I still haven't checked out game trails along the southwest hillside. Anyone?

Trail to valley bottom 600 m
From the Y-junction as mentioned in the second section, turn left onto a rising trail that crosses the hillside above a big cliff. Step over much deadfall. A gradual descent above another drop-off precedes the plummet — a definite design fault in trails. At the bottom, traverse right above a third drop-off, then angle fairly steeply down to the valley bottom.

The valley
For much of the way the valley is dark, old-growth forest, mossy bumpy with pools of standing water, beautiful in its way but not conducive to easy travelling. Expect tiny snippets of game trails going nowhere and lots and lots of deadfall. Most people will have given up long before they reach the meadows.

Opposite: A flat stretch of ridge between the two tops. In the background is Lower Kananaskis Lake.

Above: Returning along the rock ridge below the summit.

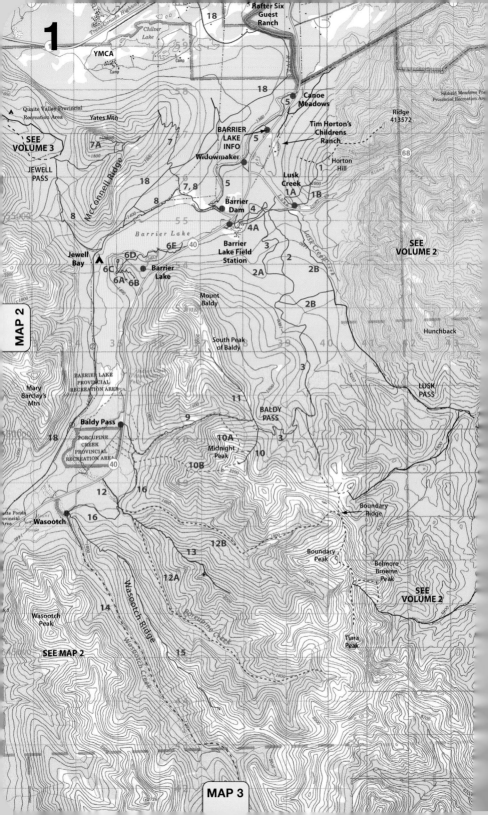

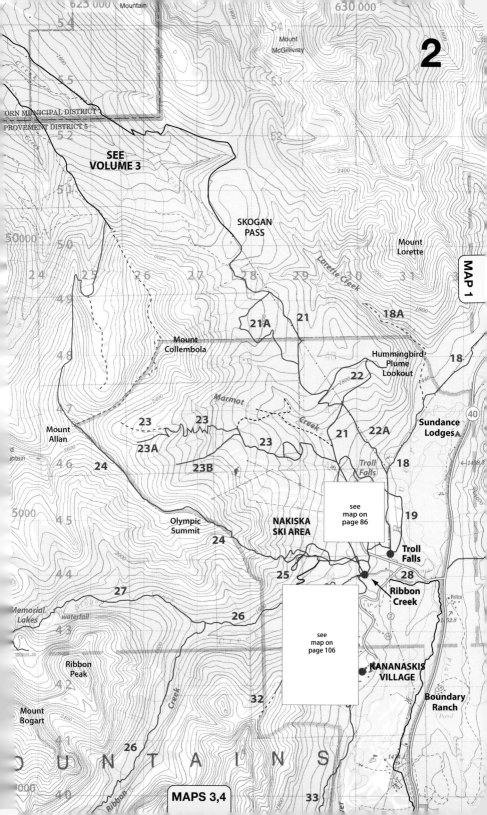

MAP 1

625 000

630 000

Mountain

Mount
McGillivray

ORN MUNICIPAL DISTRICT
PROVEMENT DISTRICT 5

SEE VOLUME 3

SKOGAN
PASS

Mount
Lorette

Lorette Creek

50000

24   25   26   27   28   29   30   31

18A

21A   21

Mount
Collembola

Hummingbird
Plume
Lookout

18

22

Marmot   Creek

40

23   23

21   22A

Sundance
Lodges

Mount
Allan

23A

23

Troll
Falls

18

ntain

23B

19

5000

Olympic
Summit

**NAKISKA
SKI AREA**

see
map on
page 86

Troll
Falls

24

25

28

27

Ribbon
Creek

Memorial
Lakes

waterfall

26

see
map on
page 106

Ribbon
Peak

**KANANASKIS
VILLAGE**

Mount
Bogart

Creek

**Boundary
Ranch**

26

32

O U N T A I N S

MAPS 3,4   33

see
map on
page 86

see
map on
page 106

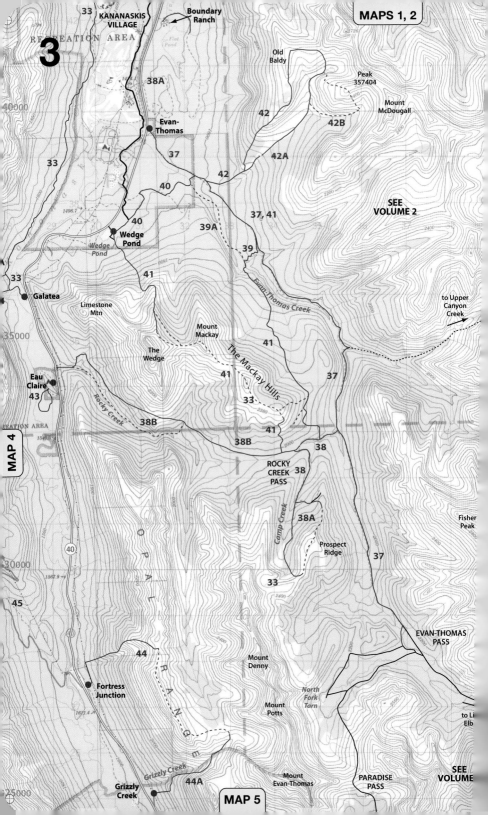

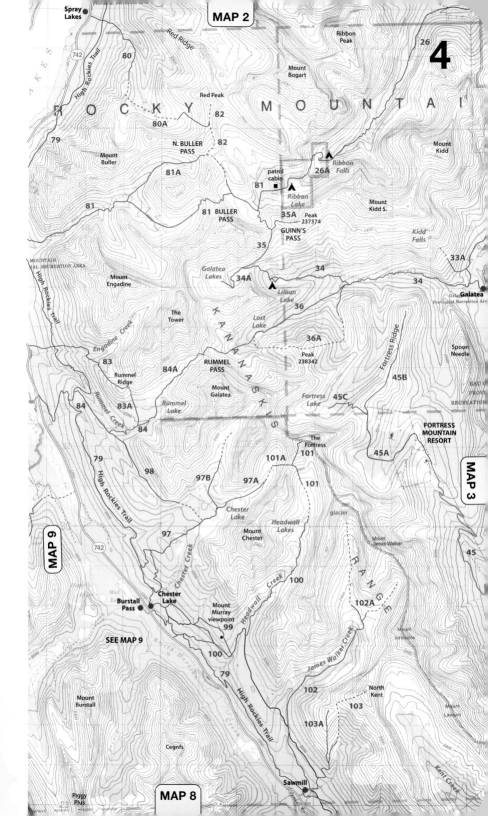

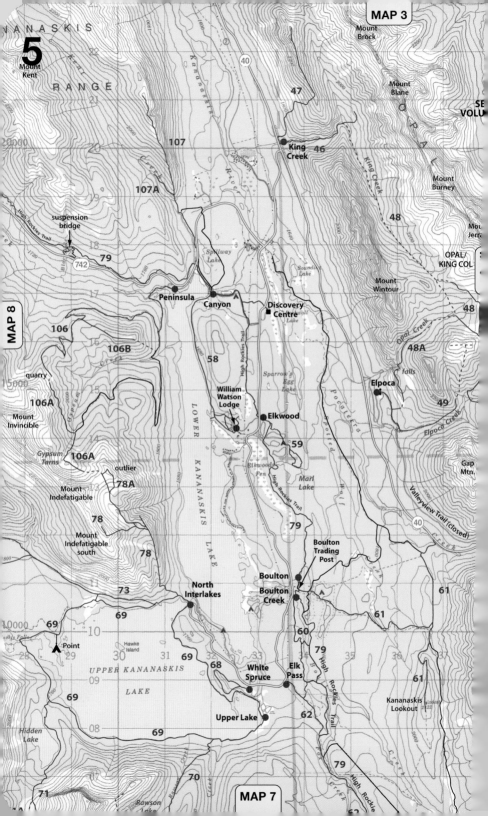

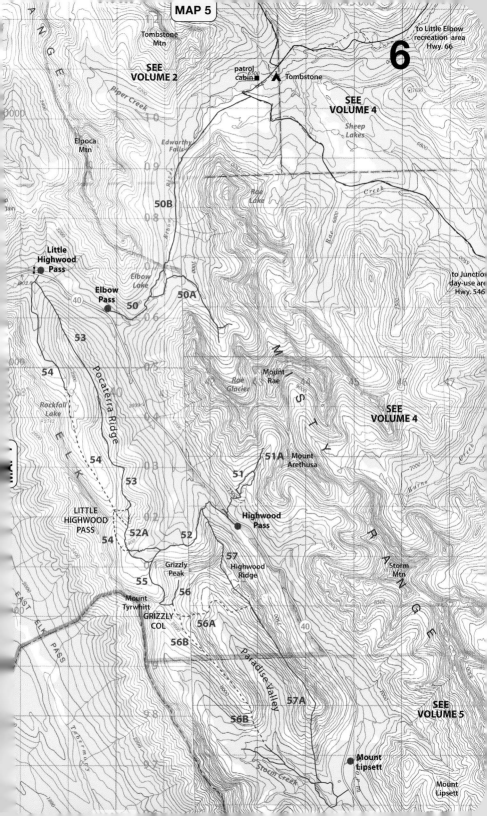

MAP 5

6

R A N G E

Tombstone
Mtn

to Little Elbow
recreation area
Hwy. 66

SEE
VOLUME 2

Piper Creek

patrol
cabin
Tombstone

SEE
VOLUME 4

Elpoca
Mtn

Edwarthy
Falls

Sheep
Lakes

Rae
Lake

50B

Rae Creek

Little
Highwood
Pass

Elbow
Lake

Elbow
Pass

50

50A

to Junction
day-use area
Hwy. 546

40

53

M I S T Y

54

Rae
Glacier

Mount
Rae

SEE
VOLUME 4

Rockfall
Lake

54

53

51A

Mount
Arethusa

51

LITTLE
HIGHWOOD
PASS

E L K

R A N G E

54

52A

52

Highwood
Pass

Storm
Mtn

55

Grizzly
Peak

56

57

Highwood
Ridge

40

Mount
Tyrwhitt

GRIZZLY
COL

56A

56B

Paradise Valley

EAST ELK PASS

57A

SEE
VOLUME 5

56B

Mount
Lipsett

Storm Creek

Mount
Lipsett

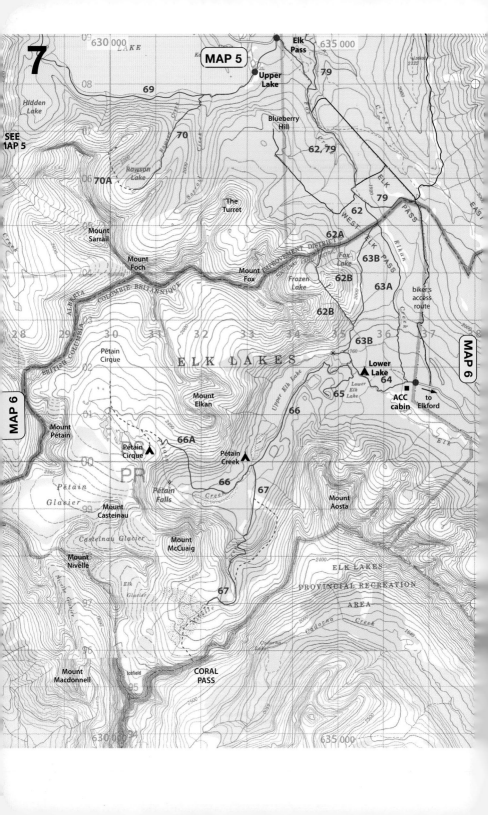

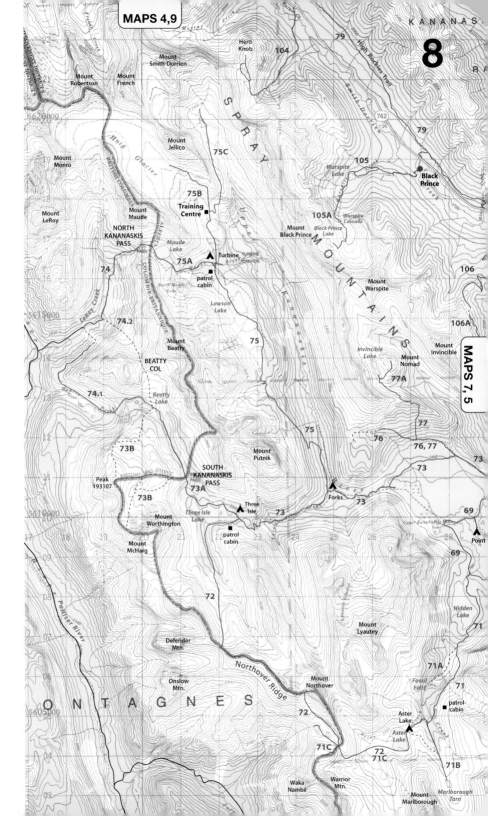

MAP 8

INDEX

CONTACTS

For **Alberta government establishments** use the toll-free line 310-0000, which is available from 8 a.m.–6 p.m. weekdays only.

Kananaskis Country Head Office
(Alberta Tourism, Parks and Recreation) in Canmore 403-678-5508

The Friends of Kananaskis Country
403-678-5593, kananaskis.org

Kananaskis Country Information
403-678-0760

On-line Info
Kananaskis Country and trail reports
kananaskis-country.ca
Gillean & Tony Daffern's blog site
kananaskistrails.com

Wildlife Sightings
To report sightings 403-591-7755

In an emergency DIAL 911 and tell the operator you have an emergency in Kananaskis Country. Or contact Kananaskis Country Emergency Services at 403-591-7755.

Campground Reservations
Campgrounds 1-403-678-0760, reserve.albertaparks.ca
Mt. Kidd RV Park 403-591-7700
Sundance Lodges 403-591-7122, info@sundancelodges.com

Facilities
Boulton Creek Trading Post 403-591-7226
Boundary Ranch 403-591-7171, 1-877-591-7177, info@boundaryranch.com
Crosswaters Resort, 403-591-6255, 1-833-440-1964
Elk Lakes Cabin run by the ACC at 403-678-3200, info@AlpineClubofCanada.ca
Fortress Junction 403-591-7371
Summit Restaurant, Kananaskis Golf Course 403-591-7070
Kananaskis Outfitters at Kananaskis Village, 403-591-7000
Kananaskis Wilderness Hostel at Ribbon Creek, 403-762-4122. info.sa@hihostels.ca
Mount Engadine Lodge 587-807-0570 Mountengadine@castleavery.com
Nakiska Ski Area 403-591-7777, 1-800-258-7669, info@skinakiska.com
Pomeroy Kananaskis Mountain Lodge 403-591-7711, 1-866-432-4322
Stoney Nakoda Resort Casino 403-881-2830
William Watson Lodge 403-591-7227

Further Reading
The first two books cover harder scrambles in K Country, the other three, trails in areas adjoining K Country and Elk Lakes Provincial Park.
Alan Kane *Scrambles in the Canadian Rockies (RMB)*
Andrew Nugara *More Scrambles in the Canadian Rockies (RMB)*
Brian Patton & Bart Robinson *Canadian Rockies Trail Guide (Summerthought)*
Dustin Lynx *Hiking Canada's Great Divide Trail (RMB)*
Janice Strong *Mountain Footsteps (RMB)*